Some Revelations in
The QUEEN of MEAN

* Leona apparently pressured Harry Helmsley into marrying her by inventing a rival lover—complete with diamond engagement ring and love letters proposing marriage.

* Leona's family members suspect that her 1973 stabbing in the Helmsleys' Palm Beach penthouse may actually have been done by Harry—not the female intruder in a "World War gas mask" that Leona reported to police.

* Jay Panzirer, Leona's son, died during an extramarital tryst with a furniture saleswoman—despite the obituary that claims he died during a business meeting.

* Leona not only refused to pay for major items like TV sets and house renovation; she also demanded freebies from her suppliers including toilet paper, cleaning supplies, and toothbrushes.

* Leona used a computerized Scitex machine to take decades off her face and inches off her figure in photos of herself for her hotels' international advertising campaign.

* Her insensitivity extended to her own family. Her daily vituperative phone calls to son Jay likely hastened his death. When her sister Sandra lay dying in the hospital for two weeks, Leona never even telephoned—and she did not attend Sandra's funeral.

The
QUEEN
of
MEAN

*The Unauthorized
Biography of
Leona Helmsley*

Ransdell Pierson

BANTAM BOOKS
NEW YORK · TORONTO · LONDON · SYDNEY · AUCKLAND

THE QUEEN OF MEAN
A Bantam Book
September 1989

ISBN 0-553-28558-0

Published simultaneously in the United States and Canada

Bantam Books are published by Bantam Books, a division of Bantam Doubleday Dell Publishing Group, Inc. Its trademark, consisting of the words "Bantam Books" and the portrayal of a rooster, is Registered in U.S. Patent and Trademark Office and in other countries, Marca Registrada, Bantam Books, 666 Fifth Avenue, New York, New York 10103

PRINTED IN THE UNITED STATES OF AMERICA

KRI 0 9 8 7 6 5

The
QUEEN
of
MEAN

One

"Mama's on her way! Mama's coming!" a security guard announced into the telephone the instant Leona Helmsley's stretch limo pulled out of her Park Lane Hotel carport and headed into midtown New York City traffic. Nine blocks away, at Fiftieth Street and Madison Avenue, a front desk manager at the Helmsley Palace Hotel gave thanks for the warning. Within seconds, he activated step two of the early warning system by relaying the advisory to department managers throughout the fifty-one-story Palace.

In Paul Revere fashion, Palace managers took up the cry: "Mama's coming!" "Clean up that dessert cart!" "Take out those dirty trays!" "Get this carpet cleaned!" "Leona's on her way!"

The Queen's imminent arrival quickly filtered down to legions of Palace employees, who braced themselves for the worst. In the "back of the house"—the gritty work areas of the hotel where guests seldom stray—a flurry of cleaning, sweeping and mopping ensued. In the "front of the house," primping and fluffing raged apace. Maîtres d'hôtel straightened their collars and their postures, bathroom attendants sopped up unsightly counter puddles, and housekeepers rushed through the lobby plucking gnarled cigarette butts from every ashtray stand in sight. A half dozen waiters vanished into the kitchen where they performed useless chores rather than be seen idle in the not-yet-busy Le Trianon restaurant. The staff knew they had seven minutes at best to get the city's tallest hotel in ship shape. Perfection, or at least the illusion thereof, was restored in the $110 million hotel tower as the Queen's chauffeur snaked the bulletproof Cadillac through the noonday gridlock.

The dark blue luxury sedan was home free once it passed the twin marble spires of St. Patrick's Cathedral at Fiftieth Street and Fifth Avenue. A block to the east stood Leona Helmsley's pride and joy. Her Palace of 961 rooms soared high above the stately Gothic cathedral, within hi-fidelity earshot of its chiming nineteen bells. Just six hundred feet away, her guests could look down at the rectangular lawns and privet hedges of Rockefeller Center's roof gardens. Saks Fifth Avenue was equally close. For the view and the unbeatable location, guests were willing to pay $210 a night for an average room (plus a 13¼ percent sales and hotel tax), a tidy bundle even in cost-berserk Manhattan.

As usual, the chauffeur wheeled the limo into a private driveway that abuts the Fiftieth Street side entrance to the hotel. Two bodyguards in business suits slid out of the car and prepared to move, like bird dogs, in whichever direction Mrs. Helmsley led them. Instead of walking directly from the garage into the Palace—certainly a lackluster entrance—Mrs. Helmsley backtracked to the sidewalk and invested fifty extra steps for a proper entrance under the two-tiered bronze and glass marquee.

Thanks to the early warning system, doormen were standing ramrod straight in their custom-fitted khaki uniforms and plumed Australian digger hats as the Queen approached. Slumped shoulders, dirty fingernails and high-water pants were an evil trinity in the Queen's stylebook, and many an employee had been dressed down for forgetting that fundamental truth.

The billionaire proprietress entered with a flourish, her green eyes, impeccably coiffured hair, full scarlet lips and high Slavic cheekbones gleaming under the immense Baccarat chandelier in the grand foyer. The exotic cheekbones were her true beauty marks and distinguishing facial feature. But all eyes were fixed on the Queen for another, more elemental reason. It was her posture that *commanded* attention. Her absolutely faultless— yes, regal—posture. Shoulders and heels in perfect vertical alignment. A marvel of carriage that mothers and West Point coaches can only idealize for their young charges. Posture was the linchpin of her overwhelming presence, and gave Leona Helmsley the appearance of absolute invincibility.

Employees broke into glued-on, Pavlovian smiles when they caught sight of the mercurial 66-year-old hotel matriarch, who looked barely a day over 50, thanks to some eerie stroke of genetics or good fortune. The Skin and Muscle Tone God, if one exists, certainly stored up his blessings for Mrs. Helmsley. Her firm legs, fluid movements and seemingly unlined face contradicted the very passage of time. A rapid-fire sailor's vocabulary (complete with Brooklyn accent) would banish any

2

remaining idea that this was a garden-variety senior citizen.

The Queen had good reason to be proud of her hotel, for it was like none other in the world. Here, in one of the planet's most exclusive neighborhoods, the wrecking ball had been spared so that twentieth-century comfort could tenderly embrace nineteenth-century romance. The hotel was really two structures married on the altar of historic preservation.

Developer Harry Helmsley had erected the unadorned fifty-one-story aluminum-and-glass tower in 1980 and grafted it at the ankles to the Villard Houses, one of the city's finest brownstone mansions. The mansion was in fact a U-shaped cluster of six connected townhouses (disguised to look like one residence), inspired by Bramante's sixteenth-century Palazzo della Cancelleria in Rome. The complex had been designed a century earlier, in 1882, for financier and New York *Post* owner Henry Villard. Its large south wing, along Fiftieth Street, Villard saved for himself. He sold the other five houses to friends, who would steer their four-in-hands into a magnificent cobblestone courtyard that looked across Madison Avenue to the backside of St. Patrick's.

In 1886, after suffering business reverses, Villard sold his wing to Elisabeth Mills Reid and her husband, Whitelaw Reid, publisher and editor of the New York *Tribune*. Reid hired architect Stanford White, Irish-born sculptor Augustus St. Gaudens, painter John La Farge and the finest craftsmen of the day to create rooms fit for lavish social gatherings. The result was a palatial array of vaulted ceilings, murals, gilded wood and plaster, marble mosaics, detailed bronze and intricate marquetry.

For good reason, Helmsley proclaimed his new hotel tower a "Palace" when he opened it on September 12, 1980. With seamless surgical skill, his architects had linked it to the Villard Houses, which Helmsley had leased long-term in 1974 from the most recent owner of the historic complex: the Archdiocese of New York. The magnificently restored public rooms of the Villard-Reid wing afforded all the allure of older grand hotels. And the guest rooms encased in the modern tower ensured the comforts of up-to-date plumbing, heating and wiring. It was a hotel hybrid, aimed at combining the best of the old and new worlds. To ensure a unified Edwardian flow, public areas of the new hotel were fitted with pastel moiré wall coverings of an earlier era, coffered ceilings, hand-woven English rugs and

French walnut paneling. As an added historic touch, specially commissioned portraits of bygone European royalty were hung in elevator lobbies and the hallways of each guest floor. Many details, such as the sunburst chandelier design in the elevators—against a sky-blue ceiling—were a *bit* gaudy. But the hybrid seemed to work.

It was Leona Helmsley's own Renaissance dollhouse, and she examined it closely as she headed for an elevator to her command post—an ultra-feminine pink candy box of an office on the fifth floor of the tower. A salmon-pink silk Hepplewhite loveseat, English reproduction chairs, blush-tinted Oriental carpet and oval cherry partner's desk gave the office just the right aura of executive luxury. Over the mantle, and dominating the room, was a giant framed photograph of her husband. Like Gainsborough's "Blue Boy," Harry Helmsley's crinkle-eyed, benevolent gaze seemed to hit every spot in the room.

The Queen was in a decorating mood on this summer day, and she summoned her top executives for a discussion of new room designs. She instructed them to meet her in a conference room down the hall from her office. It was a convenient hideaway that doubled as her private dining room. There Mrs. Helmsley could have a quick lunch without the fuss of traveling downstairs to the formal Le Trianon restaurant.

In fact, she would often dine alone at the giant conference table, surrounded by a dozen empty chairs. Waiters would wheel in a cart laden with food under silver covers and tastefully decorated with fresh flowers. It was a feast for the eyes and a stimulant to the royal appetite. But who would serve the Queen? Somebody had to whisk off the silver covers with an appropriate flourish. Most waiters shrank from the daunting task, or betrayed their fear by approaching with rattling teacups. What if they made a wrong move? What if a drop of coffee was spilled into the royal lap?

There was the story of one brave waiter who declared himself fit for the task. He proudly lifted the silver tray and served properly to the left. The service plate was carefully set in the central position, the butter plate and roll basket on the left. Coffee cup and saucer were deftly placed on the right, with the handle of the cup pointed precisely at 3 o'clock. The coffee spoon, of course, was nestled in its proper home beneath the handle. Everything was down pat and the meal had been consumed in utter peace. Only coffee remained. In his research, the waiter had learned that protocol obliged him to fill no more than half the Queen's cup. "You know I don't like a full cup of coffee!" she had bellowed to many a waiter in the past. "It will get cold before I can drink it!"

Forewarned, the waiter smugly lifted the shiny silver Reed & Barton coffeepot and prepared to pour exactly one-half measure of Jamaican Blue Mountain coffee. *But nothing came out!* Not a single drop! It was empty!

The waiter's perfect little scenario came crashing down immediately when the Queen looked up directly into his face with a sneer: "I like my coffee a *little* darker!" she said. After giving the message ample time to sink in, she added, "Mister, you have one foot out of the door here! I'd be very careful from now on." Several months later, the servant joined the legions of ex–Palace employees.

Armed bodyguards were never far away in case an uninvited guest somehow gained entry into the Queen's inconspicuous private dining room. Security had been an obsession with Mrs. Helmsley since she and her husband were stabbed during a bungled 1973 burglary of their Palm Beach, Florida, vacation apartment. The puncture wound to her chest had healed, but memories of the attack made the billionaire survivor wary to the extreme.

"She often talked about her fear of being attacked," recalled one former top aide. "She felt there were a number of people who might want to do her harm. She felt people would love to hurt her because of enemies she had made and employees she had fired. She viewed the private dining room as a special security risk because often she would have outsiders in there for meetings and knew very little about them. Her security guards always had small handguns and walkie-talkies."

No such concern weighed on Mrs. Helmsley this summer day, for known entities had been invited to join her at the table for decorating strategy. Decorators and financial aides were the first of six male executives to arrive for the noontime powwow. Also present was Milton Meckler, executive vice president of Deco Purchasing and Distributing Co., a Helmsley subsidiary that provided supplies and furnishings to the Palace and two dozen other Helmsley hotels.

As materials and fabrics were discussed, hunger pangs grew stronger, and at 1 P.M., Mrs. Helmsley asked one assistant, "How about having sandwiches brought up?" The food order was phoned in to the kitchen, and for the umpteenth time the diet-conscious Queen of the Helmsley Palace was having tuna fish.

And not just any tuna fish. The chef was under strict orders to use only Bumble Bee fancy albacore tuna, packed in water. Bumble Bee packed in vegetable oil was verboten, and waiters had been berated for serving it in the past. The water-packed Bumble Bee tuna was then to be prepared with just a dollop of real mayonnaise, some lemon juice and finely chopped onion. Finally, it was to be served on dry rye bread. The chef also knew that the Queen loved, in fact demanded, a mound of rock-hard jalapeño peppers alongside her sandwich. The same jalapeños that would make grown men cry or gag, the Queen would eat like popcorn.

Two waiters and their food supervisor arrived, looking regal in their neatly pressed maroon jackets, and laid out a platter of offerings, each sandwich accompanied by a simple lettuce garnish. The servants then stood erect, almost at attention, while Mrs. Helmsley and her aides filled their plates.

Suddenly and completely without warning, a shriek pierced the silence just as everybody was ready to dig in. It came from Mrs. Helmsley, who yelled, "Wait a second! Don't touch your food!" She was almost gasping for breath. "Don't you see what's wrong?" When none of the group could find an answer, Meckler screwed up his courage and asked, "What *is* wrong?" With a withering scowl, Mrs. Helmsley ordered: "Look at the lettuce! Don't you see there's water droplets on the lettuce?"

Water droplets! The outrage had completely escaped the diners' notice, "but we kept totally quiet and didn't dare laugh," Meckler said, "because she was three pitches above her normal tone, which meant we were in for a scene."

Mrs. Helmsley then heaped all her fury on the three servants, screaming: "Don't you see what you've done?" With veins bulging from her neck, and her face twisted into a gargoyle grimace, Meckler recalled, "Mrs. Helmsley went around and picked up everybody's lettuce off their plates" and approached the servants like a general inspecting her troops. "Then, armed with the clump of lettuce, she went into a convulsion-type atmosphere, shouting, 'How dare you do this?' and she shook the lettuce, like a wet sponge, and sprayed each of them in the face. She went up and down the line and sprayed all of them and said, 'I should fire all of you right now!'

"The servants just stood there and said nothing," Meckler added. "Everybody in the room was so embarrassed for them.

6

It was so demeaning to these guys. I was hoping someone would take the lettuce and tell her to shove it. But they were young Hispanics and needed their jobs, and kept quiet."

The executives had witnessed dozens of the Queen's rages since Harry Helmsley—the living legend of New York real estate—had made his wife president of Helmsley Hotels in 1980. But water droplets! Never had they witnessed such an esoteric rampage. The lettuce scene set off warning bells. Mrs. Helmsley's notorious daily tirades were becoming even more frequent and irrational. Unknown Furies were gnawing at the Queen, sapping her concentration from the Palace, five other Manhattan hotels, and seventeen out-of-state inns known as the Harley hotel chain. These days, it seemed, her explosions almost ran into one another, and anyone could wind up on the royal slaughterhouse floor.

Irrational or not, however, Leona Helmsley's power was very real. Just months before, on April 18, 1986, her 77-year-old husband had won front-page headlines for donating $33 million to New York Hospital. The *New York Times* reported that the gift would enable the 215-year-old hospital to complete a thirty-six-story staff residence which would be called the Helmsley Medical Tower.

Harry Helmsley made no bones about his reason for parting with the $33 million, the largest charitable contribution made by any American that year. "I'm trying to make myself one of the important people in New York and so I wanted to do something for New York," the tycoon said bluntly to the *New York Times*.

Readers of the article might have been confused. How could Harry Helmsley, New York's wealthiest man, publicly admit to his desire to be "important"? How could this living legend, near the end of a fabled career and with an unimaginably huge pile of real estate, feel like the rawest arriviste?

To be sure, the six-foot-three-inch real estate mogul would never set the mega-trendy metropolis on fire with his unassuming personality or his bland poker face. It was a genial face dominated by wire-rimmed glasses, narrow pushed-back strands of gray hair, a pointillistically thin mustache, and rather large protruding ears. On occasion, he was described as a "big rabbit."

However, by Gotham's overriding criterion—the standard of wherewithal—Helmsley had *already* achieved importance beyond compare. He owned the city's greatest fortune: $1.1 billion, according to the 1986 Forbes Four Hundred list of wealthiest Americans. A flamboyant 39-year-old rival, "Artist of the Deal" Donald Trump, was far behind on the Forbes scorecard, although he snared more headlines for his wonder-boy accumulation of hotels and casinos. Unlike Trump, who is the son of a multimillionaire developer, Helmsley started from nowhere. From scratch, he had become one of the largest property owners in New York City, a city which remained the trade center of the nation and financial heartbeat of the world. Skyscrapers are the true mountains of Manhattan, and Harry Helmsley owned or controlled some of its most venerated peaks. King Kong's lofty perch, the 102-story Empire State Building, had long since fallen into Helmsley's hands. And for fifty blocks, the focal point of Park Avenue was the double-arched Helmsley Building: a magnificently gold-leafed thirty-five-story tower that straddled the elegant thoroughfare like a Colossus of Rhodes.

His hotel portfolio included six Manhattan hotels with four thousand three hundred rooms, and a three thousand five hundred–room chain of seventeen Harley hotels (supposedly named by joining the first syllables of Harry and Leona) sprinkled in eleven states from Florida to Wisconsin. Nationwide, Helmsley also controlled no fewer than fifty thousand apartments and fifty million square feet of commercial space. With inflation and Manhattan's rapidly increasing land values, his fortune was leaping in value by millions of dollars each week.

As the second wife and heir of the childless tycoon, Leona Helmsley was automatically one of the important people on Manhattan island, the twenty-square-mile cultural and commercial heart of the city. Yet, like her husband, she seemed to need public recognition of her high standing. And a great acknowledgment had just been paid. Ecstasy would be too mild a word to describe the surge of pleasure the Queen must have felt when she opened the freshly printed August 1986 issue of *New Woman* magazine. There for all the world to see was a vivid testimonial to her success as president of one of the nation's largest independent hotel operations. In full-color glossy format, the article described her perfectionist streak and her storybook marriage to the sultan of Big Apple real estate.

"She raised the picky-picky theory of management to an all-time high," the article enthused, "and is arguably one of the most powerful women in America—to say nothing of the wealthiest!"

Recognition indeed.

"But when it comes to her love life, she's part of a new breed of old-fashioned women—tigers in the boardroom, pussycats in the bedroom—and they don't bat an eye when it's time to change roles."

Sexy copy.

"Demanding, perfectionist Leona, who is almost never satisfied when it comes to plushness of towels and firmness of beds, didn't stop touching Harry. When they walked, she held him—held on to him, to be precise. When they talked, she absentmindedly ran her fingers along his arm. She stroked him as they listened to the guest of honor's speech. She reached up and pressed her fingers to his face when they left the party and thought no one was there to see. Leona, in a nutshell, really digs Harry."

(It might be noted that the Helmsleys good-naturedly allowed the press to dispense with the stiff, formal titles of address. No need for "Mr. " or "Mrs." Helmsley. Just call them Harry and Leona in the fun spirit of the make-believe Queen and her palace.)

Leona, flushed with excitement, summoned Tad Distler from his office down the hall from her pink command post. Distler, as the account executive from Beber Silverstein & Partners advertising agency, was in charge of buffing the Queen's public image to the highest possible luster.

Distler, a trim, blond 50-year-old Yale graduate, sped to the royal sanctum as fast as his tassled loafers could carry him.

Mrs. Helmsley handed him a copy of the flattering article and ordered him to have 250,000 reprints made as soon as possible. Distler had experience in these matters and knew exactly what to do. He would get reprint permission from the magazine and then hire a private printing company to produce a truckload of the reprints on magazine-quality paper in oversized pamphlet form. A copy, with the Queen's smiling scarlet lips and perfectly coiffed hair on each cover, would be placed on the dresser of every hotel room in the Helmsley domain. Every guest could become almost friends with the Queen.

Distler's Miami-based firm, Beber Silverstein, had conceived the brilliant advertising theme that made Leona Helmsley a household name to millions of Americans. Partners Joyce Beber and Elaine Silverstein, owners of Florida's largest ad agency, named Leona "Queen of the Helmsley Palace" in a 1982 national advertising blitz. "The Only Palace in the World

Where the Queen Stands Guard" became a motto for the hotel and also underscored Leona's personal commitment to quality control at her other hotels.

By 1986, the agency was spending $5 million annually in print ads to continue the Palace slogan, as well as to advertise her other hotels. The *New York Times* alone ran $1.5 million worth, frequently with three separate rapid-fire ads on consecutive pages of its widely read Sunday magazine supplement.

The *New Woman* article was a special coup because it was incredible *unpaid* advertising. It was the biggest burst of free recognition since March 12, 1984, when *New York* magazine—like *New Woman* a Rupert Murdoch publication—ran an even lengthier queenly tribute entitled "Life with Leona." *New York* writer Bernice Kanner described the Queen's "whip hand" rule over the Palace. "Faster than a guided missile," Kanner wrote, Mrs. Helmsley "bore down on the maîtresse d'. 'Is this your room?'

" 'Yes, ma'am.'

" 'Don't yes ma'am me; I'm furious with you. This place is a disgrace. These dirty ashtrays aren't going to walk out by themselves. I want you in this room until it's straightened up right. And I am going to come back tomorrow and tomorrow, and if I see it again, heads will roll.' Then, almost pleadingly, 'Please don't make me do this.' "

The article described the Queen as an absolute "bug on details," who resents hanger hooks that are welded into the closet, plastic drinking glasses, inadequate bathroom lighting, small vanity mirrors and tepid coffee. "You know that she can't get by without a phone in the bath, or get dressed without a full-length mirror."

Leona loved the *New York* portrayal of her as whiplashing taskmaster. At least 1.25 million reprints rolled off the conveyor belts at Optima Press, the Manhattan firm that ordinarily printed menus and stationery for the Helmsley hotels. At 20 cents a shot, the $250,000 reprint job was expensive luster indeed for the Queen's public image. The glossy reprints were placed in the racks and lobbies of the hotels and, of course, were continually replenished in every guest room.

"It was a big expenditure," Distler said, but as far as the Queen was concerned, "If it's about her, nothing's too big."

The *New Woman* article temporarily lifted Leona out of the unexplained funk that seemed to have enveloped her that summer of 1986—a season that marked the one hundredth anniversary of the Statue of Liberty's presence in New York harbor. Publicity had a way of soothing Mrs. Helmsley's jangled nerves; it had an almost medicinal effect on the mercurial Queen. Yet no single burst of fanfare—neither the *New Woman* article nor the weekly *New York Times* ads—could serve as anything more than a short-lived tonic. Fame was an addiction that required ever larger doses to satisfy the Queen's craving. Like Narcissus gazing into the pool, Mrs. Helmsley scanned the newsstands for evidence of her image.

Distler, as royal ad man, was the hired hand responsible for generating the images in geometric profusion. Earlier that year, in January, a novel idea had come to his attention that he would later curse each remaining day of the year. Eastern Airlines had approached Beber Silverstein to ask if it would consider a joint advertising campaign between the airline and Helmsley Hotels. The idea was a simple one. The two organizations would jointly advertise on thousands of decks of playing cards and share the 47-cent cost of producing each deck. The cards would then be handed out on Eastern flights.

Distler took the idea to Mrs. Helmsley, but "for fun" he first cut out a photo of her and pasted it on the queen of hearts of an ordinary deck. "I thought this was rather amusing and that she might go for it." To his surprise, Mrs. Helmsley sorted through the cards and immediately declared: "Well, I think we should put me on *more* cards!"

Leona had gotten his little practical joke, all right, and had decided to expand the punch line. Distler was tempted to laugh, but replied earnestly: "I don't think Eastern will go along with a lot of pictures of you if you want them to pay for part of this promotion."

To appease her, Distler made up a dummy deck with photos of over a dozen hotels; to perhaps twenty-four other cards he affixed different full-color photos of Leona that had been borrowed from the advertising files.

"She looked through this and saw that all the hotels were pictured and she said, 'Well! You haven't put in that wonderful picture of me by the piano! You haven't put in that wonderful picture of me by the ballroom! You haven't put in that wonderful picture of me doing this, or me doing that!' "

Weren't twenty-four photos enough? Just how many pictures of herself did the Queen want? Then, as Distler scanned her office, the full weight of his blunder hit him. There were—count them—seventy-three framed photographs of Leona scattered about the sanctum.

Distler could have kicked himself for pasting up Leona's picture in the first place. Now he was forced back to the drawing board in a desperate bid to satisfy a royal ego. He returned with his handiwork. "I pulled out our files," he explained to her, "and got all thirty-six pictures of you that we have ever taken and put them on the cards. And when there weren't enough pictures of you, I filled in with the important hotels."

He then advised Mrs. Helmsley that "if you're going to fill up every card with your pictures, we should of course put Harry on the kings." Although the thought had never occurred to the Queen, she readily agreed.

As Distler expected, Eastern bowed out. With the airline out of the picture, Mrs. Helmsley ordered Distler to proceed independently, and with all speed, on the project. Like all good executives, she could adapt to changing circumstances. Instead of being handed out on airplanes, her playing cards would be distributed as party favors at her annual Fourth of July birthday bash at Dunnellen Hall, the Helmsleys' baronial $8 million Greenwich, Connecticut, estate. Distler was given strict orders to meet the deadline. Thousands of other decks would be printed and put on sale in the lobbies of the Queen's various hotels.

Distler soon learned that he had embarked on a virtually impossible task. Cost, for one thing, had become a major stumbling block. From 47 cents a deck originally, the price had skyrocketed to $7 a deck because of unforeseen manufacturing problems. He learned that few card companies are equipped to produce the four-color reproductions Mrs. Helmsley wanted on each card. "Usually they print only in black, red and yellow," Distler explained, "so it got to be a very expensive proposition." How would the frugal Queen react to the financial conundrum? After all, this was a 1500 percent cost overrun. Distler held his breath as he imparted the news. "I don't care," she responded to his amazement. "The cards look wonderful. It's fun! It's wonderful! It's fun!"

Months of negotiations ensued with card companies. Delays arose when Mrs. Helmsley unexpectedly changed the pictures she wanted on the cards. More time was eaten away when Mrs. Helmsley suddenly found fault with the size of the cards. "I came in with a deck one day," said Distler, "and she complained, 'These are too small!'"

"Now, wait a minute," Distler replied. "Cards are all the

12

same; these are standard bridge cards."

"No, you're wrong!" Leona insisted.

"Well, if I am, please prove me wrong," Distler answered.

The Queen then immediately dispatched her secretary to the store with orders to bring back "a fresh deck of pinochle cards." The secretary returned with a pinochle deck and indeed they were bigger and wider. Distler knew another three weeks would be wasted taking new bids for the larger cards, so he gave the Queen a pitch for keeping the bridge cards.

"The type of people who come to the Helmsley Palace will play bridge; they won't understand these bigger cards."

The Queen, a little unsure of the merits of Distler's argument, needed an adviser. "Call Lerigo!" she screamed out to her secretary.

Into the room, in sartorial splendor, walked Geoffrey E. P. Lerigo, executive vice president and arbiter of taste for the Helmsley hotels.

Lerigo, scion of a British earl, was the unseen power behind the throne of Leona Helmsley. This elegant gentleman in banker's pinstripes was the *only* employee in the Queen's hotel domain with true job security. He was an absolutely invaluable resource to Harry and Leona Helmsley, and now his advice was needed on the matter of playing cards.

"Which do you like better, Lerigo?" the Queen asked while displaying the two sizes of decks.

Lerigo scrutinized the choices for a judicious period and announced: "The bridge deck is quite elegant enough. But since I wear glasses, I like the larger size—the pinochle deck—better."

Distler, foiled again in the maddening card crisis, could have shot Lerigo on the spot for unwittingly siding with the Queen. There was no use pursuing the debate any longer, however, for Lerigo had spoken. Distler requested new bids from the card manufacturers for larger decks. Weeks slid down the drain, new bids arrived, and Distler returned to the Queen's pink sanctum.

"All right, we are about to go to press," he told her. "Is there anything else you want on them? Do you want the edges gilded? If you do, it's going to raise the cost another dollar ninety-five up to nine dollars a deck." To which the Queen replied: "No, I don't want the gilding; that's it." No sooner had production begun than Leona issued another royal stop-work order. In addition to the fifty-two cards, she now commanded that two of her favorite cartoons be reprinted and used as jokers.

In one, from *The New Yorker*, a well-to-do housewife vents her frustration as her husband reads the paper in front of the fireplace. "Why can't *you* buy some hotels and make *me* your queen?" she demands to know. The other cartoon, from the *New York Times*, was a crude drawing of the U.S. Capitol in which the House and Senate have been displaced by separate Leona and Harry wings.

Leona Helmsley was capable of laughing louder than anyone else at her own pretense to American royalty. And Warren Miller's *New Yorker* cartoon tickled her funnybone like no other caricature of her lifestyle—so much so that a blowup of the ink drawing hangs on her office wall.

Distler had to remind his boss that regardless of how humorous they were, the cartoons couldn't be reproduced without permission.

"And her attitude was, 'Of course they can; they're about me!'

"I replied that the *Times* and *The New Yorker* copyright these things and they don't care who you are!"

One thing was for sure. There was no way to secure copyright permission and print the jokers in time for Leona's birthday party. The day of the party arrived, and her guests received the fruits of Tad Distler's six-month struggle: a copious assortment of Leona Helmsley poses on jokerless, pinochle-sized playing cards. On the four of clubs, she stokes a Palace fire in the massive Augustus Saint-Gaudens marble fireplace without charring her gold lamé dress. Looking like a silver butterfly in a feather-trimmed sequin gown, she reaches on her tiptoes to light a candle on the jack of spades. On the eight of diamonds, she holds a gigantic shrimp aloft like a trophy dripping cocktail sauce. Wearing a tiara and a gold lamé raincoat, she heads for inclement weather on the ace of hearts. Harry, by contrast, is relegated to the same brown suit and same pose—he squints into the camera while adjusting his glasses—on the four kings.

The birthday party came and went, but alas, the card crisis was far from over. Another 10,000 decks remained unprinted, and Mrs. Helmsley wanted them pronto—with jokers. Distler realized that his little joke had been taken literally to heart. "The cards had become the Queen's cause célèbre of 1986; they were her equivalent of the Manhattan Project or the Wollman Rink."

In a July 29 memo to Beber Silverstein, Distler reported that he met with Mrs. Helmsley that morning and received a warning: "If the jokers aren't ready, she's going to make a joker out of me. We need at least three or four weeks to resolve and get permission from both the *New York Times* and *New Yorker* magazine. Will you please mention the copyright problem to Mrs. Helmsley? I have brought it up repeatedly, but she chooses to ignore it." The next day, Distler drafted another memo advising that Mrs. Helmsley's corporate sales staff would use the playing cards as "door openers" when they solicited accounts in the field.

After some delay, the *Times* and *New Yorker* gave permission to reproduce the cartoons and 10,000 of the decks were printed. Grateful that the trying project was now at an end, Distler triumphantly carried several of the decks to Mrs. Helmsley's office. But within seconds, the triumph fizzled.

"When I took them in, she started throwing them all over the office" in a wild fury. The cards fell like four-color rain in Leona's version of 52-Card Pickup. She then screamed, 'These don't have gold edges!'

" And I said, 'You didn't want them gilded!'

" 'Yes, I did!' she insisted.

"And I said, 'It would have cost a dollar ninety-five extra per deck!'

" 'I don't care; I want them gilded,' " she demanded. Before embarking on the enormous gilding job, Distler had one deck of the cards gilded and brought the sample to the Queen for her approval. She was ecstatic.

"While playing with the gilded vs. the white-edged cards on her desk," Distler noted in an August 11 memo to Beber Silverstein, "she claimed the gilded cards were a much better quality paper, even though there's absolutely no difference. Indeed, the gilded ones were white-edged several days ago."

The memo also noted that "Mrs. Helmsley wants the two cartoon jokers to be packaged on the outside of the box. We will immediately proceed to put this plan into effect." But the crisis remained unsolved: who could be found to gold-plate the remaining decks?

In desperation, Distler fired off an August 27 memo to Beber Silverstein advising that "Mrs. Helmsley's main thoughts are still focused on the playing cards. We *must* get them gilded and to her, even on a piecemeal basis, <u>ASAP</u>. Please push this and I will do the same here in New York."

By some miracle, Distler managed to find "a little 85-year-old bookbinder" who agreed to remove each of the 10,000 decks from its cellophane wrapper, individually place each deck in a vise and gild it. Then he would re-encase the decks in new cellophane wrappers and repackage them.

In a September 11, 1986 memo to Miami headquarters, Distler reported that the first big batch of gilded playing cards had come in "and Mrs. Helmsley cannot understand why she doesn't have all 10,000 of them at the same time. I tried to explain, but she lost interest."

Weeks passed before the gilded, jokered, pinochle-sized decks finally reached the newsstands of the hotels, marked up to $12.95. (The price soon rose to $15.) Distler said hotel customers were astounded by the souvenirs. "They were a novelty item. Nobody had ever done a deck of cards with a picture of themselves on every other card." When guests asked the point of the whole exercise, Distler could only joke out loud: "Where else but in a deck of cards can so many of Leona's pictures be displayed, and in such an easy-to-carry form?"

The public might scoff, but the cards were a surefire hit with the Queen. "She was just crazed by them. She would put them in baskets with fruit and wine that went up to the rooms. She would send them to VIP guests."

The Queen of the Helmsley Palace, who stands guard over 5,000 employees and a $1 billion hotel empire, had given the cards her unflagging attention for ten long months.

"It was the most time-consuming project of the year by far— by far!" Distler said. "It just drove me crazy. For months I was fretting about those playing cards. I was working with so many different companies and they all said, 'We can't do it this way; we can't have it that way.' It was like doing fifty-two different magazine ads. Each card had to go through the same four-color process as an advertisement in the *New York Times*. It was so...well, so...out of the norm."

Like the magazine tributes, the playing cards had only a temporary calming effect on the Queen. As the month of September wore on, employees on the fifth floor saw tensions build like a gathering storm. The Queen was unbelievably volatile by nature; everyone knew that. But the space between her tantrums—the cooling-off periods—was becoming noticeably shorter.

Mike Randall, a young receptionist at Beber Silverstein's fifth-floor Palace office, was the target that month of one such frightful tirade.

One afternoon, he pleasantly answered the phone with the

singsong greeting: "Be-ber Sil-ver-stein," and was confronted by a hard-edged, growling voice.

"This is Leona Helmsley," the gruff caller said. "What's your name?"

Randall said the voice at the other end of the line "was pure Brooklyn truckdriver. It was such a deep *husky* voice, maybe from too many years of smoking cigarettes. And she was not in a pleasant mood."

"Mike Randall is my name," he answered.

"What do you do there?"

"I'm a receptionist."

"I don't care if you swing from the chandeliers," she growled. "Get up here to Greenwich and get these recipes!"

Randall had no idea what recipes his gravel-voiced Queen was referring to, but was certain "that this woman was psychotic, crazed."

He quickly learned that the recipes were for a new "Low-Salt, No-Cholesterol Gourmet Menu" Mrs. Helmsley was planning for the Palace. The "gourmet" part of the title seemed a bit contradictory, he thought as he dashed about in search of a car for the thirty-two-mile drive northeast to Greenwich.

Within thirty minutes he skidded off the Merritt Parkway onto Round Hill Road, the most blueblood street in the ultimate blueblood suburb of Greenwich. A few moments later a security guard waved Randall through the swinging wrought-iron gates of number 521, and Randall walked around to the back of an immense hilltop mansion right out of *Town and Country* magazine. He could count eight chimneys on the sprawling roof, and no telling how many acres sloping down toward Long Island Sound.

There, at the kitchen door, was a casually dressed woman holding a handful of index cards.

The vision was just as shocking to Randall as the voice he had heard on the telephone. Was this the same glamorous Queen he had spotted before in the fifth-floor corridors of the Palace? The radiant Queen who shone forth every Sunday in the magazine section of the *Times*?

But it was Leona Helmsley, Randall said. "She was wearing cheap jeans, a white polyester blouse that I could see through, and tennis shoes with no socks. She had no makeup on at all, and her face was all lined. Her cheeks were all wrinkled, real deep lines. And she had big pouting lips that go down.

"I'm here to pick up the recipes," he announced, and Mrs.

Helmsley handed them to him. Just as quickly, he said, "she yanked them back and said, 'I'm not going to give you my recipes! What are you going to do about it!'"

"I was shaking in my boots," Randall recalled, having no idea what on earth the Queen meant by the curious challenge. "I thought she wanted me to come inside and have sex with her, quite frankly. So all I could answer was, 'I have no idea.'"

Mrs. Helmsley then reached inside for a yellow legal pad and pencil and handed it to Randall. "I'm not going to give you my original recipes," she repeated. "You start copying them down and I don't give a good damn if you stand here all day!"

She led Randall inside to the kitchen and told him to lean up against a kitchen cabinet and start writing.

"After I was writing for over an hour without a chair or a table," Randall recalled, "she came and got the index cards from me and gave them to a black servant. And she told the servant, 'Photocopy these for me.'"

Randall could scarcely believe his ears. *She has a Xerox machine and just made me write down all her recipes!*

Mrs. Helmsley then approached Randall and said, "I could have photocopied these for you an hour ago, but I had to teach you a lesson."

A lesson? What kind of lesson Randall couldn't imagine.

"Do you understand?" she asked.

Randall replied, "I don't think so."

She then said, "It's three-thirty in the afternoon and you had all goddamned day to get here!"

Randall thought to himself, "She called me at two o'clock. I got here in less than thirty minutes. I couldn't have gotten here quicker by helicopter."

Rather than argue the issue, he took the photocopied recipes and said, "It's been a real pleasure meeting you, Mrs. Helmsley."

"No, it hasn't," she shot back.

Randall drove off thinking to himself, "What a sick encounter. This is white trash that has sort of a brain. And with all her money, she wears polyester. I could see her bra."

He immediately reported his encounter to his superiors at Beber Silverstein. But just a week or two later he found himself again face-to-face with the Queen—made up and looking a decade younger this time—in a cramped elevator at the Palace.

"I was carrying a bundle of packages, and all of a sudden she grabbed one out of my arms and ripped it open to see what was inside. She had no idea who the package was for or whether it pertained to her or another account. Beber Silverstein had four other accounts in New York, and it just happened to be a Helmsley account. It was frightening. It was so disturbing I had nightmares about it."

The next day, Randall phoned Joyce Beber in Miami and confided the experience to his shockproof, approachable boss. "I told Joyce: 'Don't ever involve me with her again.' I said if I ever saw Leona Helmsley again I would tell her in public what a sick bitch she is, and that I would have told her that in Connecticut but I was afraid she would have had her bodyguards cripple me."

The last day of the month, on September 30, Leona Helmsley escorted her husband to New York's Eye and Ear Infirmary, where he was to undergo surgery to correct severely inflamed lower eyelids. The condition is not uncommon among men of advanced age, and Harry Helmsley was midway into his 77th year. He was to spend at least two nights in the hospital at 310 East Fourteenth Street, and Mrs. Helmsley hired Charmaine McFarlane, a 33-year-old private-duty nurse, to be in attendance. As double insurance that he would receive the best possible care, Leona herself was determined to be at her husband's side every minute.

It would become one of the most memorable times in the life of the nurse, who had never heard of the Helmsleys before the assignment and never really understood *how* prominent the couple were until the scandal rocked the city two months later. But it was an experience she decided she would just as soon forget.

McFarlane recalled that Mrs. Helmsley, dressed in a checkered double-breasted suit with gold buttons, was the picture of hospitality the first night.

"She was so nice. She came up and took my hand and said, 'I'm Leona Helmsley.' She chitchatted with me, and when I was reading a *Cosmopolitan* magazine she remarked that she thought it was all trash."

The nurse noted, however, that the sweetness seemed to disappear when Mrs. Helmsley got on the telephone for business calls. "Then all of a sudden she was so crude."

From the first moment she met the billionaire couple, McFarlane felt an overwhelming sense that Mrs. Helmsley had a strange, absolute control over her husband.

To begin with, she was surprised that "Mrs. Helmsley

checked into the same room and wouldn't leave at all, not even to take a walk down the hallway. She even followed him into the bathroom when he needed to go, instead of me going with him as a nurse." Mrs. Helmsley's constant hovering was surprising, McFarlane said, "because Mr. Helmsley was only in there for minor surgery. He wasn't there for heart surgery or anything like that."

The nurse said Helmsley's eyelids were turning in toward the eyeballs, and he had huge bags under his eyes. Discomfort was the greatest problem, but his doctor had no doubt the condition could be easily corrected by surgery.

"Mrs. Helmsley then proceeded to tell the [female] doctor what to do," McFarlane recalls. "She told the doctor she wanted the eyes prepared in such a way that her husband did not lose that *'He-e-lmmsleee look.'* "

When the doctor proceeded to take Mr. Helmsley's medical history prior to surgery, McFarlane "found it very funny" that Mrs. Helmsley answered the questions, as if by proxy. "The doctor would say, 'Mr. Helmsley, have you had any prior surgery?' And she would say, 'Remember, honey, you had such and such an operation ten years ago.' And he would say, 'That's right.' And she would say, 'See honey, it's a *good* thing I'm here.' If the doctor asked, 'Are you having pain, Mr. Helmsley?' she'd say yes or no without him answering. Maybe she has ESP. Isn't that strange? I think she totally controls him."

In fact, said McFarlane, thirty minutes before surgery—at 11:30 A.M.—Mrs. Helmsley "had this man doing exercises. 'Honey, come on. Let's work on the chin now. Let's do this.' She had him doing exercises! Everyone knows before surgery you should be relaxing. And she had this man working up a sweat.

"He does whatever she tells him to do. If he sits and crosses his legs, she'll say, 'Okay, uncross your legs, my darling.' He did whatever she said like he didn't have a mind of his own. I can see how it happens because she showers him with all this love and attention and makes herself so indispensable. For instance, if he takes off his watch or his shorts, before he can even put them down properly, she has already scooped them up and put them where she wants to put them. So when he starts looking for it later, he has to go to her. 'Honey, I just put my watch down. Have you seen it?' And she'll say, 'Oh yes, I have it!' Whatever he wants, he has to go through her."

For breakfast, the Helmsleys would have bialys, oatmeal and

Blue Mountain coffee. When McFarlane proceeded to feed Mr. Helmsley, his wife stepped in and said: "No way!" Only the Queen could feed the King.

The operation took place as scheduled on October 1, and Mr. Helmsley spent several hours in the recovery room. "I was in the recovery room with him alone," said McFarlane, "and he was very pleasant." She said it was the only brief span of time "that Mrs. Helmsley was apart from him, and that was because he was in the recovery room where she couldn't go."

In the meantime, to keep herself occupied ("She has a lot of energy and can't keep still"), Mrs. Helmsley played endless games of backgammon with one of her security guards. The healthy Queen also managed to conduct a prodigious amount of business from her own hospital bed. "She made a lot of phone calls, a *whole* lot, constantly," the nurse recalled. "She was talking to one hotel manager about seventy rooms that had old carpets, and she was trying to put in new carpets. She got on the phone and said the samples he sent her weren't good enough. She asked him how many people he had in the office and she said, 'I want everybody out on their cans today looking for samples and I want the samples within twenty-four hours because you're trying to ruin my hotels. And before you ruin my hotels, I'll make sure you're ruined first!' "

And McFarlane thought to herself, "How can this guy on the other end of the phone work for her?"

Mrs. Helmsley also killed lots of time, McFarlane said, applying her makeup. "It took her two hours. She's very meticulous. Everything had to be just, just right. She just sits there and admires herself. She sits in front of the mirror. She puts on this eye shadow and then takes it off. She put it on and took it off ten times. She looked at her expressions. She smiled, and then she put on a sad face. She'd laugh at herself in the mirror. And she'd look serious. Then she'd laugh and look sideways and look at her profile. She'd look all sorts of ways to see how she looked with different expressions. It was good entertainment."

Rather than eat hospital fare, Mrs. Helmsley phoned one of her hotels to order a hot meal delivered to the hospital room. Uniformed waiters, possibly from the Park Lane Hotel, promptly arrived with silver platters loaded with chafing dishes of food and china.

At that very moment, just as the waiters were laying out the movable feast, Mr. Helmsley returned from the recovery room.

McFarlane said Mrs. Helmsley saw him on the stretcher, jumped to her feet as if the room was on fire and began barking orders drill-sergeant style.

The nurse couldn't believe the rudeness of the Queen's commands: " 'Okay now,' she shouted to the waiters. 'Out! Out! Out! Get out, all of you,' like she's talking to a pack of dogs. I couldn't believe how nasty she was, because just a few minutes before that she was all subdued.

"It was like Dr. Jekyll and Mr. Hyde behavior," said McFarlane, who added that she knew at that moment "that my turn would come. I knew she would eventually have to turn on me like she had turned on the waiters."

Once Mr. Helmsley was comfortably restored to his bed, the waiters were beckoned back inside the room. "They stayed there and waited on her. They poured the coffee, served this, or did that."

Another outburst came only hours later when Mrs. Helmsley lambasted the hospital's engineering department for failing to get the chill out of her room. "She thought it was too cold," McFarlane said, "although it seemed very comfortable to me. She kept calling the engineers on the phone and they came up to adjust the air conditioner four times. But no matter what they did, they couldn't adjust it to her liking. She turned on them and kept saying, 'Don't you know what you're doing?' "

The Queen was further discomfited by the hospital's overhead paging system, which echoed through the hallway every time a nurse or doctor was paged by the hospital switchboard. With each new announcement, the Queen grew more furious and finally asked McFarlane to call the hospital operator and order her to cease paging the staff "because it was disturbing her husband. I told her I couldn't do that, and she got nasty about that."

Another curious thing, the nurse noticed, was that in the midst of all the acrimonious incidents, "Mrs. Helmsley constantly, tenderly told her husband—a hundred times a day— how much she loved him and how much she admired him. She kept telling him all the time he was a genius. You know, like convincing him he made the right choice in marrying her. Every second word that came out of her mouth was how she made the right choice by marrying this genius. And I found it highly unusual for someone with her status and her power to be convincing this man he made the right choice."

To McFarlane's utter confusion, Mrs. Helmsley could immediately switch gears during the middle of a cooing session with her husband. "All of a sudden a tyrant would come out when she got on the phone with her employees. It was like she had several different personalities, like a schizophrenic."

Between her bouts of anger, Mrs. Helmsley insisted on applying the ice compresses to her husband's eyes following surgery, although McFarlane was hired to do it. "She took the compresses I had on his eyes, she put them back in the ice and reapplied the same dirty compresses instead of using a sterile new one. I told her I'm supposed to do that, and nurses try to be as sterile as possible."

Mrs. Helmsley turned to McFarlane and sneered, "Talk to me about sterile! Do you know how many hotels I own and how much food they cook every day?"

"What does that have to do with sterility?" the nurse answered. "Food doesn't have to be sterile!"

The Queen, who apparently was not accustomed to such democratic give-and-take, then told McFarlane she did not like the nurse's way of doing things.

" 'There are three ways of doing things.' she told me. 'There's the right way, the wrong way and the Helmsley way.' And she wanted it done the Helmsley way."

McFarlane said she started to chuckle at the novel concept— "I just couldn't help but laugh"—and Mrs. Helmsley took offense at the less-than-reverential response. "She wanted to know what I was laughing about, and I told her I didn't learn anything about the Helmsley way in nursing school."

The unintentional insolence put a bee in the Queen's bonnet, McFarlane said, and "she really got up and came towards me and started pointing in my face. She wanted to know if I knew who I was talking to. I thought she was really going to strike me. She was really coming up, shaking her finger and stamping her feet like a child with a temper tantrum. And at that point her security guard jumped in between the both of us and told me, 'I think you better leave right now.'

"And I said, 'I'm not going to leave until I'm paid my fee.' I wasn't going to let her talk to me that way. I was the professional there, not her. She didn't even wash her hands."

What surprised McFarlane was Mr. Helmsley's complete obliviousness to the whole scene. "He said nothing at all when his wife was ranting and raving. He must have known that she was wrong. He just lay there with his eyes closed and didn't say a word. And when she refused to pay me, I said, 'Mr.

Helmsley, is there any way you can arrange for me to be paid?' He didn't answer at all, even when I was leaving. I said, 'Mr. Helmsley, it was a pleasure working for you.' And I totally ignored her.

"And he didn't even answer. He just lay there. Not a 'goodbye' or a 'good night.' Not anything! He just lay there like a big dummy." McFarlane said she left and later phoned Mrs. Helmsley's office "several times to get my money. And after that, I decided to call Mr. Helmsley's office." After many fruitless calls, the frustrated nurse said she was given a frightening bit of news by Mr. Helmsley's secretary, Celia Fried.

"The secretary told me that Mrs. Helmsley wanted me to know that if I continued to call the office, she would see that I don't work at another hospital in New York." McFarlane, a black Jamaican, said she took the threat seriously for fear of being blackballed from a livelihood. The immigrant nurse figured the odds and backed off. How could she, living practically hand-to-mouth in a healing profession, hope to prevail against a woman who owned entire hotels and who had bodyguards and liveried waiters at her beck and call?

Let it go, she figured, and she never picked up the phone again to demand payment for services rendered to New York City's wealthiest couple. "I'd hate to lose my nursing license for a three-hundred-dollar fee," she decided, and tightened her budget to compensate for the financial loss.

"I never called back because I know this lady has a lot of power."

TWO

> "A lot of people are proud of their humble origins, but not Leona. She doesn't want to acknowledge *anybody* from the past. That's her posture. That's her manner. That's her philosophy. That's her insecurity."
>
> LONGTIME FAMILY FRIEND

Leona Helmsley, as befits an American queen, was born neither to the manner nor the color purple. Instead, she grew up in gray discomfort as the child of poverty-stricken immigrants. Her mother, Ida Pupko, had arrived in the United States from Vilna, Lithuania. Ida's father, Abraham, had laid the groundwork by immigrating to New York in 1898. Abraham Pupko went to work in a wholesale fish business and became a U.S. citizen by 1902. With these preparations completed, the young immigrant then changed his name to Popkin and sent to Russia for his young wife and six children, including John (Zelig by birth) and Ida. They finally joined him after making the grueling transoceanic voyage in 1907.

Yiddish and Lithuanian were the two languages of Popkin's *shtetl*, but in America his children quickly learned English by reading New York street signs and working on their alphabet at home. At 13, just a year after reaching Ellis Island, John landed a job as an errand boy for the Postal Messenger Service on Fifty-seventh Street. Three years later he was big enough to join his father's fish business as a truck driver. In rapid succession, the energetic lad then tried his luck as a boxer, auctioneer and duck breeder before opening one of Manhattan's most famous jazz clubs—the Hickory House—in 1933.

John's sister, Ida, had followed a far humbler path by marrying a poor Polish immigrant hatmaker, Morris Rosenthal, and raising four children in the Coney Island section of Brooklyn. Rosenthal was among the approximately 40 percent of Jewish immigrant families who earned their livelihoods in garment shops on Manhattan's Lower East Side or in other immigrant sections of Brooklyn or the Bronx. For most, the garment trade was just a stepping stone. Within fifteen to twenty-five years in the U.S., half the hardworking Jewish immigrants achieved white-collar status. That was not the case, however, with Morris Rosenthal. Until his death from heart disease in the 1940s, he struggled mightily at the sewing machine to keep his family fed and clothed, according to surviving relatives.

Sylvia, the eldest child, was seriously overweight much of her life, but was extremely popular because of an unshakably sweet and sunny disposition. She was the peacemaker in the family. Sandra, born in 1918, was the family beauty—a strawberry blonde with a porcelain complexion. Leona Mindy Rosenthal took her first breath at 6 A.M. on July 4, 1920, in Marbletown, New York—a dot on the map approximately one hundred miles north of New York City in rural Ulster County.

Her father, according to the birth certificate, was working at the time as a hatmaker in nearby High Falls. The family moved back to Brooklyn soon thereafter. Leona blossomed into a pretty and spirited brunette, but was highly competitive—particularly with her older sister Sandra. Alvin, plump like his sister Sylvia, was born in 1928. Of her four children, Ida Rosenthal was particularly close to Alvin, the baby.

According to school records, the Rosenthal family lived in five different houses in the Coney Island area before Leona reached 13, including ones on Mermaid Avenue and West Thirty-third Street. Coney Island—once a wilderness of wild rabbits—was the beach resort and amusement center of Brooklyn. Over a million sun-lovers would flock to its shoreline on hot weekends and holidays. It was also the home of thousands of Jewish families who relocated from the crowded Lower East Side of Manhattan after the new subway unlocked the door to urban expansion between 1914 and 1921. By 1933, according to school records, the Rosenthals moved slightly inland to Bensonhurst, a Brooklyn community heavily populated by first-generation Italian and Jewish immigrants. There, Leona Rosenthal attended Seth Low Junior High and had an "extraordinary talent in English and communications subjects," school records show. She took pride in being the first in her gym class to shinny up a rope and had a crush on a working lad named Iggy, who pushed a laundry cart. The Rosenthal family hopscotched to another Brooklyn home several years later, and Leona enrolled in Abraham Lincoln High School. As an adult, Leona would proudly recall having won a medal there for her recitation of "The Highwayman" and still remembers fragments of the school anthem she sang at graduation ceremonies. An official of the school, however, suggests that Leona stayed "only a short time" at this secondary school.

One of Leona's closest surviving kinsmen (who does not wish to be identified) said Morris Rosenthal supported the family by making hats, military pins and insignia for the U.S. Army. His small shop, however, produced only meager earnings. "In listening to family stories, I know they were not well-to-do; they struggled." As an illustration of the poverty, the kinsman described the time Leona, or one of her siblings, "had the chicken pox. The children had an ice cream cone, but they were so poor that they all had to share it. The way the story went, because they all licked the same cone, all the kids got sick.

"There wasn't much money; they just got by." Money notwithstanding, it was a fairly tight-knit immigrant family with bright dreams of better days to come. Leona's mother had little interest in business, but was a very strong, opinionated immigrant who taught herself to speak fluent English. Having endured the voyage from Lithuania and suffered the privations of immigrant life, she constantly pushed her three daughters to attain the success that eluded her and her husband. And for girls in immigrant Jewish neighborhoods, the expressway to success was marriage and motherhood.

Leona, the youngest daughter, could not afford to wait patiently for a favored suitor to come along and better her humble circumstances. As a teenager—possibly one who dropped out of high school—she hit the pavement in search of a job to help supplement her family's income. Decades later, after marrying Harry Helmsley, Leona recalled that she lost one of her very first jobs—selling handbags—after asking for a raise. Next, according to the often-cited résumé, she attempted to become a showroom model but was rejected at 16 because she was "undeveloped." Mrs. Helmsley recalled that she raced to Woolworth's, bought a bra and stuffed it with cotton, and was hired after returning with improved cleavage.

Indeed, Leona often made proud claims to a successful modeling career, but there is little evidence to support the assertions. According to a longtime acquaintance, one of Leona's earliest jobs was as a girl Friday for the Ceil Chapman dress company. "She would sit there and answer the phone, like a secretary. Maybe a few times a customer would come in and the boss would say, 'Leona, try the dress on so he can see what it looks like.' Then, all of a sudden, Leona starts to think she's a model."

Relatives confirmed that Leona, as a teenager, did work in some capacity for Chapman, a designer and manufacturer of "dream dresses" on Seventh Avenue. Besides dramatic décolletage, Mrs. Chapman and her husband, Sam, stressed tiny waistlines, elaborately draped bodices and either very bouffant or very slim body-revealing skirts. The job apparently gave Leona an opportunity to build up a nice wardrobe. The form-fitting styles soon caught the eye of a young Brooklyn athlete named Lester Belmuth, who convinced Leona to become his sweetheart. "She was always dressed at the height of fashion," Belmuth clearly recalls after the passage of a half century. "[But] you looked at her because she was beautiful; you didn't look at her because she wore crazy clothes."

Belmuth was a 20-year-old carpet salesman from the Flatbush section of Brooklyn, making $50 a week, when he started dating Leona in 1938. "Her name was Leona, and my mother's name was Leona, and my mother never liked her,"

Belmuth recalled. "We went out anyway, quite a bit. And she was the most wonderful, charming girl I ever met. We had a relationship that was almost perfect. When you were with her, she integrated herself; she didn't try to take over the situation. She was sweet and charming."

Belmuth remembered feeling "too poor" to take out such a beautiful young lady, but Leona was "considerate and easy to be with. She never demanded to go places; she was a wonderful girl." He noticed that Leona was popular with other girls. "She was never obnoxious and always entered into conversations, and they always wanted to know, 'Are you bringing Leona?' She had tremendous manners. You could take her any place....We didn't socialize with the elite, but I knew darned well that wherever I took her, I was always comfortable with her."

Another memorable trait was her posture. "She was regal. She looked great when she walked. You felt like a million dollars being with her....She exuded confidence. She knew she was good-looking.

"She loved riding to Jones Beach with the top down under the moonlight" in Belmuth's convertible. "It was just normal fun times. There were no sexual encounters. She was romantic, but not sexually. We walked arm in arm; that was romantic enough for us. I was not interested in sex at the time. I was a health nut, and was more interested in football, baseball and lacrosse. We went out and had dinner and would drink milk and Cokes."

Belmuth recalled that his family had been wiped out by the Depression only five years earlier, and times remained tough. He never bought Leona flowers, even once, "because I didn't have enough money." Nor was there enough money to take out-of-town trips.

But Belmuth did have enough pocket change to gas up the convertible for Saturday-night trips to Manhattan, where the couple would fox-trot, waltz and Charleston the evening away on the roofs of the Astor and McAlpin hotels and the Rouge Room of the Pennsylvania Hotel. They also danced as Glen Gray and his Casa Loma Orchestra played "Under a Blanket of Blue," "Night and Day" and other ballads at Glen Island Casino, a public pavilion on Long Island Sound in suburban New Rochelle.

As with many romances, however, there was competition. Leona was dating other young men, and eventually—Belmuth couldn't remember exactly how—their courtship ended. He was left with only a faint recollection of Leona's family or her simple childhood home in the working-class Bensonhurst section of Brooklyn.

Belmuth did recall, however, that the family name was actually Rosenthal, and that Leona had adopted "Roberts" as a surname. Like many other children of Jewish immigrants, Leona had no doubt given herself a less ethnic surname to smooth her way in a more anti-Semitic era. "Rosenthal" evoked thoughts of the Lower East Side and other Jewish enclaves in the outer boroughs where millions of immigrants continued their struggle for financial security in a new homeland. By contrast, "Roberts" was neutral in every regard. It was one of the commonest surnames in the overriding white Anglo-Saxon Protestant landscape of America.

Not long after putting her stuffed Woolworth bra to good use, according to Leona's past statements, she scored a home run in her teenage modeling career by showcasing her sensuous legs as a Chesterfield girl in magazine advertisements. The ads, sometimes with a girl on a swing, introduced millions of 1930s readers to the brazen notion that it was perfectly acceptable for women to smoke. Like Leona's high school graduation, however, the modeling coup may never have happened. Carol Jova, spokesperson for Liggett and Myers Tobacco Co., noted that "there were a lot of Chesterfield ads done in the 1930s" when Leona claims to have been a teenage model, but virtually all of the ads were artist's renderings—not photographs. "Photography ads that we commonly refer to as using 'Chesterfield girls' were not done until the 1950s, so it is not likely that Mrs. Helmsley was in one of those" as a teenager.

Joyce Beber, of Beber Silverstein, the Helmsley ad agency, said she was always suspicious of the Chesterfield girl claim because, "Whenever I asked Mrs. Helmsley about it, she quickly changed the subject. Never once did she offer any details," nor did Mrs. Helmsley ever show her any photographs from the Chesterfield days.

Regardless of whether Leona *actually* worked as a model, she undoubtedly had the looks and the carriage—if not the opportunity—to succeed in that profession.

Her résumés might hark back to teenage glamour, but as Queen of the Helmsley Palace, Leona would look back with great pain at her Brooklyn roots, Beber said. "She would complain that it was rough in the sense that she hated the people around her—the ethnicity, the older people struggling to get by. The *need*—she hated that. She talked about how they didn't have things, and it almost disgusted her.

"They had food, but they didn't have luxuries in any way, and I think that sort of disgusted and offended her and it was a sickening thing to her."

Leona's mother, Ida Rosenthal, was dirt poor but she was graced with "this perfect posture," one of Leona's relatives recalled. "She had a sense of presence. She walked into a room and you knew she was there. She had a very regal way about her." And like her daughters, "she was a very charismatic person; Sandra has a lot of charisma, and Leona, for sure. There was always this spark, and I think they were all born with it." Likewise, the kinsman said, the mother and her two youngest daughters "were in great shape, and despite their poverty, all three of them were always absolutely beautifully groomed."

Leona, while not as stunning as her sister Sandra, was still a beauty. Her carved features were guaranteed to attract attention, especially from older men who could fully appreciate the fashion plate's sense of style. About the time Belmuth fell by the wayside as a boyfriend, Leo E. Panzirer, a high-spirited lawyer approximately ten years Leona's senior, came on the scene. "Some friends of mine got us together," Panzirer recalled. "We were a bunch of guys going out on blind dates and she was an attractive brunette—yes, *very attractive*. I'm a young guy, and she's a young girl. It was the end of the Depression." The year was 1939 and the city was abuzz with excitement over the opening that fall of the New York World's Fair at Flushing Meadows, in the adjoining borough of Queens. The theme was The World of Tomorrow, a rather ironic motif given the fact that Hitler was already on the move in Europe and would soon dispatch his panzers into Belgium and the Netherlands.

But the horrors of World War II were still to come and the worst of the Great Depression had passed. The fair was a glorious emblem of the city's return from the depths of financial despair. Thirty-five million people, certainly including Panzirer and 19-year-old Leona, visited the futuristic Trylon and Perisphere exhibits as well as a fairyland of fair buildings on the shores of Flushing Bay.

Just as the fair was a bridge into a hopeful new world beyond the Depression, Panzirer was Leona's crosswalk out of poverty.

He was a self-employed Brooklyn attorney, six years out of law school. Although he was "a young lawyer getting into everything," Panzirer's income was quite modest in those early days of his career. Nevertheless, he said, "I was a good catch for Leona because I was a lawyer. Maybe she was trying to catch me because she was an ordinary girl" aside from her natural beauty.

After a year of courtship, the couple married and moved into Panzirer's two-bedroom apartment in the Flatbush section of Brooklyn. Like Leona's previous neighborhoods to the south in Coney Island and Bensonhurst, Flatbush was a magnet for second-generation Jewish families. Unlike those working-class sections of Brooklyn, however, Flatbush was an upper-middle-class enclave of Jewish businessmen and professionals. Just fifteen years earlier, the neighborhood had sprung abruptly from sprawling fields in the heart of the borough. Newspaperman Leon Wexelstein described the happy results of the mid-1920s construction binge of modern homes and apartment houses. "Residents of Flatbush are looked upon with envious eyes by those living elsewhere...[It is] a picturesque, open and delightful place in which to make one's home."

The move was definitely a step up for Leona and she quickly adjusted to her improved circumstances. For the first time in her life, she had a maid to pick up after her and a car to run her errands. She also enjoyed meeting her husband's professional acquaintances and friends, and seemed determined to master the social graces. "Maybe she married me because I moved in certain circles. She liked to be up there. She'd try to move in circles where she'd meet nice people. And she did meet nice people."

But while Panzirer was at work, Leona had a surplus of time on her hands and no real interests to fill her day. "She wasn't interested in my law practice or anything else. I don't think she was interested in anything at that time. As far as intellectual pursuits, I don't know of any. I don't know of any hobbies she had. She didn't play bridge; she didn't play golf; she didn't play tennis." Nor did he remember her being an avid reader or theatergoer. "She had her mother, and she had her sisters. And she had one or two girlfriends that she would spend time with. But otherwise, I don't think she had any real interests."

Panzirer soon noticed, however, that his wife indeed had one abiding passion—shopping—and it soon became a sore spot in the marriage. "She was always looking for nice things; she always dressed well. She was as glamorous as my income allowed. She couldn't buy a thousand-dollar dress or a fifty-thousand-dollar diamond ring. But she dressed nicely. She always kept herself in pretty good shape. I could afford to pay some of those bills, so I paid them. But I would have had to be an idiot if I didn't resent some of her spending."

A year into their marriage, on November 8, 1941, Leona gave birth to her first and only child: Jay Robert Panzirer. The little brown-haired, brown-eyed baby drew the couple closer together and was a special joy to Leona's father, Morris Rosenthal. Panzirer said Rosenthal "used to love to come to our house to play with the baby. He was very sweet-spoken and quiet. He was a hard-working guy and a lovely man."

Despite the unifying influence of their child, Panzirer said only "about two years" passed before the magic wore off the marriage. "We were incompatible, that was it. We just didn't agree. Maybe I thought she was spending too much money on certain things. Let's just say I think she had a lot of respect for money. In her mind, there was perhaps a problem with money." It was a problem that Lester Belmuth had never noticed in Leona, perhaps because she had never had the opportunity to buy luxuries until her marriage.

Although Panzirer didn't see much intellectual strength in Leona, he said she had powerful "street-smarts. 'Intellectual' is not the word I would use for her. She was smart. She was *cunning*. You've heard that word before? I think she's more cunning than shrewd or smart. In other words, she sees the *opportunity*. That's my opinion. She'll see the opportunity, and then try to move into it some way. Maybe I was an opportunity."

In any case, "Chemistry broke down. I wasn't interested. She wasn't interested. She had certain ideas. And I'm a pretty strong-headed guy and I don't take b.s. from anybody. So we just made up our minds this was it."

He said they agreed, however, to remain under the same roof in a state of peaceful coexistence for the sake of their young child. "I decided to be sensible and keep her around for the boy's sake. I wanted to keep the marriage going to let the boy get older—old enough to understand the breakup. We had an understanding. We didn't stay in each other's way. It was done in an intelligent way like two normal human beings should do it. Maybe she had somebody else; maybe she didn't. I didn't care. Maybe she thought I had someone. But it was done intelligently. There was no animosity of any kind. We stayed in the same house and there were no problems. It was not a lovely relationship, but it worked until we got out. It was an agreement to disagree. I held no animosity against her. She didn't do anything in any way that would make me say: 'That little son of a bitch!' "

After Jay's tenth birthday, sometime in 1952, Panzirer said he realized the time had come to part company with Leona. "The boy was getting bigger, and I was tired already." Another factor was Panzirer's deepening suspicion that his wife was romancing another man. He said he sat Leona down and quietly told her: "Look, I think we've had it. Let's go. Let's do it in a nice way and get through with it." He said he then "sent her to Mexico for a quickie divorce. It only took seventy-two hours in those days. I think it was Juarez. There was a Mexican judge and a Mexican lawyer. Las Vegas takes six weeks and I couldn't wait that long."

Panzirer agreed to move out and pay Leona's rent on the Flatbush apartment for a year after the divorce. He allowed her custody of Jay, and consented to pay a nominal amount of child support. In later years, the Queen of the Helmsley Palace would complain that it amounted to only $25 a week and forced her to go out to work immediately to support her little boy.

Leona was a survivor, and a proud one. She endured to tell a tale of victory over the trauma of divorce and unexpected poverty. As a former spouse of the Queen of the Helmsley Palace, Leo Panzirer would rate scarcely a footnote in the imperial scrapbook. His existence, but not his name, was noted when newspapers and magazines recited the highlights of Leona's boilerplate résumé and her yellow brick road to Harry Helmsley's threshold.

New York magazine, in its March 12, 1984 issue, ran a typical synopsis: "Her father, a milliner and manufacturer of army caps, died of a heart attack at 52. Her mother took care of Leona, her two sisters…and a brother. She studied English at Hunter College for two years.…She also modeled clothes, married a Manhattan lawyer whose name she won't reveal [Panzirer] and bore a son, Jay."

Predictably, every article would then describe how Leona divorced the unidentified lawyer and immediately "barreled into real estate" to support herself and her young son. "She and Jay were living in a tiny studio apartment when she talked her way into a typist's job" at a prestigious realty firm, one long profile explained.

But something was missing.

In a truly royal case of amnesia, the Queen always omitted the matter of her seven-year marriage to, and subsequent two-year reunion with, Joe Lubin—the "other man" whom Panzirer had suspected. She blocked the entire decade out of her life.

It was an amazing rewriting of history for such a public figure as the Queen of the Helmsley Palace—a "marriage coverup" that went totally undetected for years by hordes of journalists. It was the kind of public relations deception that could only have been achieved by a person with few friends and, thus, easily severed links to the past.

"I worked as closely with Mrs. Helmsley as anyone for eight years," recalled ad executive Joyce Beber, "and she never once mentioned the marriage [to Lubin]." Beber said she had been curious that such a beautiful and charismatic woman as Leona would have gone unmarried for so many years before meeting Harry Helmsley in the late 1960s. "When I asked her how she could have been single all those years, Mrs. Helmsley told me, 'Why should I get mixed up with lowly garment center types?' It was such a strange comment," Beber said.

Not so strange, however, in light of the fact that her "secret" second husband, Joe Lubin, was a garment center type. When they met in 1951 or early 1952, Lubin was 33 years old and already married. As an executive for his parents' company—Amity Dyeing and Finishing Co. of Glendale, Long Island—he was also rich.

Lubin said he "fell head over heels" one Saturday afternoon that year at La Martinique—a famous dance club on West Fifty-seventh Street where stripper Gypsy Rose Lee occasionally paraded her black lace panties and bras. It happened when Lubin gazed across the dance floor at one of the most striking women he had ever seen. "Her face was the main thing," seemingly carved with classical proportion. "She had very high cheekbones, a good almond complexion and generous lips. She was *very* attractive. I fell in love with her because of that face." The object of his admiration was sitting at a table with another woman, engaged in conversation.

"This place was a matinee pickup joint," Lubin said, and he was determined to meet the young lady. So he went over and asked the brunette to dance with him as Noro Morales—the Puerto Rican "Monarch of Rumba"—cranked up his fourteen-piece orchestra. When she stood up, Lubin could see "that she had stature. When she walked, she walked tall." Lubin—balding, trim, and five eight—stood eye-to-eye with his rumba partner and noticed immediately that she was very much at home on the dance floor. And close up, her statuesque features were a sight to enjoy. After several dances, Lubin said he wasn't about to bid a polite adieu to his new acquaintance. "I asked her to dinner, but she said she couldn't."

"Why not?" Lubin asked, and was told, "I have to go home."

"Why?"

"Because I'm married."

"If you're married," Lubin said, "what are you doing *here*?"

"Just fooling around. I just came to dance."

Lubin walked the stunning-but-married creature to the front door and watched as she dropped coins into a telephone in a sidewalk booth. A second later, Leona Panzirer was speaking to her husband, Leo.

"I've been shopping," she told him. "I just came out of Saks Fifth Avenue."

A few minutes later, Lubin heard the tail end of the conversation, "I'll meet you at seven at the St. Moritz," Leona said and then hung up the receiver.

She then turned to Lubin and said goodbye, but not before he had a chance to slip her a crumpled piece of paper bearing his phone number. "Call me if you get a chance," he asked.

But Lubin had laid plans to see her again that very evening. His apartment, on Central Park South, was just a few doors from the St. Moritz Hotel. "So I decided to go have dinner there, just to frighten her." At 7:30 P.M., Lubin strolled inside the hotel's Café de la Paix, an elegant dining spot with gold-leaf ceilings and walls of Brazilian rosewood. He spotted Leona, looking just as luscious and statuesque as before. She was sitting with Panzirer, a lanky, gentle-looking fellow with bushy eyebrows who seemed a shade less energetic than his dinner companion.

Lubin took a seat at a nearby table—not too close, not too far—and cocked eye and ear to take in the proceedings at the Panzirer table. "She saw me and smiled," Lubin recalled, but she ignored the intrepid eavesdropper for the rest of the meal.

Lubin's mischievous gambit must have worked, he said, "because she came down to see me in the middle of the week. We met and had dinner at the Pierre, and started seeing each other from then on." He said they met secretly twice a week, usually in Brooklyn. "They were Saturday-night screws. Panzirer was playing gin rummy every time she went out, and Leona had acquaintances who covered for her. They'd tell Panzirer they were playing with her when she was out with me."

It became clear to Lubin that Leona was the head of the Panzirer household. "She told Panzirer what to do. If she told him, 'We're going here,' that's where they went. He had little to say in the house. Leona said he was like a vegetable. She'd say, 'I run the show.' "

Leona complained constantly that Panzirer "didn't part with spit. He gave her only seventy-five dollars a week for house money." Out of the blue one evening, Lubin said, Leona came to him with a startling proposition.

"If you give me the same amount—seventy-five dollars a week —I won't have to take Leo's money," Leona said. "I can stop sleeping with him...I can't give him taxation without representation."

It was too preposterous for words. Was Leona telling him there was a *specified price* for her sexual favors to her own husband? That she would withdraw those marital favors if Lubin *matched* Panzirer's weekly allowance?

"My answer to her was, 'Do not deprive him. He's your husband.' "

Leona then burst out, "Well, I'm going to get a divorce!" But first, Lubin said, "she wanted to make sure I was hooked on her—that I would tie the knot with her. And I was hooked, I admit it. Look, she was a good-looking woman."

Lubin promised that if she divorced Panzirer, he would divorce his own wife of twelve years, Lillian.

"I'll take care of that pronto!" Leona replied. "Leo and I are going for dinner tonight at Lundy's," a noted seafood restaurant overlooking Sheepshead Bay in Brooklyn. "I'll tell him tonight! I'm finished with him!"

The announcement was so abrupt that even Lubin was caught by surprise. Unlike Panzirer's version of the divorce, Lubin said it was Leona who pulled down the curtain on the marriage. "The average woman would say, 'I don't want to hurt him,' and take it slowly. But she was brutal. Cold turkey, she sat Leo down at Lundy's and said she was divorcing him. And then she kicked him out of the apartment. And it hurt Leo. It had to. I feel he was in love with her. She told me he was in love with her. For Leona to dismiss the marriage was like you going to the john. It was meaningless to her. It was a big step, but to her it was nothing.

"Leo was not high-caliber enough for Leona. He was just a nice lawyer and a sweetheart of a guy. That didn't cut the ice with Leona. Panzirer was a lawyer, but not worldly. He didn't understand that she planned to fall into bigger things." Lubin said Leona had outgrown Flatbush, as well. "She said she was tired of living in her second-floor apartment—that it was 'very, very plebeian.' She thought it was a slovenly neighborhood. She hated the neighbors' sitting in front of their houses. She didn't like the class of people. She didn't climb to the top by luck. Leona was an opportunist and knew that I was rich.

"An opportunist is one who recognizes the big break. If you're an opportunist, and I'm not, and we both meet 'Mr. A,' the opportunist will figure how to use Mr. A and the non-opportunist will just take it as a meeting and say, 'Nice to meet you.' The opportunist stores it in her computer. And Leona had a big computer. This is a *cunning* woman. She went after the smaller fish like Panzirer and me first. Harry Helmsley would be her bonanza.

"She's no novice, Leona. She knew the womanly wiles necessary to capture a man. Total charm. She'd go to dinner with you and put cream in your coffee. 'Let me pour your coffee for you.' She'd light your cigarette. If she had to go for something, she'd pour on the charm. She was a woman who wanted to climb the ladder."

The charm worked on Lubin as well as anyone. He went home and told his wife that he was seeing another woman "and she slapped me with divorce papers. But Leona got her divorce first."

Leona's own version of her divorce from Panzirer, told in later years, was that it was inevitable because she had only married the lawyer because "my parents thought I should." At the time, "everyone was doing it," she told another magazine. Only later, she said, did she realize they were hopelessly incompatible. "He was tone deaf and I love music, which gives you an idea of our relationship." Despite Leona's slighting references to her first husband, it is interesting that Panzirer never stepped into public view to return the fire. Instead, he quietly contented himself with a devoted new wife and a prosperous law practice.

In 1953, Lubin said, he and Leona exchanged wedding vows in an elaborate ceremony at Hickory House, the Manhattan jazz club owned by Leona's uncle, John Popkin. They then moved into a seven-room penthouse apartment at 750 Kappock Street in the exclusive Riverdale section of the Bronx. The neighborhood was just north of the Harlem River, the eight-mile-long tidal channel which separates Manhattan from the Bronx, the northernmost of the city's five boroughs. In the postwar period, many Jewish immigrant families left the old neighborhoods of Flatbush for the softly rolling hills of Riverdale. With them they brought delicatessens, bakeries and butchershops. As the fields of Flatbush were filled in, it had lost much of its earlier suburban character and came to be a crowded part of Brooklyn proper. Riverdale, however, was real suburbia, with wooded areas to rival leafy Westchester County to the north. It was another step up for Leona Mindy Rosenthal.

The swift developments were confusing for 12-year-old Jay Panzirer, who found himself living with a new father in an unfamiliar neighborhood. Lubin said the lad quickly adjusted, however, especially because Leo Panzirer faithfully picked the child up every Sunday for daylong trips about the city or to Panzirer's new apartment in Brooklyn Heights.

When the child asked about the divorce, Lubin said, "Leona told him she left his father because he wasn't up to her standards." Lubin said the boy "was a spoiled brat when he came to live with me. He faked headaches to get out of everything. Leona tried to be very stern, but Jay overpowered her." Eventually, after a year or so, the child warmed up to Lubin "and hung on me like his real father. He was like my own son for the next ten years. Leo was not a kid at heart; I was. I liked children and was an athlete. I played baseball and basketball. I gave him discipline."

Lubin never got a chance to meet Morris Rosenthal, Leona's father, who had died from heart disease several years before the marriage. But he soon became close to the rest of her family.

Leona's beautiful older sister, Sandra, immediately took over her dad's business after his death and transformed the ailing company into a money-making venture, according to relatives. Sandra's business skills were so keen that she soon was able to move her mother, Ida Rosenthal, from Bensonhurst to a comfortable two-bedroom apartment in Flatbush on Avenue L, near Ocean Parkway. A few years later Sandra married a clothing manufacturer, William Shulman, and gave him her personal savings of over $200,000 as a wedding present. Shulman died, however, just four years after the marriage, leaving her with a son and a daughter.

"Sandra kept Leona's family together," said one of Leona's

relatives. "Sandra stepped in to run the company because there was nobody else to run it. And it did well enough that she was able to take care of Ida and the rest of the family. Thank God it ensured that Ida didn't have to go to work." The kinsman said Sandra also took it upon herself to finance her younger brother's—Alvin's—college education. "She sent Alvin to college in California, I believe, and then he returned to New York." Alvin would eventually become principal of a Brooklyn high school.

Leona's eldest sibling, Sylvia, had married Irving Roman, a professional photographer with a very modest income. "They lived in Seagate, on the tip of Coney Island," the relative said, "and Roman was a terrific guy—just as warm and caring as his wife." Unfortunately, Sylvia had multiple health problems. She had struggled her entire life with obesity, only to develop diabetes in middle age. They had two children.

"Sylvia was a Pollyanna," Lubin fondly recalled. "She agreed with everybody. She only loved to cook and have company in her home. And she portrayed herself as not being as worldly as the other two sisters. She was happy in life." Lubin said Sandra and Leona, however, "ridiculed Sylvia from day one for marrying Irving Roman. He was a loner and didn't have much money. She didn't marry somebody with bread. Maybe that—bread—was the ultimate goal of the mother and sisters. That was their beef, except for Sylvia.

"Why didn't Sylvia care? Maybe because of her obesity. Maybe she was happy with Irving Roman because that was all she could get. She was better off because she was happy."

In contrast to Sandra and Sylvia, the kinsman said Leona was never a caring relative. As far back as the early 1950s, the relative realized that "if you needed something, Leona was not the one you would go to. She was very self-centered; very much into herself. Maybe you'd see her on holidays, but that was about it...She wasn't someone you could get close to." On the other hand, the kinsman said Leona had charm, "a fun streak. She had a great sense of humor. Maybe I thought she was fun because she wasn't a disciplinarian. She told off-color jokes. But I don't think she really cared too much about anyone else. Leona will always be into Leona, to the exclusion of anyone else. As a child, I knew she had a phony warmness. She was a fun person in general, but she really didn't give a shit." The kinsman recalled, "Leona came to stay at my house one weekend when I was a youngster and I begged my parents not to let her stay. Overall, it wasn't pleasant being with her."

The relative said when Leona was around "there was always friction. She was never an easy person, either with her family or her relatives. Nothing was ever good enough for her. No price was ever good enough, either. If someone said, 'I'm going to charge you five dollars for this,' she'd say, 'No, you're not— I'm paying two dollars!' It was meanness—the kind of person who enjoys picking wings off flies. There's something very, very bad there."

Leona's relationship with her sisters was very inconsistent, the kinsman said. "Things might go smoothly for several years, and then Leona would break off communication for six months or a year, or longer, with one or both sisters, depending on who she was fighting with. Some days you were in; others you were out. One day she loved you; the next day not." The relative said Leona's erratic treatment of family members was most upsetting to Sylvia. "Sylvia always tried to keep the family together. She hated to see the family fighting.

"Long before Leona came into big money, she was erratic," the relative said. "Something was always missing and I don't think anything could change her. The way she is, she is. And she seems real comfortable with the way she is."

Leona often wrangled with her baby brother, Alvin, but never broke with him as she did with her sisters. Alvin was only slightly more affectionate than Leona, the kinsman said, and took little interest in his relatives. "Alvin is definitely wrapped up in Alvin. He's definitely not a warm person, but he's not a mean person. I think he's a mixed-up person who often doesn't know the right thing to do."

After marrying Leona, Lubin would often eat at Ida Rosenthal's home, "which was strictly kosher. She abided by the laws—you don't mix meat with dairy; separate dishes for meat and dairy products. She adhered to all the Jewish tradition."

As for Leona, however, "she didn't care one way or another. There was no religiousness associated with that person. She never gave it much thought." Like many American-born children of immigrants—a generation removed from the Jewish *shul* of Eastern Europe—she had strong cultural ties but was not religiously observant. The synagogue, so important for fostering ties among neighbors, was visited only occasionally.

Lubin described Ida Rosenthal as "a very plain East European immigrant. She couldn't read or write well." But what she lacked in cosmetic appeal or polished prose, she more than made up for in common sense. "She was *sharp*. That I can assure you. She showed her smartness in practical ways."

After his marriage to Leona, for instance, Lubin said Ida "always favored me over Sylvia's husband because Sylvia's husband [Irving Roman] didn't make much money. She felt I was very wealthy because of where we lived. She hooked on to me. So you see, Leona's mother was also the opportunist."

But Sandra, who inherited a sizable estate from her husband, was treated best of all, Lubin said.

"Ida favored Sandra over Leona because Sandra was independently well off. And that was another thing that got Leona pissed off. Ida was always bragging how 'Sandra did this,' 'Sandra did that,' 'Sandra called me,' 'Sandra bought me these things.' Sandra had been getting all the attention, and Leona was second. And Leona didn't want to be number two. She didn't want to be Avis. But that's where her mother seated her in the tournament of life and that bothered Leona. She was not seated in first position."

Leona nursed more than a pinprick resentment against Sandra, her better-appreciated sister. "She was tall, about five eight, had a nice figure, and a gorgeous face like Mary Astor. Stately, high cheekbones. She was beautiful—more beautiful than Leona—and Leona was aware of it. Leona's aware of everything."

To vent her frustration, Leona constantly ridiculed her older sister face to face or behind her back. "Leona claimed Sandra was beautiful because she had a nose job. She wanted to take her down a peg—but later, who could count how many face jobs Leona would have."

A former executive of Leona Helmsley's hotel chain recalled that as late as 1980, Leona still harbored deep resentments against Sandra. "Mrs. Helmsley often complained that in growing up, Sandra was the better-looking one and thought she was everything. She said that Sandra's husband was richer and that she was always in her sister's shadow."

The two younger sisters had "lots of fights," Lubin said. "It all had to do with Leona accusing Sandra of doing the wrong thing because she had money. Leona would try to put her down, and it all stemmed from Sandra having the money while Leona didn't." Lubin said Leona's resentment was such that he "should have known then and there the gal would go to the top! Psychologically, if you were to analyze it, people who have very little self-confidence usually go to the front and rule the roost. Just like she dominated Leo Panzirer, her first husband."

Similarly, "If Leona was buying something, she would talk down to the sales clerk. She was a little nasty. She'd always take a shot at you if she had the upper hand."

Sandra was independently wealthy, but with an affluent husband, Leona was now in a fairly good position herself to step out into the good life. Creature comforts were the best revenge, *provided* an audience was on hand to witness her good fortune. "She's the biggest showoff," Lubin said. "She wanted two maids instead of one, because that would be better than anyone else in the neighborhood. It was a three-bedroom house, with three people, but she wanted to make a spectacle.

"She never learned the old rule: you never try to be outstanding in someone else's ballgame. Then you become a target. If I went to Monte Carlo, I wouldn't be the best dressed. I'd be a target. The other guys wouldn't like it. You're supposed to live laid-back. That's smart. She's just the opposite. She's got to put on a show."

Although comfortably off, Lubin was no multimillionaire. Nevertheless, "Leona wanted me to buy her twenty-five-thousand-dollar diamond necklaces on Forty-seventh Street. I told her, 'That's not necessary.' She said, 'I want it.'

"You're not going to get it!" Lubin insisted. Vanquished, Leona "would pout a couple of days and forget it." He said Leona seemed to soften when she *knew* that she could not dominate the scene. But she would continually test the bounds of her own control over the purse strings. "She didn't know the rule: you can be a zillionaire and still wear a cloth coat. Leona thought you had to wear all your wealth on your back. You can't do that. High society people don't show off all their diamonds. She's ostentatious." Lubin curbed her spending demands firmly. "Deep down, she liked the discipline of not getting her way all the time. She knows that you can't have two chiefs. She likes a man in control—if the man knows what he's doing. But if she realizes he's weak, she takes over."

In marriages, "a woman might be a lamb with one guy, but outrageous with somebody else. Liz Taylor was the biggest rat alive with Eddie Fisher. She was the boss; he was a weakling who carried her bags around. With Richard Burton, she was the lamb because he was the boss. When you get rid of the yoke, you take over and the real you comes out. Panzirer was weak. I was strong. When we split up, Leona took over again, because

Harry Helmsley was weak, too."

Lubin's older brother—a short, bespectacled man who, at 80, still manages his own fabric store in New York's garment district with unbridled energy—had few good memories of his nine years of contact with his former sister-in-law. "Money was everything with Leona. It was the most important thing. She would not stop to ask, 'Can we afford it?' She always felt like she had to be better than the next person. You could see it in her manner. The way she said, 'I like this fur. This is the latest style.' Your mother or sister might make do with an old coat for the winter, but not Leona. If the style was purple fur, that was it!"

He said Leona "never learned the meaning of the word *shalom*....That means 'peace.' A lot of Jewish people of Eastern Europe were taught to live their lives by that concept. My parents came over from Poland, and they taught us *shalom*. If you fight and argue, what do you win out of the argument? You don't win anything. You get your way, yes. But that doesn't mean much. *Shalom* means let's keep peace; let's make peace. Let's not fight. But Leona always wanted it *her way*, take it or leave it!"

Joe Lubin said his ex-wife aspired to climb the social ladder but always tripped over her own aggressive manners. Instead of being gracious about a differing viewpoint, "she'd want to show how smart she was. It takes talent to act like something you're not. That's her failing with nice society."

Even when she knew she was wrong, she would firmly hold her ground. An extreme example, he said, was after dinner with another couple one evening at the exclusive Four Seasons restaurant. "It was the best place to go—the most expensive place in town. As we were leaving, I [stayed behind] to pay the check, and the maître d' came over to me and said, 'I don't want to embarrass you, sir. But occasionally people steal the silver salt shakers.' "

Confronted by what appeared to be an accusation, Lubin demanded an explanation.

Instead, the waiter diplomatically replied, "I'll add it to your check."

"Before you do," Lubin said, "shouldn't I check with my dinner guests to see if one of them took the shakers?"

Lubin then went outside and said to his friend's wife: "Did you take the salt shakers?" and she shook her head. "The maître d' said one of us took them," Lubin explained. He knew he and his male friend didn't have the shakers. "That only leaves you, Leona," he said.

"I don't have them," she replied. Lubin then went back inside and told the maître d': "Charge it to me because I know who has them." He returned to the car and informed the trio he had settled up with the restaurant. "Why did you pay for them?" Leona demanded. "They don't know I have them."

Lubin said he then reached in and found the shakers in Leona's handbag.

"I said, 'Why didn't you tell me you had them?' and she kept repeating, 'They don't know. They don't know.' " The surprising thing, he recalled, was how she calmly brushed aside an episode that should have been profoundly embarrassing. Her face-saving approach was just to *explain it away* to herself as much as to others. "It was in her genes. She had this feeling that she could always get *her way*, that nobody could stop her. Even the Godfather has fear of being caught. But apparently Leona doesn't have any fears. She is beyond—above it all."

Lubin ascribed Leona's innate aggressiveness, in part, to her competitive family background. "I think it was because Sandra was the all-important one for the greater part of her life. Sandra was rich. She had class. She was an austere person who liked the finer things in life. She liked the classics. Her friends were a little better strata because she had money from an earlier age and lived very well, and I'm sure Leona was jealous of this. She would make fun of Sandra, that she bought this and spent money frivolously.

"When Sandra married Shulman in the late 1940s, he was a millionaire from the clothing business. Sandra was no longer average anymore. She left the strata. She went to another plateau and Leona didn't like it."

When Shulman died, Lubin says, Sandra invested her husband's fortune in AT&T—"the famous 'widow stock.' It was steady. She was conservative about money. She bought three acres in upstate New York and built a tremendous house from the ground up. The walls were all walnut. She later sold the house and moved to the Upper East Side. It made her the important one. Everyone now catered to Sandra because of the money. She was the rich sister. Leona couldn't be top dog and I guess she wanted to be top dog. She had to get even then. Her aggressiveness didn't just develop all of a sudden. But after she got a taste of her own money, you had to go along with what *she* said. She wanted her share of respect finally. If you didn't agree with her, you had to go along with what she said anyway."

Things appeared to be a substitute for life itself, perhaps in revenge for Leona's poverty-stricken childhood and Sandra's irritating prominence in the Rosenthal family.

Material goods, not relationships, were the avenue to success. "I don't know of one person, one old friend or classmate, that ever came to the house to see Leona," said Lubin. "She had no friends except Leo [Panzirer], who came every Sunday to pick up Jay."

A memorable example of Leona's material ambitions came in 1953, not long after their wedding, when Lubin's father died. He said his mother inherited Amity Dyeing and Finishing Co. in Long Island, but Leona quickly stepped forward with a plan to take control of the garment company. "Leona tried to have me go to my mother and convince her to give her half the business. I had one brother, and Leona wanted the brothers to take the money. She told me, 'I don't want you to work for your mother! I want you to own the business!' " That way, Lubin said, "Leona would have been the wife of the owner. Then maybe someday she'd take over. I told her, 'What difference does it make if my mother has it? It will eventually be mine.' "

Leona wanted, however, to eliminate the possibility of any unforeseen complications. She wanted to know, "What if your mother remarries someone? Then we might lose out."

Lubin was amazed to see firsthand "how her mind operates. See how cunning? The average wife wouldn't think along these lines."

To effectuate her plan, Leona "would buy my mother gifts. Leona figured if she got Mother on her side, she could tighten up the loose ends. But it didn't work because my mother could see right through her. She would play Dicky the Dunce, but she wasn't going to be fooled. Leona didn't give a damn about anyone. We found out about her. She didn't give a damn about me. She only gave a damn about getting to the top.

"I have drive, but it's not that strong," Lubin said. "I'm as happy as a pig in shit today. I do whatever I want. I can settle. You cannot win every battle. But Leona's like the general who can't lose a battle. And when she's losing, she throws everyone out. Money was her god."

It was the exact phrase—"Money was her god"—that Panzirer had used to describe his former wife.

Lubin said he realized that "Leona never had enough. She never will. Her idea is 'never stop.' Her family was poor; they always needed money. I know she was not happy about being poor. So let's face it: money gave her a chance to pull herself up. She wanted money and power. Maybe she was trying to be as good as her sister Sandra."

Lubin said Leona and her son, Jay, "fought all the time because they couldn't agree." As a mother, Leona "tried to be overbearing" but didn't have a clue as to how to discipline her headstrong school-age son. "She would put him down and try to enforce penalties or try to ground him. But there was no grounding Jay. Impossible!"

The boy occasionally ran away from the Lubin household, and would end up fifteen miles away on his father's doorstep in Brooklyn Heights. "I was single and had a suite of rooms at one of the hotels," Panzirer recalled, "and Jay would come running to me. I'd come in from work, and there he would be sitting in the lobby, and everyone at the hotel knew it. And I'd say, 'How did you get here?' And Jay would say, 'I hiked out.'

"Leona would call me up hysterically, saying, 'Jay ran away!' And I'd have to calm her down: 'He's here; I'll bring him home tonight.' Then I'd raise a little hell with Jay and remind him that 'She's your mother.' "

Tensions between Leona and Jay eased in 1956, when the lad was sent off to Cheshire Academy in Cheshire, Connecticut. Lubin's own son happened to be the same age as Jay and also attended the prep school. Leona saw Jay once a month after that, Lubin said. Besides making things quieter at home, the boarding-school solution was a badge of prestige for Leona "because her son was going to a classy school. She bragged about it."

The school was an expense Lubin was happy to pay for the sake of Jay's education, not to mention his own domestic tranquillity. After graduation, Lubin encouraged Jay to follow in his own career path, and sent his stepson off to college in the fall of 1959 to the Philadelphia Textile Institute.

Over the years, Lubin also frequently gave a financial helping hand to Leona's younger brother, Alvin Rosenthal, who struggled for years on a teacher's paycheck in Brooklyn.

Lubin said on two occasions he tried to get Rosenthal started on entrepreneurial projects in the fabric business, hoping that Rosenthal would then have a means to supplement his teaching income. Both efforts failed miserably, Lubin said, "because

Alvin had no particular talent—no business acumen.

"I was supplying him nylon-mesh fabric and he was making belts out of it. The fabric was like a gift—he didn't have to pay me up front, not until after the belts were sold." Rosenthal rented loft space on West Twentieth Street, Lubin said, and "after his classes in Brooklyn, he would go to Manhattan in the afternoons. It was a one-man operation. He would send the fabric out for the belts to be made." The problem came after the finished products arrived. "After he lined up customers, he couldn't make the sales," and the belt effort collapsed.

In another project, "I sold Alvin fabric which he was supposed to resell. But that only lasted a year because he didn't have time." Although Rosenthal was inept at business, Lubin said Leona's rotund brother—five feet nine and almost two hundred pounds—was "a genius at food. He's a gourmet. He knows how to cook. And apparently he has teaching ability. But he had zero business sense."

After seven years of marriage, in 1960, Lubin became an owner of a dye plant in Lumberton, North Carolina, and made plans to move South. Leona, however, adamantly refused to accompany him. "She said it was too small. I guess she thought these people in Carolina weren't citified enough." After many arguments over the merits of pulling up stakes Lubin said Leona struck out for Alabama and obtained a quickie divorce. "On her own she went there and got an overnight divorce," he said. "I could have contested it," he said, "but I figured if someone didn't want me, I wasn't going to fight it." He moved South as planned and sent Leona $300 a week "for about six months." Lubin stopped, he says, "because I found out she was running around."

The cutoff left Leona financially alone for the first time in twenty years. At the age of 40, the divorcée had no choice but to go live temporarily with her aging mother in Brooklyn.

Later, after Lubin and Leona reconciled, she bitterly complained about having had to endure her mother's constant *kvetching*. "She told me it was all my fault," Lubin said. "It was a poor atmosphere. Her mother kept asking her questions—kept goading her. She probably told her, 'You broke up your marriage! Look what you got!' " Blanche Slauson, one of Leona's few traceable former close friends, recalled her protest: "I did my penance. I went home to live with my mother."

With finances an urgent reality, Lubin recalled, Leona implored her sister Sandra for advice. "Sandra was involved in properties, stocks and bonds, and Leona respected her opinion." Lubin said Sandra's immediate recommendation was that Leona "go into real estate because Leona had no trade. She didn't know how to do anything." Real estate was one of the few professions at the time where women, even those without high school diplomas, could grind out a good living. Leona gave Sandra's advice some thought, but wasn't yet ready to take a plunge into that rough-and-tumble arena.

In 1961, only a year after the divorce, Lubin returned to New York and patched up things with Leona. He said he then moved in with his ex-wife, who had scraped together enough money to leave her mother and rent a one-bedroom Manhattan apartment near Forty-eighth Street and Second Avenue. "We were living under one roof again, but we didn't bother to get remarried. We were shacking up." But why would Lubin, after so many previous go-rounds with Leona over money and her overbearing personality, want to renew the relationship? "Look," he said, "she was still a beautiful woman. I was still in love with that face. I figured I could put up with the bullshit."

Family life resumed its course, with Leona and Lubin moving into a larger, two-bedroom apartment a block south. Jay was now 20 years old and six feet tall, with an already receding hairline. His educational stature, however, tumbled when he dropped out after completing his sophomore year at Philadelphia Textile Institute in 1961.

Then, only a year after Leona and Lubin were reunited, she had reason to feel the entire rug go flying out from underneath her when the "shack-up" with Lubin ended. Lubin said the last straw came when his son called the apartment one afternoon in 1962 and Leona answered the phone. The college-age lad asked Leona if he could speak to his dad. "No, your father can't come to the phone," Leona replied.

"Why not?" young Lubin demanded of his stepmother.

"Why do you want to talk to him?"

"Because he's my father."

"Well, I'm your mother!" Leona replied.

"No, you're not!" Lubin's son shot back.

That evening, Lubin said Leona came to him in an agitated state and informed him: "I'm very upset! Your son insulted me on the telephone. He told me I was not his mother."

Leona then laid down the law, Lubin said, telling him in no uncertain terms: "Your son can never come in this house as long as I'm here!"

Without blinking, Lubin made it very clear where his first loyalty rested. "Fine! That means he can come whenever he wants, 'cause I'm kicking you out of the house! Pack up your shit and get the hell out! Get the hell out of here by morning!"

Lubin speculated that later, as Queen, Leona banished him from her résumé because "she thought it would be smarter to say she was only married once before marrying Harry Helmsley. If you're married twice or three times, you're not stable. How could a woman tell such a massive lie? She omits a marriage. If she shut me out, how could she shut out a nine-year existence? How do you fill in the nine years?" Lubin wonders to this day. "Do you think Harry Helmsley knew?"

Lubin also took issue with Leona's continuing claim that she attended Hunter College. "This is all nonsense. She never went to college a day in her life that I'm aware of." (Hunter has refused, for confidentiality reasons, to confirm or deny whether she ever enrolled.)

A longtime friend of the Rosenthal family also scoffed at the elevated claims on Leona's résumé. It would have been more apropos, he said, had she mentioned her past employment at her uncle's restaurant, the Hickory House. Johnny Popkin—the brother of Leona's mother, Ida—opened the supper club in 1933 at 144 West Fifty-second Street. Thanks to a huge circular music bar, within a year it became one of the hottest jazz clubs in America. Jam sessions were invented at the bar in the early '30s, with Louis Armstrong, Duke Ellington and Benny Goodman "just sitting in" on any given Sunday afternoon. The club served some of the best steaks and chops in Manhattan. Hundreds of pounds a day were seared over an open grill fueled by cured hickory logs. Popkin burned a forest of hickory over the years, and bookmakers and loan sharks of every stripe were among his best customers.

The family friend said Leona worked at the club "in the early fifties," possibly during a financial crunch between her marriages to Panzirer and Lubin. "As I remember, she worked in the cloak room and walked around the restaurant and sold the cigarettes. Maybe she needed the money, and Johnny gave her the tobacco concession."

In the 1940s and 1950s, the family friend said, "Leona was just a little nobody." In one respect, however, Leona stood out even in those early days. "She was a pusher. She was always an aggressive woman; she would come on like gangbusters. She'd come on very opinionated."

When the layers of mythology are lifted from Leona's résumé, it becomes clear that she did not begin to assemble any real career credentials until 1962, after her "second fling" with Lubin came to its stormy end. Pressed for money, the middle-aged divorcée then broke into real estate and began her professional ascent. Until then she had been just an unexceptional housewife.

Three

Alone again, Leona moved into a one-bedroom apartment on the Upper East Side of Manhattan. The apartment, at 35 East Eighty-fifth Street, near Madison Avenue, was small and poorly lit, but it was a comfortable, attractive dwelling place for a single woman. Furthermore, her widowed sister, Sandra, also lived in the building, having moved to Manhattan after selling her home in upstate New York. A longtime acquaintance of Leona's recalled that the sisters "clashed tremendously over silly things like money and clothes." Another possible irritant was the relative size of the sisters' apartments—a matter of no little importance to space-starved Manhattanites. "Sandra's place was far larger, maybe twice as big—at least a two- or three-bedroom." Sibling rivalry aside, however, the roots of family still tied them together.

Without alimony, there was no recourse. Leona had to go to work. She applied for a receptionist position with Pease & Elliman, a Manhattan real estate brokerage firm. For a little edge on the competition, she included faked typing samples with her job application. The deception worked, and she got the job. ("It was desperation; it wasn't chutzpah," she would recall in later years. Leona would claim that at the time she landed the Pease & Elliman job, she and Jay had been living in a tiny studio apartment—leaving the impression that she was a young mother with a young son at the time. Jay was, in fact, 21 years old by then; Leona was 42.)

Being a woman was handicap enough in the days before sexual equality became an acknowledged employment goal. But as a divorced woman with little education, the odds were stacked triply against Leona in the marketplace. Given those realities, she perhaps felt lucky to land the receptionist position, however unglamorous it might be.

Real estate, then, would be Leona's bread and butter after the final breakup with Lubin. Although they soon resumed communication, Lubin offered no financial help to his ex-wife. She was strictly on her own. And as a receptionist at Pease & Elliman's real estate office at 60 East Fifty-sixth Street, her paycheck was minuscule.

"Leona started out not even as a secretary," said one former female Pease & Elliman broker. "She was just a receptionist sitting up front answering the phone for all the brokers. People barely knew her name she was so unimportant." Another former broker recalled that Leona's job became somewhat more challenging when she assumed limited clerical duties for eighteen brokers in the office. "She was appointed to serve as secretary for all of us. Most of us did our business by phone; we didn't write many letters. She was there supposedly to help us with our correspondence and answer the phones."

Within a year, 1963, the firm assigned her to work as an on-site receptionist at the Parc V (pronounced "Park Sank"), a white brick apartment house then under construction on the corner of Sixtieth Street at 785 Fifth Avenue, next door to the venerable Sherry Netherland Hotel. The eighteen-story building, when completed, would boast sixty-six of the city's most expensive cooperative apartments. The builders—a partnership of brothers Larry and Zachary Fisher and shipping magnate Daniel K. Ludwig—selected Pease & Elliman to sell the individual apartments. According to the former broker, Leona's job was to sit in the unfinished building's lobby and handle receptionist chores such as keeping track of telephone calls.

Before long, Leona took the real estate salesman's test and got her license. The test was a fairly simple affair, with none of the formal classroom preparation required of today's incoming sales troops. Then came a promotion from receptionist to on-site saleswoman at Parc V.

Simultaneously, the former broker noticed, a pivotal career development had taken place. Leona, she recalled, somehow had become "very close" to Robert Neaderland, the 62-year-old owner of Pease & Elliman. In no time, other secretaries and brokers spotted Leona and the boss at real estate dinners. And whispers echoed through Pease & Elliman's corridors as Leona paid increasingly frequent visits to Neaderland's office—and closed the door behind her.

The broker couldn't understand how Leona, so beautiful and youthful, would date such an old and unattractive man—however rich—as Neaderland. He was a generation older, but looked more like her grandfather because he was grossly over weight and completely bald. His face was perfectly round except for a lantern jaw, and his jowly neck seemed to sit directly on his shoulders. He looked like an elderly Humpty Dumpty.

Furthermore, from personal experience the broker knew that Neaderland sexually harassed his female employees. "He was very suggestive to me. Everything had to do with sex." One day, she said, "he called me into his office—remember, he was the owner—and wanted me to look at pictures of his new apartment. He asked me, 'What do you think of my bedroom?' and I said, 'I don't see it.'"

Neaderland replied, "Well, you'll have to come see it. It has mirrors on the walls and ceiling." The red-faced broker made a hasty retreat.

She said Leona, by contrast, got as close to the boss as she could. "Neaderland was crazy about Leona; we could all see it. They were dating. Any real estate function he would take her to." Other brokers couldn't stop talking about the pair, but Leona was oblivious of their stares. "It never entered her mind what the brokers thought. She would just wiggle her behind up through the office, and everybody knew what was going to happen—that Neaderland's door was going to close. It wasn't like a secretary going into the boss's office. Nobody else got behind those doors."

Another broker recalled that "Leona was always in Neaderland's office talking to him. She knew exactly what she was doing. She was a calculating woman. Neaderland was single, and when she came on the scene she took him and manipulated him. The door would be closed, and I'd ask, 'Who's in there?' and his secretary would say, '*Who do you think?*'"

Joe Lubin was more surprised than anyone when he saw his ex-wife and Neaderland having a quiet dinner together one evening at Reuben's, a late-hours theatrical spot on East Fifty-eighth Street, shortly after Leona landed the promotion to sales agent at the Parc V. "She came to see me a couple of times after I kicked her out," Lubin said. "We were on a friendly basis and we would talk. And I asked her what she was doing with this guy because it was a terrible mismatch. It was Beauty and the Beast.

" 'Don't make fun of me,' Leona replied. 'He's my sweet-

52

heart, and I might own the company someday. He's very good to me. He's a bachelor, and if I marry him I'll show him how to run the company.'

"She zoned right in on him," Lubin said. "Everybody pays dues, but these dues were pretty stiff. She wanted the company." For her new career, Lubin said, she had resurrected the name "Leona Roberts" because there was considerable anti-Semitism in the real estate business in the early 1960s, although a good many brokers and real estate executives were Jewish. "Each broker advertised in the *New York Times*," Lubin said, "and they weren't about to use the name 'Rosenthal.' "

"The whole town is full of people who shorten their names," said a male real estate broker who once worked with Leona in the mid-1960s. "Those were the days when Jewish people weren't allowed to move into a lot of buildings in New York. A lot of buildings *still* don't want any Jewish people. New York may have the world's largest Jewish population, but there's still more WASPs. It was a part of the business in those days and still is to some extent." Similarly, Jewish brokers might not be welcomed with open arms in the same buildings, and a name like "Roberts" would not complicate things.

In no time, Leona was promoted from selling apartments at Parc V to also running the sales departments of other new apartment houses. In addition to a salary, Leona would also get an automatic "override," or bonus, on each apartment sold. "She had such power with Mr. Neaderland," the female broker said, "that she was always given first shot to be in charge of selling apartments in new buildings." Leona would sit in a sales office in the lobby of the yet uncompleted building and show floor plans to prospective purchasers as they came in.

A pattern developed, the broker said, that whenever other brokers brought customers to see the building, Leona would steal the customers away. "You had to introduce your customer to her because she knew which apartments were available, and then *she* would take them to show them the apartment." She said Leona typically would then steer the customer to other properties handled by Pease & Elliman, and keep the customer—and the sales commission—for herself. "She was such a forceful broker that customers would transfer their loyalty to her. She was absolutely unscrupulous with other brokers, and was able to get away with it because she had such power with Neaderland. Any of the rules that applied to anyone else didn't apply to her. We said, 'What will she do next?' She didn't have any feelings about it. As long as Neaderland was in power, she held on to him and had her own power base." Lower-level employees also suffered Leona's highhanded behavior. "She was terrible to secretaries. She bossed them and made them cry from being so critical."

Brokers complained to Neaderland that Leona was appropriating their customers, but he continued to let her "do whatever she wanted to do. It was he who gave her what she needed to get going with. He was in a position to do it. The other brokers had no recourse whatsoever." They stayed at the firm, however, "because this was not their total business. There were plenty of other buildings" where Leona was uninvolved. Not surprisingly, "Leona's name was poison to her co-workers. She had absolutely no loyalty to anyone but herself. Any time you had a hot customer, she would steal them away—every time. We could have murdered her at any moment."

In April 1964, Neaderland sold his firm to real estate entrepreneur Armand Lindenbaum, a stepson of Max Stern—the founder of the Hartz Mountain pet supplies empire. Neaderland remained on board as president of Pease & Elliman, however, and kept Leona aboard at Parc V.

Lindenbaum said he found the brunette divorcée "very abrasive. She was struggling to make a living to support herself and her son. She had a tough background and was therefore interested *only* in making money—not for wealth, but to pay bills and live a comfortable life." At the Parc V, he said, she proved herself a certified sales champ. She was more aggressive than most brokers, but more important, "she was able to get buyers to close—she could charm them into signing, whereas other brokers might let their customers waver. She'd pick a date, close it, and move on to the next one. That was her secret talent. She never impressed me with her intellectual abilities, because I don't think she had any. But she was a fine closer. She was selling to some of the richest people in New York and was able to get the deals done." Among those who purchased apartments at Parc V were Daniel K. Ludwig, one of the building owners, and real estate financier Lawrence Wien—Harry Helmsley's closest business partner.

All of a sudden, while practically a novice in the field, Leona found herself making a "respectable income" of perhaps $40,000 a year, Lindenbaum said.

Call it luck, call it hard work, or call it dirty pool. But it could not be denied that Leona—the poor girl from Brooklyn—

was breaking into the big time. Mermaid Avenue, Flatbush and the hills of Riverdale were only dim mileposts now. She was in the thick of "million-footed Manhattan"—the city of the world—an island of glamour and ruthless competition. And she was making bold strides in one of the most ruthless professions of all. Thanks in great part to Leona's newly proven sales ability, Parc V was a sellout by 1964.

The following year, developer Marvin Kratter made real estate history by building the St. Tropez, the first condominium of new construction ever built in New York. Old buildings had been converted to the condominium form of ownership in previous years, but no condo tower had ever been built from scratch until Kratter erected his thirty-four-story building at 340 East Sixty-fourth Street.

In cooperatives, such as the Parc V project, residents do not own their apartments outright. Instead, they own a proportional share of the building, and surrender management control to a shareholders' board of directors. Condominium apartments, by contrast, are individually deeded—thus allowing their owners far greater control over their own residences and their own lives.

Kratter selected Pease & Elliman to sell all 301 condominiums in his bold new tower. Without hesitating, Lindenbaum picked Leona Roberts as on-site manager of the St. Tropez because of her earlier achievement at Parc V. "She had been really successful, so I decided to move her around," Lindenbaum recalled.

He said he also chose her because Leona was not suited for the riskier, more lucrative field of free-lance brokerage. Freelancers sell apartments in already existing buildings, hopping from one building to the next as units become available. "They make the most money because they advertise, generate their own business, and build their own clientele."

Leona preferred, however, the safer route of staying in one location and "babysitting" an entire new building. She would be paid a much smaller commission on each apartment sold—perhaps 2 percent—but knew she would have "at least some minimum income that way. She wouldn't have to go out and struggle for customers like the free-lancers. She would have traffic from the street and wouldn't have to worry about eating. She had to have a building as a base to operate; she needed that base—that comfort—because she had nothing else to lean on.

"The St. Tropez job was very hard because it was something

new and revolutionary," and Leona had to be taught the basic differences between the cooperative and condominium concepts of ownership. She was not a quick study, however, Lindenbaum recalled. "I had to have a lot of patience explaining the condominium concept to her. It was hard because she wasn't an intellectual giant. I had to spend more time with her than anyone else, making sure she understood the nature of her work. The building was important to the firm and we had to make sure it was done right." On the other hand, Lindenbaum said he had the utmost confidence that she would ultimately succeed because "Leona had tremendous street smarts, even in those days."

Leona opened an office in the lobby of the St. Tropez as cranes and workmen continued apace above her. Several secretaries and clerical workers were transferred to the site as her personal staff, "and she ran these people very hard," said Lindenbaum. "A lot of them couldn't get along with her. She couldn't get along with them."

Marvin Kratter's secretary, Alicia Heatherton, recalled that Leona "had to be the top dog and nobody could take that away from her, especially other females. Everything had to be lower than her—in personality and money and everything else. You could see the seeds of her ego when she would come wafting into the St. Tropez office at 9 A.M. in a full-length white mink coat, carrying an attaché case. She was stunning. It was as though she was walking into the White House. It was a putdown on everyone else."

Leona worked practically around the clock, seven days a week, to fill the building with her own customers. At the age of 45, she was working at a pace that would wilt the average 20-year-old. Heatherton, in fact, assumed Leona was in her mid-30s. "She looked fantastic. The woman was another article. She's fifteen years older than me, and I never knew it. Sometimes when you come out of a poor background, you have taste. And that's why I admired her. She was an elegant lady. She was right off the cover of *Vogue* magazine. She had to be a very disciplined person to take care of her body, her nails and face through the years. That takes discipline."

Although glamour and appearance were important, those concerns in no way distracted Leona from her job. After learning the basics of the condominium concept from Lindenbaum, she nailed it down to a science and went to work like a whirling dervish. "She was always very well spoken, and excellent with the customers," said Heatherton. "She could twist them. If they were doubtful when they walked in, they were knocked out when they left. She had a way with people. She was very, very determined in what she was about to do and did it with class, with good manners and a soft, charming voice. If she had to get tough, she did it in a very, very nice way. She knew exactly what she was talking about and the customers left *knowing* that she knew it. She had the personality for the job, and was a brilliant woman. The clients never knew what hit them when Leona started with them. She had them wrapped around her finger. They instantly believed what she said was God's truth. They would do anything; they would sign on four dotted lines."

The insuperable charm would vanish, however, as soon as the customer left the premises. To employees, Heatherton said, Leona "was a real nasty lady. She was cutting. The tone of her voice would cut right through you. Other brokers stayed their distance, too, because she could turn on you in two seconds with her mouth. She was the hotshot sales agent, and we didn't want to rattle her cage."

Heatherton said territoriality was too mild a word to describe Leona's salesmanship. "There may have been a few outside brokers who brought customers to the St. Tropez, but the minute they walked through the door they were Leona's. Leona had a contract with Kratter that anybody that comes through the door was hers. Brokers came not knowing anything about condos, and probably thought they could get a piece of the action. If they came in blind, they went out blind." Heatherton added: "It takes a certain amount of talent to hog it all. It's a cutthroat business."

Heatherton believes the fire that motivated the workhorse broker "was money. She had to bring up a son as a single parent and she wanted to bring him up in the best way possible. I admire her wits to get up there and stay there. That little boy was her world. He was what she was out there for. He was going to have everything she didn't have as a youngster." (Heatherton, like virtually every one of Leona's former business acquaintances, assumed Jay Panzirer was still a child at the time.)

One former Pease & Elliman executive recalled that Leona "had her negatives and positives, just like anyone else. But her biggest negative point was her distrust of other people. She never trusted anyone. Her distrust was intense. That was the undercurrent that kept coming through her personality." He said

Leona's suspicions ran so deep that "she couldn't even accept an advantageous position. If you tried to give her a better deal, she'd think it must be a bad deal. She'd be suspicious of your motives." He noted that other brokers distrusted Leona as much as she distrusted the world. *"She couldn't be trusted, so she didn't trust anyone."*

In 1967, two years after Leona's triumphant sellout of the St. Tropez, a Washington, D.C., developer, Gustave Ring, erected an equally exclusive apartment house at 980 Fifth Avenue. The twenty-six-story cooperative tower would have only forty-five apartments, but they would have price tags in the $300,000 range—making them among the most expensive cooperatives in Manhattan.

Robert Neaderland, still president of Pease & Elliman and Leona's frequent escort, was a very close friend of Ring's and convinced the developer to allow his firm to sell the luxurious apartments. As before with the St. Tropez, Leona was picked as on-site manager of 980 Fifth Avenue and set up a small sales office in its lobby. And again she brought with her a small support staff of secretaries and clerical help.

Lindenbaum, as owner of Pease & Elliman, authorized Leona's appointment even though many of her co-brokers and staff members detested the hotshot saleslady who seemed to run roughshod over everyone except her clients and superiors. Immediately, Lindenbaum said, "she distinguished herself again. She was hard-working and aggressive, and talented in closing the deals." And not unexpectedly, "she was abrasive and tough to control. On petty things, she was a tough taskmaster to other people working in the office."

Leona's administrative assistant at the time, Sofia Kalfas, verified that "she was tough on everybody—I almost quit every week." But unlike so many other professionals who wince at the very thought of their past associations with Leona, Kalfas said she came to feel an abiding affection for her haughty taskmaster. "In fact, I loved her. I still love her," said Kalfas, now 66 and living in Montreal.

Kalfas recalled that her former boss had a tunnel-vision obsession with business that left little room for life's nurturing diversions. "Leona couldn't be a woman with friends and a social life—just enjoying her life. *Everything* had to be business. She was just too busy in her business. I don't remember her chitchatting with people. She was just too busy working and keeping appointments. Most of her social life was just meeting people and talking business."

Kalfas said Leona managed to sell "almost all the apartments" at 980 Fifth Avenue herself by working virtually round the clock. While the building was merely a rising concrete-and-steel skeleton, Leona would thread her way through construction debris to show raw floor space to potential buyers. "Very wealthy people would come to the site without gloves, and we'd have to lend them our gloves," Kalfas said. "We'd take them up the outside construction elevator and point out the space and then the apartment would be built according to the purchaser's own specifications." Leona would then work with decorators, contractors and the apartment owners to complete the apartment.

To Leona, Kalfas said, selling apartments was a thrilling opportunity—the first such in her life—to be noticed for her considerable talents and energy. "She had been a middle-aged secretary, and then very quickly she enjoyed success on a much higher plane. It was starting a life more glamorous than anything before. It was the attention—*she had the floor!* She was the speaker. Everybody was listening to her. People were being dependent on her. It was not just money. It was her job and her life."

One former Pease & Elliman cooperative saleswoman said Leona quickly got herself in the good graces of Gustave Ring, developer of 980 Fifth Avenue, "a tough guy" perhaps ten years her senior. "She had him in the palm of her hand. She could make her own rules. She could take off, come in and go off whenever she wanted." Another broker said that during construction, Ring stayed at the Stanhope Hotel at Eighty-first Street and Fifth Avenue—directly across the street from the Metropolitan Museum of Art—and had frequent conferences at his hotel with Leona. "She ingratiated herself with Ring and was really involved with him. She was on the job and talked with him day to day. She was spending a lot of time with him. She got very friendly with him."

Although brokers seemed to hate Leona, Kalfas said few of them were able to get close enough to her to see her real virtues. "There was plenty to love about her." Kalfas's most touching memories were Leona's unfailing attention to her aging mother, then about 80 years old, who frequently phoned the office at exactly the wrong time—when Leona was in the middle of hectic negotiations with developers or customers. "I've always admired her because she never forgot her mother. No matter how busy she was, whenever her mother called, she had time to talk. 'Yes, Mother, I'll call you....Yes, Mom....I'll call you later, Mother.' And her mother would continue to talk and she would continue to listen. That touched me because when other people called when she was busy, she wouldn't talk to them." Many times, Kalfas said, Leona would send her mother away to resorts on the weekends.

Kalfas said brokers often unfairly singled out Leona for "using" Neaderland and other men to advance her career. In a cutthroat business like real estate sales, "doesn't everybody 'use' other people to a certain extent? When you play tennis with someone, don't you want to play with someone better than you so you'll learn? Maybe Leona was like that. You can't knock her for that. It's true that men helped her. She just had a way about it. She'd call a man and they'd give her information. She was attractive. She had a nice smile; she had a nice way of saying it. She had personality. Isn't that part of being a woman who's smart? That's a woman, isn't it? Leona was no different than the others."

Although Leona "was tough on everybody," Kalfas said she was always fair and trusting to her. "She'd say, 'Sofia, take care of this, you know how to do it.' She'd just let me do it. She wasn't bossy." Other brokers couldn't understand Kalfas's loyalty to Leona. "They told me I was foolish to be doing so much for her." Among her duties was taking care of Leona's personal checking account. "It wasn't enormous. I paid the bills, and most of them were for clothes."

Unlike her habits in the married days, when Leona's spending money came from her husbands, she was thrifty as a working woman. "She would buy one nice thing at a time, which is what a smart businesswoman should do. Leona believed you should look prosperous when you're out there, but she didn't go on spending sprees. She'd say, 'Ummm. I should buy a dress,' " and Kalfas would instantly tighten the purse strings, telling her, "No, wait till next month."

With the exception of her fur coats, Kalfas said Leona veered toward subtle, understated clothes in her early career days. Her favorite store was Women's Haberdashers, on Madison Avenue, which specialized in what might now be described as "early businesswomen's attire." There she could find classic—but not dowdy—styles and fine tailoring at prices a notch below those at better-known stores along Fifth Avenue. "She wore black, brown, beige, subdued green. They were very plain lines—

maybe a loose raincoat with a simple swerve. She dressed smartly. She could wear the same suit for years and years because Women's Haberdashers' clothes never change. She'd wear a suit with a flair, with just a simple pearl necklace or costume jewelry. If she bought a scarf, it was a good scarf to go with many things." The only garments that were ever "a little flashy were her chiffon evening gowns," which Leona bought wholesale elsewhere.

Indeed, Leona's tendency to buy wholesale, and in enormous bulk, was one of her most curious personal habits. From her earliest career days, one former associate said, "She was terrified of being overcharged." To guarantee she got the rock-bottom unit price, Leona "would buy hundreds of the same thing" at discount although the collection could not be used up even in a lifetime. In effect, dollars would be wasted in order to save pennies on the few items she really needed. Even if the bulk transaction was ill advised, Leona would have the satisfaction of knowing she got the "best possible deal." One memorable purchase, he said, "was the time she bought one hundred combs." Fifteen years later, as Queen of the Palace, Leona would joke: "I'm still using the combs!"

Kalfas couldn't remember a white fur, but recalled that Leona had a beautiful mink coat that excited the envy of other female brokers. "They assumed that other people bought it for her. When a successful broker like Leona comes into the office and has made a deal, and the one next to her hasn't made a deal, that's when envy occurs. She had beautiful buildings and they sold well." When brokers made false accusations about Leona's "gifts," Kalfas would set the record straight. "Absolutely not!" she would protest. "I pay her monthly payments on them."

Leona confided few details of her private life to Kalfas. "Her son was never around. She wasn't a very open person about her life."

Indeed, Leona had failed to mention that by 1966, her son had married and taken his bride, Myrna, to live in Queens. A year later, on November 1, 1967, Myrna gave birth to Craig Stuart Panzirer, Leona's first grandchild! Nor did Leona mention a tragic feud that sliced her out of Jay's life even as little Craig heard his first nursery rhymes. According to a former in-law, Myrna barred Leona from her home almost immediately after marrying Jay. The bad blood started "when Myrna invited

Leona for Sunday dinner and Leona showed up two hours late. Myrna went ahead and served without her and Leona took it as a personal affront and created a terrible scene. So Myrna kicked her out. 'See the door? Don't let it hit you on the derrière on the way out.' Leona was never invited back. Craig never missed her because he never had a relationship with her." In any case, the in-law said, "Leona was single and searching for a husband. She didn't want to be known as a grandmother."

Although secretive and standoffish, Leona sometimes welcomed Kalfas to her apartment on Eighty-fifth Street for lunch. Kalfas recalled that on those rare occasions, "when you were away from the office with her, she was a completely different person. She wasn't under strain. She would take me to her apartment building for sandwiches and have her hairdresser cut my hair in the apartment. At times like that, you could see that she had a personal touch. I thought she was very natural." The one-bedroom abode was modestly furnished. "The most elaborate thing she owned was a simple hi-fi which I paid for monthly. I didn't notice any elaborate paintings or antiques. It was just a simple, clean apartment."

When Kalfas left the firm in 1967, she said Leona hated to see her go. "She told me, 'Remember, there will always be a door open if you want to come back.'" Kalfas said the kind assurance "gave me the courage to go out and get my own New York real estate salesman's license. I knew that if I ever ended up on the street I could go back and get a job."

A female broker who was briefly one of Leona's bosses—during Leona's days as a secretary/receptionist—described herself as one of the very few Pease & Elliman brokers who were able to recognize both Leona's "intense ruthlessness" and her "warm, caring side."

By the time Leona landed at 980 Fifth Avenue, the broker said it was obvious to everyone in the office that "Leona had it in her to be ruthless if anybody got in her way. I saw it in little ways. She would be unpleasant to the workmen. She adopted an imperious manner as she became powerful. She was going to knock away anything that got in her way. She was only spending her time and attention on what would get her money and fame. Neaderland was president of the firm and she would play him for what she could get. She wasn't overwhelmingly friendly to the other brokers. She was hostile; she didn't want to be bothered. They weren't in her program. This woman had a single goal in life and everything was confined to that. She didn't waste any time going to lunches with anyone. She wasn't a palsy-walsy person. She stayed in her cubbyhole."

The broker said Leona constantly battled with brokers for the slightest advantage, "but when I saw she really wanted something, I'd step aside and let her have it. I don't believe in fighting over a bone. But to Leona, it was so vital. She *had* to have it. I could look into her and see this terrible craving she had for these goals that were beyond her." The former broker, however, could see—as Sofia Kalfas had seen—"how good Leona was to her mother and her son. She couldn't be warmhearted to other brokers, who were her rivals, but she was to those who depended on her. She was loving to her family; that was real.

"One of my greatest insights into her," the broker said, was the day Leona "went around and introduced her mother to everybody at work." The broker described the elderly Ida Rosenthal as a very plain, matter-of-fact woman "who was not educated in American ways. She wasn't the gracious person trying to curry favor, but was a very solid—kind of 'I am what I am'—type of person, take it or leave it. If she had been a grand, elegant lady, that would have fit in with Leona's image as a businesswoman on the path to glory. Instead, she was a foreign-born woman of no importance in the worldly sense. But that didn't matter to Leona at all. In spite of her own worldly dreams, she was not going to downplay her mother. She wasn't going to make her mother a person of no account. She introduced her to everyone, and was damned proud of her."

By 1967, five years after going to work at Pease & Elliman, Leona found herself alienated from most of her co-workers because of her lioness manner. She grew close, however, to Steven U. Leitner, a broker ten years her junior who became her confidant at the firm. "She had an incendiary temper, which she never turned on me, thank God," Leitner said. "Basically she was a very vulnerable, sensitive person. She was a wonderful lady and I can't speak too highly of her."

He, too, recalled that her attachment and sense of responsibility to her mother and her son, Jay, were enormous. "Her mother, who was kosher and Jewish Orthodox, always came first." By the mid-1960s, he said, Ida Rosenthal had been placed in a kosher nursing home in Far Rockaway, Queens, "and Leona felt it was her duty to provide her as much comfort as possible in her last years. All her efforts were towards taking care of her." Next on Leona's priority list, Leitner said, was

Jay. He recalled that one of Leona's greatest concerns was her 26-year-old son's rapidly receding hairline. (A balding son apparently would undercut her own youthful image.) "She was worried about what she could do to preserve his hair. I told her not to make it an issue—don't make him self-conscious. It came up every day—either her mother or her son."

Gerald Kadish, Leona's hotel factotum in later years, said the Queen of the Palace often recalled how surprised her mother had been at her daughter's rapid, lucrative success in real estate. Kadish said he doubled over in laughter at one of Leona's favorite anecdotes. "She [Leona] would tell the story of how one Sunday she was visiting her mother and her mother said, 'Leona, you're making a lot of money. Tell me, are you doing it legally?' " Mystified at Leona's new-found resources, the mother added, "What do you do? What do you sell?"

Leona replied, quite matter-of-factly: "I sell condominiums."

Her immigrant mother mistook the multisyllable response for "condoms," and replied: "Ah! I knew it had to be something like that!"

Leona relished a good story. Indeed, her sense of humor was perhaps the saving grace that enabled the hard-charging broker to stay in the saddle while alienating most of her staff and fellow workers. It enabled her to stay in the good graces of the people who counted—her bosses and building owners, and long-suffering employees like Sofia Kalfas.

Leitner agreed with other brokers that Leona was "cutthroat" in her work, but even so, he said, "I can't hold it against her because all the top sales people in this business are cutthroat. It's highly competitive. I've been with brokers who stopped talking to me in the middle of lunch because they overheard a broker at the next table giving a property listing. Whatever Leona did, if it was legal, everyone else did it, too. There are people with money that are cutthroat, and there are people who are poor who are not cutthroat. She was poor and cutthroat."

At the time, Leitner said, Leona frequently negotiated with wealthy developers and owners of apartment buildings in hopes of winning contracts for Pease & Elliman to sell their apartments. "The problem was that many of them wanted to date her because she was so attractive. I never saw her dress as if she hadn't stepped out of two hours of primping and makeup. Everything about her looked absolutely perfect. Even when she was poor, she looked like Elizabeth Arden. Her hair was always coiffed perfectly, without a strand out of place. Whenever I went on the street, men turned around and looked at her. There was something in her posture. The way she moved. She was like Rita Hayworth, a natural beauty. It didn't require much work. Anyone with normal sexual appetites could not have looked at Leona without visualizing having sex with her. *You could imagine this would be one beautiful body to jump all over!* Let's just hope she didn't claw you to death afterward."

To keep the tycoons on their good behavior during business dinners with Leona, Leitner said he often agreed to trail along—a third wheel—as "a kind of chaperon. She would often drag me along on her dates because she had this attitude that she didn't want to be corralled into a sexual liaison with these businessmen. She wasn't looking for that. She was looking to make a living and not submit to the indignities that maybe a beautiful woman feels pressured into."

Benno Bordiga, a wealthy Manhattan landlord, recalled taking Leona out on several dates in the mid-1960s after meeting her on a Pease & Elliman business transaction. "I took her out for dinner a few times to see if there was any mutuality," he said, but romance failed to flicker. She may have looked like Rita Hayworth on the outside, "but there was nothing soft about her. She was a tough Brooklyn broad. She was single-minded about making a go of her real estate career. Most of the women I dated were soft and friendly, but she was tough. She had a good figure and had striking good looks, but that was all. She didn't strike me as a sexy lady because she was not soft and gentle. She wasn't feminine. I thought she was a challenge, but then I decided 'Who needs challenges?' " Another problem, he recalled, "was that Leona wore a lot of makeup in those days—maybe one-eighth of an inch thick. I didn't think it was very conducive to snuggling."

Leitner, who was single, said Leona invited him to chaperon so many business dinners that they became "like brother and sister. She was delightful company. She was very normal, funny and a lot of fun."

Even though Leona was making more money than she had ever dreamed of—perhaps $40,000 or $50,000 a year—she was far from being able to buy the jewelry that she had yearned for since her marriage to Lubin a decade earlier. As a compromise, Leitner said she would shop at Jolie Gabor, a Madison Avenue store that specialized in good imitation jewelry.

"One day she called me and said, 'I have an important date and need some earrings. Let's go to Jolie Gabor!'

"The problem," Leitner recalled, "was that Leona was on a budget of one hundred dollars." When he escorted her inside, Leona immediately started trying on the largest and most garish earrings in sight. "Anybody who knew jewelry would know they were fake. You just knew the settings weren't right. They were too much. She was picking things that Mrs. Ford or Mrs. Getty would buy, if they were real." Leitner advised her to "pick something modest, with imitation diamonds and emeralds. I picked out a semi-antique piece with small stones and said, 'Leona, if you wear this, people will think it's real because it's modest and small enough. They'll think it's an heirloom.' So she bought it, and paid about fifty-three dollars, and it looked like it was worth six thousand. She had picked out stuff that would look like five hundred thousand, parading as a millionaire. I had to protect her from herself."

Leona and Leitner continued to hop and shop around town together and it became clear that Leona—the fire-breathing workaholic who seemed too busy for friends—indeed had a pal. On many a Sunday she invited Leitner for brunch at her second-floor apartment on East Eighty-fifth Street. The one-bedroom apartment faced a back wall and had little sunlight, but "was very pretty. It was decorated in blue and white." During one such brunch, he realized that Leona might have wanted their relationship to move a step beyond. "She was making scrambled eggs and bagels, and came out to serve me in a negligee, with a lot of veils. She must have been disappointed because I only wanted to talk business." They had been "brother and sister" too long to change the game plan.

Brokers at the office believed, however, that Leona and Robert Neaderland's relationship was anything but platonic, Leitner recalled. For several years, the pair had been considered an office item. Neaderland, then 65, "was a bachelor and dragged Leona around as a date. Everybody assumed he was, as they'd say, dorking her." Neaderland did little to discourage the impression of a sexual relationship by "putting his hands on her" and proclaiming Leona's virtues in public.

When the public displays became bigger and bigger talk around the office, Leitner said Leona felt embarrassed enough to come to him with a denial. "She told me, 'He [Neaderland] insinuates things about me, and he puts his hands on me in public. You know I wouldn't touch him. I don't like it because people think the best I can get is to go out with Bob Neaderland.' "

Other brokers were repelled by the very thought of an affair with Neaderland because of his lurid office reputation. Leitner said the Pease & Elliman president "loved to talk about sex—sordid sex talk. I couldn't repeat the things he said. He was a dirty old man, but he was a scintillating character. He wasn't amorphous. He was a personality. He was old and ugly. He looked like Winston Churchill three years before he died." Leona couldn't help but catch his eye. "She was beautiful. She wasn't a hothouse flower. She was a *sunflower*."

Neaderland had been indicted by a federal grand jury years before, in 1961, for allegedly evading $27,550 in taxes by vastly overstating his business and entertainment expenses. In 1965, he was acquitted on the basis of insufficient documentary evidence. Leitner said Leona came to him in an excited state with the news that the Pease & Elliman president had beaten the rap. "Can you imagine the old coot got off!" she said. "You know he must have fixed the case," she speculated, noting the federal judge had dismissed the jury only three days into the trial.

Neaderland was "a very pompous man," Leitner said, and he couldn't help but think that Leona "patterned her own personality after him" as she grew more powerful in the man's world of real estate. Independent of any ulterior career motives Leona might have had with "the old coot," Leitner said the pair got along fabulously "because Neaderland was so similar to Leona to begin with. He was basically a loner, and so was she. They were both witty and funny and would break up laughing over little things in a business meeting." Like Leona, Leitner said, "Neaderland was Jewish from modest beginnings, with no college education and no real background."

And most important, "Neaderland became a self-made millionaire by being all bluff and bravado. He knew that everybody, regardless of how rich, wants to make more money. So he knew that, cold turkey, you could call any tycoon—the Donald Trumps of this world—on the telephone and say, 'I have a property for you.' He knew that he could get through to them once—that one time they'll listen to see what your offer is. If you made a fool out of yourself, they'd never talk to you again, but they'd listen that once. Neaderland was a dumpy-looking man and yet he could get on the phone and dial up anyone." Bluff and bravado required another ingredient, however, to get results. "Neaderland thought *appearance* was everything. He'd have his secretary place the phone call, and say, 'Mr. Neaderland will be right with you.' It made him seem important." Leitner recalled that "when Neaderland was only three weeks from bankruptcy once, he threw a party for forty executives at the Sherry Netherland." Appearances were crucial. "Leona picked up on that and said, 'If people don't think you are successful and aren't envious of you, they won't do business with you.'"

Neaderland was Leona's own Norman Vincent Peale, her inspiration and role model. "He taught her that the whole world could be your own little oyster if you have the chutzpah to go out and get it. And I think Leona embraced his attributes herself because she really thought they were the secrets of his success."

Like Neaderland, Leona would publicly humiliate employees or shopkeepers at the slightest whim, as if the ear-piercing broadsides validated her own importance. If Neaderland was her mentor, however, she exceeded him in nastiness. "You could go into a restaurant with her," Leitner said, "when she had limited funds, when she was on a budget supporting her son. And if the waiter or waitress wasn't to her liking, she'd *explode*. She'd say the crudest things, and I'd have to tell her that she was embarrassing me. And she would defend her outburst by telling me, 'I work hard. Why can't they learn to do it right!' She was a perfectionist, and when you didn't measure up, she had a scowl that could freeze you or drop you dead." Then after the meal, Leitner said, "Leona would go into another room and look at me and laugh out loud about the whole thing, saying: 'That's over. I showed them!' As if she had put on a little performance."

Leitner said he considered Leona's smaller outbursts as her "Brooklyn Catskill Mountain Humor. They were meant to be humorous. A lot of people take offense at Leona, but from her point of view she's funny. She sees herself as a comedienne in life. She always did. She thought of herself as a female Charlie Chaplin, although she didn't look like Charlie Chaplin—as a little girl who stamps her feet, who has fits, and then leaves the room after she's gotten what she wants. And then smiles and says, 'Look what I did. Look how it worked.' I saw her do it all the time. She'd shove clothes back at the dry cleaner's and order them to 'Give me my money back or do it again!' That hasn't changed. She had the same personality and mouth then" that she had twenty years later as mercurial hotel Queen.

Humor was important, but Leitner sensed that anger and frustration over her earlier years were the dominant forces underlying Leona's aggressive manner. "Everything she does is like fighting back at her own sad and unfortunate" beginnings. Emotionally, "she felt destroyed in her life and left alone without any real help and understanding. That's the real Leona. She's not a person that could enjoy, even when living well. She's always felt hurt, humiliated, or like a clown" pretending to be on top of the world. The humiliations didn't end, moreover, when she hit a successful real estate career, but piled up higher. "Not being wealthy," Leitner said, "she had to deal all day long with these rich people who put her down. She told me stories about women looking at million-dollar apartments and she would say, 'Look at the marble bathrooms.'

"And they would say, 'You don't know anything, honey. This is lousy marble! I want it ripped out. I want Carrara marble!' She felt they demeaned her, as though she was not their equal— like she was just a saleswoman." Instead of becoming more sensitive as a result of the mistreatment, Leitner said she became further hardened. In fact, just as she took cues from Neaderland's bravura style, she began to copy the haughty manners of her customers. "The way she is acting today, as irascible Queen of the Helmsley Palace, is only parodying the way wealthy people treated her. They say children often imitate their parents later in life and that wife-beaters were beaten as kids. I think years of working with impolite wealthy people possibly got to her and she felt this is the way you have to act once you've become successful."

Leona spared the airs, however, with a few trusted souls like Leitner and her secretary, Sofia Kalfas. She was also her more fun-loving self with an aristocratic Jewish investor by the name of Willard Malkan. The two were dating about 1967 and encouraged Leitner to join them for quiet evenings around town. Leitner said Malkan was as distinguished and elegant as Leona was beautiful. "They were a good match. He was very well mannered, very laid back, tall and neat. He spoke beautifully and dressed impeccably. You couldn't say anything about him except that he was a gentleman." And unlike Neaderland, "Malkan was Leona's age or younger." Leitner said Leona "was looking for someone wealthy, but not a millionaire. I didn't ever think she would marry someone like a Harry Helmsley. I always thought she would have been happy with Malkan," who was wealthy from investments in cable television stations but was no mogul.

The threesome, and a divorced businessman who was

Malkan's roommate at the time, would spend evenings together at Gino's—a crowded, inexpensive Italian restaurant near Bloomingdale's on Lexington Avenue.

Frequently, they would stop off for a drink at the Carlton House, a deluxe sixteen-story residential hotel on Madison Avenue owned by a partnership headed by developer Harry Helmsley. "Being a broker is backbreaking work, and very often you don't get paid when you've worked very hard. So after work, Leona loved to go to the bar on the ground floor of the hotel. It was a local broker's place. She said she would love to be able to live in a place like this, or own a building like this—that it would be such comfort. It never dawned on her that it would come to pass."

Leona's dreams of grandeur were abruptly interrupted in late 1967, Leitner said, when trouble struck at Pease & Elliman headquarters. "One day she came into my office and broke down crying," Leitner recalled. "I was alarmed because I had never seen her in such a state. She was never like that."

"I've just been fired!" she announced, wiping tears from the corners of both eyes. "Armand [Lindenbaum] called me into his office. He just fired me!"

"What's it all about?" Leitner asked.

"I can't believe how hard I've worked, and now they want me out." Leona broke into tears again and said she feared Lindenbaum would keep the approximately $50,000 in commissions she had earned from sales at 980 Fifth Avenue and other cooperative projects.

"They want to cheat me out of my commissions! They're going to beat me out of my money."

Leitner said Leona told him she demanded the commissions, and Lindenbaum replied: "If you want them, just sue."

Leona implored Leitner to intervene. "Please talk to Armand. Tell him I'm entitled to my commissions." A few minutes later, Leitner said, "Leona left the office and never came back." Leitner said he felt guilty ever afterward because "I was one of the top salesmen at the time, and I thought I could have probably gone in there and fought her battle for her" with Lindenbaum. Instead, he had the impression that Leona hired a lawyer and eventually collected her back earnings.

Lindenbaum insists, however, that Leona was never fired: "I didn't ask her to leave." He says that Leona left the job on her own accord after 980 Fifth Avenue was sold out and no new buildings became available for her to supervise as on-site saleswoman.

Leona, by now, was too accustomed to being in charge of individual buildings, with buyers waltzing in the door. She was unable to go out and find her own customers. Lindenbaum said she adamantly refused to free-lance and instead demanded "a guaranteed salary which was much more than we could afford." When he turned her down, he said she walked out the door. Lindenbaum said he eventually paid Leona all her commissions—"There were no threats of litigation"—and they remained "very good friends."

A female broker who once worked for the firm said Leona's departure was an emotional blow to Neaderland—her mentor and career booster for the previous six years at Pease & Elliman. "At real estate dinners, she was no longer with him, and he yearned for her at the table after she left. He would complain how much he missed her."

Leitner sensed that Leona felt a deep bitterness about "being shunted out of Pease & Elliman." He said she was forced to hit the pavement in search of a job. Opportunity struck quickly, in May 1968, when three owners of an aggressive new commercial real estate firm, Sutton & Towne Inc., decided to diversify into apartment sales. More and more landlords were converting their apartment buildings to cooperatives—selling individual units to tenants at specified prices and conditions. Under state law, an owner had the option of converting if 35 percent of a building's tenants agreed to buy their apartments. Holdouts—tenants who refused to buy—could be evicted at the end of their current leases in order that outsiders be allowed to purchase their units. As the trend caught on, real estate brokerage firms realized that cooperative sales might be a lucrative addition to their business.

Sutton & Towne decided to get into the act by forming a subsidiary, Sutton & Towne Residential, Inc., which would specialize in conversions. The subsidiary would harvest hundreds of commissions by selling tenants their individual apartments. The conversion field was relatively new, however, and there were few seasoned cooperative experts to run such a subsidiary. David Wilshin, one of Sutton & Towne's three owners, was casting about for such an expert when a friend mentioned a hotshot cooperative saleswoman by the name of Leona Roberts. She had sold hundreds of apartments in newly constructed buildings for Pease & Elliman, and presumably could also work her sales magic in older apartment buildings targeted for conversion.

Wilshin arranged to meet her at luncheon and laid out a proposal. He and his partners would finance the new subsidiary and hire her to run the show as executive vice president. She would receive no commissions on sales; instead, she would be given a salary and a guaranteed share of the annual profits. In effect, she would become a full partner without investing any money of her own. Her skills as a saleswoman would be her capital investment in the new enterprise.

The offer was too good to pass up. The income potential of sharing fully in the profits was superior to working on commission, as she had done for years at Pease & Elliman. She took the offer, recruited a small sales staff and moved into Sutton & Towne's office at 300 Madison Avenue.

Her career shift was duly noted by the *New York Times* in a May 27, 1968 announcement under the headline "Sutton & Towne Elects Woman to a Key Post." It was accompanied by an elegant profile photograph of Leona, looking prosperous and wearing a strand of pearls. The following month, the New York *Post* cited her as a sales "specialist" in an article entitled "Inflationary Spiral Fuels Popularity of Cooperatives."

Miss Roberts believes more and more people are recognizing the vast investment potential of cooperatives in today's rental market....The purchase of a cooperative apartment today, according to Miss Roberts, represents a tremendous hedge against inflation. She noted, for example, that the value of real estate historically rises during periods of inflation such as now exists.

Miss Roberts, who has sold millions of dollars' worth of cooperative apartments in recent years, said that rising rentals have also made the purchase of cooperative apartments extremely appealing because tenants can claim a sizeable percentage of their carrying charges as a tax deduction while building up equity in their investment.

While the newsprint was still wet, Wilshin realized he had made the right hiring decision. Sutton & Towne Residential landed contracts to convert two prime buildings immediately after Leona introduced him to builder Jerome Minskoff and members of the Anthony Campagna real estate family.

Minskoff wanted to convert the Brevoort, a late 1950s apartment house at 11 Fifth Avenue, between East Eighth and East

Ninth streets. The Campagnas wanted to sell the 150 apartments in their building at 35 Park Avenue, near Thirty-seventh Street. Wilshin said Leona didn't have enough confidence to negotiate the deal alone, so she brought him along. It became clear to him that she was a fairly able negotiator in her own right. "When she wanted to be charming, she could charm the hell out of anyone. She convinced both of them to give us the selling agency," Wilshin said.

The building owners submitted conversion plans to the state attorney general's office and received approval to attempt to convert the buildings. In a marvel of salesmanship, Wilshin said, Leona and a pair of sales assistants managed to sell out both buildings within ninety days after getting permission from Albany to launch the conversions. "Leona was responsible for the sale basically of all four hundred apartments," at an average cost of approximately $7,500 per room. "She ran back and forth between the two buildings and was involved in just about every sale. She was there to supervise the sales staff and answer questions. She worked seven days a week, day and night. She never complained about being tired; she was really driven." Wilshin said Leona was a magnet that attracted customers like iron filings "because she was very glib and very charming. Without Leona, as far as I'm concerned, Sutton & Towne Residential was worthless."

Seymour Rabinowitz, an attorney who helped convert both buildings, recalled that Leona's performance was utterly remarkable because "in those days, real estate was a man's world. There weren't that many successful woman brokers in the field. You could have counted them on your fingers and toes but Leona was as strong as a man. She had the strength of a man—the forcefulness." He said she was indeed the *only* outstanding cooperative saleswoman in all of New York. "She could stand up, knowing what it was she was looking for, and from a business viewpoint she knew what was needed and she wasn't about to give in. She wasn't going to accept less than success. She wasn't going to compromise when she thought she was right." Most of all, "she had the ambition we all have to get the good things in life and go after it." A keen sales instinct, moreover, helped her rack up the business. "When she showed an apartment, she knew women would be interested in the kitchen and their husbands would care more about the views. If a couple came in, she would know who was the dominant one, knew how to sell him or her. She also knew when to stop talking and say, 'It's time to sign on the bottom line.' That's the essence of a good salesman—knowing when to stop talking." Also important, Leona was good at supervising her own sales staff "because she had the intuitive ability to sell and recognized it in others."

Good timing was also a critical factor, Rabinowitz said. "She got going in business for herself at the exact right moment because conversions were just beginning to proliferate. Luckily, she had gotten enough prior experience at Pease & Elliman to lead the pack."

As with earlier sales triumphs at Pease & Elliman (particularly the St. Tropez and 980 Fifth Avenue), however, Leona was loath to share her rewards with others. Wilshin said Leona's breathtaking sales record at 35 Park Avenue and 11 Fifth Avenue was in large part due to her hardworking sales assistants. Despite the team triumph, however, Leona "never suggested that any of them get a bonus. She was running the operation, and I don't ever remember her offering something that she didn't have to offer. We sold the buildings a lot faster than we thought possible, and she never thought about rewarding the people with her. Not surprisingly, most of the people that worked with her did not get along with her after a while."

Leona's parsimony to staff was particularly upsetting because "she made tremendous demands upon them and wanted them to work the hours she worked—eighty hours a week—without recompensing them. She had people in our management department working every night, preparing schedules and forms. She would insist on her sales department working excessive hours. She was the antithesis of kindness. She ranted and raved and didn't know any other way or care for any other way. And she expected the staff, for their salary, to put in the extra time." If it were possible, Wilshin said, Leona "would have liked to have kept 110 percent" of the rewards for herself.

Sarah Plesser, Leona's top salesperson at the time, recalled, "I was doing the best of anyone in the division, but I didn't get any bonuses—nothing except my commission." Nevertheless, Plesser said she was more grateful than resentful because Leona hired her knowing full well she had nary a shred of sales experience. Bonus or no bonus, "she gave me a chance to learn, and I picked it up quickly." Plesser recalled that Leona was "a tough personality—a business personality—who used to wear *very strong* perfume. Every time she passed by, you couldn't help but notice."

Although she was a taskmaster to all her salespeople, Wilshin said Leona seemed to have been harder on her three male brokers than her five female brokers. "I think it was possible she had it in for men. Remember, she was not a young woman even then, and had been divorced. She probably felt men had used her through the years. It wasn't as though she went out of her way to abuse her male employees—it was just the way she behaved. I think part of it was painful memories."

When Leona agreed to set up Sutton & Towne's cooperative sales division in May 1968 and become its executive vice president, she convinced Wilshin to hire an acquaintance, Richard Meyers, as president. Only six months later, Wilshin recalled, "Leona came running to me and demanded that I fire this fellow: 'I can't stand him! Either fire him or I'm leaving!' " Wilshin was astonished by the ultimatum. "It was such an unusual request because she had brought him to the company and helped him get an equity position in the company as well as an employment contract. For her to become disenchanted with him so quickly was unreal." Wilshin said that because Leona "was actually running the division and since we had major contracts to convert two buildings (35 Park Avenue and 11 Fifth Avenue)," he and the other owners acceded to the demand. When Meyers filed suit for breach of his employment contract, Wilshin said, the firm paid him a cash settlement.

The swift dismissal, Wilshin said, was typical of Leona's impatience with management employees, particularly men. "Emasculation was how she did it. She made demands that were unreasonable, and in the long run it's not a good way to run a business. From a sales standpoint, if you're looking to hit and run, it might be okay to upset a lot of people. But if you want to run a business long range, I don't think we would have stayed in business."

As it turned out, Sutton & Towne Residential abruptly folded anyway in the summer of 1969, less than a year after it opened for business.

The shutdown was not the result of bad employee morale, bankruptcy or a downturn in the housing market. It was probably the only real estate division in history that would trace its demise to a dinner dance.

Four

On the night of April 16, 1969, Leona Roberts took time from her busy schedule to attend the annual dinner of the Realty Foundation of New York. Each year, hundreds of real estate brokers, salesmen, investors and their escorts filled the giant ballroom of the Waldorf-Astoria to renew old ties and discuss new endeavors.

The biggest names in the real estate pantheon attended the bash each year. The Lefraks, Zeckendorfs and Fishers could huddle over dinner and discuss the next $100 million deal, or waltz with their wives or secretaries across the giant dance floor. The biggest titan of all, Harry Helmsley, had just turned 60 but could outwaltz and outlast even the most spirited dancers in the room. At work he was a dull numbers-cruncher in an old brown suit. But in a tuxedo on the dance floor, he was Fred Astaire. Dancing was perhaps his biggest passion in life next to acquiring and managing more buildings for Helmsley-Spear Inc.—his $2.5 billion real estate management company. He always had a problem at these dances, however. His wife, Eve, was a retiring woman who preferred to stay at her suburban Westchester County home rather than contend with the crush of wheeler-dealers and all the business chatter. Harry, without a date, had to stand up at his front table, near the dais, and scan the room for dance partners. He would stop by the various other company tables and occasionally ask an attractive candidate to join him for a waltz.

On this fateful evening, Leona Roberts sat with a dozen other Sutton & Towne brokers way off to the back left side of the ballroom. Several diners recalled that Leona's gown became quite a topic of conversation at the table when the late Powell Winston, another Sutton & Towne salesman, jokingly proclaimed it a "*shmata*," the Yiddish term for "rag." Winston, whose family made gowns for some of Hollywood's most glamorous film sirens, immediately recognized Leona's gown as an antique creation of designer Ceil Chapman. She was apparently wearing a well-preserved keepsake from her job with the Chapman company a generation earlier. "Winston was telling her the dress she was wearing was twenty years old," recalled Paul Steinbock, a former broker in the firm's commercial division. Leona became very defensive at the remark, but soon regained her composure.

Then, Steinbock recalled, "Leona asked us if we could point out who Harry Helmsley was. Her intention was to meet Harry Helmsley." The brokers singled out a rather nondescript gray-haired man—very tall and slim, with a mustache and glasses—at the front of the room. "As soon as we pointed him out," Steinbock said, "Leona made a beeline for him."

Within minutes, everyone at the table noticed Helmsley leading Leona smoothly and gracefully across the dance floor in a perfect waltz. The amazing thing, another broker recalled, "was that they danced the entire evening" as conductor Al Wayne led the Mark Towers Orchestra. "Leona never returned to our table." Even so, the broker said, "there was no thought about what would happen. No one said, *'There goes the Leona ship—it's sailing!'* "

Shmata or no *shmata*, a waltz apparently was the perfect introduction to Harry Helmsley. Only weeks later, Leona went to David Wilshin's office at Sutton & Towne and announced she was resigning. She explained that she had been offered a profit-sharing position at Brown, Harris, Stevens, Inc., a Helmsley subsidiary that specialized in the sale and management of expensive New York apartments. Helmsley had asked her to become director of cooperative sales and a senior vice president of the subsidiary, which was making little money. It needed Leona's expertise in the profitable new field of converting apartment buildings to cooperatives.

"She came to me and told me it was a wonderful opportunity," Wilshin recalled. "She asked me to release her from a five-year employment contract so she could take the job." He agreed to let her go, on the understanding that Leona would forfeit any accrued profits Sutton & Towne still owed her from her one-third ownership interest in the firm. In addition, the Sutton & Towne Residential subsidiary would close up shop and the two buildings it managed—35 Park Avenue and 11 Madison Avenue—would henceforth be managed by Leona at Brown, Harris, Stevens. "She took the management of the buildings with her and we parted amicably."

Bringing 35 Park Avenue to Brown, Harris, Stevens was a logical move not only because Leona had converted the building in the first place, but because one of the building's most prominent residents was Leon R. Spear. Spear had been one of

Helmsley's closest associates since 1955, the year Helmsley's firm—Dwight-Helmsley—merged with Spear's management company to become Helmsley-Spear. He was 75 years old and still an active senior vice president of Helmsley-Spear in 1969, when Leona converted his Park Avenue apartment house to a cooperative. A friend of the late developer recalled that Spear had been hugely impressed with Leona's performance. "He thought she was a top-drawer salesperson and had done a very good job with the building. He was so impressed, in fact, that he told me he went and told Harry [Helmsley] about 'this very bright lady.' " That being the case, the name Leona Roberts presumably had a familiar ring to Helmsley when she introduced herself at the Realty Foundation soirée.

Wilshin said he assumed "there was no romance with Harry" when Leona left Sutton & Towne Residential to join Helmsley's subsidiary. "It was strictly business. Leona was business oriented and was interested in a move that would benefit her financially."

Leona's own recollection of how she met Harry is quite different from the dinner-dance memories of her former Sutton & Towne colleagues. In numerous later interviews, she claimed Harry demanded to meet *her* after learning she was a powerhouse broker and a millionaire in her own right. "During three months in 1968, I earned $450,000 in commissions," she boasted in one *New York Times* close-up. "Harry heard of my reputation and he told one of his executives, 'Whoever she is, get her.' When he finally called, I told him, 'You can't afford me; I'm in a bad bracket now.' " Reluctantly, Leona added, she agreed to become a senior v.p. of his Brown, Harris, Stevens subsidiary, but only after Helmsley guaranteed her a $500,000 annual salary. "He didn't hire me. He was fortunate enough to get me to join him in his organization," she told another reporter.

Leona's story, however glamorous, just doesn't stand up to scrutiny, according to Wilshin. Far from earning $450,000 in just three months of 1968, he estimated, "She probably earned around $75,000 for *the entire year*" at Sutton & Towne, a worthwhile sum but no king's ransom. "She was not at six figures." He estimated that the total revenue of Sutton & Towne Residential, Leona's division, was only $750,000 for the year, from which rent and the salaries of eight brokers and staff members also had to be paid. Rexford E. Tompkins, the former president of Brown, Harris, Stevens, who hired Leona at Harry's insistence, laughed at Leona's memory of pulling down a $500,000 salary. "She was hired as a broker like anyone else when I hired her. Unless she was on Harry's private payroll, which I can't imagine, it would have been impossible. It would not be like Harry Helmsley to pay anybody a half million." However outlandish, Leona's claims were accepted as fact and parroted breathlessly by the media, thereby dampening any jaundiced speculation that Leona was a gold digger.

The New York *Post*, in a June 27, 1969 news blurb, reported that Leona Mindy Roberts, "who successfully organized New York's first condominium, the 35-story St. Tropez," had joined Brown, Harris, Stevens.

Leona, as her ex-husband Joe Lubin liked to say, could never be content in the "Avis position." With claws bared, or retracted for strategic advantage, the lioness broker always aimed for highest possible ground. And she knew that the potential rewards of working for Harry Helmsley—the very best in the business—totally eclipsed those imaginable at Sutton & Towne.

From scratch, Helmsley had built one of the nation's largest real estate empires over the course of almost half a century. This soft-spoken man with the "rabbit-like" face was the unequaled Renaissance man—an acknowledged master of virtually every facet of the business. As a property-finder and appraiser, he was without peer. At the negotiating table, his wily, hard-nosed skills invariably prevailed. As a property manager, he was on intimate terms, sub-basement-to-spire, with dozens of Manhattan's tallest skyscrapers.

While still a child, Henry Brakmann Helmsley heard opportunity knocking loudly at his door. At age 16, the Bronx lad was already soaking up the knowledge that would take him to the top of his profession. Harry, as he was known, went right to work after graduating in June 1925 from Evander Childs High School. He had no choice, for his father's career as a buyer in the wholesale dry-goods business had faltered in spite of the vibrant overall economy. Young Harry's earnings were needed to help support his parents, Henry and Minnie Helmsley, and Harry's 10-year-old brother, Walter.

The family had been living at 1478 Grand Concourse, at about 175th Street. The 180-foot-wide thoroughfare was the Park Avenue of the Bronx. There, before his family's economic crunch, Harry grew accustomed to seeing uniformed doormen in front of the six-story apartment houses. Living along the

Grand Concourse afforded a kind of gracious, relatively un-cramped lifestyle that would have been unthinkably expensive in comparable residential districts of Manhattan. Another affordable advantage was a good secondary education. At the time, New York City boasted one of the country's finest public school systems, with high-caliber teachers and firm discipline. Like his Bronx classmates—a good many of them from affluent Jewish families that had left the Lower East Side behind—Harry was serious. According to school records, he completed Evander Childs with good scores on his regents exams, particularly in economics, law, advertising and French. Yet, along with so many other promising students of the day, economic realities prevented him from going on to college.

Instead, as Helmsley would often recount in later years, he took his mother's advice and sought out a real estate job. Since her own father had been a modestly successful apartment landlord, Minnie Helmsley was able to cite firsthand at least a few advantages of the business. If Harry learned the basics, maybe someday he could also be a property owner.

He started out at the bottom, pitching letters for $12 a week in the mailroom of Dwight, Voorhis & Perry, a small property brokerage and management firm that traced its beginnings back to 1866.

As young Harry worked indoors, construction crews braved ice and blistering heat in a race to create a new, towering Manhattan skyline. That year, 1925, the largest office building in the world, the Graybar Building, began to rise on a site just east of Grand Central Terminal at Lexington Avenue and Forty-second Street. The four-hundred-foot-tall behemoth would advertise one million square feet of rental space, more than enough room for twelve thousand workers.

Nearby, steelworkers erected other giants on the heels of a landmark 1916 zoning ordinance which carved Manhattan into distinct commercial, residential and unrestricted sectors. Thanks to the new law, lower Manhattan and its teeming Wall Street hordes would now have competition from new business districts, including one then emerging around the rail transport hub of Grand Central Terminal. The ordinance not only opened up specified districts for commercial developments, but foretold the tapering "skyscraper" shape of future office buildings. To guarantee that neighboring buildings got their fair share of light and air, the ordinance provided that a tower could no longer rise straight up from a building site. Beyond a certain height, it would have to be set back from the sidewalk—thus the terraced "step-back" design of skyscrapers.

Land-hungry developers also cast about feverishly for building sites farther north, particularly along the elegant blocks of Fifth Avenue south of Central Park. The commercial juggernaut, combined with the burden of steep city property taxes, convinced the avenue's most illustrious families to deed over their sprawling mansions. In 1924, the era of great houses came to an end when demolition crews razed the medieval replica of the Château de Blois, built at Fifty-second Street and Fifth Avenue in 1881 by William K. and Alva Vanderbilt. A year later, Willie's sister-in-law, Mrs. Cornelius Vanderbilt II, sold her Fifty-seventh Street version of Fontainebleau for $7 million. From her mansion's rubble rose an elegant block of shops principally occupied by Bergdorf Goodman. The exodus of other Knickerbocker families along Millionaires' Row soon sealed the transformation of that stretch of Fifth Avenue into a commercial district.

Vanity Fair magazine denounced the mansion-razing craze, warning that the city's aristocracy was passing the social baton to investors and speculators "who only ten years ago boasted no fortunes at all.…In place of a society restricted to a few hundred people of good breeding, we now have a social fabric widening into the thousands, most of whom have inherited no very traditional creed of conduct or behavior." Business savvy, not pedigree, had clearly become the passport to the era's unbounded riches. Opportunity was open to anyone with the power to dream and the skill and determination to make dreams come true.

This democratic trend was sweet encouragement for young Harry Helmsley, one of the lowborn "thousands." The enthusiastic Dwight, Voorhis & Perry mail clerk soon got a raise and a ticket outdoors, where he could see the action for himself. He became the firm's rent collector for properties in the notorious Hell's Kitchen section of midtown Manhattan. He was also given brokerage duties, which would require him to help owners find tenants for their commercial space.

Hell's Kitchen was an unsightly hodgepodge of freight yards, stock pens, tenements, garages and factories between Eighth and Twelfth avenues and Thirtieth and Fifty-ninth streets. Armed gangsters had terrorized the area between 1868 and 1910, when a special police force organized by the New York Central Railroad finally restored a semblance of law and order.

But it was still a tough area when young Harry began knocking on doors and demanding rent. Luckily, what the fresh-faced boy lacked in years he made up for in height. At 18, he could command a little respect with his six-foot-three-inch frame. He was almost legally blind in one eye, and his spectacles also lent an air of maturity that must have been helpful in winning the confidence of commercial tenants.

While other fellows his age were still enjoying baseball and the delights of the Coney Island boardwalk, young Harry was having equal fun mastering the intricacies of property leases and renewal options. Real estate had became his recreation as well as bread and butter for the budding businessman and his Bronx family. He familiarized himself with every building in Hell's Kitchen and those in adjoining areas as well. Only by becoming familiar with buildings—and getting to know their owners—could Harry hope to bring new brokerage business to Dwight, Voorhis & Perry. It was hard homework, but he had a dream to fulfill. Even as a youngster, Helmsley would later recall, "I knew what I wanted. I've always wanted to be the biggest real estate man to come down the pike."

Harry's youthful optimism endured even when the stock market crashed through the floorboards of Wall Street on October 24, 1929. In the first few years after the crash, many economists assumed they were witnessing merely an extended financial panic that would soon go away. In that hopeful spirit, industrialist John Jacob Raskob set out in March 1930 to build the tallest building in the world at Thirty-third Street and Fifth Avenue, on the site of the demolished Waldorf-Astoria Hotel.

Three hundred steelworkers—"sky boys"—raced to erect the Empire State Building's 57,000-ton skeleton. More than three thousand other workers hustled to fasten the limestone façade and to install fifty-one miles of pipes, seventeen million feet of telephone cable, seven miles of elevator shafts and an enormous ventilating system capable of pulling one million cubic feet of fresh air into the building every minute. It was a herculean job, and fourteen workers lost their lives in the scramble. On May 1, 1931—barely thirteen months after structural work began—President Hoover inaugurated the completed 102-story tower by turning a key in Washington which lit the building. The streamlined 1,250-foot-tall creation was an engineering, as well as an aesthetic, masterpiece. In high winds, it shifted no more than one-quarter inch off center.

Several other renowned Manhattan skyscrapers exist only because their construction began in the months before Black Thursday. In fact, the Empire State Building shattered the world height record of 1,046 feet set just a year earlier by the spired Chrysler Building at Lexington Avenue near East Forty-second Street.

Not as tall, but powerfully dramatic, was the headquarters of the New York Central Railroad, which assumed its straddle position over Park Avenue (at East Forty-sixth Street) in 1929. The double-arched thirty-five-story tower, connected at each side by fifteen-story wings and crowned by a baroque cupola, became an instant landmark.

Yet, pleased as builders were at their daring new contributions to the skyline, they were unable to fill them with tenants in the stubborn Depression economy. Journalists nicknamed Raskob's tower "The Empty State Building" because it was only 46 percent rented upon opening in 1931, and only 68 percent occupied in subsequent years.

At the depth of the Depression, in 1933, the country's gross national product had plummeted to $56 million from $103 billion in 1929. It was the worst of times for sixteen million unemployed, about one third of the available national work force. But it was the very best of times for 24-year-old Harry Helmsley, who for the remainder of his long career would unfailingly prove himself an expert in spinning great riches from a ravaged marketplace.

When the Depression struck, demand for office space dwindled with the declining work force. Building owners were unable to meet their mortgage payments. The value of properties plummeted, and thousands of properties were repossessed by their mortgage holders—particularly banks and giant financial institutions like the Metropolitan Life Insurance Co.. With fortunes wiped out and little capital floating around, the banks could expect few buyers to step forward and relieve them of their unwanted smorgasbord of foreclosed properties. Yet, until the economy improved and buyers could be found, someone had to manage the buildings.

Helmsley's experience thus far had been as a leasing broker, but the Depression decimated that end of the business. Property sales also dried up. Rather than give up the ghost, Dwight, Voorhis & Perry backed away from brokerage and turned its sights to managing foreclosed properties for banks and companies like Met Life.

By shoe leather and subway, Helmsley began making trips at the beginning and end of each week to Met Life's headquarters at Madison Avenue and Twenty-third Street. He'd be there promptly when the company posted its biweekly lists of the latest foreclosed properties. Then, like a good salesman, Harry would quickly negotiate a contract with Met Life assigning his firm to manage more buildings.

Getting just the management contract—if not the building itself—would become the oft repeated theme of Helmsley's future success. In addition to management fees, such contracts would prove invaluable in numerous other ways. They would enable Helmsley to learn the economics of good property management—from budgeting electrical and insurance expenses to cleaning a limestone façade. Most important, by keeping his ear glued to the management grapevine, he would be among the first to hear of any affordable investment opportunities that might arise.

Such an opportunity appeared in 1936, when the owners of a ten-story office building on East Twenty-third Street were about to default on their $100,000 mortgage. Thanks to the cost-trimming expertise he had acquired as a property manager for Dwight, Voorhis & Perry, Helmsley knew he could make the building profitable by eliminating certain expenses. That invaluable knowledge gave him the confidence to go after the deal—not on behalf of his firm but as his very first personal investment.

Always careful with a buck, the young property manager had squirreled away just enough savings to "do" the deal. "They were willing to let me buy their mortgage for $1,000—my only $1,000—and I took over the building's debt," he would recall decades later in a *New York* magazine interview. "The mortgage at the time was 3 percent, and it cost me $3,000 a year, and I remember I had a hard time, but I was confident that I would be able to turn the building around. I was in the management business. I could watch the building better than its previous owner." Indeed, by paring costs to the bone and filling vacancies, Helmsley steered his investment into the black. "I watched the building's expenses such as fuel, electricity, and the payroll. I made sure there wasn't one extra man on the staff. One extra employee could cost $3,000 in those days, and that made the difference as to whether I could pay the mortgage." Nevertheless, the 27-year-old landlord left room in his budget for a new building superintendent: his unemployed father. Henry

Helmsley had lost his job in the Depression, Helmsley explained in another interview, and "I was supporting him anyway. One of the reasons I wanted to buy the property was so he could get a job."

(Helmsley sold the building for a $65,000 profit in the late 1940s after his rent roll rose in the expanding postwar economy—a dandy return on his initial $1,000 investment. Instead of spending his windfall, he invested the profits in other buildings.)

"The worse the market, the better to buy" was the lesson Helmsley took to heart from his continuing Depression-era deals. He also learned the beauty of "leveraging" savings, of buying a six-figure property with a four-figure down payment and watching it balloon in value. Those financial lessons, combined with Helmsley's firsthand knowledge of property management, enabled him to instantly recognize an undervalued piece of property. In the late 1930s, he was already one of the best appraisers in town.

By 1938, Helmsley bought into the firm, which was renamed Dwight, Voorhis & Helmsley. As a partner, he was then able to hire his younger brother, Walter, who would continue in his employ for the next three decades.

Hard work was first nature to the fast-rising real estate operator. But Harry Helmsley had at least a drop or two of romance in his veins. In between deals, he was introduced to Eve Ella Green—a blonde, blue-eyed widow who shared his love of dancing. Mrs. Green had been widowed a short time earlier when her young husband, Arthur Green, was killed in an accident. Alone and pregnant, the tall young woman returned from Boston to New York to be close to her parents, Eugene and Eva Sherpick of Mineola, Long Island. Tragedy struck again several months later when her infant son died a day after his birth. "At the time, I wondered if it might not have been the best thing for the child, because he came into the world without a father to help raise him," Eve recalled. One of her friends tried as best he could to help the widow through her grief, and occasionally played the role of matchmaker. On one especially strong recommendation, Eve said, she agreed to go out with an ambitious real estate broker named Harry B. Helmsley. The blind date with a man four years her junior was a little unusual for a woman of that era.

"When Harry met me, the first thing he said was, 'Let's go dance!' " Eve, whose college-age brother had taught her every conceivable dance step when she was only nine years old, eagerly consented. "So you see, that was a major attraction. Harry really loved to dance, and so did I."

Although the couple were as one on the dance floor, they were separated by a wide gulf of differences in educational and family background. Helmsley, son of a humble notions buyer, had not been able to go to college. He was reared in a Lutheran family that attended church only on occasional Sundays. Eve, by contrast, grew up as a fervent Quaker in a comfortable, highly educated family. Her father was a physician in general practice who returned to Columbia University in mid-career to study pharmacy. "He gave up his medical practice because his health was not good," Eve said, "and thought pharmacy would be physically less demanding. No calls in the middle of the night." She said her mother was also "brainy" and "wanted everything Columbia had to offer. Any time someone in the family got a degree she'd say, 'I want one too!' " It came as no surprise, then, when Eve's mother followed her husband's footprints to Columbia and became a pharmacist as well. Together, her parents opened a pharmacy in Brooklyn, and were easily able to send Eve through four years of Barnard College. After graduating with honors, she taught English briefly at Teachers College—Columbia University.

Among Eve's earliest words as a child were "meeting" (the Quaker term for church or church service) and "First Day" (Sunday). The Sherpick family belonged to the Twentieth Street Meeting House, an austere two-story Italianate building on Manhattan's Gramercy Square where Quakers had worshiped since 1859. In keeping with the Quaker emphasis on simplicity, its brownstone façade was devoid of ornament except for a beautifully proportioned triangular pediment. Inside, there was no altar or other visible focal point because Quaker worship is directed toward neither the actions nor the words of others. Instead, it is directed toward the shared prayer of the gathered group, who wait in silence for the "inner light"—the voice of God in the soul. Nor was there any liturgy, pulpit, sermon, choir, sacrament or priest to distract the Sherpicks or other members from "digging deep" inside themselves for divine guidance.

When she came back home as a widow, Eve resumed going to meeting each First Day at the Twentieth Street Meeting House and avoided immoderate materialism or vanity. On that first blind date, she must have seemed a rare individual indeed to a property-hungry real estate executive like Harry Helmsley.

"Harry Helmsley never knew there was such a thing as Quakers until he met me," Eve recalled. "He thought something must have been crazy about my whole family." Yet there was a chemistry. At the end of the date, Helmsley asked if he might take her out another evening. "But I told him, 'I can't come. I have to go to meeting.' "

"All right," the young squire replied, "I'll go with you. I've got to go and take a look at that."

Soon, Harry began accompanying Eve to the Twentieth Street Meeting House on a regular basis. "He was quite willing to do anything I did," she recalled. "I don't know if he was spiritual; I think it was a matter of stringing along with me to please me. He couldn't get over it at first—that there was such a thing as a Quaker meeting—with nobody kneeling or anything like that." After a succession of First Days together, Eve realized that beyond courtesy's sake, her tall suitor had a tolerable interest in this new-found Society of Friends. "He was very impressed by it and could understand a lot of it. But some of it, I could tell, just didn't go over."

Even if it wasn't exactly a case of spiritual rapture, Eve said Harry was intrigued by the Quakers' unconventional but highly practical "spin" on standard notions. "Quakers have interesting angles—turns of thought—and Harry would say, 'I never thought of that before.' He was quite amazed at that. He never knew that people did turn their minds."

Quaker writers, for instance, frequently cautioned members about the dangers of striving *too earnestly* for perfection in a human world. It's good enough just to live up to one's own "measure of light"—to the individual's particular talents or spiritual understanding. "If we are faithful to that, we shall be given more." In fact, to strive prematurely beyond one's personal reach might be tripping headlong into the vanity pit. "To go beyond our measure and imitate persons who have a greater measure than we have, is to be deceitful and to represent ourselves as something more than we are," wrote Howard H. Brinton.

In countless ways, Helmsley learned that Quaker nonconformity offered worldly as well as spiritual advantages. Its focus on simplicity in dress, architecture, furnishings and overall lifestyle meant that money that would otherwise be wasted on fripperies could be invested in more important things.

Simplicity also meant genuineness and sincerity. Quakers went to great extremes to tell *the exact truth*. Plain and spare language, a related Quaker characteristic, was a virtue Helmsley had already acquired beforehand. When practiced in the business world, such plain speaking was a great asset in winning the trust of others.

The Quaker doctrine of equality meant equal respect for everyone, regardless of racial or social distinctions. (Even before the Quakers became pacifists in 1661, they were dismissed from Oliver Cromwell's army for refusing to treat their officers as superiors.) Helmsley could extrapolate as well as anyone the doctrine's value in the real world. The lowliest employee, when afforded unexpected courtesy, was motivated to return the respect in the form of good work performance.

Eve Helmsley said that during her courtship it was apparent that Harry "got a lot out of going to Quaker meeting. He was with a different crowd all of a sudden; before, he was used to strictly business people. He found himself with a group of kind, loving people who weren't all out for a buck."

The 29-year-old Lutheran broker and the 33-year-old Quaker widow exchanged wedding rings in the presence of their immediate families on the evening of February 25, 1938 in the Lutheran Church of the Transfiguration in Manhattan. Walter Helmsley, 23, stood as best man for his older brother, but there were no bridal attendants at the simple ceremony. A short three-paragraph item in the *New York Times* noted that the newlyweds then boarded the ocean liner *Europa* and sailed for France, Austria, Italy and Switzerland.

On their return, the Helmsleys took an apartment at 31 Park Avenue, near Thirty-sixth Street, in the Murray Hill section of Manhattan. It was an upper-middle-class neighborhood with a sprinkling of baroque brownstone mansions amid tall new apartment buildings. Weather permitting, the Twentieth Street Meeting House was a reasonable twenty-minute walk away. By July 20, 1940, according to meeting records, Harry Helmsley had been "convinced" and officially joined the Quaker congregation.

For convenience's sake, the Helmsleys eventually moved to an apartment at 45 Gramercy Park North—literally a stone's throw from the Meeting House. The apartment was, moreover, only a short hike to Helmsley's corner office in the Flatiron Building, at Broadway and Twenty-third Street. Then, as now, the Gramercy Park district was a relatively secluded enclave of expensive brownstones and prim red-brick townhouses surrounding New York's only surviving privately owned park. The district's creator, Samuel B. Ruggles, wooed the rich by laying out the oblong two-block greensward in 1831 and restricting its use to neighborhood residents. The Helmsleys and their neighbors were issued keys to a handsome iron gate which allowed entry to the preserve of beautifully tended flower beds.

Harry Helmsley was too busy, however, to spend much time smelling the roses. His real estate career had blossomed perhaps beyond his own dreams during the hangdog years of the Great Depression. Already, in his early 30s, Helmsley had become a full partner in an ambitious real estate firm and was collecting rental income from his own office building. With Pearl Harbor and America's entrance into World War II in 1941, billions of dollars in defense spending jolted the economy out of its ashes. Helmsley, who was exempt from the draft because of his poor eyesight, had ideas aplenty of how he would spend the war years. The appraiser extraordinaire knew beyond a shadow of a doubt that New York's many half-vacant office buildings would soon welcome returning tenants as the economic pendulum swung back. When rent rolls inevitably shot up, the value—and therefore, the future cost—of commercial properties would increase commensurately. No leap in logic was required to understand the wisdom of buying quickly while the getting was still cheap. During the ensuing war years, Helmsley acquired fifteen modest properties from banks forced to sell by a state law forbidding them from holding foreclosed buildings more than ten years.

His early purchases were good investments because he controlled every aspect of the buildings down to the door squeak. To keep costs down and ensure efficiency, he personally hired the cleaning crews and the boiler repairmen and he dealt with the tenants directly. Keeping a tight lid on costs was already Helmsley's hallmark, even at a time when it cost only 60 cents a square foot to operate a building (compared to about $12 in 1988). In choosing his buildings, Helmsley adhered almost to formula. In appearance, they tended to be "plain Jane," with façades lacking the carved and sculpted grace notes of more expensive properties. Yet they tended to be superbly functional, with newsstands and good restaurants in the lobby. Many were located near train terminals and subway stations, which explains why Helmsley's company still owns or manages scores of buildings near Forty-second Street, Thirty-fourth Street and

Lexington Avenue.

But the most important ingredient in the early Helmsley formula was one he would eventually raise to an art—the ability to acquire property with little or none of his own cash. It generally took a 10 percent down payment to take title to a loft or office building. Helmsley, however, routinely was able to pay only 5 percent. Since he was usually the sales broker as well as the buyer his brokerage commission would serve as half the down payment. As time went on, he was often able to substitute his broker's fee as his *entire* cash "investment."

As the number of his investments grew during the war years, Helmsley occasionally found his name printed in brief news articles. In a January 25, 1942 item in the *New York Times*, he predicted an upswing in loft rentals due to the national defense program. Curiously, in a burst of wartime patriotism, Helmsley severely parted company from his pacifist Quaker brethren. He enthused that "New York, with its thousands of small manufacturers, will at last be given a chance to prove that it, too, can produce for the defense of the country and it will convert its machines to war production." The draft-exempt investor went on to tell the *Times*, "All this effort will require loft space which can be provided in New York at fair rentals."

Again, in a February 15, 1942 news brief in the *Times*, Helmsley placed patriotism—or perhaps economic motives— ahead of the predominant Quaker belief in pacifism. He argued that the military could obtain thousands of tons of scrap iron if New York would raze the then remaining section of the Second Avenue "El." "The eyesore, which long ago ceased to have an indispensable value, is going to be torn down eventually anyway," Helmsley added. (Real estate values skyrocketed, of course, once the elevated rails were scrapped, thereby restoring light and quiet to the avenue.)

Despite his periodic utterances in newsprint, Helmsley was a virtual unknown to the city's biggest real estate players. His acquisitions were unremarkable and in neighborhoods avoided by the city's most prestigious firms. Many of his tenants were small-time Jewish businessmen and manufacturers. In fact, Dwight, Voorhis & Helmsley, which became Dwight-Helmsley Inc. in 1946, was deemed a Jewish firm with Jewish brokers and a Gentile boss.

Until the war, big-time real estate in New York was controlled by old New York families. Perhaps the most illustrious stars were Frederick Brown, who built the Sherry Netherland Hotel at Grand Army Plaza, and the Rockefellers, who cleared six midtown blocks of crumbling townhouses and erected Rockefeller Center during the years 1931 to 1939.

However, Helmsley did have a certain style—a low-key presence and sincere manner—that gradually enabled him to stand out in a business notorious for its sharks and hustlers. "Harry Helmsley was always a straight shooter. His word was his bond," said Henry Baker, a pioneer broker of cooperative apartments. Baker said Helmsley "was the same all the way through. When he was starting out and when he finally got billions of dollars, he was always very conservative, very honest, and very plain and humble. I always respect a person that answers your calls. He was not the type that was ever too busy or too wealthy to talk to anybody."

Being a Quaker—with the reputation for bending over backward to tell *the exact truth*—no doubt boosted Helmsley's credibility yet another notch. Despite her husband's furious work pace, Eve Helmsley recalled that he made time to help her with Quaker charity projects.

Eve's favorite charity was a Harlem shelter for black homeless families—the New York Colored Mission. At least one day a week for fifteen years, she took a subway or taxi to the mission to donate her services. Most of the indigent residents, she recalled, "were Southern women making their way north and looking for jobs. They had just arrived from the South with their children and were pathetically poor. There were two wonderful black women who ran the place; they were so good it makes me want to weep. And we gave these homeless families a room until they could find themselves an apartment. I loved them all and they loved me and it never occurred to me that they were black people at all. But I got him interested and he was sympathetic to their cause." When the mission's pipes froze or its doors came unhinged, Helmsley would send his own commercial plumbers and carpenters to repair the damage. "Harry would just say, 'I'll take care of it, my dear.' Harry's a very generous, kind man. He enjoyed seeing these people get somewhere with their lives and loved to be helpful to them. He recognized that I was right wanting to give my time and money to these people."

Eve said the biggest proof of Harry's generosity came in 1944, when Eugene Sherpick died. "When my father died, Harry insisted my mother come live with us. He was devoted to her and so good to her." For eight years, until Eve's mother died in 1952, Eva Sauer Sherpick was a pampered member of the Helmsley household. "When Harry came home from work he'd say hello to me, and immediately run to my mother and give her a hug. On Sundays, if we were planning to go out for dinner, Harry would always tell my mother: 'I won't go unless you come along.' We loved her. We were crazy about her." If the Helmsleys' lifestyle was quiet before, it became even more subdued with the inclusion of the new household member. "Mother would read and then retire early." With no children to enliven their home, Harry typically would dive eagerly into his real estate documents for the rest of the evening while Eve gratified her love of reading philosophy and history.

"I never really wanted children," Helmsley said in a 1980 interview. "They appeal to me, but I think it's a woman's decision." Eve Helmsley, who was 33 when they married, said the death of her infant son from her first marriage was not a factor. "Harry and I had no conscious decision to have or not to have them. It was just as well that Harry had no children because he was the busiest person I have ever seen."

If indeed Harry ever felt true paternal longings, they were easily sublimated by his love of work. When a business partner once questioned Helmsley's insatiable appetite for new properties, he replied: "Don't spoil my fun. When I get into a deal and it's full of machinations and complications to work out, it's like having a grandchild."

After the death of Helmsley's own mother, Minnie, Harry's father often visited the Gramercy Park apartment and became fast friends with Eve's widowed mother. "We would all have luncheons together. Mother got along so well with Harry's father because he was a simple man with a nice sense of humor. He was down to earth—not the kind of guy who would want a million dollars. He'd have thought that was silly. He wouldn't want to be bothered by the complications of wealth." Henry Helmsley, tall and thin like his son, "just didn't want to be involved with frivolity on the edge of everything. He was just happy to work as a handyman for Harry. Harry used to say, 'Why don't you do this [chore], Dad?' and he'd answer very cheerfully, 'Anything you say, Harry.' "

Despite Harry's growing affluence, Quaker simplicity prevailed in the home. "We lived comfortably; we did some traveling. But it was all done in a very nice way. Nobody was boasting about anything." Eve realized, however, that her husband yearned "to make a lot of money" even though their lifestyle precluded heavy spending. "His family didn't have a lot and I think he made up his mind when he was a little boy, 'Well, believe me, I'm going to make a lot of money! I'll show 'em! I'm not going to be poor!' That's the way little boys are."

As with many little-boy dreams, Helmsley's was to come true when he crossed paths with another stargazer. The fateful match-up came in 1949, when the 40-year old broker was introduced to Lawrence A. Wien, a Columbia University–trained real estate attorney. The pair would become the "Rodgers and Hammerstein of New York real estate," with Helmsley finding and negotiating for properties and Wien supplying the cash.

Both men were hungry for giant real estate deals, but initially lacked sufficient capital to jump into big-league action. In the '40s, only financial institutions and very rich individuals had bank accounts big enough to acquire the best parcels. And banks and insurance companies weren't interested in making loans to small investors like Wien and Helmsley.

But Wien, after finding an obscure Ohio case, invented a formula for making untold riches in real estate. In essence, he refined the already existing concept of syndication—raising money from large numbers of investors—in such a way that investor earnings would not be subject to the stiff corporate income tax. With the formula in hand, Wien was then able to raise capital to his heart's content.

For any given property, Wien would convince numerous investors to contribute a set amount toward its purchase in return for a specified annual return—often 12 percent—on their investment, plus a share—usually 50 percent— of any additional profit. (If a $200,000 cash payment was needed to buy an office building, for instance, Wien could raise it by selling a $10,000 share to each of twenty investors.) At a time when interest rates were less than 4 percent, the 12 percent guaranteed annual return was an irresistible inducement to many investors.

Not surprisingly, the tax feature was an equally powerful lure. Annual profits would not be subject to corporate taxes. And the individual participants would also share in the deferral of taxation as a result of permissible deductions for depreciation or amortization of their cash investment and any mortgage on the property. The investors, after buying the property, would immediately lease it back to a separate operating group owned or controlled by Wien and Helmsley. The operating group, as the lessee, would run the property, collect the rents, and issue monthly checks to the investors. Because the investors were merely collecting rents and not "engaged in business" in the eyes of the IRS, they escaped paying the hated tax.

Wien and Helmsley were happiest of all because their operating leases benefited disproportionally from increased income due to improved operations and inflation, even after sharing that increased profit with the ownership syndicate.

Helmsley's role was to find Wien the best properties and negotiate the best purchase price. As his reward, Wien would allow him to buy a piece of the property's lucrative operating lease or sublease—usually no more than 25 percent—for little or no money. Helmsley, repeating a cash-saving technique from his earlier career, would simply forfeit his 5 percent broker's fee as a substitute for his required share of the purchase price of the lease. In addition to profits from the operating lease, Helmsley was almost always allowed to assign his real estate firm (and its later subsidiaries) profitable contracts to manage and maintain the properties. Thus, without spending a penny of his own money on a single transaction, Helmsley could expect to earn huge leasehold profits as well as eventual multimillion-dollar management fees.

For evaluating the proposed deals submitted by Helmsley, lining up the syndication investors, advancing contract deposits, and assuming the financial risk of general partner, Wien would control the operating leases and his law firm would be royally compensated with seven-figure legal retainers.

Besides office buildings, the pair also set their sights on hotel acquisitions. Rather than managing them, however, they would sell profitable long-term leases to experienced hotel owners.

In an interview a few months before Wien's death in December 1988, the 83-year-old financier vividly recalled his introduction to Helmsley four decades earlier. Despite advanced cancer, the silver-haired, blue-eyed patrician remained in full command of the memory which had helped him build a $350 million personal fortune.

"In June of 1949, I was buying a two-story building at 161 Columbus Avenue," Wien said. "And I went to the closing and was introduced to Harry Helmsley," who brokered the sale for an out-of-town owner. "Harry—a guy about six foot three—was the head of Dwight-Helmsley Inc. And with him was his brother, Walter Helmsley, who was six foot five. And the third man with them was a chap who took care of all their physical property— Jim Early—who was six foot six and he looked like a linesman for Notre Dame. I was overawed by this group of young giants."

Wien, standing five foot nine, said his life was forever changed when the ranking giant, Harry Helmsley, asked him the magical question: "Mr. Wien, are you interested in acquiring other properties?"

"Yes, I am," replied Wien in his perfect diction, adding that he had already acquired forty or fifty different parcels, mostly apartment houses. Wien explained that he really wanted to expand his sights to large commercial buildings; in fact, he had developed a special formula to finance their acquisition.

Luckily, the real estate market was still in a heavy slump in the wake of the Depression, despite the intervening economic boost of World War II. "At that time, the banks, insurance companies, investment houses wanted to have nothing to do with real estate. Most of the financial institutions had suffered very badly during the Depression," and were in no great hurry to re-enter the real estate game.

As a result, said Wien, "You didn't have the competition that you have today—when groups are angling for themselves and foreign clients for any major piece of property that makes sense." Virtually every building in Manhattan, in effect, was ripe for the plucking at bargain-basement prices. Using his formula, Wien could buy the best bargains as long as Helmsley could point them out and negotiate a good purchase price with their owners.

"In short order," Wien said, "Harry came up with the Brewster Building in Queens," where Brewster bodies were once built for Rolls Royces. Without catching his breath, Helmsley then went back to the streets "and worked very hard and very effectively" to bring Wien other investments. "In every case, Harry found the deal and I provided the money. One of the reasons Harry was so effective was because I told him to act as though he was investing his own money. He could tell building owners, 'I want to buy this. I want to buy that.' "

On April 1, 1950, Wien and Helmsley closed on their first major syndicated deal, a twenty-story building at 501 Seventh Avenue in the garment district. Only eight months later, on December 1, they picked up the Toy Building at 200 Fifth Avenue, a major property in whose showrooms more than 90 percent of all the nation's toy orders were placed each year.

Flushed with success on an unanticipated scale, Helmsley could feel justified in indulging a few personal curiosities. He had spent his entire life in the fast-paced city, and Eve Helmsley recalled that Harry "thought it would be fun living in the country. He wanted to try it on for size because he had been a city boy right from the beginning." So in the fall of 1950, the couple purchased a hilltop site at 61 Ridgecrest Road in the wealthy suburban Westchester County village of Briarcliff Manor. There, with a sweeping view of the Hudson River, they built a simple three-bedroom ranch-style house for themselves and Eve's elderly mother. A small swimming pool was dug in the back yard. Helmsley, always a careful scout, had selected the site not only for its front-porch river view but because of its convenient location just above the eighteenth tee of the Sleepy Hollow Country Club. "He had his golf on the weekends," Eve recalled. After a while, however, Helmsley realized he wasn't crazy about the game. "He thought it was basically a waste of time parading about the golf course."

Helmsley, like his neighbors, would leave his car at the Scarborough station every workday morning and take the train to Manhattan. Barely an hour—and several newspapers—later, he'd arrive at the Flatiron Building for another day's wheeling and dealing. He'd return by rail with his briefcase and settle in for a quiet evening with his wife and mother-in-law. For relaxation after dinner, Helmsley had little use for television or the stereo. Instead, there was no greater enjoyment than unsnapping his briefcase and diving headfirst into pending deals. "He brought home a sheaf of papers every night to go through," said Eve. "He would do what he had to do with them while I would read. If he had to make a choice between reading a novel and work, he would work. It was his livelihood and his fun."

After Eve's mother died in 1952, the Helmsleys spent more weekday evenings in Manhattan, dancing at the St. Regis Hotel or the Rainbow Room at Rockefeller Center. They also continued to worship at the Gramercy Park meeting house until it was closed in 1958 because of declining membership. The Helmsleys, like their displaced Friends, then became members of the nearby Fifteenth Street Meeting House on Stuyvesant Square. There Helmsley was named to the Trustees of the Murray Fund, a $200,000 Quaker foundation which earmarked its annual accrued interest for assistance to blacks, American Indians and the poor. The responsibility must have been easy work for a real estate wizard with a mushrooming stake in New

York City.

In the early 1950s, backed by Wien's money-raising formula, Helmsley burned up the town with a buying spree of major properties. Noble skyscrapers fell into his hands like so many shelftop souvenirs. In February 1953, he negotiated Wien's purchase of the thirty-two-story Shelton Hotel at Lexington Avenue and Forty-ninth Street; in July the well-known twenty-six-story Fisk Building at 250 West Fifty-seventh Street; in 1954, the fifty-three-story Lincoln Building at 60 East Forty-second Street; and in 1955, the twenty-seven-story Hotel Lexington at Lexington Avenue and Forty-eighth Street.

Henry J. Forster, a 98-year-old retired residential broker who once headed Brown, Harris, Stevens, recalled that it was a buying binge unlike any before or after. "Helmsley and Wien personally guaranteed a 10 percent or 12 percent annual return for two years *absolutely on their names*. And the public thought if these fellows are willing to guarantee with their personal signatures, it must be pretty safe. And that went over very big— and that was new. Nobody had ever done that before. And it took off, and they syndicated a hundred buildings.

"Things were going ahead so fast that they were making a million dollars a minute. And it was going ahead so fast, multiplying so fast, that you couldn't keep up with it."

Perhaps even more impressive than the number of acquisitions, Forster said, "was the amount of attention they were able to give to those hundred buildings. The problems! Every one of these buildings was a problem—by definition, every building is a problem. And there just aren't enough hours in the day to handle over one hundred buildings and get rid of all the problems that develop every day. It would drown most people. But they were able to stand up under it."

As Helmsley's portfolio of operating leases and management contracts mushroomed with each new deal, he realized he had to expand his firm to keep up the pace. Fifteen years earlier, in 1940, he had hired Alvin Schwartz, an extremely personable, high-spirited broker who was second to none in loft sales and leases. But Schwartz left Dwight-Helmsley in the late '40s to go to work for brokers Leon and Maurice Spear, brothers who owned Spear & Co. The job switch was understandable because Schwartz had recently married Maurice's daughter, Dorothy. Nonetheless, Helmsley never got over the loss of his star broker, and now he needed him more than ever.

To get him back, Helmsley bought out the smaller firm from

the Spear brothers in 1955 for $500,000 and merged it with his own company. The new entity, Helmsley-Spear Inc., immediately moved into larger quarters in the Lincoln Building, catercorner to Grand Central Terminal. Leon Spear remained on board as a broker, but neither he nor his brother retained any equity in the firm.

David Wilshin, a broker for Spear & Co. at the time of the 1955 merger (and future boss of a broker named Leona Roberts), recalled his "immense awe" at joining forces with Helmsley—whom he recognized at that early date as a legend well in the making. "Harry was already a superstar; from deals with Wien, he was personally making several million dollars a year by then." In addition to the Wien revenue stream, Helmsley was making a killing from his full-service brokerage company.

From the start, Wilshin added, "Harry had stature. He had a reputation of being a great negotiator and of being totally absorbed by his business. He left the office with a briefcase full of papers. I don't think he had any other interests." Wilshin speculated that because Helmsley had no children, "there was something missing, and he compensated with business. He had no sons and daughters, so he became a father figure to his employees." Wilshin said Helmsley's office was off to the southwest corner of the fifty-third floor, with the Empire State Building looming full-frame into his picture window.

The corner office was certainly more for the quiet and stunning view than for segregating himself from his brokers, Wilshin said. "Harry's door was usually closed, but he was available. He was always very personable and encouraged people to come talk to him if they had a deal."

Although personable, the master dealmaker seemed most comfortable totting up columns of financial data. "Harry always wore a tie. I'd say in those days, he was stiff. He used to love to dance with his secretary, Celia Fried, at the Christmas party. That was the only time you'd see him let his hair down all year." Wilshin noticed that Helmsley's wife, Eve, "rarely came to the office. I don't think she had much interest in his businesses." Wilshin also recalled that the boss could hold on to a dollar for dear life. "I don't think Harry was ever generous with employees," except for cutting brokers in on deals. "He was pretty frugal. He couldn't hire clerical staff for less than the prevailing wage, but he didn't overpay anybody." Nor did Helmsley seem to waste any money for his own comforts.

"When I worked for Harry in the mid-'50s," Wilshin said, "he was still driving an old '30s Buick. And you couldn't have called him a dapper dresser."

Wilshin recalled that Helmsley-Spear grew rapidly "once more management and leasing people came aboard. Helmsley and Wien continued to buy more buildings that had to be managed. And, of course, there was more space to rent out. The firm expanded in all facets," and was equally adept at buying, leasing and managing commercial properties. Growth was also fueled by energetic brokers who raced to bring potential new acquisitions to Helmsley's attention. As their reward for finding the deals, the boss frequently gave his top brokers partnership positions in the purchases—an incentive policy that made many employees happy millionaires. Leading the pack were Schwartz and another hotshot broker, Irving Schneider: they both would quietly become Helmsley's full partners at Helmsley-Spear and among the wealthiest real estate men in America.

With a bigger management company of his own and Wien's bottomless financial backing, Helmsley went into a full-tilt buying fever. "We were doing as many as ten or fifteen deals a year," Wien recalled. "We were creating investments not to sell, but to keep for future income. Harry became part of the operating lease group and developed positions which have become of tremendous value because these leases have prospered. He was a great negotiator, a brilliant man and a great analyst. He could evaluate property and its potential. He knew more about operating costs than anybody else that I ever met."

In December 1957, a Wien-Helmsley syndicate bought the Taft Hotel, a 1,400-room behemoth that occupied the entire block front on the west side of Seventh Avenue between Fiftieth and Fifty-first streets. In a January 1958 syndicated deal brokered by Helmsley, Wien agreed to pay $16.5 million in cash for forty parcels between Thirteenth and Fifteenth streets and Union Square and Sixth Avenue. The area was irresistible to Helmsley because of its rich network of subway stations and bus stops. Where transportation lines crossed, Helmsley knew, convenience-conscious tenants tended to seek out commercial space. Indeed, the Transit Authority had reported collections of 63 million bus and subway fares in the vicinity during the preceding year.

Early in 1958, Wien investors paid developer William Zeckendorf Sr. an estimated $4 million for his sublease to operate the Graybar Building, a 400-foot-tall linchpin of the

Grand Central business district. The Wien syndicate then leased the monolith — known for its façade of sculpted rats, grasshoppers, albatrosses and fifteen-foot Assyrian figures representing Transportation and Electricity—back to Zeckendorf's firm. A few years later, in yet another financial flipflop, Helmsley paid a scant $1 million for the Zeckendorf operating lease, which gave him the opportunity to run the building and make a profit on it. Alone, the 1958 syndication agreement would funnel tens of millions of dollars in profits to Helmsley's coffers over subsequent decades.

The same busy year, a syndicate headed by Wien bought the Equitable Building at 120 Broadway, the thirty-eight-story former headquarters of the Equitable Life Assurance Society of the United States.

A particularly elegant coup came in November 1958, when Wien heeded Helmsley's advice and bought the city's "wondrous" hotel, the Plaza, from the Hotel Corporation of America. The price tag on the Renaissance-style landmark overlooking Central Park was $21 million, the highest ever recorded for a single hotel.

As he scanned the skyline in search of more acquisitions for Wien, deals galore continued to sprout from Helmsley's fingertips. It was clear to all observers—including the emerging tycoon himself—that Helmsley was addicted to dealmaking. "If I were a girl," he once told an interviewer, "I'd be pregnant all the time. When someone comes in with a good deal, I can't say no."

It was an enchanted investment era, recalled Alvin S. Lane, Wien's former law partner in the firm of Wien, Lane, Klein and Purcell. "You could buy very reasonably because nobody else was buying real estate. You couldn't make such returns on investments today unless you bought Impressionist art."

Timing was crucial, but so were brains and expertise, and Helmsley had both ingredients in spades. "He was a man," Lane said, "who came into a meeting with a lot of bright people and just shined. He had total recall. You could ask him what happened to a little space on the sixteenth floor of a building, and he didn't have to turn to an aide. He could tell you who the tenant was and if there were negotiations going on for the lease. There was little you could ask him about in real estate that he didn't know. He's the brightest in the world in his field."

Wien was also equipped with an awesome memory, and shared Helmsley's renowned affinity for mathematics. "They spoke a language of numbers without a calculator or a pad," Lane recalled. "If you were in a room with them, you wouldn't know what the hell they were talking about. It was sort of a volleyball game of numbers. Not many people can do that. Perhaps it is one of the aptitudes of real estate people."

Rexford Tompkins, who was to work for Helmsley years later as head of Brown, Harris, Stevens, recalled that "Harry was an incredible figure man. He had a capacity for detail. Because he knew the ratios, he could analyze a building's operating statement and know immediately if it was well run. He knew right off the bat whether your heating bills were out of line, or whether the taxes were unduly high or low. Part of his genius was his ability and willingness to pore over building statements. He must have done it by the hour to pick up those details. He'd send notes in his personal writing asking you to investigate a departure—for instance, whether too much was being spent on miscellaneous supplies. He wouldn't look at just the bottom line; he'd check to see if the bottom line was valid. You couldn't fool Harry Helmsley!"

Stephen W. Brener, a broker who started at Dwight-Helmsley in 1952, said Helmsley's numerical skills enabled him to look at an undervalued piece of property and instantly "project what its long-term value could be." Knowing management inside out, he could quickly calculate how much a property's bottom line would improve if elevator service were automated and five new tenants could be found. "What few others have the ability to put even on paper, he could describe on the spur of the moment."

Because Helmsley's mental cogwheels were geared toward minimizing future costs, Brener said, he became a pioneer tax strategist. "People talk about the great tax deals of the 1980s, but Helmsley was thinking tax deals in the '50s and '60s. He thought that it was not how much you made, *but how much you can keep*. He read and studied tax bulletins all the time. He came up with suggestions, and attorneys would have to do the research. But Harry would lead them on. He would say, 'This is what should be done,' and most of the time he was right. Harry knew if he could shelter $100,000 in income, he could spend it on more real estate. If Harry has done anything to impress me, it was to take tax law as written and create the greatest 'cash-keep' flow he could."

Helmsley was also a master at the fine art of keeping valued employees. "Motivation was a secret of his," said Brener. "Everybody worked harder in that office because of him than they would have in any other office." Helmsley-Spear was run like a mom-and-pop store, with virtually no hint of bureaucracy. Employees reported directly to the top—Helmsley—or to his two executive vice presidents: Schwartz and Schneider. "Our table of organization," Brener recalled, "was like taking a pail of ball bearings and shaking it up. It wasn't a pyramid. There weren't a lot of chains of command. Harry was in the middle and everything worked around him. It didn't matter who you were; you came into Harry's office. He had pads and a letterbox for each person. He knew what he was doing for you and what you were doing for him, and he gave you instructions. It wasn't like today, where five guys sit around a table, who then talk to five other people, who get nothing accomplished. With Harry, it was one-to-one and you got fast results. You gave extra effort."

To Roderick T. MacDonald, a former property manager at Brown, Harris, Stevens, humility was Helmsley's memorable trademark. "He always made it his business if he recognized an old acquaintance to go over and shake their hand, rather than have them come to him and pay court. And at office parties, he would walk up if he didn't know you and say, 'Hello, I'm Harry Helmsley.' It's like Ronald Reagan walking up to a guy on the street and saying, 'Hi, I'm Reagan.' "

Nor could Helmsley's instinctive skills as a demographer be overlooked. With great accuracy, Brener said, Helmsley predicted the shifts in population that would trail World War II. "From the '30s until the war, real estate had taken a bath. Many buildings were foreclosed or dispossessed. But Harry always had faith in the cities. Servicemen returned. Families grew. Housing became an important item. All this led in Harry's mind to a true increase in value. He knew a mobile population would spur a true growth in lifestyle in all urban areas, and that the central cities would bounce back."

Not surprisingly, therefore, Helmsley and Wien did not confine their forays to New York. In 1959, they scooped up the Desert Inn in Las Vegas for $10 million. Alone, or with Wien and other partners, Helmsley eventually amassed such other out-of-town properties as One LaSalle Street, the Stone Container Building and the Insurance Exchange Building in Chicago; the Russell Industrial Center in Detroit; the Wilshire Comstock East and Wilshire Comstock West, luxury apartments in Los Angeles; the Three Fountains apartment complex in Houston; the Palm Beach Towers hotel; the 3,493-unit Parkmerced apartment complex in San Francisco; and the Meadowbrook apartment complex in Indianapolis.

The deal, however, that put the names of Harry B. Helmsley and Lawrence A. Wien in lights was quintessential New York. On December 27, 1961, Wien paid $83 million for the Empire State Building—the world's tallest and most famous skyscraper.

It was by far Wien's most complicated sale-and-lease-back deal, and one that would never have become reality without the keen brokerage and negotiating skills of Helmsley. It was also the pair's most spectacular example of using other people's money to swing a deal and then taking the greatest profit for themselves.

In the largest syndication ever recorded, Wien raised $33 million from approximately 3,300 investors by offering a then sizable 9 percent annual return. Helmsley and Wein were required to risk only $1,500,000 each of the deposit, but were refunded their down payments the moment the deal was consummated. To swing the deal, Wien also secured a $6 million leasehold mortgage from Colonel Henry R. Crown, the previous owner. He also obtained $29 million from the Prudential Life Insurance Company, which already owned the land under the building, by agreeing to give the company title to the skyscraper as soon as the syndicate acquired it from Crown. In return, Prudential agreed to grant the Wien syndicate a lucrative 114-year lease on the skyscraper. This financial arrangement with Prudential was basically equivalent to a mortgage, but left Wien's syndicate with the fully depreciable lease and building.

In order to exempt its profits from the onerous corporate income tax, the syndicate immediately subleased the building to the Empire State Building Company, an operating company owned by Wien and Helmsley.

On closing, Helmsley got $500,000 as his broker's fee and a $90,000 annual management contract for Helmsley-Spear. Wien's law firm raked in $1.1 million in legal and underwriting fees, plus a retainer of $190,000 a year to represent both the investors and his own operating company.

Far more significant, however, would be their income as owners of the operating lease. For their operating services—as partners in the Empire State Building Company—Wien and Helmsley were to receive the first $1,000,000 and half of any additional profits that remained after paying the investors a 9 percent annual return. This magical contract provision ensured that these two men would ultimately earn almost as much as the combined annual profits of the 3,300 syndicate investors. In 1987, for instance, the operating company made a profit of $31.3 million, of which only $17.6 million was paid to syndicate participants. Separately, Helmsley-Spear collected $2.4 million in management fees and $827,000 for insurance services; and a Helmsley subsidiary, Owners Maintenance Corporation, got $4.75 million in cleaning fees before expenses. Wien raked in $1 million in legal fees.

For simplicity's sake, most newspaper accounts of the 1961 purchase cited Wien as the skyscraper's new owner and mastermind of the $83 million deal—the highest price ever paid for a single building. By comparison, Helmsley's name—as the broker—received little if any news play. Despite his unequal share of limelight, Helmsley no doubt looked upon the Wien syndication as a deal made in heaven. At absolutely no personal expense—except his own considerable sweat in convincing Colonel Crown to sell—Helmsley had latched hold of an unimaginable future income stream.

Alvin Lane says only a fellow of Wien's financial legerdemain could have pulled together so many different layers of ownership. "The Empire State Building was a classic example of the 'Hawaiian bundle of sticks,' " Wien's former law partner recalled. "The safest investor was Prudential," which kept the land it had already owned underneath Colonel Crown's skyscraper. "The next safest thing was the building itself," which Prudential bought from the Wien syndicate as soon as the syndicate took title from Crown. "The next safest thing was the long-term lease," which Prudential sold to the syndicate; "and the least safe [but most profitable] was the operating sublease," obtained from the syndicate by Wien and Helmsley. The conceptualization and number-crunching would have reduced lesser dealmakers to bleeding ulcers. But, as always with Wien and Helmsley, numerical gymnastics was one of the most exhilarating components of any deal.

The syndication was so complex that dozens of lawyers were called to witness the transfer of title at Prudential's office in Newark, New Jersey, on December 27. "They had the biggest conference table that I have ever seen," Wien recalled. "There were probably fifty seats, and another fifty or a hundred people were standing around." Adding to the confusion, he said, were "all the television people, because it was the biggest transaction of its kind in history."

Few reporters had any notion of Helmsley's crucial role in bringing the deal to fruition. In fact, Wien said he had given up hope of buying the skyscraper after four years of unsuccessful negotiations with Colonel Crown. Then, in early 1961, "Harry began negotiating with Crown's lawyer, who didn't want Crown to sell it. And this lawyer tried to put in every obstacle that he could think of." In frustration, Wien said he urged Helmsley to stop wasting his time negotiating. "I told Harry, 'You can't do it. These people are impossible. Look, there is no sense killing yourself. Let's forget it. That's all.'

"And Harry said no, he wouldn't forget it. He would continue. And he did. He was a very good salesman and he demonstrated to them why it was desirable from their standpoint to sell. Harry negotiated and negotiated and I thought the deal was off five times."

Helmsley, decades later, explained his determination. "Number one, it's a challenge. There it stands and every morning you would look out the window and the building is staring you in the face. So, you'd say, 'Well, I gotta buy it.' "

Finally, under the weight of Helmsley's persistent appeals, Colonel Crown agreed to terms.

More than a showpiece, the building became a phenomenal cash cow for Helmsley. After taking over management, he cut costs in half by such methods as slashing the bookkeeping staff from twenty-eight to six. And thanks to inflation, rent receipts eventually dwarfed the fixed mortgage obligations.

Over the years, moreover, Helmsley acquired larger and larger slices of the skyscraper's profitable operating lease. Originally, shipping magnate Daniel K. Ludwig was to own 50 percent; Helmsley and Wien were to own 25 percent. Later, when Ludwig was forced to walk away before the closing because of unforeseen legal complications, Wien and Helmsley each emerged with 43.75 percent and a new investor, Martin Weiner, bought the remaining 12.5 percent. Eventually, Helmsley took an even larger slice after Wien agreed in 1969 to donate $1.25 million toward construction of the city's new Lincoln Center for the Performing Arts. To raise that money as well as funds for other charities, Wien said he sold Helmsley 20 percent of the Empire State Building operating lease—almost half Wien's interest—for a mere $3.5 million. "It was definitely a bargain," which today entitles Helmsley to 63.75 percent of profits from the operating lease. In the year 1987 alone, the 20 percent share bought from Wien gave Helmsley almost $3 million in operating profits.

No doubt, Wien and Helmsley realized they had bagged one for the history books when they closed title to the city's ultimate skyscraper. But, like Rodgers and Hammerstein, the energetic pair was constitutionally unable to rest on its laurels. Deals aplenty would continue. Indeed, the very day of their Empire State Building acquisition, Wien took title and Helmsley acquired the lease to one of the city's most beautiful hotels: the St. Moritz on Central Park South at Sixth Avenue. Over the years, the thirty-one-story hotel had been headquarters to such notables as Charles Laughton, Errol Flynn, James Stewart and Bing Crosby.

With deals cooking so fast in Manhattan, Helmsley decided to set aside the St. Moritz penthouse as a city *pied-à-terre* for himself and Eve. At first blush, the Quaker couple's change in lifestyle might have seemed surprisingly extravagant. In fact, however, the Helmsleys continued to use their Briarcliff Manor ranch house as their primary residence, and occupied the penthouse merely on a part-time basis. Many summers they stayed away for months at a time so the hotel could use the penthouse for paying guests.

During his nights in the Big Apple, Helmsley usually worked the hours away rather than hitting the sights. "Harry wasn't too keen on the opera or the ballet," Eve Helmsley recalled, "because he hadn't been brought up on it. He didn't know enough about it to be keen on it. Harry had many friends, but not as many as some people," she added, "because he spent a lot of time at his work. Work was more important because it was the stage where he was building his great career. He was consumed with ambition. He wanted to become a great success not only to test his financial ability but because he enjoyed it all. He liked buildings and wanted to own a lot of them. He would bring his papers home and I wouldn't interfere." But for a little spice, Eve recalled that occasionally "we would go dancing or to the theater" with Lawrence Wien and his wife, Mae. "We would go as foursomes. At the time, Mr. Wien was possibly Harry's closest friend."

Wien also had fond recollections of the outings, but noted that pumpkin hour for the Helmsleys was considerably earlier than 12:00 midnight. "Eve was a very quiet person and tended to get tired early when they went out." By contrast, Wien noted, "Harry had a *lot* of energy."

Social outings, however, were the exception to the rule. "Harry used to expend his energy on *work*," Wien said, "and would go home with two briefcases every evening and work all night."

Eve Helmsley said she knew by the early 1960s that Harry was becoming quite wealthy, but she never inquired *how rich* they were. "Harry was just a simple man; I never felt he was a big somebody. I felt he was doing very nicely and I was pleased that he had some money. But I never asked him for diamonds."

As properties continued to multiply, she said, "I thought it was comical. I don't think in terms of cash, so I never thought of it as an empire. I didn't realize that buildings cost that much. I didn't give a damn about it as long as I had enough to eat and to wear, and we could take occasional trips to Europe." Although Helmsley was making millions of dollars a year, Eve said it was hardly noticeable to her because of their simple lifestyle.

"Harry never thought clothing was the most interesting or marvelous thing. He just didn't care about a lot of flaunting of things. And it never occurred to me that Harry wanted to be a billionaire. I would have thought that was crazy. I can't count up that many zeroes! He may have been thinking about it, but he never let me know because I would have said, 'You're nuts!' "

"Harry was a simple man with a great mind for mathematics and making money," one close friend recalled. "He was not the man in custom suits and Rolex watches. He bought cheap suits in the basement." Nor was he one to lavish money on fine cuisine. "Many times we'd go out," the friend added, "and Harry would have two soups and a baked potato. And that was it."

With a few exceptions—such as the future Park Lane Hotel and the Empire State Building coup—Eve said she had little enthusiasm for her husband's beloved sport. "Real estate is real estate. It became a bore. What are you going to do about it? What are you going to say about it? It's just bricks and mortar, with a little money thrown in. I'm not money mad. I'm not interested in amassing cash; I'm more interested in giving it to some poor soul who needs a meal."

The Helmsleys occasionally would entertain in their suburban Westchester County home. One former neighbor, Edwin Walton, recalled they had "one or two parties every spring or summer, overlooking the Hudson River." They were neither grand nor extremely exciting affairs, he added, "nice intimate parties with six or seven people sitting around having finger sandwiches and a couple of drinks."

As always, business was Helmsley's favorite topic of conversation. At one party, Walton recalled, Helmsley told him: "I just figured out a way to make ten million dollars." Then, just a year later, Helmsley revealed: "Ed, now I'm going for a hundred million!"

Walton, then a director of the Bank of Commerce, said the social cradle of the neighborhood was the home of Mrs. Frank A. Vanderlip, widow of a former head of First National City Bank. For at least fifteen winters—"every other Saturday night"—the wealthy widow would convert her formal library into a ballroom and invite twenty-five area couples to dance. "I provided the stereo and the records," Walton said, and the Helmsleys usually attended. "They were wonderful parties, a group of neighbors thoroughly enjoying themselves." For refreshments after the music stopped, he said Mrs. Vanderlip would serve coffee "and a big flat cake. The wives took turns bringing the cake. It was a real community tradition that went on year after year." It was also perfect entertainment for a homespun couple like Harry and Eve Helmsley.

Red Barber, former announcer for the Brooklyn Dodgers, lived directly opposite the Helmsley home on Ridgecrest Road. Barber, who has since moved to Florida, remembered the Helmsleys as a nice, unpretentious, and definitely lackluster couple who rarely visited his home. Asked to describe Eve Helmsley, Barber fumbled for several seconds before replying, "She was a rather—I hate to use the term—*plain* person. She was just sort of a pleasant person who you saw once in a while at a cocktail party. She was not flashy at all. She didn't wear flashy clothes. She didn't make any splash or any noise."

A former business associate who often visited the Helmsleys' one-story home described it as "a simple house with very plain furniture—no antiques, nothing French or Early American. Furniture you'd get in the store, without character. But it had a nice living room with a big stone fireplace, a long porch and a little swimming pool out back." The visitor said the Helmsleys' biggest pride was a huge retractable picture window in the living room. "It faced a downsloping lawn and the Sleepy Hollow golf course. Harry would press a button and the window would go down into the basement," exposing the lifelong city native to the pure country air. "Harry loved to go into the living room

108

and turn to the window. He would lay out his briefcases on a table, and each folder was a multimillion-dollar deal. The window gave both of them such joy."

Yet, as Helmsley openly confessed, no personal pleasure—either natural or man-made—could compete with the thrill of dealmaking. Despite his wife's growing inability to share that enthusiasm, and bolstered by Wien's financing, Helmsley forged happily ahead with new acquisitions.

A significant change in their longtime partnership came in 1963, however, when Wien announced he would no longer form public real estate syndicates. Because of the increasing competition and higher prices for buildings, he could no longer guarantee investors the high annual returns which for fourteen years had been the magnet of his pioneering financing vehicle. Thereafter, Wien would finance new deals either with his own growing cash flow or in combination with Helmsley and groups of fewer than fifteen private investors. Although Helmsley would continue to find properties and Wien would continue to raise the cash for years to come, the new financing scheme ultimately would encourage the men to pursue independent investment paths.

Still very much a team, however, in May 1963 they and three other general partners paid $22.5 million for Bush Terminal, said to be the world's largest multi-tenant industrial facility. The huge complex on the Brooklyn waterfront boasts 6.5 million square feet of space in eighteen commercial buildings.

Hungry as ever, Wien and Helmsley contracted in March 1964 to buy the deluxe Carlton House from the Astor family. The sixteen-story residential hotel, on Madison Avenue between Sixty-first and Sixty-second streets, had been erected in 1951 as the successor to the famous Ritz-Carlton Hotel. The *New York Times* noted that Helmsley and Wien were "purchasing the property as a personal investment," not as a public syndicate.

Only two months later, in one of the largest downtown deals in years, Wien and American Realty Trust of Washington, D.C., paid the Clarson Company for ground leaseholds on three office buildings in the insurance district. Helmsley, who brokered the sale, participated with Wien in a long-term lease from the buyers.

As he and Wien invested for the future in more property, Helmsley's everyday income mushroomed thanks to fees brought home by his energetic brokers and property managers at Helmsley-Spear. Yet, to capture even more fees, in October 1964 he paid approximately $1 million for the Charles F. Noyes Company, a prestigious real estate brokerage firm specializing in lower Manhattan office buildings. "I needed more action downtown in the financial district," Helmsley explained. Just seven months later, for more than $1 million, he bought Brown, Harris, Stevens, Inc., the venerable brokerage and management firm which specialized in the new arena of cooperative apartment houses.

And as always, Helmsley-Spear was a conduit for more acquisitions as managers and brokers brought word of investment opportunities.

Although both men remained fairly obscure to the public, their acquisitions brought them increasingly more ink in newspapers and national magazines. No longer was Helmsley, the broker, mentioned at the tail end of news articles about Lawrence Wien, the prominent financier. As a tycoon in his own right, Helmsley received equal billing. A three-page feature in the August 21, 1965 issue of *Business Week* described the realty partners as a profitable "mutual admiration society." Thereafter, Wien devoted himself increasingly to philanthropy, as a trustee and the largest benefactor of Lincoln Center, Columbia and Brandeis Universities, and Channel 13, among many others.

With increased wealth from the appreciation of his properties and income from syndication deals, however, Helmsley became confident enough to test his independent skills as a developer. Five years earlier, without Wien's participation, he had organized a group that assembled a site on East Forty-second Street to build the Pfizer world headquarters building.

Knowing no bounds after that success, he obtained an option in 1965 to demolish his former place of worship—the Twentieth Street Meeting House on Gramercy Park—in order to build a thirty-story apartment building. The elegant brownstone, with its tall arched windows, had fallen into disrepair since 1958, when the Quaker congregation transferred most of its activities to the Fifteenth Street Meeting House on Stuyvesant Square. According to a former business leader of the Gramercy Park meeting, the congregation agreed to sacrifice the 106-year-old meeting house to Helmsley's wrecking ball "because the building was falling apart and we didn't have the money to keep it going."

Financial realities aside, wealthy neighborhood residents hit the roof when word leaked out that an unnamed "developer" planned to raze the architectural jewel. In an effort to protect it, the building was quickly designated as one of New York's first official landmarks. The anonymous developer— Helmsley—abandoned his plan when a group of residents led by retired publicist Ben Sonnenberg paid $400,000 for the building. (In 1975, it was purchased and restored by another displaced congregation—former members of the Brotherhood Synagogue on West Thirteenth Street.)

Brendan Gill, a writer for *The New Yorker* and one of the city's most stalwart preservationists, recalled that Helmsley had "no sentimental feelings whatsoever" for his old meeting house. "It is one of the remarkable buildings of New York state and he was determined to knock it down and build a high-rise apartment house overlooking Gramercy Park. The Quaker meeting house remains standing only because of Benjamin Sonnenberg and other good public-spirited citizens."

Helmsley's indifference to the historic Quaker site was perhaps indicative of his true feelings for the Society of Friends itself. Indeed, to some former members of the Gramercy Park meeting, Helmsley's attendance seemed more a matter of pleasing his wife than abiding personal interest. "He married a Friend, and joined the Friends. But he didn't take an active part in meeting; I never heard him speak," recalled "Eileen," who traced her own Quaker roots to seventeenth-century England. "I don't think there was too much there. Maybe to him, being known as a Quaker was a stepping stone. Maybe it gave him a little standing, a little background" in the business community. "But he never seemed like a Quaker in background or principles." Rather, "there always seemed to be a climbing and making of money," out of keeping with the Quaker emphasis on moderation. "You don't find many Quakers who would say the whole game is to make as much money as you can. Harry certainly wasn't a devout Quaker wearing a dark suit."

Although Helmsley attended meeting and helped administer several small Quaker charitable funds, Eileen recalled that the tall, poker-faced broker was somewhat aloof from other members. "He and Eve would come back from trips and would show slides. That didn't tell much about him." Yet Eileen recalled that Helmsley was capable of mustering enthusiasm for occasional Quaker social affairs. "He would collect eighty-five cents with great glee for our dinners."

Although thwarted at Gramercy Park, Helmsley accomplished even bigger plans in 1967 with the completion of a sleek fifty-two-story black tower at 140 Broadway. Helmsley had commissioned architects to build the million-square-foot building on a block bounded by Broadway, Liberty, Nassau and Cedar streets. Its distinctiveness was assured by a plaza formed from 60 percent of the site, which opened the canyons of the financial district to light and air. Elegantly marking the spot is Isamu Noguchi's 1968 "Red Cube," a 24-foot-high steel sculpture balanced on point.

Alvin Lane, one of Helmsley's investors in the project, recalled that it was an astonishingly ambitious venture for someone with so little prior development experience. "Harry was amazing. He didn't start out by building ranch houses. His first projects were skyscrapers." Although the rental market was in the doldrums at the time, Helmsley-Spear filled the new building with such prestigious tenants as Marine Midland Bank (for which the tower was named) and the investment firm of Morgan, Stanley & Co. "One-forty Broadway was an ideal investment," Lane said. "I got my money back immediately."

Helmsley demonstrated his credibility with the financial community in 1968 by forming his own real estate investment trust. With Irving Schneider, one of his two trusted lieutenants at Helmsley-Spear, Helmsley borrowed $78 million from Chase Manhattan Bank to buy the Furman-Wolfson Trust, a collection of thirty-three properties in seven states valued at $165 million. Keeping some buildings for themselves and putting in others of their own, the two men then sold the rescrambled twenty properties (renamed Investment Properties Associates) to the public in participation units of $1,000 each. With the proceeds, they were able to repay the initial loan. In addition to clearing their Chase debt, the newly established trust ensured the partners substantial continuing fees for its operation.

Returning to his new love—development—Helmsley erected two more buildings in the Wall Street area: 22 Cortlandt Street, with 600,000 square feet of space; and 10 Hanover Square, with 465,000 square feet. In 1972, he earned his credentials as a mega-developer by completing One Penn Plaza—a fifty-seven-story behemoth with 2.4 million square feet of office space adjacent to Pennsylvania Station. Lawrence Wien, as Helmsley's partner in the deal, lined up $90 million in construction loans from three commercial lenders and each put up one-half of the equity/risk investment.

By then in his early 60's, Helmsley was cutting deals and mastering new specialties at a pace that would have physically and mentally drained far younger men. With equal enthusiasm, Helmsley simultaneously cast his acquisitive gaze on the housing market. Hoping to convert his purchases to cooperative apartments, Helmsley scooped up rent-controlled apartment buildings by the hundreds.

In September 1968, a syndicate headed by Helmsley agreed to pay $90 million for Parkchester in the Bronx, the nation's largest apartment complex. In addition to its 12,271 apartments in 171 buildings, the complex included a shopping center with one hundred stores, a two-thousand-seat theater, banks, a library and a post office.

"There is a certain glamour to buying a city within a city," Helmsley, the proud new owner, told the *New York Times*. According to a later article in the *Daily News*, the Helmsley group actually laid out only $9 million for the sprawling mini-city. In keeping with Helmsley's credo of always using other people's money, the remaining $81 million or so "came from a mortgage generously provided by Met Life, which was anxious to quit the landlord business."

After the ink dried on the deed of sale, Helmsley made thousands of enemies by socking tenants with a 14 percent "hardship" rent hike (allowed under rent control laws only for extraordinary landlord expenses) and revoking Met Life's previous practice of paying interest on security deposits. He also announced plans to convert the 3,985-unit "north quadrant" of the complex to condominums, whereby each individual apartment would be separately purchased, owned, taxed and mortgaged. By *Daily News* calculations, the Helmsley group stood to earn a cool $28 million net profit on the resale of just those apartments as condominiums. By also eventually converting the majority of the remaining 8,286 units, the paper added, "the syndicate stands to make an obvious killing." Helmsley severely underestimated, however, the firestorm of tenant opposition that would greet his condo plans. In late 1972, John Dearie, head of the Parkchester Tenants Association, predicted that fewer than 2 percent of the tenants would opt to purchase their apartments. "It's not economically feasible and the place is too old," he complained.

Despite tenant resistance, Helmsley remained overcome with apartment fever. In June 1970 he formed a new syndicate which bought another "city within a city." For $36 million (only a fraction in cash), the group bought Tudor City, a quiet Manhattan community of 2,800 apartments on a dramatic five-acre bluff overlooking the United Nations. Its eleven Tudor-style red brick buildings, some as high as thirty-two stories, covered parts of four blocks west of First Avenue between Fortieth and Forty-fourth streets. In 1929, a year after the enclave was built, *The New Yorker* cited its community gardens—where "children could play … out in the open air"—as among its greatest amenities.

The peaceful setting meant little, however, to Helmsley. Almost immediately after taking title, he shocked tenants and city alike by vowing to close Tudor City's two private parks and build two skyscrapers, one twenty-eight stories and one thirty-two stories, on the beloved carpets of green. Although the park controversy would rage unabated for another decade and severely tarnish his public image, Helmsley ignored the din of condemnatory headlines and editorials.

Alvin Lane said it was typical of Helmsley's nonchalance in the line of fire. "He never gave a damn what people thought! If he felt he wasn't doing anything illegally, he didn't care if tenants screamed. It didn't affect him. If a newsperson wrote about tenants angry about him taking their park away, he could care less!" Instead, "Harry would look strictly at the monetary figures and say, 'It's *my* park and I'm entitled to it!' Likewise, he went to Parkchester knowing he was going to get criticism. That takes a tough man."

Still expanding, Helmsley paid the New York Life Insurance Company $65 million in 1972 for its 140-building Fresh Meadows community in Queens. The same year, he also bought Park West Village—a middle-income community of 2,700 apartments extending from Central Park West to Amsterdam Avenue between Ninety-seventh and One hundredth streets—from the Aluminum Company of America.

"Just who is this Harry Helmsley?" became a question increasingly asked by journalists as the enormity of his dealmaking hit home. No longer was he playing property scout for Lawrence Wien and settling for a lucrative share of property leases. Now able to raise tens of millions of dollars on his own signature, Helmsley was the primary partner—the general partner—in many of the country's biggest transactions.

"The least-kept secret in town is that Harry Helmsley is buying New York," wrote Owen Moritz in a September 1972 profile in the *Daily News*. "Helmsley has always been the Bobby Fischer of the Monopoly board, the real estate grand master who calculates his every move.…What's news is that Harry

Brakmann Helmsley, all $3 billion worth of him, is on a new building collection spree, and this one just might change the map of New York." In contrast to the image of flamboyant entrepreneurs, Moritz added, Helmsley was "quite low-key and plainspoken" and "studiously avoids newspapermen."

According to the *New York Times*, estimates of Helmsley's personal income in the early 1970s ranged "from $6 million a year (possibly tax-free because of depreciation rules) to $1 million a month. He says, 'Only the I.R.S. knows for sure.'

"The only way to keep score in business," Helmsley instructed the paper, "is to add up how much money you make. If you're a good player, you get rich."

By 1970, according to *New York* magazine, "Helmsley-Spear had become the largest real estate management company in the country. And Helmsley had become the thirteenth largest landowner in New York City, ranking just below the Prudential Life Insurance Company and just above Rockefeller Center."

As important as he was, the average New Yorker wouldn't have known the publicity-shy tycoon from Adam. Only especially alert citizenry could pick him out of a crowd.

In the late 1960s, one such cognoscente—a long-haired, college-age kid named Donald Trump—recognized the tall, lean figure walking along a city sidewalk.

"I was 20 and had my own car," Trump recalled, "and for some reason I saw Harry Helmsley and had the nerve to offer him a ride." Trump said he was surprised when Helmsley accepted the offer. "He was the king of the real estate business and had never heard of me. I was honored." Helmsley squeezed his six-foot-three-inch frame into Trump's front seat and gave the youngster instructions to drive him up Madison Avenue.

When the car arrived at its destination, Trump said he caught an unforgettable glimpse of Helmsley's personality. "Harry didn't want to get out on the passenger side because traffic was on that side. Most people would run out and beat the traffic." Instead, Trump recalled, "he wanted me to get out my side. So I got out and Harry slid all the way over," and cautiously exited from the driver's side.

"I was impressed," Trump said. "I knew this was a very conservative man. This is a man who will never get himself in difficulty. He was right. He didn't want to beat the first wave of traffic at fifty m.p.h. It was very smart, very logical, very conservative. Of all the people I've ever known, here's a man who knows how to stay away from problems."

Five

Soon after Leona Roberts arrived at Brown, Harris, Stevens
fresh from her waltz with Harry Helmsley, shipments of pink
furnishings began arriving at the firm's headquarters at 14 East
Forty-seventh Street.

"None of us ever heard of her until she landed on our doorstep," one former member of the firm recalled. That changed
as soon as Leona took over an isolated, vacant upstairs office
"and decorated it very gaudily. It was done in beigy pink, and
had a mishmash of very bad French reproduction furniture. It
was done in dreadful taste." Understandably, word spread fast.
"Everybody used to laugh." It was more of a *salon* than an
office.

That summer of 1969, few of Leona's new colleagues were
familiar with her past triumphs at Pease & Elliman and Sutton
& Towne Residential. But she soon made it clear, in her own
imperious way, that she was somebody of importance. "Leona
was hoity toity with people," the former co-worker recalled,
"which made her very unpopular with other brokers. She arrived from absolutely nothing as far as I was concerned. And
when people come from nowhere, they get pretty elegant. She
was pretty elegant up there," with a secretary and perhaps two
brokers under her command.

And who could have guessed that the youthful new broker
was a grandmother? Indeed, only months earlier, on March 27,
1969, Jay and Myrna had a second son, David Bevan Panzirer.
Because of the couple's continuing feud with Leona, however,
it's doubtful that she attended the baby shower.

When Helmsley had purchased Brown, Harris, Stevens four
years earlier, in 1965, it was one of the city's most prestigious
firms in the sale of "upper-end"—the truly expensive—Manhattan apartments. He installed his top residential broker,
Rexford Tompkins, as president of the firm with high hopes
that he would increase its lackluster profits. Tompkins recalled
his surprise earlier that summer when Helmsley phoned him
with orders to hire Leona as head of a brand-new cooperative
conversion department.

"I hired her basically at Harry's request, because I wasn't even looking for brokers at the time," Tompkins said. "Harry had heard about her and said she was a good broker." From the start, Leona was practically a lone wolf in the firm. Virtually all the residential brokers worked on the third floor, a world away from her fifth-floor salon. "I let her operate pretty much on her own because there wasn't a lot of conversion work going on," Tompkins recalled. At the time, "the conversion phenomenon was barely beginning and there weren't that many buildings being co-oped. What you see today [in the late 1980s] is at least ten times the activity we had back then."

The independent setup was similar to Leona's earlier profit-sharing contract at Sutton & Towne Residential. In effect, Tompkins said, Miss Roberts was an "independent contractor who was allowed to hang her hat" at the firm only because of Harry Helmsley's special request. Using her cooperative sales license, she would make sales under the Brown, Harris name and enjoy the fancy title of senior vice president. In turn, Tompkins said, she would share her profits with the firm, "but was not under any supervision from me."

George E. Transom Jr., a former Brown, Harris, Stevens broker, said he never pegged Leona as a great asset to the firm. "Harry became enamored or fascinated with her. He brought her into the firm not because we needed her but because he wanted to park her someplace. Without Harry, she would have been lost in the woodwork. Rumor had it that Harry was walking her up and down the boulevard. He was romancing her, or she was romancing him."

Whatever the circumstances, in the blink of an eye Leona snared a contract to convert the Brevoort East, a twenty-six-story apartment house at 20 East Ninth Street in Greenwich Village. The white brick building had been erected as a huge addition to the Brevoort at 11 Fifth Avenue, which Leona had successfully converted the previous year for the Minskoff family through Sutton & Towne Residential.

As with earlier rent controlled buildings, under state law she needed to convince 35 percent of the tenants to sign up to buy their apartments in order to convert the apartment building to a cooperative. With the required number of signatures in hand, the building owner legally could then evict all nonpurchasers and sell their apartments on the open market. To succeed in her conversion effort, therefore, Leona had to sign up more than 100 of the 325 apartments at prices in the $35,000 range.

She soon found out that times were changing in New York. Tenants had grown more sophisticated as conversions became more common. They were no longer as terrified of ending up on the street for failure to buy. Instead, they banded together in tenant committees and decided for themselves whether the "offering plan"—the sales program offered by the building owner—was to their advantage. If so, they bought. If not, they balked, demanding better terms or purchase prices.

At 20 East Ninth Street, the tenants balked, particularly the elderly residents on fixed incomes. Quite simply, they preferred to hold on to their cash. Why buy? With rent stabilization—a form of rent control placed on newer buildings—they could coast along forever at predictably affordable monthly rates. In addition, they had no way of knowing that the apartments were sensational investment opportunities. How could they have predicted that Manhattan real estate values would soon streak into the stratosphere, increasing the value of their apartments by over 500 percent in barely a decade? All things considered, the building's tenant committee decided that continuing to rent was a far safer and more affordable alternative to buying.

When Brown, Harris, Stevens's hard-driving saleswoman, Leona Roberts, arrived on the scene, the tenant committee made it quite clear to her that she could take her conversion plan and shove it.

But Leona, one of the city's pioneer conversion experts, was not about to take no for an answer. Her reputation and scorecard were on the line. The fabled real estate wizard didn't hire her to take marching orders from a band of obstreperous tenants. Her job was to bring home the bacon—to come up with the 35 percent of sales needed to tilt her client's buildings to cooperative status. All it would take was a little "friendly persuasion."

Julian Menken, a businessman who was co-chairman of the tenant group, recalled that Leona set up a sales office in the building and immediately began to browbeat the tenants into submission. "She was hellbent on succeeding, no matter what. Every apartment counted, and she was determined to achieve the co-op. She wasn't intent on anything but getting her way."

Appearance was as important a tool as friendly persuasion. "She was well turned out, always very attractively dressed in tailored suits and a lot of jewelry around her neck," Menken said. "She wasn't exactly glamorous in those days, but she was a good-looking working girl." At 49, she looked a decade younger.

Menken said Leona was "on the premises all the time" chasing down prospective buyers. "She went to the weakest point, to people who didn't have much security—particularly older widows who could be easily intimidated. She used to ride the elevators and tell these nice old ladies that the building was going co-op and that there was an imminent danger they would be evicted unless they bought their apartments. She created a panic among the older women. She rode herd on them and did many unscrupulous things." In addition, he said Leona peppered the tenant committee with threats in the hope of breaking its spirit. "She would tell us to our faces, 'You think you're going to succeed, but you're going to fail!' She was letting us know we were up against an impossible force—that she could not be overcome because the pressure of vested interests would defeat us."

Menken's mother-in-law, Sylvia Dissick, was 69 years old when she moved into a separate apartment in the building that year following the death of her husband, a Manhattan physician. Mrs. Dissick recalled that Leona accosted her one day, having no idea she was related to the strongman of the tenant committee. "She met me on the elevator and found out that my husband had died seven months before. She told me the building was going co-op immediately. She said, 'Come to the office right now and I'll help you sign the papers. Do it right now. Don't take any time or you'll lose your apartment.' "

Mrs. Dissick said she was horrified by the prospect of losing her new apartment and ran to her daughter, Joan Menken, for advice. "My daughter told me to calm down, that this woman was a fake and was crooked. The apartment house was not going co-op after all and she [Leona] was just trying to get money." Dissick said one of her elderly neighbors received the same scare treatment. "It was a pattern. It was very calculated. It sounded very honest. She was very sincere. It was like a thief at work."

Marvin Miller, former executive director of the Major League Baseball Players Association, was the other co-chair of the tenant group at 20 East Ninth Street. He said Leona was a bird of prey who swooped down unmercifully on tenants, particularly elderly "empty nesters" who had sold their homes in suburban areas like Westchester County and moved to the city. "These were people who didn't want to buy their apartments or couldn't afford to. But Leona Roberts told them she had an eviction plan, and they could be on the street when their leases were up. It was a real threat and she played that line for all it was worth. The stories I got from tenants and crying widows were too numerous to record." He said threatening phone calls were another form of "constant harassment. She kept phoning tenants and saying, 'You know what's going to happen to you if you don't buy your apartment!' " He said she also became a pamphleteer, slipping "strongly worded" tracts under tenants' doors at night. "They would say, 'We're going to get the 35 percent—there's no doubt about it. And you *know* what the result will be.' "

Menken said Leona may have managed to reduce the tenants to tears and fears, but the residents ultimately defeated the conversion plan by sticking together. Without the necessary tenant support, "Jerry Minskoff had to fold his tent and keep the building a rental. Leona Roberts's reckless pressuring tactics just didn't pan out. Her six months of work went down the drain." (Not until several years later, under a different offering plan, was the building finally converted.)

Despite her failed efforts on the first offering plan, Minskoff remembers Leona Roberts as an invaluable workhorse. "She would work twenty-four hours a day; time was no problem for her. She was very reliable and the best broker around. I like her as a person." He refused, however, to discuss specifics of the conversion project, or allegations of Leona's almost warlike aggressiveness with tenants.

On another conversion project in 1969 — a twenty-two-story apartment house at 525 East Eighty-sixth Street—Leona's pressure tactics with tenants became a concern even to members of her own sales staff. One of Leona's former star brokers resigned in early 1970 after deciding that Leona was learning too many tricky sales techniques too fast for comfort. In fact, the broker said, "I knew what she was doing was unethical. You could smell trouble. I respected her very much for her drive and success, but I knew what she was doing was going to lead to trouble. I decided I didn't want to be part of her downfall, so I quit."

Leona's superstar reputation was blemished by her conversion failure at 20 East Ninth Street and the defection of her broker at 525 East Eighty-sixth Street. An opportunity to redeem herself arose in April 1970, when the owners of a twenty-two-story apartment house in the silk-stocking environs of Sutton Place hired Leona to convert their building into a cooperative. The owners of 345 East Fifty-sixth Street hoped to reap an approximate $2 million profit by selling the individual apartments at prices ranging from $15,000 for a two-and-half-room studio to $85,000 for a three-room penthouse, with maintenance charges of $120 up to $682 a month.

Immediately, Leona found herself up against the same obstacle that defeated her at 20 East Ninth Street: a tenant committee unwilling to play ball. All over town, it seemed, tenants were getting wise to the new co-op game. They were learning they could remain renters — and hold on to their savings — by jointly giving the raspberry to their landlords. They could simply band together and refuse to buy their rent-controlled apartments. Once again, the trick was to prevent the owner (known also as the "cooperative sponsor") from signing up the 35 percent of apartments needed to make his conversion plan effective. Tenant solidarity was a trend maddening to landlords because the conversion scheme was often the only way they could make a profit on their buildings. A maze of local rent control laws made it impossible for some owners to just break even on their brick-and-mortar investments. It was often easier to shuck the whole deal — to unload their buildings and flee the rental business — by selling to tenants through the medium of cooperative conversions. That way, owners could wring out a last-ditch profit and kiss their rent-control headaches goodbye.

Confronted with a tenant blockade at 345 East Fifty-sixth Street, Leona opened a sales office in the yellow brick building on March 31, 1970 and began the uphill task of persuading tenants to buy. To help her, she brought along two brokers from her Brown, Harris, Stevens cooperative division. They knew it was going to be a long, hard fight.

By summer, the sales team realized the tenants were an immovable force. More pressure, it was clear, was needed to persuade the tenants to buy. Out of the blue, eleven longtime residents began receiving letters in the mail advising them that outside investors had signed contracts to buy their apartments out from underneath them. But the letters — on Brown, Harris, Stevens letterhead stationery and signed by "Leona M. Roberts, Director of Cooperative Sales" — also held out a glimmer of hope. In sober, legalistic language, Miss Roberts wrote that they could keep their apartments after all *if* they bought their apartments — that is, if they matched the purchaser's offer — "within 15 days from the date of mailing of this letter." Then, returning to the original threatening spirit of her "match offer," she concluded: "If you fail to execute a Purchase Agreement … on or before fifteen [15] days … you will have lost your right to purchase your apartment."

Doris Goldstein, a tenant with a studio apartment on the third floor, said she shook like tapioca when she received her threatening letter on August 31, 1970. "It was very scary being told you're going to be without a home because somebody's going to take it away from you. Where do you go, what do you do when someone says 'I've sold your apartment' and you have to move?" Goldstein, a public relations specialist, said she had no idea who Leona Roberts was or what she was up to. After talking to the tenants' committee and learning a few details about Roberts, Goldstein said her mind rested a little easier. "I realized the letter was an absolute bluff, that there was nobody who really intended to buy my apartment. It was a scare tactic that this Roberts lady concocted to frighten people away who might have been gullible or who might not know their legal rights. The tenants committee assured everybody it was a bunch of bull."

Goldstein assumed that Leona "must have pulled this stunt at other places, or maybe this was a new scheme of hers she thought up. I was mad because it was my home, and here I was being led to believe I was being uprooted and thrown out. She was preying on people's ignorance and fear."

Leona's sales in the Sutton Place building progressed miserably through the summer of 1970. Things were not going well for Harry Helmsley's hand-picked sales champ. Surprisingly, however, her lackluster performance in no way diminished her clout at the office.

Quite the contrary, Tompkins said. In fact, the company president said he was surprised to discover that whenever Leona would criticize office policy, "Harry would mysteriously call me up to talk about it. He would say, 'How about so and so?' I wasn't about to discount Harry's advice." It was clear, Tompkins concluded, that Leona "was going over my head to Harry. Something was going on between them.

"I had no specific knowledge of their relationship when I hired her. I didn't realize there was anything in the wind. Then I realized it might be more than just a case of Harry asking me to hire a big broker. I realized she had *access* to him." There was no denying it. All the atmospheric conditions pointed to romance.

It was simply improbable that Helmsley—the gentle, colorless, happily married workaholic — would have the inclination or zest for an affair, particularly one with such a rough-edged broker as Leona Roberts. She was 50, but had the spunk and vocabulary of a 35-year-old longshoreman. At 61, an age when some men retain the look and air of youth, Helmsley was a gray eminence. For years, newspapers had run the same dull snapshot of the magnate, he of the unchanging silver mustache, sober countenance and inscrutable gaze behind wire-rimmed glasses. Physically, thanks to his lifelong love of swimming and walking, he was slim and vigorous. But his image was frozen in time: an inconspicuous fossil of high commerce publicly dusted off with the announcement of each new real estate coup.

Brokers began to gossip quietly about "the affair" between Helmsley and Leona, even though evidence was only circumstantial. Those who knew Leona's history — particularly her past association with Robert Neaderland at Pease & Elliman — were not surprised that she might be romancing an older, wealthier man like Helmsley. But Harry's associates, who considered him anything *but* a Romeo, were less willing to accept as fact mere speculation that he was involved in an extramarital romance.

One of Helmsley's closest former aides said the reality was that by early 1971, Leona had moved into a cozy penthouse apartment at 77 West Fifty-fifth Street, a nineteen-story building known as the Gallery House. It was a convenient arrangement because Helmsley had a financial interest in the building, located on the northwest corner of Sixth Avenue.

"The Gallery House is where Harry and Leona had their rendezvous," the ex-aide said. "Harry didn't just meet Leona one day and marry her the next. They dated for a year and a half or two. It was all sub rosa." The aide said Helmsley's wife, Eve, "had no idea what was going on the whole time."

Before moving into the apartment in March 1971, Leona hired a carpenter to build special closets, bookcases and kitchen cabinets. The craftsman from Long Island City, Queens — Nick Pantazis — also provided a long list of custom touches such as lining all the closets with white tile. The overall result, alas, was so unsatisfactory to Leona that she filed a $50,000 lawsuit against Pantazis in June, alleging that he wrecked rather than renovated the penthouse. Among her claims were that he "improperly installed a buffet table in [the] dining room, with the result that the drawers continually fall to the floor." She also charged that "a tool box for the terrace and chains on the doors which were to have been supplied were never delivered." Pantazis countersued Leona for failing to pay his $3,011 bill and the dispute was apparently settled out of court.

The penthouse was decorated in a casual style, with a bohemian curtain of blue and green glass beads separating the dining and living rooms. White and blue Chinese rugs were scattered about on a hardwood floor that was regularly varnished and buffed to a mirror sheen. Drawings of horses hung on the living room walls.

One of Leona's former acquaintances who visited the apartment described it as "a lovely little two-bedroom penthouse with a wraparound terrace. It was a very cute little apartment, but not a 'drop-dead' apartment. It was the kind of place that if you visited, you wouldn't be overwhelmed, but you would say, 'What a nice apartment!' "

Leona and Harry would frequently repair to the penthouse terrace, the acquaintance said, for a scenic barbecue overlooking midtown Manhattan. "Leona had an electric hibachi out there, and she would barbecue kosher hot dogs for Harry." Thanks to Leona's mink coat, even in the wintertime she could roast the weenies outdoors. The acquaintance said Helmsley "kept a very low profile in those days," and could visit and leave the building without arousing any attention. "Unless you were in the real estate business, I don't think many people knew who he was. He was somebody you read about every now and then in the newspaper." He said during one visit to the penthouse in the summer of 1971, "Leona told me her boyfriend, a Mr. Helmsley, was coming for dinner." Upon leaving the building shortly thereafter he said, "I noticed a limousine pull up front and a very undistinguished older man got out." The elderly gentleman apparently was a frequent visitor because the doorman stepped smartly up to the limousine with a "Good evening, Mr. Helmsley."

For diversion, Harry the boss and Leona the broker would dine by candlelight at a back table at Georges Rey, a French restaurant located at 60 West Fifty-fifth Street, just a few doors east of the Gallery House. "That's where a major part of their courtship seemed to have taken place," one of Helmsley's former aides said. "I met them there once and you could tell it was their hideaway because the staff knew them well. It was quite clear they were regulars." The restaurant was a lure not only because of its convenience to Leona's penthouse, but for its decidedly romantic ambience. They could dine in the soft glow of sconces and chandeliers. The walls were covered with large murals depicting Parisian scenes. With its nostalgic street lamps and live accordion music, the couple might well have imagined themselves dining along the Seine.

During the meal, the aide recalled, Leona kept nuzzling up to Harry and showered him with sweet nothings. "She tickled his chin and said, 'Isn't he gorgeous?' 'Isn't he beautiful?' " The aide said he was revolted by the effusive display. "It was so overdone. It was like a Las Vegas hooker who tickles the chin of a pot-bellied businessman and makes him feel like a movie star."

The aide said Harry sopped the attention up "because he didn't know any better." In matters of real estate, Harry Helmsley was perhaps the shrewdest and toughest bird in town. "But when it comes to women, his expertise lies somewhere else. He was not experienced with women. He was not a man about town—a bon vivant. He wasn't a person who gallivanted around town with a roving eye. Harry never looked at other women." The former Helmsley executive said it was clear to him that "Leona was strong, and just bulldozed over Harry" with her charms. "He fell into the clutches of a pro."

George Transom said he and other brokers assumed that Leona was in the process "of busting up Harry's marriage" to Eve Helmsley. "Most people in the office thought Leona had some kind of whammy on Harry—some inexplicable hold."

What brokers could only assume, a longtime friend of Leona's family heard straight from the horse's mouth. The friend, who had known Leona's family for over a generation, said Leona boasted to him in 1970 that "she was going to *capture* Harry Helmsley. She said he was going to be hers. She indicated that he was her target and she was going to acquire him. She was going to co-op him just like she co-oped all those buildings. She was a determined broad to begin with. She was tenacious. It didn't happen to her overnight. She had to have a successful campaign. It took a lot of cunning for a Jewish broad to try to split up a Quaker couple and succeed."

David Wilshin said Leona's campaigning would have fallen short, however, had Harry and Leona not shared a common obsession. One of Leona's biggest attractions in Harry's eyes was that "she was extremely interested in the real estate business, and he could relate to her businesswise. I think that was the catalyst that got the romance going."

Regardless of how intimately the pair danced on the same

wavelength, however, Leona had to stay respectfully in the background when Helmsley opened Manhattan's newest luxury hotel in May 1971. Instead of Leona, Helmsley's wife, Eve, had the thrill of swinging open the wide gray doors to the glittering Park Lane Hotel. The forty-seven-story building, with 640 rooms, was the highest structure on Central Park South; it had been four years and $30 million in the making. It was the first new luxury Manhattan hotel since the Regency had opened on Park Avenue seven years earlier. A promotional brochure touted its "elegance" and "the understated world of rich marbles and wood." Velvet brocade wallpaper and gilded French provincial furniture had been personally approved by Eve Helmsley far in advance of the grand opening.

The Helmsleys had decided to plant firmer roots in Manhattan by moving into the new hotel, and they had set aside its duplex penthouse for themselves. But unlike their former *pied-à-terre* at the St. Moritz, the Park Lane apartment would be for their permanent year-round use. They would hold on to their ranch house in suburban Briarcliff Manor as a country getaway. The Park Lane penthouse was a breathtaking aerie, but Eve decorated it in the unpretentious style befitting their Quaker faith.

It had to be apparent to Leona Roberts that Harry and Eve Helmsley were embarking on an exciting new chapter in their thirty-three-year marriage. They were living literally atop Manhattan's newest real estate sensation and relishing Harry's latest accomplishment. From their cloud-draped windows, the Helmsleys would be able to look down on Central Park and watch the change of seasons.

Although she was not a major player in her husband's career, in little ways Eve Helmsley made her own valuable contributions to his legendary success. "Eve helped him start his business," one of her longtime friends said. "They discussed everything together. Harry had the investment know-how. He had the savvy. He looked for a potential property in a good area and Eve would go along with him to visit properties. When he started acquiring little commercial buildings, Eve would go to Macy's and buy curtains and fix the buildings up and get them painted."

Eve became less involved and consciously stayed out of the limelight as Harry's empire grew larger. "We Quakers prefer to stay in the eelgrass," she said. "Quakerism teaches you to stay in the background and not boast about what you have or what you've accomplished. And that's what Harry and I did."

No celebrity profiles were written about tycoon Helmsley's wife. She preferred her country club tennis court to the Manhattan media whirl. Yet in spite of her basic indifference to real estate, occasionally she become enthusiastic enough about a particular endeavor to offer strong advice.

On one such occasion—motivated by a personal desire to return home to Manhattan—it was Eve Helmsley who pointed out a "perfect little site" on Central Park South to build a major new hotel. "I decided to build the Park Lane," Eve recalled, "and Harry said he didn't have time for such a major project. So I told him, 'Fine! You're a hundred times busier than I am, so let me plan it out for you.' " Without any construction experience of her own, Eve said she "went ahead anyway, and proceeded as though I was someone with the know-how. I told Harry, 'I'm going to build a decent building, and we're going to have a pool up top.' " Taking her cue, Helmsley instructed his professional development team to draw up blueprints for a forty-seven-story hotel tower. The front section of the site was occupied at the time by two small apartment houses at 36 and 38 Central Park South, with a combined frontage of 75 feet. At the rear of the site—with a combined frontage of 127 feet on West Fifty-eighth Street—were a handful of four-story brownstones that would also have to meet the wrecking ball to make way for the hotel.

Eve's dream became a reality the first week in May 1971, when the hotel opened for business. Prices were competitive with other luxury hotels such as the Plaza and Waldorf-Astoria. Small single rooms, facing the park, cost $32 a night. A two-bedroom suite on the forty-sixth floor commanded $140. The best accommodations, of course, were set aside for Harry and Eve. Their duplex consisted of approximately ten large hotel rooms with park views—five on each of the forty-sixth and forty-seventh floors—and three smaller rooms on the forty-sixth floor. A pool on the forty-seventh floor—the top floor—would allow Harry to engage throughout the year in his lifelong passion for swimming.

It was a luxurious setup for a couple whose previous byword had been frugality. Eve recalled, however, that she had no guilt pangs over the luxurious digs. After all, she and Harry had lived the simplest of lives for thirty-three years of marriage. Harry was approaching 62 and she was four years older. They were nearing the age when most people consider retirement. It was time, perhaps, to reward themselves for decades of work and accomplishment. "It was expensive, perhaps," Eve recalled, "but it was money innocently spent. Even Quakers like a certain amount of luxury. That's normal, don't you think? I would hope that if there's a Creator, he would say, 'Let them do what they want as long as there's no harm in it.' "

Perhaps the only person who could imagine any harm in the arrangement was Leona Roberts. After dating Helmsley for many moons, the brass-knuckled broker surely realized that his wife was still very much the center of the tycoon's life. It was a stalemate that relegated Leona—the secret friend—to second-class citizenship.

The Park Lane move-in must have been the final straw. What clearer evidence could there be that Harry Helmsley was in no hurry to sever his thirty-three-year bond with Eve? The time had come for a showdown.

Within three months—by early August—Harry Helmsley returned home to the Park Lane with a heartrending announcement. Their marriage was over, he told Eve, because he had decided to marry a Brown, Harris, Stevens broker by the name of Leona Roberts.

To Eve, so happily ensconced with Harry in their new penthouse, the declaration was a thunderbolt. "I couldn't imagine that this was happening," Eve recalled. "Harry and I had had such a nice life together. I had loved his parents, and he loved mine. We were so close. We never had brawls of any kind. And then this woman—this Leona—came along. I had never met or seen her. Maybe I knew there was a Leona at one of Harry's offices, but I didn't know it was anything serious."

Although Eve knew nothing of Leona Roberts, she received detailed descriptions from real estate friends. "Nobody had anything good to say about Leona. Everyone in the world knew she was a floozy. People said, *'Wait till you see her! Wait till you hear her talk!'* She was a floozy, and floozies go after old men. They want them to hurry up and die so they can get their money."

Eve said she couldn't imagine "how this woman could interest Harry. We are complete opposites. I am educated and have several degrees. From what I've heard, she [Leona] has no real education, except maybe grammar school or a high school degree." Equally inexplicable to the shaken wife was why Harry would fall head over heels "for a woman that I heard was hated by her peers."

One of Eve Helmsley's closest friends said the unexpected marital crisis "was absolutely shocking because Eve and Harry seemed absolutely compatible. It was the last couple in New York I thought would be divorced. Nobody had an inkling. Friends felt idiotic to see these people two or three times a week and everything's fine. And then, boom!"

Helmsley had been able to hide the romance for so long, the friend said, "because he's not a very open person. Harry is not a great talker or jokester, or someone who would pinch someone. So he's doubly hard to read.

"Maybe with Harry the seven-year itch took thirty-three years. Maybe he wanted to come out of the shell that Eve's religion put him in. Maybe it's more fun on the way up than on top. With all his money, maybe he finally wanted to break free and have some fun. He was a very wealthy man and never flaunted it. Maybe Harry finally wanted the recognition." Whatever the motivation, "you can't force a human being into anything they don't want. Apparently there was something in Harry that wanted it." The friend speculated that Leona Roberts "just beguiled this man. She must have worked very hard to come to this point. Obviously, she won out."

Even more surprising, the friend said, was Eve's calm acceptance of her unexpected fate. "Eve told me that when it all came to an end, Harry told her everything. He told her he had been seeing Leona, and told her about Leona's apartment at the Gallery House. At first Eve was sad, but she managed it very well. She's not the kind to put up a fight. She's the kind to say, 'If this is what you want, I'll go.' "

Before calling it irrevocably quits, however, the friend said Harry "had daily conversations with Eve discussing the whole situation. Eve was a reasonable, sensible woman and they talked the whole thing out." Following one such discussion, the friend said Eve came to her with a revelation as alarming as Harry's earlier announcement.

The friend said Eve informed her that Harry—the wiliest of businessmen—was being suckered into marrying his real estate broker. "Eve said she had asked Harry if he was committed to his decision to proceed with the divorce. And if so, was he sure that Leona Roberts was the right woman for him." A red alert went up when Harry replied that he didn't have much time to make up his mind, because *another man was vying for Leona's hand!*

"Harry told Eve, 'There's a man in Georgia that is so crazy about Lee [Leona]. He sent her a letter and a diamond ring and told her she had ten days to make up her mind whether to marry him.' " Harry proceeded to reveal, "I saw the letter and the diamond, so I have only ten days to decide" whether to beat the Georgia rival to a marriage proposal.

Eve, astounded that Harry would swallow such an improbable ultimatum, told her close friend: "Can you believe this man believes this hogwash?"

Years later, the friend said she discussed the entire episode with Leona's sister, Sandra, who moved South around 1968 after marrying an Atlanta businessman, Jerry Kaufman. "I asked Sandra if she knew who this guy was in Atlanta who sent the diamond and the letter."

"Are you kidding? We sent them!" Sandra cried. (A kinsman also remembers Sandra's telling him that she "filled Leona's apartment with flowers" for the same purpose.) With a gale of laughter Sandra then added, "Not only did we make the letter up, it was a *fake* diamond." Sandra, who had since fallen out with her sister, then added: "Xaviera Hollander [author of *The Happy Hooker*] could take lessons from Leona." Eve's friend was stunned by Sandra's revelation. The implication was too shocking even to contemplate: Leona Roberts and her sister had concocted a fake love letter—complete with engagement ring—to excite Harry's jealousy and spur him into action. They had fooled New York's canniest real estate operator into divorcing his wife and tying the knot with Leona. And with such a preposterous ruse!

Eve Helmsley said she recalls having heard about the ten-day ultimatum but can remember no details after seventeen years. "I remember hearing about that. Yes, I recall hearing the story. It has been a long time since Harry and I parted—1972—and I put aside things like that. I've seen and heard men do very strange things that I don't think a woman would have done, and it never occurred to me to dwell on this. I thought, 'That's what a man would do.' I always dropped things like that."

Even though her former husband was a business wizard, Eve said Harry would not have been immune to such a seemingly transparent ruse. "I think a lot of men would fall for it. That's a fairly common story, isn't it, in situations like this? I don't mean to deride men, but sometimes I think they swallow things more easily than women do. I may be maligning men without reason, but I think we're a little cagier."

Leona's version of her engagement was a far different tale. Blanche Slauson, who came to know the hotel queen in later years, said "Lee" was fond of describing how Harry begged for her hand after dinner one evening. "Lee said he proposed to her on his knees. But Lee demanded, 'Tell it to me with your eyes!' And she said Harry wiggled his eyes and she told him, 'I know that you mean it.' "

Slauson said she took Leona's romantic tale at face value, and could only imagine "this big, tall man doing that—rolling his eyes for her." The story, real or fanciful, was typical of Leona's "little-girl" seductiveness. (The "little girl" became a grandmother three times over on June 5, 1971, when the stork brought Meegan Jill Panzirer to Jay and Myrna's door.) In one interview, Leona said her marriage to Helmsley was perfect. "The only thing I would change, if I could, is that I would have married him when I was two. " She told another reporter it was love at first touch when they "just fit" together during their first dance and Harry sang romantic songs in her ear. Leona also revealed that Harry included a strict requirement in their wedding plans. "During a time in our courtship when we were having problems, I lost a pound a day for twenty days—twenty pounds I lost for my Harry, and I kept it off."

Regardless of how cagey or coquettish Leona had been in winning Harry, Eve said she decided it was fruitless to fight back. Numbed with shock and pain, she decided to fade gracefully into the sunset rather than try to hold on to a husband with a much younger, obviously more vivacious woman on his mind. "I wasn't going to go into a tailspin about anything. I decided that it was good enough to feel very satisfied about having had a nice marriage for so long to a nice man. He had fine attributes and was strictly honest. I'm willing to give him his praise. You cannot have a breakdown about everything."

As if to prove her mettle, during the long Labor Day weekend Eve invited her best friends from Westchester County to come take a first admiring look at her Park Lane penthouse. "I didn't lay the bricks or set the windows, but I was proud of the hotel because I was so involved in making it happen. So I brought my friends for a tour and then took them upstairs to the apartment. 'How do you like the pool?' I asked them. They voiced their approval.

"Then I told them, 'I just wanted you to have a good, long

look *because I'm going to divorce Harry now!'* "

Gasps and shrieks of disbelief filled the air. The suburban housewives deliberated: was it some kind of joke?

No, Eve assured them, it was for real. Her attorney was already drawing up the divorce papers. The inseparable Helmsleys had somehow come unglued.

In hindsight, Eve said, "It was probably unfair of me to break the news in such a fashion. My friends had just gotten such a kick out of the hotel, only to be terribly shocked by the anticlimax. They didn't comprehend it, and I wondered if I did."

Leona Roberts, however, must have been able to comprehend her good fortune when Harry Helmsley went ahead and asked her for her hand in marriage. The only thing standing in their way was a little time—the time it would take him and Eve to amicably dissolve their marriage.

Meanwhile, Leona was still a working woman with a job to do. On September 8, a few days after Eve's poolside bombshell, Leona could tell Harry that she had finally succeeded in converting 345 East Fifty-sixth Street to a cooperative. On that day, the owners of the twenty-two-story Sutton Place apartment building filed an affidavit with the state attorney general declaring that they had obtained purchase agreements from sixty-five tenants—four more than needed to fulfill the 35 percent conversion requirement. Thanks to Leona and her Brown, Harris, Stevens sales team, the conversion was now "effective"—or completed.

The conversion declaration meant that *all* tenants—not just the eleven like Doris Goldstein who received Leona's threatening "match offers" in previous months—were in danger. Everyone had to buy their apartments or get out. Somehow, Leona had prevailed over the building's stalwart tenants' committee. On the heels of her failure at 20 East Ninth Street, the Sutton Place conversion was a sweet, redemptive victory to show Harry.

Yet, as sometimes happens with victories, Leona's Sutton Place triumph unexpectedly slipped through her fingers only two months later, on November 17, 1971. That crisp Wednesday morning, State Attorney General Louis J. Lefkowitz filed a motion in Manhattan State Supreme Court to enjoin the owners of the building from selling their 172 apartments.

In an unprecedented civil action, Lefkowitz charged that the owners and their sales brokers had engaged in a slew of "fraudulent practices" and misrepresentations in attempting to convert the building. The accompanying motion papers alleged that "the major perpetrator of these fraudulent acts and practices was and is defendant Leona M. Roberts."

Other defendants included Leona's two on-site sales agents from Brown, Harris, Stevens—Olga Anna Bogdan and Marion S. Terr—and four owners of the building, Albert C. Drucker, Arthur Katz, Paul Goldin and Rhoda Schaffer.

Lefkowitz alleged that thirty-two of the sixty-five sales agreements obtained by Leona and her sales team were not bona-fide purchasers under the city rent stabilization law. Instead of signing up actual tenants, Lefkowitz alleged that the defendants obtained their 35 percent quota by "loading" the building through "sham sales" to friends and relatives of the building owners.

It was the first time ever in Manhattan that state officials had gone to court to challenge the sworn declarations of those "purchasers" making up the 35 percent quota needed to put a conversion plan into effect.

In scathing language, Lefkowitz also alleged that the defendants attempted to "fraudulently coerce at least 11 tenants" to purchase their apartments through "match offers" by outsiders. In fact, he charged, "the outside 'purchasers' either never paid the required consideration for their 'purchase,' received a refund at a later date, or paid with bad checks that were not corrected. Defendants concealed the true facts from the tenants." Moreover, "These acts and practices constitute a blatant form of coercive harassment. Most of the above tenants are still under the apprehension that their apartments have been sold and that they will be evicted by the outside 'purchaser.... ' "

Furthermore, Lefkowitz charged that the defendants "harassed at least 12 non-purchasing tenants by threatening them with eviction based on false allegations that these tenants were refusing to show their apartments to interested purchasers."

Leon and Penny Kachurin, a couple on the sixth floor named in Lefkowitz's court pleading, said Leona singled them out for double harassment. Not only did the couple receive a threatening match offer, Mrs. Kachurin said, but Leona also warned them "that she had access to our apartment whenever she wanted." It was an unnerving thought. The saleswoman could barge into their apartment like a storm trooper at any unexpected moment of the day or night in order to show it to a potential buyer. Mrs. Kachurin said that fifteen members of her family were seated for dinner during Passover when Leona banged on her door and shouted: "We want to show the apartment!" The Kachurins were enraged, thinking the atrocious timing could not have been accidental. "Forget it!" Penny shouted back equally loudly. "You want to see my apartment—make an appointment!" Penny said the entire family was upset "because she intentionally picked a holiday to harass us. She figured if she made us uncomfortable enough for long enough, she could get us out. She wanted us to know that we didn't have the sanctuary of our own home, and that we didn't have any rights."

Had there not been a strong tenants committee, Mrs. Kachurin said, "a lot of us would have been tricked out of our homes. Leona Roberts was making money one way or another, hook or crook. It was just a very dirty thing all the way around."

In response to the aggressive sales shenanigans, Attorney General Lefkowitz asked the court to declare the Sutton Place conversion "null and void." He also demanded the drastic remedy of permanently barring Leona Roberts and her two sales agents, Bogdan and Terr, from selling cooperatives in the state of New York. In effect, Lefkowitz was demanding that Leona be driven out of her specialty—selling cooperative apartments—forever and a day. It was like ordering a painter to hang up his brushes for life, or denying a carpenter the continued use of hammer and nail.

Even worse than the medicine, however, was the timing. The woman accused of being the "major perpetrator" was none other than the bride-soon-to-be of Harry Helmsley, the respected dean of New York real estate. Luckily for the lovebirds, however, their engagement two months earlier was never announced in the newspapers. The *New York Times* noted on page 37 of its November 18 edition that a broker named Leona M. Roberts was in hot water with the law, but even the newspaper of record had no idea of her preordained importance.

Lefkowitz's action was in the form of a temporary restraining order, a civil action taken to immediately stop a perceived wrong from continuing. If the judge saw possible merit in the attorney general's initial arguments, the next step would be a full-blown civil trial where Leona would have to fight the fraud charges and battle to keep her state license to sell cooperative apartments.

The likelihood of a trial had to be a frightening possibility. With a trial—by definition a public spectacle—the word might get out *just who* was being charged as "the major perpetrator" in an important test case for the attorney general. The *New York Times* and no telling who else might make the connection. They might learn that the chief defendant in the fraud case was in the process of emptying her hope chest for an approaching wedding date with Harry Helmsley. If the word got out, there would be a firestorm of ruinous publicity. Headline writers at the *Daily News* and the *Post*, no doubt, would have a field day. Hundreds of thousands of copies, with headlines such as "Real Estate King Engaged to Fraud Queen," would be anything but helpful to Helmsley's real estate career. Smelling blood, reporters certainly would dig deeper in order to uncover more of Leona's past history. It was also the kind of potential adverse publicity that could derail a marriage proposal.

Damage control was of the essence. Leona and her two sales assistants hired a prominent New York lawyer, Charles G. Moerdler of the firm of Stroock & Stroock & Lavan, to do battle with Lefkowitz. Moerdler filed a salvo of counter-motions, including an affirmation alleging that Lefkowitz's charges were "dishonest, materially misleading and do not warrant the grant of any relief." He still defends Leona's "match offers," saying she had informed him that bona-fide outside purchasers, not sham buyers, had put down deposits to buy apartments occupied by tenants in the Sutton Place building.

In recalling his old case, Moerdler said the allegations against his three former clients were "chickenshit." The lawyer said he believed that Lefkowitz pursued the case because co-operative conversions were a new trend in the early 1970s and the attorney general needed "a hot potato" to prove he was performing his watchdog role over the industry. Sexism was also at the heart of the prosecution, Moerdler charged. "Here was the first strong woman in the real estate field [Leona], and that in itself raised a lot of jealousies in the industry. This was a male industry at a time when women were not considered more than hostesses in the process of conversions. Leona was a pioneer in every sense of the word and she was drawing a lot of heat for that. She had obtained a position in one of the most prominent firms in town—Brown, Harris, Stevens. She had received a senior status and this was an assault on that kind of status."

Alan M. Parness, the young deputy attorney general who handled the case for Lefkowitz, has a less benign recollection of the case. At the time, Parness was Lefkowitz's special assistant in charge of enforcing state laws regulating cooperative conversions. Of hundreds of cases he handled between 1970 and 1973 involving alleged harassments by landlords and selling agents, he said virtually none was destined for trial. "Most cases involved anonymous complaints against brokers that led nowhere." The sales tactics in Leona's case, however, were "the straw that broke the camel's back. It was one of the first times we had sufficient evidence to bring a case of harassment and fraud in connection with a cooperative conversion. This case involved killer-type allegations." He added that there had been "a number of previous complaints to the attorney general's office about Leona Roberts and her sales tactics—a lot of harassments and misrepresentations."

Although Moerdler continued to swamp the attorney general with countermotions, by January 1972 Lefkowitz was as determined as ever to take the test case to trial. The possibility of a public spectacle was becoming a probability. Simultaneously, Eve Helmsley was in the process of packing her keepsakes from a somehow ruined thirty-year marriage. She would retreat from the Park Lane penthouse in favor of a smaller penthouse at her estranged husband's Carlton House hotel at Sixty-first Street and Madison Avenue.

Harry Helmsley's plan was to exchange rings with Leona and install his younger wife in Eve's prized creation—the Park Lane penthouse. No longer would Helmsley sleep alone in a separate bedroom from his wife, as he had with Eve. Carpenters would erase Eve's memory by transforming her blue-and-white bedroom into a wood-paneled library. Helmsley's bedroom, meanwhile, would be doubled in size to accommodate a bed for two. But his wedding date with Leona would have to be on hold until she resolved her legal woes with Lefkowitz. It was an infuriating wait for a tycoon like Helmsley, so used to fast results at the snap of his fingers.

It must have seemed to Helmsley that an extra layer of damage control was needed. A bribe was obviously out of the question. But a carefully placed word on Leona's behalf would be invaluable. Since the day Alexander Graham Bell uttered, "Mr. Watson, come here; I want you," businessmen have realized the value of a phone call. Helmsley did not waste his nickel. In his dire need, he phoned the perfect man for the job.

On a wintry January day, with marriage as his New Year's resolution, Helmsley beseeched Alton G. Marshall to come to his rescue. As president of Rockefeller Center, Marshall was connected to the state's political and financial elite. Of crucial importance was Marshall's intimate association with the Rockefeller family itself, particularly Governor Nelson A. Rockefeller. He had served as the Governor's secretary from 1966 until he took the Rockefeller Center post in early 1971, and had run Rockefeller's successful 1970 re-election campaign. During his five years at Rockefeller's side, Marshall, of course, had also formed close friendships with the top shelf of state officials—including Attorney General Louis J. Lefkowitz.

Marshall recalled that Harry phoned him in an out-of-character agitated state. "I got the call and Harry was very much concerned because he was getting a divorce and fully intended in his own mind to marry Leona. It wasn't just a question that he was just in a divorce and this was a female member of his organization. He intended to marry her. He was concerned she might be convicted, and that of course would have been a *bitch* because Harry was then considered one of the top real estate figures in the city and the country. This was before the Trumps or anyone else were on the scene.

"Yes, that would have been a bitch. That's what he said in his call—that it would be a source of embarrassment, maybe even difficulty, for him in his real estate business to marry someone who was found guilty of these charges, who was *also* in the real estate business. You know, it would have been one thing if it was a charge of shoplifting or something. But Leona was in the real estate business, and for her to be found guilty of the various charges in the real estate business would have put Harry in an uncomfortable, if not untenable, position."

After explaining his predicament, Helmsley worriedly asked Marshall what influence he might have with Lefkowitz. Judging from Helmsley's tone, Marshall said, "It looked as though the charges must have been quite a serious concern. He was very worried he would be marrying into the industry, so to speak, marrying someone who might have an *identifiable record*."

At the time, Marshall said, he knew little or nothing about Helmsley's fiancée. "I'll be blunt. She was not that big a deal when she was Leona Roberts. She might have been quite successful in the trenches, but she certainly was not Mrs. Harry Helmsley, from the standpoint of visibility."

Marshall said it would have been difficult for anyone to deny any favor to "a man as reliable and honorable as Harry Helmsley. As an individual, he was always a very decent—

humble is not an overstatement—gentleman. He was a quiet, not a boisterous, kind of guy. And I liked him. I considered him a friend." Marshall said he immediately phoned Lefkowitz and rallied for Helmsley's embattled sweetheart.

"I told Louie that Harry had called me and that Harry had this concern. I repeated to Louie that, 'Look, Harry is getting a divorce and planning to marry this Roberts woman and your department has some charges brought against her and Harry feels it would be a terrible source of embarrassment if his new wife-to-be is convicted. And he's very much concerned about it.' "

Lefkowitz was familiar with the case, Marshall said, "but couldn't rattle off the details. And he said, 'I understand.' " Lefkowitz did not give Marshall any specifics to report back to Helmsley. Nor did he disclose "how his department was going to handle it. But knowing Louie, I would guess that he might have called the assistant attorney general in charge, and said, 'Look, this is what Harry's concern is. This is his prospective, future wife. Let's be damned sure of what we have.' Having been in the middle of a lot of those things, I would guess that's how Louie handled it."

Immediately after the conversation, Marshall recalled, "I reported back to Harry that I had made the call to Louie Lefkowitz. Harry said he appreciated my help and told me, 'It isn't just everybody that would get involved.' "

Approximately a month later, on February 7, Lefkowitz' office agreed to remove the names of Leona and her two assistants—Terr and Bogdan—as defendants in the continuing civil action. In exchange for letting the trio off the hook, the three Brown, Harris, Stevens sales agents, while denying any wrongdoing, signed a consent withdrawing themselves as present or future selling agents in the Sutton Place building.

As stronger medicine, according to Parness—Lefkowitz's special deputy—Leona offered to relinquish her license for a year in order to avoid trial. "It was a settlement where Miss Roberts agreed to drop out of her business. She was about to marry Good Ol' Harry, so I guess she figured she wouldn't need the license anyway."

Alton Marshall said he never knew for sure whether his call to Lefkowitz was a determining factor in bringing the case to a relatively painless conclusion. But he said both Harry and Leona thanked him on several later occasions for his helping hand. "Whether I deserved it or not, they gave me some credit for it. I guess they had a right to assume that as long as things turned out right, the call certainly was not hurtful. At a maximum, it was *very* helpful." Lefkowitz, now an attorney in private practice, said he had no recollection of the case.

A week after settling the case with Lefkowitz, Leona could celebrate Valentine's Day with Harry, safe in the knowledge there would be no trial and no spotlight to interfere with their wedding plans. They picked April 8 as the date, and decided to make it an extremely private ceremony in the Park Lane penthouse.

Helmsley's closest associates, mindful of Leona's close scrape with Lefkowitz and her earlier reputation as a meatgrinding broker, became alarmed by the certainty of the approaching marriage. Sure, she was off the hook. But her reputation was none the better among Helmsley-Spear insiders as a result of the legal action. They pulled Helmsley aside and privately cautioned him to think before he leaped into wedlock with his controversial fiancée. Even Leon Spear, who had recommended Leona as a "top drawer" saleswoman three years earlier, apparently voiced misgivings about the imminent marriage.

Gerald Kadish, one of Leona's top hotel executives in the early 1980s, says Leon Spear confided to him that he had strongly opposed the marriage a decade earlier. "Spear thought that Leona was a miserable person. He thought she was an ingrate, just not a nice person, and that she was just using Harry. Spear said that before the marriage he cautioned Harry that he was being taken in by her, and that he was afraid she was going to be bad for him."

One of Harry and Eve Helmsley's closest friends recalled that Harry's other important partners—Irving Schneider, Alvin Schwartz and Lawrence Wien—had concerns of their own. "Before he married her, they had been familiar with Leona for years and were rather outspoken about this lady they knew through the real estate circles. They knew about her days at Pease & Elliman and a million other things. In general, all of Harry's friends suggested that he not marry her."

The entreaties, however insistent, fell on deaf ears. Helmsley may have been indecisive about the marriage months earlier, when he revealed his intentions to Eve. But once he made up his mind to marry his vivacious broker, the realty maven's word was final. "I think it was her voracity and love of life that appealed to me," Helmsley recalled later. He had simply too much to look forward to to turn back now.

According to published reports, Harry gave Eve a cash settlement of $7 million as part of their separation agreement. One of Eve's former lawyers, however, scoffed at the figure, saying, "It's way too low." She also received $500,000 a year in alimony and was allowed to remain for a nominal rent in her penthouse apartment at the Carlton House. Most important, according to one of Harry's former estate lawyers, the tycoon also consented to set aside approximately 10 percent of his eventual estate for Eve. "It was the basis for their separation agreement." In effect, Eve Helmsley retains a vested interest in Harry's continuing real estate career. Upon his death, she will, if she survives him, share his wealth from projects built or acquired long after their divorce, including the Helmsley Palace.

Eve Helmsley might never have understood why she was shunted aside for a rawhide-tough, less educated woman like Leona. With the benefit of hindsight, however, Eve said, "Harry must have wanted the recognition. He worked so hard for so many years. Maybe he wanted to be a hero and get credit. I realize now that I kept him down, away from the spotlight, and he just accepted it for years. But I think all men have a yearning to be The Big Shot. Harry never talked about it to me because he thought, 'She'll think I'm crazy.' Maybe I didn't get him enough publicity. A wife like me maybe spoiled it for him. Maybe I should have said, 'We should write a book about you!' "

Leona didn't make the same mistake. By contrast, she *bombarded* Helmsley with the ego stroking he must have yearned for. In courtesan fashion, she literally cooed over Helmsley in front of his friends before their marriage—describing good looks, even "gorgeous feet," that nobody else could spot. Helmsley soaked up her compliments like a paper towel, even though he claimed to know better. Years later, he frankly speculated that Leona was attracted to him not because of his sex appeal but because of "my power. I think the ability to use power constructively—to build a Park Lane Hotel ... to put together a combination to buy the Empire State Building—certainly gives you a certain amount of power. I think women are attracted to men with power, like Kissinger. But he doesn't have power because he's been elected to something. He has power because he's smarter than the next guy. Same way with me. I don't think where I'm so attractive to women, and if I were and acknowledged it, I'd have my head cut off. So for my well-being, I'm telling you I'm not attractive to women."

If power was an aphrodisiac, as Helmsley suggested, Leona Roberts had ample reason to swoon in anticipation of her wedding. She had aimed straight for the top target. Harry Helmsley had spent forty-five painstaking years building one of America's greatest real estate empires. Now, at 50 and with only ten short years in the same industry, the twice-divorced housewife was about to assume co-command over Harry's hard-won empire. And if he died she would inherit it. According to one of Harry's closest former friends and business associates, there was no prenuptial agreement.

In preparation for marriage, Leona filed a petition with the state supreme court in Manhattan praying for leave to change her name. In the December 10, 1971 petition, she informed the court that her legal name remained "Leona Mindy Rosenthal" although she had adopted the name "Leona Mindy Roberts" years earlier without bothering to make it official. She asked the court to officially change her name to "Roberts" because "it is and can be a source of embarrassment for Petitioner's [Leona's] legal name to be different from the name by which she is known and which she uses."

Consequently, Harry's signature on the five-dollar wedding license appeared next to that of Leona Mindy Roberts—not Leona Mindy Rosenthal.

As the day approached, excitement was palpable. Leona and her sister Sandra scurried to Tiffany's to shop for Leona's wedding silver, recalls one of Leona's longtime acquaintances. Sandra grew impatient with an inattentive salesman and scolded him: "Don't you realize who this is? Her future husband owns the Empire State Building!"

On the afternoon of April 8, 1972, Leona Mindy Roberts and Harry Brakmann Helmsley became man and wife in a simple ten-minute ceremony performed in the living room of the Park Lane penthouse. For her third wedding day, Leona wore a beige organdy dress accented by a satin bow and a long double strand of pearls with matching earrings. Harry dressed as soberly as ever, in a dark suit with a striped gray tie. Below, in Central Park, another transition—between winter and spring—could be seen in the form of millions of buds. Only a handful of guests were invited to witness State Supreme Court Judge Theodore Kupferman perform the nuptials. They included Helmsley's 57-year-old brother, Walter, and his wife, Terry. Also present were Leona's older sister, Sandra, and her husband, Jerry Kaufman.

Conspicuously absent was Leona's son, Jay, and her three grandchildren. Also missing were the bride's brother, Alvin, and eldest sister, Sylvia. Her mother had died a year or two earlier.

After the exchange of vows, the tiny gathering sampled finger sandwiches and sipped champagne before repairing to the La Forêt room of the Pierre Hotel for dinner and dancing. There, one witness recalled, "the mood was relief that they made it. Leona wanted it so badly. Certainly she realized she had become a multi-multimillionairess. She accomplished it at that earlier moment." For the rest of the evening, the newly-weds "danced like the First Couple."

Leona's fairest fairy-tale dreams were coming true. "All my life I wanted to go on a cruise in a chiffon dress with my hair blowing," she once said. Using a check instead of fairy dust, Harry made the dream come true by renting a 136-foot yacht for their honeymoon. As the vessel left port for the Greek Islands, Leona Mindy Helmsley had to know her ship had come in.

Six

The sumptuous Park Lane penthouse was like none Leona had ever seen or sold in her real estate career. And now the new Mrs. Helmsley, still tanned from her honeymoon cruise, could call it home. With over 10,000 square feet of space, the apartment was truly gigantic—five times the size of Leona's previous aerie at the Gallery House.

Leona acquainted herself with the rooftop pool on the forty-seventh floor, as well as an outdoor terrace that wrapped around the north, west and east sides of the hotel. Yet, as grand as the layout was, it did not suit the new lady of the penthouse. It was devoid of color, reflecting Eve Helmsley's unadorned taste. "It was furnished like a hotel," recalled one visitor, "just basic, nothing really decorative. Leona, who is a rather vivacious individual, decided to make it pretty.

"The pool area," the visitor said, was her biggest priority. "It was utilitarian, more like a gymnasium, with just a pool, yellow brick walls, and a terra-cotta floor. She wanted to make it homey." To the rescue came Clyde Wachsberger, a 27-year-old

Manhattan artist whose stock in trade is trompe l'oeil art, especially phantasmagoric murals. Leona summoned him to the duplex and pointed out the bare front wall of the pool area. "She asked me to create something in a fanciful style as a focal point for the room—nothing realistic or formal," Wachsberger recalled. "It was a recreation area, and she wanted it to be a lighthearted area where she and her husband could spend casual time. She wanted it to be fantasy, childlike and playful. And she wanted it in bold, primary colors of red, yellow and green. Almost comic-book colors."

Using layers of plexiglass for three-dimensional effect, Wachsberger created a tall, bebopping Manhattan skyline, dominated by the Empire State Building, the Flatiron Building and other Helmsley landmarks. "There were yellow taxicabs with wings on them as if they were flying creatures. Buildings were transformed into botanical elements. They became almost floral patterns." And in homage to Central Park below, "Mrs. Helmsley asked me to include Wollman Rink." As Leona had hoped, the mural breathed life and personality into the nondescript space. "Mr. and Mrs Helmsley were extremely pleased."

Before dismissing the artist, Leona asked him to perform similar magic on a wall that abutted the spiral staircase leading to the pool terrace. "She said, 'I'd like something here, something romantic.'" Wachsberger suggested that he draw a matching balustrade on the wall, adding Central Park lampposts, and foliage fading off into the distance. To the artist's surprise, Mrs. Helmsley pleaded, "Can you have it by next Friday, because Mayor [John] Lindsay is coming for dinner?" Already, politicos and captains of commerce were making their way to Harry Helmsley's door to personally congratulate the tycoon and his newlywed wife. Leona Helmsley, the rough-and-tumble broker, had reached an elegant new plateau with attendant social obligations. Wachsberger assured her, and completed the dreamscape in time.

Color, and lots of it, meanwhile, was also desperately needed downstairs in the huge L-shaped living room. With time on her hands, Leona rummaged through antique stores in search of the perfect carpet. Nothing was big enough or spirited enough. Finally, after finding a tattered Aubusson rug with the perfect floral design and combination of colors, she ordered Scalamandré Custom Carpets of Manhattan to create a giant copy of the French sample. A detailed artist's drawing of the design was sent to Scalamandré's mill in Hong Kong. Nine months later the handmade carpet—at least twenty-two feet long and dominated by shades of rose—was delivered. The finished creation was worth the wait, one visitor recalled. "That carpet was her main objective, and it was a beautiful copy that virtually filled the living room." The pellucid northern rays from Central Park highlighted each of its twenty-five colors, setting the Helmsleys afloat on a pastel sea. Once again, and in steady progression, Leona was brightening up Harry's life.

She complicated it, however, by filing a lawsuit, with Harry as co-plaintiff, against one of the companies involved in the penthouse spruce-up. It was a flashback to two years earlier, when Leona, while dating Harry, filed suit against a carpenter for allegedly botching renovations to her Gallery House apartment. This time, in 1973, Leona went to battle against a Queens firm, Marshall Construction Co., which had been hired to modify three closets in the Park Lane aerie. Trouble began when the firm completed the job and submitted its $6,900 bill. The Helmsleys refused to pay. The construction company, using a time-honored collection strategy, then filed a mechanic's lien against the penthouse. Leona retaliated by filing suit in state court, accusing the firm of using inferior materials and overcharging her by $3,400. She also alleged that the firm submitted "grossly exaggerated and inflated bills" in connection with subsequent work. In all, the Helmsleys demanded $600,000—$100,000 in compensatory damages, with interest, and $500,000 in punitive damages. Tempers eventually cooled, however, and the case was settled out of court.

Once she had surrendered her real estate license to state authorities, some of the energy Leona had burned for years in work had to be channeled in other directions. She lived only a half block off Fifth Avenue, so shopping was a natural outlet. And Harry, unlike Leona's earlier husbands, opened the purse strings. Clothes became a major priority, recalled one acquaintance. "Leona went wild with clothes after she married Harry. She was terribly interested in being social. She was making her entrance and needed a wardrobe. Dresses were being made daily. Everything was custom made—nothing off the rack." Luckily, she had discovered a talented Cuban dressmaker, Julia, who was happy to make the same dress in half a dozen colors. The fittings were fast and efficient "because Leona had been a model and knew what she wanted. She'd say, 'Julia, make the sleeves bigger. How about a collar? Lower the neckline.' They played with it."

The expensive necklaces she had pined for in the Panzirer and Lubin years were purchased in abundance. "She was always buying jewelry at Van Cleef and Arpels," the swank Fifth Avenue store. "Harry never complained," the acquaintance said. "Leona needed it to go out to parties. She was like a child in a candy store. You suddenly have so much money and you can buy anything you want. She's not a woman who reads many books; materialism was her outlet."

Harry, like Leona, had been too busy or too preoccupied to develop many true pals. Consequently, the couple's immediate social circle was heavily weighted with business associates. But charity events and the party circuit kept the newlyweds in circulation. People noticed that Leona continually hung on to Harry, pampered him, and never let him out of her sight. Such fervent attentions raised eyebrows. "It was so gauche, such poor manners," recalled one socialite. "People just don't comb their husband's hair in public or say, 'Isn't he gorgeous!' It's just not proper." The observer also noted that Leona was unwilling—or unable—to temper her hard-driving broker personality in polite society. She came on as strong as ever. "She'd say, 'Let me tell you!'" And once Leona's closets and jewelry boxes were properly stuffed, she pronounced herself an arbiter of taste. "She would tell other women, 'You should dress this way! This is wrong! Why don't you go to Julia?' She was pushy and insulting."

From the start, dancing was the Helmsleys' favorite sport, a former Helmsley aide said. "When they went to other people's houses, the first thing they wanted to do was dance. They would get up and dance in the living room, to a radio if necessary. She always wanted to dance with Harry, and he loved it." The aide said it was such a habit that "I assumed it was their way of trying to get away from people and avoiding discussions." He said Helmsley "never cared about being social" during his first marriage, and perhaps felt awkward at parties. "Dancing kept them busy for a while."

Dancing and shopping, however diverting, were merely pastimes. Leona must have missed the hum and rattle of the real estate business. Although her sales license was on ice, she paid occasional visits to her cozy nook at Brown, Harris, Stevens. Ann Heywood, a former broker at the Helmsley subsidiary, recalled Leona's first appearance after marrying the boss. "She came in with a diamond as big as a house and a lot of necklaces and chains. She was gathering all kinds of jewelry and parading it in front of everyone. She wanted us to know she got the prize. It was a triumph for her." Heywood, however, was more amused than impressed. "It reminded me of the joke about Mrs. Shapiro, the lady with a huge diamond, who says her diamond has a curse on it: *Mr. Shapiro.* Leona had to live with Harry, who would not have been my cup of tea. He was a man strictly interested in acquiring money."

Another former broker said Leona sequestered herself upstairs when she visited the firm. "She was compiling lists or something, but I don't think she sold any real estate. She always had vast lists of names—boxes and boxes of names of business contacts. She would follow up with them so they would remember her. She just wanted to have a little power of her own and a place where she could keep up her contacts. She didn't want to be a housewife, regardless of how grand the home. She wanted to be outside." Leona seldom strayed down to the third floor, however, where most of her ex-colleagues worked. It seemed sad, the broker said, that Leona didn't reach out to them. "If I had lost my license, I'd want a few friends. I'd want to have a few brokers friendly and speaking to me. But that wasn't Leona's way. She worked absolutely alone and secretly. She was always a loner."

Although she conducted little if any official business at Brown, Harris, Stevens, at home Leona quickly became one of Harry's most valued advisers. Unlike his former wife, Leona had the background, the interest and the real estate lingo to follow Harry's beloved deals. "Harry often told me that he could talk to Leona twenty-four hours a day on business and that there were few people he could do that with, particularly women," recalled one key former aide. "So there was a strong practical side to their marriage."

Although she had few formal duties, when the need arose, Harry designated Leona as his troubleshooter. One of her first assignments, according to a former senior Helmsley aide, was to investigate a kickback scam that had been discovered within Helmsley-Spear's purchasing department. The aide said "old timers" in the department had been taking kickbacks from a stationery vendor, and in turn "fixing prices and paying for about $1.5 million worth of stationery that was never delivered. If it had been delivered it would have filled up the whole building." The aide said he had warned Helmsley eighteen months earlier that there were no internal cost controls at Helmsley-Spear, but the mogul brushed off his warnings. "Then it blew up, and that's when Leona got involved." He said Leona ordered one Helmsley subsidiary, Owners Maintenance Corporation, "to give her a list of all vendors they bought stationery from, and a sample of each product." In a short time, the aide said, "the nest was cleaned out and the crooked vendor was fired," although the value of Leona's detective work was unclear.

A short time later, the aide said, "Two or three female bookkeepers walked away with a couple of hundred thousand dollars from Helmsley-Spear," and were caught. He said it was ironic that Helmsley was a bloodhound property manager, who could spot at a glance whether a dollar was wasted maintaining any given building. But when it came to cost controls within a score of Helmsley-Spear administrative offices scattered around the country, "Harry could be a dupe. Sure, he could look at a report and say, 'The Empire State Building's electric bill was higher this month than last.' That's not difficult. But one of his own little bookkeepers slipping five thousand dollars into her personal account—he can't see that unless it's brought to his attention."

Harry sought Leona's expertise again in the summer of 1972, another former top aide recalled, concerning his plan to convert to condominiums the first four thousand apartments of his Parkchester complex in the Bronx. Leona called a meeting of several brokers and top Helmsley-Spear executives "to give them sales pointers since she was a conversion expert." The aide said Leona had given a similar sales talk six months earlier, before marrying Harry, "when she was a regular broker at Brown, Harris, Stevens." He said the executives noticed "a somewhat dramatic change in her attitude now that she was Mrs. Helmsley. Once she was in that exalted position, her treatment of people changed. During the earlier meeting she was subdued; she was the listener. Now she was the talker at the head of the conference table. She would stand up to make a point. She knew she was the power. The soft edges disappeared. Her tone changed from conciliatory to contemptuous. She singled out people and made them uncomfortable. She would unnerve or embarrass a person. She might say, 'I don't know why you're selling. You don't belong in this business!' She would insult you on the basis of what you were wearing. 'You should lose weight. You're getting fat!' " The aide said he saw the handwriting on the wall. "I knew then that she was going to be a much tougher and harder person—a different person." Leona also projected the forceful image during periodic inspections of her husband's Manhattan hotels, including the Park Lane, her home base; the St. Moritz; and the smaller Carlton House, Windsor and Wyndham.

Her work assignments were relatively few, however. There was plenty of time to relax, and she convinced her aging husband to also slow down a bit after forty-seven years of empire building. Beginning in February 1973, the Helmsleys began flying to Palm Beach almost every other weekend to enjoy the sun. They moved into a penthouse of the Palm Beach Towers, a sprawling Florida hotel that Helmsley had converted to three hundred condominiums that year. The six-story complex, located near the center of the exclusive resort island, was a dream retreat. Their penthouse directly overlooked Lake Worth, the waterway that separates Palm Beach from the mainland. With a five-minute hike to the other side of the island, past the golf course of The Breakers hotel, they could plunge into the Atlantic surf. But there was no need to leave home. Each morning the Helmsleys would churn out laps, forty at a time, in their condominium's teardrop-shaped outdoor pool. Harry was a lifelong swimmer, and Leona had enthusiastically taken up the sport both to keep him company and for its health benefits. After drying off, they could stroll in the gardens in the shade of giant royal palms and enjoy an ocean breeze perfumed by yellow roses, fuchsias and mango trees. Other elderly residents, quite likely in white safari hats, might happen along by foot or bicycle.

The penthouse was a simple affair compared to the Helmsleys' Manhattan duplex, with one bedroom, a small dining room and a glass-enclosed sun porch. "The furniture wasn't gorgeous, just mass-produced everything," recalled one guest. "And there were atrocious plastic flowers all around." Décor could slide because the natural scenery was sublime. The apartment's grandest feature was an enormous rooftop terrace, carpeted with astroturf. White umbrella tables and lounge chairs were sprinkled around a much used barbecue pit. With its view of Lake Worth, the terrace was like the topside of a giant ship, graced by an authentic captain's wheel which Helmsley loved to show off.

Besides swimming, dancing was the activity for the weekending couple. "Palm Beach has more dance bands than any other city in the U.S.," claims Vern Casanave, a hoofer who has taught his skills for twenty years to the cream of local society. "The people who retire here—New Yorkers, Chicagoans, Philadelphians—grew up in the ballroom era where they did the cha-chas and merengues." He said Harry and Leona glided into his Palm Beach dance studio in 1973, wanting to expand their repertoire. "Harry was already a better-than-average dancer, and wanted to dance all the time. Leona really followed him very well. They were interested in learning all the dances, the Latin and swing." Casanave noted that Harry had brought his first wife, Eve, for lessons in earlier years when they visited town. "Eve was pretty good, too, but was a quiet, Midwestern type. I guess you might say Leona was better. Leona's outgoing and a leader." At hot spots like the Ta-Boo Lounge on Worth Avenue, Harry and Leona could practice their steps to a live orchestra without a trace of self-consciousness. Millionaires are a dime a dozen on the island, and many a couple far better known than the Helmsleys was politely ignored. And unlike Eve, who tired at 9 P.M., Leona could keep up the pace well into the wee hours. All of a sudden, Harry was a man revived. In a decade known for its teenage disco ducks, at 64 he was a foxtrot firebird burning up the night.

Occasionally, the Helmsleys took vacations to Las Vegas with Leona's sister, Sandra, and her husband, Jerry Kaufman. The newlyweds also spent frequent weekends at the Delray Beach, Florida, home of Walter and Terry Helmsley. (Walter had retired in 1966, at the age of 51, as vice president and treasurer of Helmsley-Spear.) Then, in their second year of marriage, relatives and close business associates noticed a change in the Helmsleys' social pattern. Although Leona had opened up Harry's personality and kept him in the party circuit, she began shutting out his closest acquaintances and associates. "She started taking over Harry's personal life," said one of the tycoon's closest former aides. "Harry didn't have many friends to begin with, but anyone who was close went. Gradually, she got rid of everyone," including golfers he had stayed in touch with from his days at the Sleepy Hollow Country Club in Westchester County. The aide, who was among those pushed aside, said Leona "was smart enough not to drop us overnight. She had to wait until she established her position as Mrs. Helmsley. I think she planned to do it all along, just like she planned to marry Harry." The aide said Leona soon felt at ease scolding Harry "for hardly anything. If he said the smallest thing she wasn't pleased with, she would go into a wild tangent. She would become hysterical. She wanted it *her way*." Rather than argue, Harry would defuse the outbursts with a gentle "All right, darling." Nor did he offer any great protests as Leona played social director, screening out his former associates.

A close relative said Leona also began restricting contacts with her family, including sisters Sandra and Sylvia, as if "to keep them away from Harry. She was very jealous of anyone being near him." Another relative said he got Leona's cold shoulder even sooner, "immediately after the marriage," and watched as she spun an ever tighter cocoon around her potentate. Yet, he empathized somewhat. "If you married a megamillionaire, don't you think all your relatives would be calling you up asking for a favor? Maybe she didn't want anybody to take advantage of her and take a piece of him." But the kinsman criticized Leona's harsh approach. "By shutting us out with the rest of the world, she forgot about the people that once helped her. She didn't feel like she owed a lot of people anything." One of Leona's most effective ways of shunning familiar faces "was to stay on the run, away from us," and the constant trips to Palm Beach filled the bill nicely.

Between Thanksgiving and Christmas, wealthy snowbirds begin flocking to Palm Beach for the winter, quadrupling its off-season population of 10,000. In 1973, that first year in their resort penthouse, the Helmsleys were in town on Saturday, November 24, at the start of the great influx. They stayed in for the evening while, across town, old-timers at the Ta-Boo danced on without them in the mock-Polynesian lounge. The night was still young at 1:03 A.M. when a police dispatcher got the call from a telephone operator at the Palm Beach Towers complex.

Within seconds, a squad car and fire-department first-aid squad were dispatched to 44 Cocoanut Row, Apartment A514, in response to a report of a stabbing. Harry Helmsley met two policemen at his doorway and stated that he had been stabbed in the lower right arm and that his wife was also stabbed. The apartment was dark as a tomb, with no power or lights. It was a clear evening, and by moonlight filtering inside, Patrolman S. R. Scott carefully steered his way through the penthouse. Another investigator, meanwhile, discovered that all the circuit breaker switches in the kitchen electrical panel had been flipped to the "off" position. When he switched them back on, Officer Scott saw Leona Helmsley lying on her bed, stabbed in the upper left breast. The room was splattered with blood and the area around the bed was covered with upholstery tacks. Red spots dotted the tiled floor, and the wires of two telephones in the bedroom and bathroom area had been snipped. A six-inch-long white cylindrical object, labeled "Paralyzing Tear Gas," was on the floor near the telephone night stand. As first aid was administered to his wife, Helmsley explained that they had retired at 11:15 P.M., and Leona was awakened by a dark shape leaning over her. Harry reached over, pushed the figure away, and went after it. The person fled, but Helmsley said he was able to knock it down at the door of the bedroom, near the television. His wife, meanwhile, joined the chase. It was here, Helmsley reported, that both he and his wife were stabbed by the intruder, who had gotten up again. He pursued the figure to where the hallway met the living room, only to see the intruder escape through the apartment's front door. Helmsley recalled seeing "a flash of light" at that moment, although the penthouse remained dark. He gave up the chase when he heard his wife cry out for help. He tried to turn on the lights, but they didn't work; the bedroom telephones were dead. He went to the living room and tried the lights, to no avail. Luckily, he told the two cops, the telephone did work, and he called the building operator to summon aid.

The Helmsleys were rushed by ambulance to Good Samaritan Hospital in West Palm Beach. Doctors, fearing a possible lung puncture and internal bleeding, went to work on Leona's $1\frac{1}{2}$-inch-wide wound. Surgery went smoothly and she was admitted in serious condition to the intensive care unit. Harry's injuries were limited to cuts on his right forearm. After receiving a dozen quick stitches and paying his $28 emergency-room bill, he was out the door.

A half dozen detectives and police officers, meanwhile, continued to search the Helmsley apartment, exterior hallways, stairwells and the landscaped grounds. Not a clue could be found. The areas were rechecked at 3:10 A.M. with negative results. Mr. Helmsley was then reinterviewed, and repeated the same story, adding a few new details. He now recalled that the intruder's face appeared to have been that of a black female, that she had "reddish, streaked" hair and was wearing a white dress, like a maid's uniform. The hair was especially memorable. "It reminded him of a maid that recently worked for him, named 'Chi Chi,'" the police report said. Finally, at 11:02 A.M., detectives found their first lead: an eight-inch knife was spotted on the lawn fourteen feet south of the building. The knife, bearing the brand name "Sabatier" on its blade, was smeared with blood. Significantly, it matched a set of black-handled knives in one of the Helmsleys' kitchen drawers.

At 1 P.M., twelve hours after the stabbing, Mrs. Helmsley agreed to be interviewed in her hospital room. Her description of the attack was similar to her husband's earlier statement, but with frightful new details. According to the police report, Mrs. Helmsley stated that "she woke up screaming when someone wearing a 'World War gas mask' with big eyes" hovered over her. "She heard the subject speak, saying 'All right, I'm going. Leave me alone.' " Although it was obscured by the gas mask, Mrs. Helmsley said she believed the intruder's face was that of a black female. She recalled that her husband hit the intruder, and that the person fled with Harry and herself in pursuit. Only seconds later, Leona recalled, the intruder stabbed her near the bedroom television, and later slashed Harry. As for the mysterious tear gas cylinder found on the bedroom floor, Mrs. Helmsley said it did not belong to her. Finally, Leona speculated that the attacker "could have been someone who worked for her, but she is not sure," according to the police report. The interview was terminated when "Mrs. Helmsley stated she could not continue. She was sedated and getting tired and sleepy." In a subsequent hospital interview, Mrs. Helmsley added the gas mask had large "glass" eyepieces, greenish in color, that the intruder had an "educated or English accent," and might have been wearing gloves.

Despite the Helmsleys' wealth, their stabbings were given only the scantiest mention in the local newspapers. On November 29, the *Sun Sentinel* noted that Mrs. Helmsley was recovering quickly from her wound. The newspaper listed her age as 42. Her hospital chart, by contrast, accurately pegged her at 53. The Palm Beach *Post*, in a six-paragraph item, noted that the intruder ran as soon as the Helmsleys woke up and that nothing was stolen. Kathryn Robinette, then an editor at the *Post*, said the stabbings were barely mentioned because "the Helmsleys weren't known. They're still not in the social scene. They made no attempt to make a social splash." Although downplayed, she said the incident "was curious because stabbings aren't that common here." Sergeant William Cypher, one of the investigators at the scene, recalled that the case was unusual for another reason. "You don't see many burglars using knives. If a burglar is coming in, normally he has a gun. A knife, you have to be close up; a gun, you don't."

The police report theorized that "whoever was in the apartment must have had keys to the two locks on the front door," because there was no sign of forced entry. Therefore, three maids who had worked for the Helmsleys in the previous year were located and questioned. Only one seemed to match the description. On the afternoon of November 26, detectives knocked on her door in nearby Lake Worth. They were greeted by a dark-complexioned, 61-year-old woman with reddish hair. She stood only five foot three, a full foot shorter than Helmsley, her would-be combatant. The former maid confirmed that her nickname was "Chi Chi" and that she had worked for the Helmsleys for nine months, quitting approximately six weeks before the stabbing. She said she left after learning the couple "were looking for someone else and were not satisfied with her work, and [anyway] she was planning to retire from work entirely." The petite suspect asserted that she had no keys to the Helmsley penthouse because she had left them "in the apartment with a note" explaining her reasons for leaving. Furthermore, she said she was at home with her husband the night of the stabbing.

According to the police report, Chi Chi then gave police a few particulars concerning the Helmsleys' lifestyle. "[The maid] stated that the [Helmsleys] were not generally on the best of terms personally and did have quarrels from time to time which she states varied in intensity. She also mentioned a drinking problem in relation to Mrs. Helmsley, but was not specific." She could not recall, however, the Helmsleys ever exchanging blows "or any other sort of attack" during their arguments. Apparently satisfied with her answers, police made no further contact with Chi Chi. The chief suspect was off the hook.

That evening, they interviewed Hank Boettcher, maintenance manager of the Palm Beach Towers complex. His response no doubt cast a heavy cloud of skepticism over the Helmsleys' account. "Boettcher indicated that he was fully aware of the reported incident, and said he had theories of his own," the police report stated. Boettcher added *that he did not believe anyone entered the apartment.*" Combined with Chi Chi's information about arguments and drinking, the theory of a strictly domestic dispute could not be ignored. Results from the Dade County Crime Laboratory, moreover, provided no clues whatsoever. No fingerprints were found in the house or on the knife, and a blood swab from the blade was inconclusive. On February 14, 1974, the investigation was closed because "all leads have been proven false." The police report concluded, "Any charge based on an internal or personal conflict between the [Helmsleys] as husband/wife would not be entertained or pursued due to the inability of having one testify against the other."

A former supervisor of the condominium complex who worked closely with Helmsley said Harry and Leona's account "just didn't look right. There were just too many things that didn't add up," especially the burglar overkill: gas mask, snipped phone wires, tripped electrical circuits, abandoned tear gas canister and the upholstery tacks, presumably sprinkled on the floor by the intruder to prevent the couple from giving chase. (Indeed, neither the police report nor the emergency room report cites any injury to either of the Helmsleys' feet.) It was like an amateur stage set of the perfect burglary. "If I was going to burglarize a place," the ex-supervisor said, "I wouldn't go to all that trouble. I'd just hit and run." Strangest of all, with such a *Mission Impossible* bag of disguises and tricks, the "intruder" somehow forgot to bring along his or her own weapon. The ex-supervisor speculated, "It could have been an argument that got out of hand. It would have been unlike Harry, but everybody has their point of stress."

Could Harry Helmsley, the gentle tycoon, have stabbed Leona? It was a question very much deliberated among Leona's family. In fact, one close relative recalled, "It was our first thought because he had such a little scratch on his arm. The family actually believed it. Look at all the bullshit this guy puts up with. Is she the most lovely person you ever met in your life? You wake up one morning and you say, 'I'm married to this woman. She's going to ruin my life.' " The relative said many family members followed the theory to an intriguing conclusion: "If Harry did stab her, she instantly gets leverage over him. Then she can say: 'Harry, you tried to kill me. If you don't walk the line, you're through!' It's not so farfetched."

The stabbing, however thought-provoking, had an unmistakable silver lining. It brought Leona and her son, Jay Panzirer, back together again after more than five years of cold silence. According to one in-law, "Jay flew to his mother's side after the stabbing. The only thing that brought him back was that he was a nice Jewish boy from the Bronx and he thought his mother was near death." Upon hearing the burglary scenario, the relative said, Jay reached his own conclusion. "He always maintained that it was Harry that stabbed her." Mother and son had much to talk about. Jay had divorced and given Myrna custody of their three children. (She eventually took them to live in Staten Island after marrying a local businessman.) Footloose and free, Jay had moved to Marina del Rey, a Los Angeles suburb, where he was making a modest income selling fabrics. He could also update his mother on his own health problems. Earlier that year, in 1973, he had suffered a mild heart attack, the relative said. Soon afterward, the 31-year-old salesman was hospitalized again in California for a second, massive coronary. "He was in bed for months listening to his heart go beep, beep, beep, waiting for it not to go beep one time. He said it was an excruciating ordeal he wouldn't go through again. Doctors were afraid the next one would kill him." Jay's diagnosis was arrhythmia, an alteration in rhythm of the heartbeat caused by short-circuiting electrical impulses.

From the moment Jay returned to her side, the in-law said, "Leona wouldn't risk losing him again." And one of the best ways to preserve the bond was to bring him into the family business. A new Helmsley subsidiary, Deco Purchasing Company, was created as his springboard into the empire. The company, incorporated in Florida on May 3, 1974 (with Leona's Palm Beach penthouse as its temporary headquarters), would make bulk purchases of furnishings and supplies to be used in approximately forty hotels owned or managed by Harry Helmsley. In addition to a half dozen Manhattan hotels, over the years Helmsley had acquired approximately a dozen others around the country, including the Colonial Plaza in Orlando and the Sandcastle in Sarasota. When a national recession began in the early 1970s, moreover, banks and insurance companies convinced Helmsley to manage dozens of hotels they had acquired through foreclosure. Rather than continuing to buy furnishings piecemeal for the mixed bag of individual properties, Deco would buy for everyone at discount. The centralized purchasing concept made economic sense; in fact, one-stop shopping was standard procedure for major hotel chains.

Leona decided to create Deco to bring Jay into the fold," recalled one of Helmsley's top former hotel aides, and she saw to it that he was named a Deco vice president and its primary purchasing officer. (Harry took the title of president.) "I think Mrs. Helmsley felt tremendously guilty for the years she let slide by without him, and it was her way of trying to make amends. And without a doubt, Jay appreciated it." It was a convenient setup because Jay did not have to leave Los Angeles immediately. Using sales contacts there, he could place orders for draperies, fabrics and other materials, and have them shipped to the various far-flung hotels. Jay knew, however, that eventually he would be spending a great deal of time on the East Coast because of a behemoth project still on Harry's drawing board. Word had leaked out two months earlier that Helmsley was negotiating with the Archdiocese of New York to lease the landmark Villard Houses on Madison Avenue. By getting the air rights over the U-shaped cluster of Italian Renaissance brownstones, the *New York Times* reported on May 15, Helmsley hoped "to erect a 50-story luxury hotel behind them."

The ambitious scheme was a pivotal, and well-thought-out, move. Helmsley had decided to focus his future energies on hotels and to forget about buying more residential properties. New York's residential rent control laws had become the bane of his existence. They limited the amount of income he could derive from his tens of thousands of apartments and forced him into pitched legal battles with tenants. At Parkchester, tenants were bucking his conversion plan, while some rents were frozen below $100, the tab for a night's stay at a good Manhattan hotel. At Tudor City, his apartment complex near the United Nations, tenants received wide publicity as they demonstrated against Helmsley's plan to build over their two cherished parks. John McKean, who has been president of the Tudor City Tenants Association since 1971, recalls that residents also publicly attacked Helmsley "for refusing to maintain the buildings. He was the world's worst landlord and one of the cheapest. All he wanted to do was collect the rent." One of the sorest complaints, McKean said, was over Helmsley's decision to eliminate the gardener in 1972. "Helmsley just let him go and never replaced him," forcing the tenants to repair fences and cut their own grass.

So, to escape such embarrassments and to enable his investments to adjust more quickly to inflation, Helmsley turned to hotels. Unlike rent-controlled apartments, hotel rates could be raised as high and as often as he saw fit.

The archdiocese had acquired the Villard Houses in 1948 and had used the complex for twenty-five years as its administrative offices, but had recently vacated them for new quarters in a twenty-story building on First Avenue. Now, according to the *Times*, the abandoned brownstones would return to life as an entranceway to a 1,000-room hotel. "Mr. Helmsley said construction would begin as soon as the lease details were finalized." Preservationists, however, took one look at architectural renderings of the proposed hotel tower and declared war. Bronze-tinted windows and vertical piers running the height of the tower, they protested, would overpower the muted brownstones. Such stylistic debates were no small matter in the Big Apple. They could take years to settle.

In the meantime, with the birth of Deco, Jay could plan for the future. His job celebration coincided with another trip down the wedding aisle. According to a relative, his second bride, Ruth, was a California real estate broker whom he had met while house hunting. They exchanged wedding vows on June 21, 1974, in Santo Domingo, and continued to live in the Los Angeles area.

Harry Helmsley was in no condition, however, to join in the celebration. His younger brother and only close relative, Walter, had died three weeks before in Delray Beach, Florida, at 59. Walter's death, at a relatively young age, was as shocking as that of his wife, Terry, who had died a short while earlier. But Eve Helmsley, who had known the couple well, said the two deaths were no great surprise to her. "Walter and his wife both spoke about not wanting to get old. They said, 'We don't want to live that long.' They looked around and saw old people who staggered around looking terrible. Walter thought it was just stupid to go on and on and on."

Harry was the end of the Helmsley line. He had absolutely nobody left, save Leona, to call family.

Despite the stabbings, Harry and Leona continued to visit Palm Beach virtually every other weekend. A former supervisor of their condominium complex noticed that the couple rebounded quickly from the bloody episode. "Everything was milk and honey between them." In fact, he said, "It seemed to be better than before. They seemed more compatible, more lovey dovey." (In later years, Leona would proudly point to her scar like a war wound and boast of beating the Grim Reaper. "I heard a brook gurgling," she told one reporter, "but it wasn't a brook. It was me." And Harry's injury would be exaggerated, from a dozen stitches to thirty-six.) The couple continued to enjoy dancing on Worth Avenue, but otherwise spent time alone in their penthouse. Mornings, they would march down to the outdoor pool and exercise. Perhaps spoiled by her private swims in New York, Leona preferred to arrive early to have the pool to herself for laps. One morning in 1974, two other wives were already taking up plenty of room in the water.

"You have to learn how to breathe! Don't hold your stomach in," said one—a hardy, gray-haired woman—to the other. Leona waited patiently for the pair to end their swim lesson, and then called out from her lounge chair to the instructor: "How do you breathe like that?" Obligingly, Blanche Slauson went through the routine again for the stranger's benefit. Afterwards, Slauson recalled, "She introduced herself as Lee Helmsley, and we had a good long conversation. I was talking to her about health and nutrition, and I could tell that was her big thing." Slauson, like everyone else in the complex, already knew of Leona Helmsley. "Everybody was embarrassed to talk to her because she was the wife of Harry. He was the one who turned this place into a condo. He was powerful. Everybody knew him and adored him, but they didn't adore her. Some people knew her from New York. She was cold. She didn't talk to anyone; nobody talked to her. Everybody moved away from her."

But Leona talked to Slauson, and Slauson didn't move away. That very evening, Slauson recalled, "I was looking out my window and saw her downstairs. I said, 'Lee! What are you doing?' She was walking all alone. She was a lonely person in those days. She had no friends here." Slauson invited the new acquaintance upstairs to meet her husband, Cidney, a millionaire from Hackensack, New Jersey, and Leona accepted the offer. Harry, whose plane from New York was just landing, was notified to meet the threesome for dinner at Providencia, a local restaurant. "We all had a wonderful, informal time," Blanche recalled, "and from that time on the Helmsleys liked our company because we didn't kowtow to them. They recognized that we didn't care about money, that it didn't mean a damned thing to us. That's how we were able to become friends with them. Harry Helmsley didn't mean anything to me. I wasn't from New York and didn't know a lot about him. Lee was just an ordinary person to me. And there was no reason for her to befriend me. I had nothing to give her."

Slauson, who once taught in the hardscrabble New York City school system, is an eminently adaptable sort. A luxurious Palm Beach lifestyle feels as natural to her as a crumbling classroom. And her brassy, no-bullshit friendliness rubbed Leona just the right way. "Like begets like," says Cidney, a lean and athletic retired lawyer who still measures his words a second or two in advance. "A great deal of that was present between Blanche and Leona. Blanche is a person who taught emotionally disturbed kids. She opens up to people and they open up to her." Soon, Leona became a constant visitor at Blanche's apartment, as relaxed as could be, resting her flip-flops on all varieties of furniture. "She would come and I might serve nothing more than some chicken and a little salad," Blanche recalls, "and she was happy. She'd put her feet up and say, 'Ya know, Harry, this is better than home.' It never occurred to me that I didn't have the linens or the silver that Lee had; as a matter of fact, I didn't care for it. She felt she could talk to us and be understood on a high level or on a low level." Luckily, the Slausons didn't get stuck in the comparison rut. "Most people," Blanche said, "feel they can't entertain Lee and Harry in the same elaborate way they live in New York with their private swimming pool. They feel they can't match it or reciprocate. In reality, Blanche said, "You must remember that Leona was not to the manner born. She's very happy to be called into one room and sit down and have a drink and enjoy a couple of jokes. One reason she holds herself aloof from other people is because they show her excessive respect or admiration. Sometimes, they cause it."

Often, Leona would raid the Slausons' refrigerator. Or rearrange the décor. "She'll go into the bathroom and say, 'This is good. That's bad. I don't like that shower curtain. I'm going to send you one.' She's like that; she's a human being. She does gauche things. I had a picture of a nude man and woman; the man had a towel around him, and the caption said, 'Shower together—don't waste water.' Well, Lee loved it! She took it off the wall and said, 'Harry, look at this! We ought to have this at all our hotels, in all the rooms.' But I thought it was kind of nervy to take it off my wall. I wouldn't do it in her house. But she loved it! She and Harry had enough money to buy anything, but they liked little clever things." Once, as a gift to Harry, Blanche recalls, "I found an old spittoon, what they used to call pots, before we had bathrooms. It was very beautiful and I thought it would be a nice present, especially because I wrote him a little poem: 'To the man who's got a lot/But has not a pot to you know what.' And Harry thought that was great. We hugged and kissed, and he laughed." In just about everything, she said, the tycoon was "gentle and sweet. He would say, 'I'm a Quaker,' with a twinkle in his eye." According to Quaker records, however, Helmsley's membership in the Fifteenth Street Meeting was dropped around January 1975 "for lack of interest and activity in the meeting."

Leona "has a sense of humor such as I've never seen in a woman," Blanche said. "Sex was nothing to be ashamed of; a lot of four-letter words. And so clever. If you mentioned her name in her presence she might say, 'Now you're on my *favorite subject.*' " Even the stabbing was worthy of a send-up. "She explained how she opened her eyes and saw what she thought was a masked man, and she said, 'Haaaaarrrry. Wake up, we got companeeee.' " More than anything else, Blanche said, Leona was "New York street-wise. It's a kind of tough competitiveness, aggressiveness and smartness. She's unusually smart. She knows how to handle everything. You talk to her and she'll know immediately whether you're motivated by something. She knows. Don't sell her short."

Blanche also noticed a flip side which was not so apparent to other condo residents. "She's a girl who needs friends, who needs to talk to people. She's soft inside. She needs to confide; she needs to cry. That could never change." More often than not, the softness bordered on maudlin sentimentality. "She would tell me anything. Most of the things she told me were sentimental. She always walked around the pool with her arms around me. When we would talk about her family, she would always have tears in her eyes—how hard it was working to support Jay. How she resented her mother, who was so dominant. My friends would say, 'How can you stand her?' and I said, 'She's wonderful.' "

Yet, as much as Leona needed friends, Blanche said, it was also clear that few, if any, remained from the past. They were ejected, or forgotten like Joe Lubin, by the time she married Harry. A shocking case in point, Blanche said, "was a very sophisticated woman from East Hampton [Long Island]" who came looking for Leona one weekend in Palm Beach. "She was elegant, the kind of woman who would have a picnic at the beach and bring champagne and chocolate mousse in a basket with flowers. She designed bras for a big company, and she and Lee were friends while Lee was divorced, and she apparently knew a great deal of what Lee was doing in those years." Instead of welcoming her, "Lee found excuses never to see her." The visitor, confused, "would call people and say 'I don't know what's wrong.' " Finally, she came to Palm Beach Towers and waited patiently at the pool for Leona's arrival, only to be totally ignored. Blanche recognized the woman and pointed her out. "Lee, look who's there! You were such good friends!" Like a block of ice, Blanche said, "Lee turned her back and said,

'We *were* good friends and that's why I don't want to talk to her anymore.' Lee just didn't want Harry to know this girl. The girl knew too much."

Blanche said Leona seldom gave gifts, and when she did, it was often without great enthusiasm. For instance, there was the time Leona prepared to take a trip to the Caribbean, and matter-of-factly asked Blanche, "I guess you want something?" On her return Leona gruffly announced she had honored Blanche's request. "Here's the hat. I had to wear it the whole way so the straw wouldn't get busted."

Leona could also be downright cheap. Harry invited the Slausons up for drinks one night, Blanche recalls, and she eagerly accepted. "I'd love to come up to your house," she replied, "because you're the only man I know who can afford Dom Perignon." An hour later, the Slausons arrived, "and they had a table full of hors d'oeuvres. Lee was quite generous, most of the time, with good food. But then I heard Harry whisper to her, 'We forgot the Dom Perignon; put it on ice.' And Lee whispered back, 'Oh, that's all right. They won't know the difference.' And they gave us some other kind of drink. I resented that. I thought it was a little tight; I always felt she was a little tight, but not Harry. He's generous. He really is. Maybe not in business, but socially he is."

Yet, when it came to matters of health, Leona could be generous and thoughtful. Like a Jewish mother, she fussed over the diets of her new friends, Cidney and Blanche, urging them to spurn salt, sugar, fats and cholesterol. "One afternoon," Blanche said, "Lee told me I wasn't eating the proper food, that I should be eating health food. So she disappeared and came back fifteen minutes later with arms full of salt-free crackers and carrot sticks." Another time, at a party, Blanche said she noticed Leona was serving "great big hot dogs, and I thought she wouldn't be serving hot dogs. And I said, 'Lee, how come?' And she said, 'These are special; they're made of veal and there's almost no fat in them. I have five hundred pounds made at a time and freeze them for the whole year.' I ate one and it was fabulous, much better than a hot dog. And I raved about it ." The very next weekend, Leona brought Blanche a shipment of the low-fat delicacies, along with a can of sauerkraut. "She said, 'Because you like it.' "

Leona's ministrations to Harry disproved Eve Helmsley's theory that that "floozy" Leona wanted him to hurry up and die. "Lee took his blood pressure every day and made sure he had his vitamins at the breakfast table," Blanche recalled. "It wasn't just his money and power; she loved him. She took the best possible care of him. She would make him laugh. She was like a little girl with him. Her pet name for him was Herschel, which is Jewish for Harry. She always called him Herschel and he smiled. They ate well and felt well. She made soup out of fifteen vegetables and a half cup of water. Lemon pie without sugar. Marvelous Thanksgiving turkey without salt." For breakfast, no cholesterol-laden eggs and bacon. "They'd have marinated snapper or pompano."

It was also obvious to the Slausons who stood where in the relationship. "Lee knows that Harry is the smart one in business," Cidney said. "He's the decision maker there. But he takes leadership from her in the emotional area," soaking up pet names such as "Pookey," "Lookie," "Gorgeous," and "Schnookey," and letting her dominate conversations and social settings.

The Helmsleys and Slausons would be seen everywhere together—sometimes with Harry stealing the show with his strawberry-colored sport coat. The foursome frolicked on the beach, sipped piña coladas and traded barbs like high school buddies. They munched carrot sticks together, instead of popcorn, at movies in the mall theater in West Palm Beach. Perhaps nobody knew the Helmsleys better than the Hackensack couple.

Earlier that year, Leona had compiled a list of the two hundred richest and most famous New Yorkers and invited them to celebrate Harry's birthday at the Park Lane. It was a bold gesture because few of the notables could have known her. But they knew Harry, or knew of him, and came in droves. That was the first of Leona's annual "I'm Just Wild About Harry" parties. Festivities always started in the penthouse with champagne and caviar as gardenias and votive lights bobbled in the swimming pool. Toward dinner time, the partygoers would move downstairs to the ballroom and wait for the grand moment. Harry and Leona would then burst into the room like Fred Astaire and Ginger Rogers while a fourteen-piece orchestra blared Eubie Blake's "I'm Just Wild About Harry." Beginning the next year, in 1975, the Slausons were expected to join in the fun each March with such regulars as Barbara and Frank Sinatra, Mary and Laurance Rockefeller, Kitty Carlisle Hart, Charlotte Ford and a host of past and contemporary mayors, governors and ambassadors. "By 4 A.M.," Blanche said, "everyone would be gone, and that's when Harry and Lee would bring out the best food. We'd stay up and sing 'La Marseillaise.' Harry sang every word, like a college kid."

But the best times together were in Palm Beach, Blanche recalls. "One afternoon, Lee called me and said, 'Do you ever go to the dog races?' And I said, 'Yes, we do once in a while.' And she said, 'Let's go tonight!'

"And we went," Blanche said, "and a doorman stopped Harry at the door and said, 'Sir, you can't go in without a tie.' "

"Gosh, I'm here; what am I going to do?," the tycoon replied.

"We have ties to rent," the doorman said, pulling out a long old-fashioned black affair. "You put this on and give me a two-dollar deposit, and on your way out you return the tie and get your money back." Harry paid up and quickly knotted the vintage cravat.

"We went in and had dinner," Blanche said, "and were having a wonderful time. We're betting and lose the first bet. And after the second bet, the results flash and we assume we've lost that one, too, so we each tear up our little ticket and Lee tore hers into about eight pieces. Then we realize that Lee had won! And she said, 'Well, I want to collect my money!' And Harry said, 'Don't be silly; all you won was about twelve dollars.'

"Well, I won it, and I want it!" Leona insisted.

"You're not going back there, are you?" asked Harry, looking toward the pay window.

"I certainly am!"

Immediately, Blanche said, "Lee went to the booth and told them she had accidentally torn up the ticket and she gave them all the pieces. Well, they said they had to put all the pieces back together and they wouldn't know until the end of the evening whether hers were the proper pieces, because you could always put other pieces together. 'Come back at the end of the races, about 12:30,' " the cashier insisted.

"So we sit down and go through all the races," Blanche continued, "and we lose every race. On the way out, Harry and Cid begin to go out to the car and Lee says, 'I'm going back to get my money.' "

"This is gonna take time," Cid replied. "Let me go get the car." As Harry, Blanche and Cidney headed outdoors, Blanche reminded Helmsley: "Harry, you've got the tie! You want your money back, don't you?"

"Harry took a look at the tie," Blanche said, "and told us, 'You know, I kinda like this tie. I'm gonna keep it.' He was roaring with laughter and he kept the tie. And we loved him for that!"

Meanwhile, Leona was hellbent on collecting her winnings. "She went back to the booth," said Blanche, and it took over forty-five minutes for the cashier to emerge with the good news. "Yes, we can give you your twelve dollars." Leona triumphantly walked outside to the dark, now deserted parking lot with her fistful of dollars. "We were terribly alone out there," Blanche recalled. "It was about 1:30 in the morning."

Cidney Slauson said the outing with his prominent Palm Beach neighbors clearly illustrates two things. "One, there's no phony baloney about Harry. A two-dollar tie? He could buy the most expensive tie in the world. And the thing about Lee is she knew what a dollar was. She worked for it. And here, when she won it, she waited an hour to get her money."

Steven Leitner knew an interesting afternoon was in store. His old pal Leona Roberts had been married to Harry Helmsley for four years, and still he had not properly congratulated the bride. The two former Pease & Elliman brokers had bumped into each other the week before at a charity function, and she read him the riot act. "You never called me to wish me well! That's not how good friends act." Leitner explained he had meant no slight. "I thought it would be inappropriate to impose on a friend with a new life." Nonsense, Leona replied. "Let's meet for lunch next week. We've got a lot to catch up on."

By 1 P.M. on the appointed day in 1976, Leitner had reserved a table at Sea Fare of the Aegean, on West Fifty-sixth Street near Fifth Avenue. As Leitner scanned the menu, a beefy gentleman in a business suit tapped him on the shoulder and announced: "I'm from Mrs. Helmsley, and she'd like to meet you at the Park Lane instead." The pair walked two short blocks to the hotel and took the elevator to the forty-sixth floor. As he entered the sprawling penthouse, Leitner couldn't help but compare it with her cramped one-bedroom apartment of a decade earlier, where Leona had invited him for so many weekend breakfasts.

Once inside, Leona took him by the hand for a grand tour. First, she walked proudly to a shelf of glass figurines and declared, "I'm collecting Steuben." Leitner, himself a collector of art glass, said he pretended to be impressed. "She had pieces that cost two or three thousand dollars and was so proud to be collecting them. She was oohing and aahing over a lump of glass that had been transformed into a transparent elephant. But there was nothing of great artistic merit. They were very kitsch." Next, she escorted him to Harry's closet and said, "What do you think of these?" Harry's tired, bargain-basement suits, the ones from his marriage to Eve, had vanished. In their place Leitner saw "beautiful hung-up coats, so neat and organized; shoes polished with precision and piled up; lizard shoes and white shoes, arrayed on shelves. There was a precision that made it look like a *House and Garden* advertisement. She was proud. I said, 'Just beautiful,' but I thought it showed a very suburban point of view. Like the young suburbanites that buy a new house in Scarsdale and are so proud, and have to show you every nail hole in the wall." As the apartment tour continued, Leitner said, "I felt it was so tragic. This is a woman of 55, so wrapped up in materialistic things of such petty value. It was her exuberance over it all! She didn't have these things before, and now she does. I was embarrassed for her. It was like the Little Match Girl that had become the princess."

But the big show seemed as phony as the costume earrings he once helped Leona select at Jolie Gabor. He had noticed the ostentation the week before at their chance meeting on the charity circuit. "Leona pulled up the sleeve of her dress and showed me a row of one-inch-wide diamonds. And she said, 'What do you think of these?' I said, 'Hello, are these real!' She gave me this drop-dead look and said, 'Of course they're real. I know So-and-so who owns Van Cleef & Arpels. I wouldn't buy anything that wasn't real.'" Then Leona, who was so apt to ignore past friends, introduced Leitner to Harry. "Harry was acting like he was in love with her. 'My wife' this, 'my wife' that. And Leona returned the endearments," Leitner recalls. It was the same tender exchange of "Schnookey-Pookeys" the Slausons so often encountered, but Leitner was skeptical. "I know Leona was trying to show me that the relationship was right. But it seemed to me like it was a marriage of convenience, without passion or real love." For years as a broker, Leitner said, "Leona was looking for real companionship, but I'm not sure she found it with Mr. Helmsley." He still pictured her, almost as beautiful now as before, with someone as debonair and youthful as Willard Malkan, the businessman she had dated a decade earlier.

Off to the side, Leitner commented: "It's unbelievable the things that have happened to you, Leona." And she surprised him by saying, "Things aren't as they seem. Things aren't so wonderful. There's a lot of things that aren't so wonderful."

Leitner avoided prying, but the comment stuck in his mind.

Now, amid the wall-to-wall gloss of the penthouse, Leona betrayed her anxiety once again. "If anything goes wrong, at least I've lived," she said. Leitner was impressed with the remark. "It showed that Leona is much more sophisticated than people think. She knows that she's an enormously wealthy woman riding the crest, like an iceberg, only a little bit exposed, and the tip could go underwater and she could go broke."

Harry Helmsley has a "secure" empire, Leitner said, because he is one of the most cautious investors going. "He's not the type to mortgage one skyscraper to the hilt in order to raise cash to buy two others." (Another titan, the late William Zeckendorf, Sr., went under only a decade earlier by playing the dangerous "pyramiding" game.) Consequently, when a painful recession gripped the city in the 1970s, one underleased Helmsley property would not signal disaster for another. In fact, to ease the city's fiscal crisis, Helmsley had been able to prepay his real estate taxes in June 1975 in exchange for an 8 percent discount on the tax bill. Yet, no empire is invulnerable, not even one with timbers as sturdy as Helmsley's. Stock markets collapse. Economies unravel.

Leitner, who had become a millionaire himself from good investments, said Leona was very mindful of such shifting sands. In truth, Leitner said, "The Helmsleys weren't worth hundreds of millions. The money is in equity, in buildings that are mortgaged for billions. Therefore, I can understand how she might feel very poor and insecure at the same time newspapers are saying how rich the Helmsleys are. Everything she owns is liened or borrowed. A person could feel, 'I'm one phenomenal fraud. Everyone who lends me money owns me, and I better live high now.'" The *perception* of danger and vulnerability, indeed, could be more real than reality itself. And with Leona's history of broken marriages, who could guarantee that this one, to Harry, would be more enduring?

Leitner said Leona bitterly complained about Harry's financial settlement with Eve, and bristled at the very mention of Harry's first wife. "She claimed Harry didn't care for Eve, and that she was giving him a better life. She said Eve already had him in an old folks' home; that she wanted him in bed by nine o'clock; that he had worked his whole life without getting any excitement or enjoyment out of it." By contrast, Leona said, "Now, we're going out every night and meeting people. That's what he deserves." Leitner said Leona told him the divorce had cost Harry dearly, and temporarily depleted his cash reserves. He quoted Leona as saying: "Eve wanted everything. We gave her millions, every penny Harry had at the time. I told Harry, 'Give her everything; then we'll be rid of her! We can start fresh. We have our know-how. You have your good name, and we'll build our own empire.'" Even the super-rich must sometimes wrestle with cash flow, the Holy Grail of the masses, but Leitner was surprised Leona still felt Eve's sting four years after the settlement.

If finances are such a concern, Leitner suggested, "Leona, why don't you take some money out and put it out of the country, in some place like Switzerland, absolutely safe? Leave it in cash or gold because real estate is so risky. You'll have enough to get by on if the roof caves in." Leona looked at him closely and smiled. "Don't worry," she said, "I'm taking care of myself. I've put some away." The penthouse was impressive, Leitner recalls, "but we both knew that all the glitz didn't mean she was liquid in all those assets, and there was no guarantee somebody like the IRS couldn't go after them. She knew it was 'Live for today.' If inflation doesn't keep up, you could end up penniless when the debts are called in. In the Depression, hundreds of thousands of people were destroyed, and she lived through that."

Seven

"Can you be at the Villard Houses at one o'clock sharp?" Harry Helmsley's secretary asked. "Mr. Helmsley wants to explore the mansion with you and Mrs. Helmsley. The three of you."

When this request came to Sarah Tomerlin Lee, a New York hotel decorator, she didn't need a crystal ball to understand what it meant. Everyone knew about Harry Helmsley's big, controversial project on Madison Avenue; now she realized she was in the running for a key role in the project. For three long years Helmsley had battled preservationists and city bureaucrats. Now, in October 1977, the 68-year-old tycoon was finally home free. He had just cleared the last major hurdle by winning a multimillion-dollar city tax abatement for his proposed Palace Hotel. Helmsley's building permit was also in place, allowing him to erect a 51-story tower behind the brownstone Villard complex. Terence Cardinal Cooke, head of the country's largest Catholic archdiocese, had given him a ninety-nine-year lease on the property, at $1 million per annum. And as hoped, the four-story, U-shaped mansion could be fused with the new tower and serve as its grand entranceway. Original plans for flashy bronze windows and vertical piers in the hotel had been eliminated in favor of a neutral black tower that would not compete visually with the mansion.

Sarah Lee's skills were needed now, however, because of another major concession that Helmsley had been forced to make along the way. To win necessary support from the Municipal Arts Society and other preservation groups, he had agreed to abandon his original plan to gut the mansion's sumptuously decorated interiors as he saw fit. In fact, he vowed to restore the very best of the rooms, those in the Villard-Reid wing along Fiftieth Street, to their original glory. The promise was crucial: although the city had declared the mansion a landmark in 1968, the designation protected only the exterior. By going the extra mile, Helmsley ensured that both sides won. Preservationists could rest easy knowing that the interior of the Villard-Reid wing would be safeguarded for the future, although only the exterior was landmarked. And Harry had finally made peace with the preservation groups, which might have been able to delay construction of the hotel years longer.

Buoyed up after receiving Helmsley's phone call, Sarah Lee announced to her staff: "I'm meeting D'Artagnan in the courtyard at one o'clock!" The decorator arrived to find her Musketeer, Harry Helmsley, standing forlornly in the midday sun. Leona was late and Harry asked her plaintively, "What do you think I should do about it?"

"I think you should call her," Mrs. Lee suggested, and Helmsley dutifully trudged down Madison Avenue in search of a pay phone. In the meantime, a shiny limousine pulled into the courtyard, and out stepped Leona looking like a movie star. "She was in a navy blue Chanel suit with a lot of sapphires, rhinestones and chains around her neck," Mrs. Lee recalls. "And dark blue sunglasses—very chic. She was dazzlingly attractive, I must say."

Without even bothering to introduce herself to the decorator, Leona asked, "Where's lover boy?"

"I don't know," said Mrs. Lee, a white-haired, blue-eyed matron of about 60 with traces of a Tennessee accent. "But if you mean Mr. Helmsley, he's gone down the street looking for a telephone because you're late!"

When Helmsley returned, a security guard admitted the trio to the Villard-Reid wing. On the main floor, ornate walls had been covered with plywood. "Fireplaces were blocked up and we couldn't tell what they were," Lee said. "It was very mysterious." Paintings had been ripped off the walls and the rock crystal chandeliers had been carted away by thieves who had broken into the abandoned mansion. The dining room once used by Whitelaw Reid to entertain European royalty had been remodeled to serve as an archdiocese courtroom where the cardinal heard church cases. Part of it had been partitioned into a maze of little cubicles "for people who were going to get divorced. A platform had been built for the cardinal to sit on, so people would have to go and look up to him for counseling." By contrast, Reid's music chamber, the Gold Room, was almost intact. Its ornate chandelier, hung in the 1880s, was unmolested. The two-story-high vaulted ceiling, amber windows and John La Farge lunette paintings representing Music and Drama were all in place and undamaged. The wall paneling, with musical instruments and garlands carved in bas relief, was unscratched. Ten plaster panels of "singing boys" cast from the fifteenth century sacristy of the Cathedral of Florence were also in mint condition. But the gold leaf covering every inch of the room's carved walls and ceiling had lost most of its sheen. Reid's triple drawing room overlooking Madison Avenue was also in fine shape, except that the chandeliers and four tall bronze sidelights had been stolen.

"You must tell us, dear," Leona told the decorator, "what we can throw out and what we can keep." Mrs. Lee advised that the interior be preserved to the fullest possible extent because of its historic nature. Only ghastly ornaments and those that had been damaged through church use should be discarded. Once they returned outdoors, Mr. Helmsley asked Mrs. Lee to meet him at his office in the Lincoln Building for further discussion.

Sarah Lee had the inside track on the prestigious renovation because her late husband, Tom Lee, had decorated the Park Lane Hotel to Helmsley's great satisfaction six years earlier. When he died in an auto accident in 1971, Sarah took command of the firm, Tom Lee, Ltd. It was a career switch for the Southern belle, a former editor at *Harper's Bazaar* and editor-in-chief of *House Beautiful*. Although she was relatively new to the field, Helmsley took one look at photographs of her recent design work and said, "I think you should do our hotel." She agreed. But such a restoration job would be expensive, Mrs. Lee warned, way into the millions. Money would be no problem, he assured her. "Just do the best possible job." She would hire craftsmen and artists to duplicate stolen chandeliers, copy or approximate missing paintings, and repair the mansion's damaged wall paneling and marble walls. For the lobby of the new hotel tower, she would order hand-loomed carpets and new marble staircases to match the adjoining landmark.

Helmsley estimated it would cost $73 million to build his hotel tower, renovate the Villard-Reid wing ("the south wing"), and gut the architecturally damaged lower floors of two houses forming the center section of the mansion. The rear facade shared by the two houses would be removed to accommodate the tower. The remaining three houses within the Villard complex, all in the "north wing" along Fifty-first Street and Madison Avenue, were deemed architecturally unsuitable for the hotel. The one at 24 East Fifty-first Street was already occupied by Capital Cities Communications, which agreed to renew its lease. The two abandoned residences at 22 East Fifty-first and 457 Madison Avenue would also be leased for rental income.

Not surprisingly, Helmsley decided to use other people's money to finance his prized hotel. Metropolitan Life Insurance Co. and Massachusetts Mutual Life Insurance Co. agreed to advance $50 million against a first mortgage on the new hotel. In April 1977, Helmsley had organized a partnership, the Palace Company, to raise another $23 million. The investors (including many wealthy Europeans), as his limited partners, would share roughly half of all future profits but incur no financial risk beyond their initial contributions. Helmsley, as general partner and developer, would be personally liable for any cost overruns or unanticipated expenses.

With financing in place for New York's tallest hotel, other decisions could now be made. While Sarah Lee concentrated on the restoration of the Villard-Reid rooms and design of compatible new public areas, Leona would begin sketching out decorating schemes for the 961 guest rooms. Deco Purchasing Company, coordinating with Leona, could begin lining up suppliers for carpeting, beds, dressers, mirrors, tables, bathroom fixtures and other furnishings. The Florida-based Helmsley subsidiary would also have to order barstools, club chairs, banquettes, dining room tables, refrigerators, ovens, pots and pans, china and silverware.

Too much was happening on the East Coast for Jay Panzirer, executive vice president of Deco, to remain in California. In September 1977, he moved from Los Angeles to Maitland, Florida, a comfortable Orlando suburb, where he opened a new Deco headquarters with a handful of office employees and traveling representatives. In addition to the proposed Palace, Deco's clients would include other hotels owned or managed by Helmsley, such as the St. Moritz and Park Lane in Manhattan and the Sheraton Sandcastle in Sarasota, Florida.

Jay and Ruth settled into a sprawling house, with swimming pool, at 66 Eastwind Road near Lake Maitland. They set up a baby bed for Walter Keith Panzirer, Jay's fourth child, whom Ruth had given birth to on December 23, 1976, just nine months earlier. Many a relative marveled that the baby, with dark hair and pink cotton-candy cheeks, was the spitting image of his grandmother Leona. Family expenses were minimal because Deco owned the house and charged little or no rent.

In three hours, Jay could make the 165-mile drive to Palm Beach and discuss business with his mother. Or Leona and Harry could fly to Orlando in true style. By 1977 they had purchased their very own jet, an eight-seater Sabreliner, and hired a pilot and copilot. It was an expensive purchase, but it gave the Helmsleys freedom to set their own flight schedules. At 68, with Leona's encouragement, Harry could rationalize spending some of his hard-earned millions to save an hour here or there.

Leona was thrilled by Jay's return, Blanche Slauson recalls, and had great visions of his future in the Helmsley empire. "Lee loved him, there's no question about it. And she told me, 'I'm going to make Jay the most important man in this country.'" Sure enough, advancement came that year when Harry stepped down as president of Deco and relinquished the subsidiary's top post to Jay. Leona continued to operate in the background. Her name was seldom mentioned in print.

Behind the scenes, however, Leona became an increasingly important participant in Harry's business affairs. "Harry would arrive in Palm Beach with three or four loaded briefcases," Mrs. Slauson recalls, " and she would be upstairs working with him. She never left him a minute." Work, as much as dancing and swimming, was the Helmsleys' shared recreation. And on the restful island, the balance between activities seemed almost perfect. "It was a time I could call Lee and get her instantly. Or she'd call me and say, 'Cancel all your appointments. We're going out for dinner!' These were their years of Camelot. They were terribly in love. Lee often said with tears in her eyes, 'My best friend is Harry. If I have a problem, I can't go through it without Harry.' They lived in a sort of fairyland."

In Manhattan, magic was in the air at Madison and Fiftieth, where actual construction of the Palace tower was finally begun on March 14, 1978, on a plot of land behind the Villard Houses. Helmsley had waited four long years for this day, and knew another two years would pass until the job was completed. Before blasting into bedrock and pouring a foundation for the tower, engineers installed special shoring in the adjacent mansion to protect its walls and ceilings from the shock waves. Seismographs were strategically placed as an added precaution.

Around the corner and five blocks south, Helmsley busied himself with yet another major project. The previous year, in May 1977, he had paid approximately $35 million for the double-arched New York Central Building at 230 Park Avenue. A provision of the sales contract required him to change its name; accordingly, at minimal expense, Helmsley simply rechiseled two letters in the facade, thereby making it the New York *General* Building. The 35-story tower, topped with a baroque cupola and straddling the avenue at East Forty-sixth Street, had been one of the city's most exuberant and visible landmarks since its construction in 1929 as headquarters of the New York Central Railroad. But its gilded crown and brick facade had become faded and grimy in the intervening years. Leona decided something had to be done to rescue the landmark from oblivion.

Nancy Weaver, a Manhattan real estate broker, recalls that Leona recommended a solution during a real estate dinner soon after the purchase. "I remember sitting at the Helmsleys' table and one of Harry's employees said, 'It's too bad about 230 Park Avenue. It's such a nice building but has so many vacancies.' Leona turned to Harry and said, 'The top of the building looks terrible! It's terrible!' Somebody else at the table asked, 'What should we do?' " Weaver said Leona thought a second "and sort of wrinkled her nose like a kid would. And then she said, 'Paint it gold!' apparently unaware that gold leaf already covered much of the roof but was hidden under years of dirt. 'If you paint it gold, it will sell. People love gold.' " When her suggestion was met with silence, Leona added, "You all think I'm crazy, don't you?" and nobody answered. "I think I'm going to get Harry to paint it gold. You watch, it will perk things up! We'll give them more amenities. We'll clean up the lobby." Weaver said Harry "sort of looked at Leona and smirked."

Within months, however, the brick façade received its first steam cleaning. Next, work crews scrubbed the cupola and rooftop ornaments. Small rectangular sheets of gold, by the hundreds, were then cemented to every accessible spot. Gilders then went to work on the Indiana limestone base of the building through which four lanes of traffic flow in an endless stream. Statues of Mercury (representing transportation) and Ceres (her grain an important railroad cargo) were bathed in precious metal, as was the monumental clock against which they lounged. Flagpole stanchions, scrolls and vines were also gold-leafed. Finally, Douglas Leigh, New York's most prominent lighting expert, intensified the 24 karat glow with a mighty emplacement of high-pressure sodium vapor lamps. As Leona had predicted, the gold perked things up considerably and rentals improved. "The building really hopped back into prominence with the gold leaf," said Leigh. "At nighttime, it lights up the very end of Park Avenue; you see it for miles head on." Once again, and perhaps more so than in its first pristine days, the tower was a dramatic "Stop!" sign over the thoroughfare.

Leona decided the "New York General Building" was too mundane a name for the glittering landmark. Instead, she suggested that it be rechristened "The Helmsley Building," in honor of Harry himself. It was almost an unthinkable proposition. For decades, even after buying the Empire State Building, Helmsley had steadfastly ducked the limelight. The *Daily News*, in a 1972 profile, noted that "he studiously avoids newspapermen" and "in contrast to the standing image of flamboyant entrepreneurs, he's quite low-key and plain-spoken." Now, when he was three months shy of his 70th birthday, Leona wanted to put his name in blinding sodium-vapor lights! Truly great powers of persuasion must have been applied, for the once publicity-shy tycoon accepted. (In later years, Leona would take full credit for the brainstorm. "I thought that was a suitable mark for him," she told the *New York Times*. "Harry Helmsley would never have named a building for himself. You don't puff.") On December 11, 1978, the change was made official at a public ceremony attended by Governor Hugh Carey. Mercury and Ceres watched from the second-floor ledge as the Helmsley name was spelled out beside them in brass letters.

With a twenty-foot shovel painted gold, Harry Helmsley

broke ground on January 31, 1979, for yet another first-class Manhattan hotel. The forty-one-story inn would be called the Harley, from the first names of Harry and Leona, and would rise on a lackluster stretch of East Forty-second Street, between Second and Third avenues. Helmsley predicted its 793 rooms would be ready for guests late the following year. If timetables could be met, he would celebrate two major hotel openings in 1980: the Harley and the Palace, a mile away in a more exclusive part of town. At the doorstep of everything ineffably chic, the Palace would aim for wealthy tourists and senior executives on carefree expense accounts. The Harley, in the workaday Grand Central Terminal business district, would cater to tasteful, but budget-conscious, tourists and business people. "Mr. Helmsley's two new midtown hotels will bring his total inventory of hotel rooms here to 4,353," the *Times* reported, and added that this would help alleviate the city's tight market for first-class lodging. It would also make Helmsley the city's largest independent hotel operator.

New York was too small, however, for the hotelier-on-the-move. In February, only weeks after the Harley ground-breaking, Helmsley paid approximately $35 million for the Hospitality Motor Inns, a Cleveland-based chain of fourteen motels controlled by Standard Oil Company of Ohio (Sohio). It was a ragtag collection of roadside inns, half of which were off the beaten path, in such towns as Enfield, Connecticut, and Willoughby, Ohio. City locations included Lansing and Grand Rapids, Michigan; Pittsburgh; St. Louis; Lexington; and Atlanta. As part of the deal, Helmsley also picked up thirty-five Dutch Pantry restaurants that had been owned and operated by the Hospitality chain. Sohio unloaded the hotel chain because of poor profits in the wake of a national oil crisis and continuing recession. Net earnings in 1977 were only $1 million on revenues of $71 million; in 1976, earnings paled at $490,000. As usual, however, Helmsley could see rainbows beyond the economic gloom. One of his close former aides estimated that the value of the hotels as real estate parcels, independent of their earnings potential, "was probably close to $50 million"—$15 million more than Helmsley paid for the chain. "So it was a good buy." Another virtue of the Sohio deal was that it almost doubled the number of hotels owned by Helmsley, giving him the ability to create a recognizable national chain. He did so by combining the fourteen Hospitality Inns with over a dozen other hotels he owned outside New York City.

He named the resulting collection the Harley Hotels, although the new chain had nothing to do with the similarly named Harley Hotel then under construction in New York. The chain was composed mostly of nondescript squat motels of fewer than 250 rooms, with executive offices in Cleveland. By contrast, the bronze-and-glass Harley of New York, rising forty-one stories on East Forty-second Street, was among seven Manhattan hotels (including the Palace and Park Lane) operated separately from the Harley chain. Nevertheless, as an advertising gimmick, Helmsley anointed the towering New York Harley as the flagship of his Harley Hotels chain. The public wouldn't know the difference, and the ploy might rub a little Manhattan glamour onto the prosaic roadside chain.

Helmsley was bursting with health and entrepreneurial vigor when Leona threw her annual bash in late February, a week before his 70th birthday. "The giant menu showed Harry wearing a space suit and benign smile as he floated over the city," the *Post* reported. "No wonder, since he owns quite a swatch of it." As usual, Leona helped select the party favors, including little red music boxes that played "I'm Just Wild About Harry." Among the guests were Governor Hugh Carey, Claudette Colbert, Charlotte Ford, former mayor John Lindsay and his wife Mary, and former mayor Robert Wagner (then ambassador to the Vatican) and his wife Phyllis.

William Hill, a former general manager of the Bush Terminal industrial park in Brooklyn, marveled at Helmsley's energy during a visit to the boss's office that year. "Mr. Helmsley was already up in age, but he began telling me about his new fifteen-year plan! I thought to myself, 'This guy thinks he's going to live forever!' " From personal observation, Hill could tell that Helmsley's negotiating skills were still razor sharp. "Just to watch him operate!" For example, there was the time Helmsley applied for a multimillion-dollar bank loan to upgrade the heating system at Bush Terminal. After six months of dickering, the loan was approved. "I was surprised," Hill said, "because Mr. Helmsley agreed to pay a high interest rate and a lot of things that I would never agree to. But who the hell was I to question him?" Hill said he then went to Helmsley and asked for permission to start drawing funds on the loan. "Oh no," Helmsley said, "we aren't going to borrow the money from *them*!"

"What do you mean, sir?" Hill asked.

"Nah, nah, nah," Helmsley said. "That document [the loan

approval] is good for two years. We're going to go to another bank now and use it as security" to borrow at the much lower prime interest rate. "And that's what we did. He worked in a way the average person wouldn't know how."

Helmsley's wit was no less sharp. "We were sitting one day," Hill recalls, "and somebody came up and asked, 'Harry, would you be interested in selling Bush Terminal?' "

Hill said Helmsley "looked at the guy kind of strange, with a cat-that-ate-the-mouse smile, and answered. 'Yes, under two conditions. First, we have to find a buyer. And second, get him released from the insane asylum!' "

On another occasion, Hill watched an investor walk up to Helmsley with a different proposition. "Harry, I've got $200 million and would like to buy some office buildings."

"Who wouldn't?" Helmsley replied, and walked off. With a personal fortune of $200 million to $300 million of his own (according to *Fortune* magazine's 1979 rankings of the rich), he could now afford to be a little cavalier. "When you're at the top," Hill said, "deals come to you. He could pick and choose his partners and investments."

Although hotels had become top priority, Helmsley did stray into other investment areas. In late July, he broke ground for the tallest condominium in Florida, a forty-two-story tower on Miami's exclusive Brickell Avenue. Like his half-built Manhattan hotel, it would be called the Palace. Because all 254 apartments were to be sold, and at prices averaging $225,000, he would have no rent control headaches. Two local brokers, Jean Inman and Alicia Cervera, were put in charge of sales. With nothing to show but blueprints, they worked out of a double-wide trailer on the Biscayne Bay property. *Miami Herald* columnist Grace Wing Bohne noted Harry and Leona's attendance as guests of honor at Inman's cocktail party following the ground breaking. "Towering over the other guests," she wrote, Harry "is remindful of the late Gen. Charles de Gaulle, but more fun. He is, confided his dynamic wife Leona, a terrific dancer who can stay on the pace at Studio 54 with madcap customers one-third his age." Although Leona was pure sugar to the society writer, one partygoer recalls that she was "disdainful to just about everyone else" after putting away quite a few drinks at the party. "She was universally able to put people down, almost as if she didn't know what she was doing."

Several months later, Leona unexpectedly showed up at the condominium sales trailer and made it clear that she was something more than just the boss's wife. "She came unannounced," Jean Inman recalls, "and nobody was in the reception area to greet her." A short while later, Inman's secretary strolled back to her desk and saw Mrs. Helmsley peeking inside the refrigerator. The secretary had no idea who the snoop was, but soon found out.

"I'm Leona Helmsley and I pay for this food!" Leona shouted at her, pointing to an assortment of cold cuts and soft drinks. "I pay for this food! I pay for this food!"

Stunned, but amused by the curious tirade, the secretary joked: "Okay, then. Would you like me to make you a sandwich?"

The offhand response set Leona flying, Inman said. "My secretary almost got fired because Mrs. Helmsley thought she had been disrespectful."

Inman said the groceries were necessary because the trailer was a long hike from any restaurant or store. "It's good business if you're selling apartments to millionaires to keep little things for people to eat and drink." Leona, however, accused the brokers of stocking the food for themselves, and carting it home. "It was upsetting," Inman said, "because when you're attempting to sell $65 million worth of real estate, you don't really expect to be questioned over a few groceries. It wasn't a wild expenditure." Yet, from that moment on, "Mrs. Helmsley watched every expenditure down to the penny. She questioned everything. She treated everyone like they're dishonest."

To Leona, the former condo sales champ, the condominium project was an irresistible lure. Now, after seven years as Harry's wife, it beckoned as a springboard back into real estate. Increasingly, to the brokers' dismay, she took personal command of the sales program. "We were in awe of working with Mr. Helmsley," Inman said, "but we never knew the extent Mrs. Helmsley would be involved." On one occasion, after Inman had flown to New York to confer with architects, Leona analyzed the broker's expenses and raised holy hell. "How dare you fly first class!" she screamed over the telephone. Inman calmly explained, "I didn't fly first class; I flew tourist." Leona had become so accustomed to her private jet that she "was out of touch with prices. She didn't know what it costs to fly like regular people." A short while later, when Leona and Harry made an unscheduled visit to the sales trailer, the heavens shook anew. Just as soon as Leona walked in the door, Inman recalls, "she started screaming and yelling at me for no reason."

"You think you're smarter than I am," Leona roared at the stunning young blonde, blue-eyed broker. "You think you're smarter than I am!" Over and over again, at the top of her lungs, she repeated the allegation: "You think you're smarter than I am!" Harry, appearing visibly embarrassed by the outburst, left the office without saying a word. "He just walked outside." Fed up with the abuse, Inman said she complained to one of Helmsley's top executives, who brought the protest to Harry's attention. Helmsley, in turn, phoned the young broker to talk it over. "Mr. Helmsley, I'm confused," Inman told him. "I don't understand why I'm being questioned about these things." The mediator told Inman that Helmsley immediately went to his wife and ordered a cease-fire. "Mr. Helmsley told her to leave me alone and to stop arguing over nickels and dimes when we were dealing with millions." Inman could only speculate about the cause of Leona's anxiety. "She was a little bit paranoid about any woman that had access to her husband, especially women younger than herself." Inman based her theory on previous conversations with Leona. "Mrs. Helmsley referred back to the fact that when she met him she was selling real estate. So I think she might have been leery of any real estate woman who had any conversation with him about anything."

Although Harry seemed visibly uncomfortable about Leona's outbursts, Inman said it was also evident "that she made him happy. If you saw them together, you might have a bit of compassion for her because she makes him happy. It's something she's done right." If only, Inman often commented, Leona could enjoy her marriage and riches "instead of making life miserable for everyone else. You'd think her money would be revenge enough; isn't living well the best revenge? I couldn't understand why she wouldn't just buy a yacht and disappear somewhere. She sure doesn't need to work."

Need, however, is a far cry from desire. Seymour Rabinowitz, who had given real estate legal advice to Leona a decade earlier, said he was anything but surprised by her long leap back into the business. By 1979, he had joined Helmsley-Spear as a specialist in residential law, and witnessed firsthand her expanding role in Harry's deals. During the early part of the marriage, Rabinowitz said, Leona had busied herself with secondary activities such as decorating several Manhattan hotels, including the Windsor, Middletowne and St. Moritz. Then, the time came "when she wanted to prove to Harry she was a good *businesswoman*. Harry is a brilliant businessman and she wanted to show she had some of that brilliance too."

Time was no problem. Leona had little or no contact with her four grandchildren and no preemptive diversions. Family ties were weakened further when Jay Panzirer divorced on September 29, 1979, and gave Ruth custody of little Walter, 3.

Soon, Leona was making the advertising decisions for the high-rise Palace condominium. That summer, Jean Inman introduced her to Joyce Beber and Elaine Silverstein, owners of Beber Silverstein & Partners, an innovative Miami ad agency. It was a case of instant chemistry, and Leona assigned them the account. Beber, a kinetic blonde, and Silverstein, a calm and unhurried brunette, had a style and *chutzpah* (they still drive matching Jaguars) that Leona could identify with. Aged 41 and 37, respectively, Beber and Silverstein were also known for the fresh angle. With eye-catching ads for the Miami *Herald* ("Have you ever tried reading the *Miami Herald* on I-95?"), Pottery Barn, and many national accounts, their firm was fast becoming the state's largest ad agency when Leona signed them up.

Beber said she had driven to Leona's Palm Beach apartment to pitch the account. "I didn't even know who the Helmsleys really were," she said, "except they were building two Palaces—a hotel in New York and the Miami condo." Once inside, Beber showed the Helmsleys examples of her previous ad work "but Harry's mind was wandering. He was thinking of other things. I don't believe he knew the difference between one ad and the next." But Leona, Beber recalls, "picked up on everything! I didn't know whether she would like the good stuff or the mediocre stuff, and she picked up on everything that was good. So I naturally started relating to her." Leona particularly liked an ad that showed a spoiled little boy surrounded by waiters in a formal hotel dining room. It read, "Billy Wiggins ordered a peanut butter and jelly sandwich, and he got it. At the Boca Raton Hotel that's not our normal cuisine, but our guest gets what the guest wants. We never forget that you're the guest." Beber said Leona zeroed right in on the ad. "I like that! I like that campaign! That's what the hotel business is about," she exclaimed. Beber could tell that Leona, by instinct, "was a good salesperson and knew that advertising meant selling.

"There was a certain sweetness in the meeting," Beber said. "In the middle of things, I'd be showing her the ads and she would break in and say, 'Where did you get those high heels!' It was a femininity that was not competitive at all. It was very nice. She'd say, 'Can you stand in them?' " She also liked Beber's cheeky air, and remarked, "You're not so dumb, are you?"

Nor was Leona dumb. "She was a very smart broad," Beber said, "a smart business lady, the smartest." When Beber suggested that floor plans of the Miami condominium be printed on high-quality paper for prospective customers, Leona improved upon the idea. "Usually, floor plans are done to quarter-inch scale," Beber explained. "But Leona insisted that her floor plans be done only to half-inch scale. She knew these large apartments would look even bigger if done in twice the scale." The drawings were made and packaged in transparent Lucite tubes "and they were extraordinarily successful," Beber said. "They were talked about everywhere, and the reason was because of Leona's idea, and later many developers switched to the half-inch scale." In addition, Beber ran newspaper and magazine ads stressing the fact that Helmsley, "the man who owns the Empire State Building," was now building a Palace in Miami. "People wanted that Helmsley assurance," Beber said, "that he wasn't a fly-by-night, because the building wasn't built. It was just floor plans we were selling from." The ad campaign was a fast winner. "In six weeks, we sold every apartment."

Inman and Cervera, the brokers, had to remain in the sales trailer until contracts were closed and payments received. Cervera recalled that Leona was always "intense" during her visits to the construction site. "How intense? On a scale from one to ten, she's ten. She told me when she was a broker in New York, she worked all the time, even at parties. She was always thinking of her business, that her business was very important to her. She thought the only way to be successful at something was to take it full-hearted, not half-hearted. In her love for her husband, she's intense. In her relationship with people around her, she's intense. She can be very strong with people." Cervera recalls the time Leona walked into the Palace lobby, once the condominium was completed, and noticed a bare-headed security guard talking on the phone. Without introducing herself, Leona raced to his desk. "Why don't you have your hat on?" she demanded to know. "If you're paid, why do you have your cap in the drawer? And is that a personal phone call?" She then told the astonished guard, "You're doing two things wrong—no hat, and having a personal call on working hours!" Cervera said the guard, a Nicaraguan refugee, looked at Mrs. Helmsley as if he could kill her.

"I think this man should be fired, Alicia," Leona summarily announced. Cervera acknowledged the order, but never carried it out "because the man never knew Mrs. Helmsley was his boss." By contrast, Cervera said, Harry Helmsley was a patient listener who made ironclad decisions in the quietest possible manner. "I don't think he put his ego into his business at all," she said. "He's a businessman, and the best thing is to *think* about what someone's telling him. He gives them the opportunity of giving their opinion. But when he makes up his mind, it doesn't go any further. He listens, he comes back, and that's it." When Helmsley smiled, she said, "he smiled with his eyes. His eyes go a little slanted like the Chinese—they close a bit. Absolutely a smile that has nothing to hide." Despite his charming smile Helmsley betrayed an ungenerous streak in discussions with Cervera about money and power.

"A millionaire should not give to charity," he said. "The only thing you can ask from a millionaire is the opportunity for them to give you a chance to work." Helmsley added, "People should not approach me to give them a hundred dollars or a thousand dollars just because I'm a millionaire. But if I come to Miami and build a forty-story building, that's something you should appreciate." Indeed, Helmsley was not known for philanthropy at an age when his longtime partner Lawrence Wien and other real estate magnates were joyfully giving away large chunks of their wealth. An occasional contribution to Lincoln Center, Manhattan's new performing arts complex, was noted in the press. Otherwise, charity and the Helmsley name were seldom mentioned in the same breath.

Helmsley was quite candid, indeed callous in his choice of words, in a November 1979 interview with United Press International. When asked if he had ever considered devoting his acumen and expertise to revitalizing ghettos in Harlem or the South Bronx, he said, "That has no appeal to me whatsoever. I think I'm performing a very valuable service, providing the best luxury hotel in the world [the Palace]. Besides, he added, saving Harlem "would not be a profitable deal." In an interview with financial columnist Dan Dorfman the same month, Helmsley said he had no interest in building housing for middle-income families. "So what's middle-income America to do?" Dorfman asked. "There's always trailers down South and used houses, though not in the best areas," Helmsley replied, "and this is what a lot of people are going to have to get used to."

On January 12, 1980, Leona found herself in a rare gathering with all four of her grandchildren at Jay Panzirer's home in Maitland, Florida. Craig, now 13; David, 10; and Meegan, 8, had traveled together from Staten Island for their father's third wedding. Walter, a rambunctious 3-year old, was also on hand amid familiar surroundings of the house he had been uprooted from such a short while earlier. Along with Harry Helmsley, they watched as Panzirer exchanged vows with Mary ("Mimi") Doyle, a transplanted Connecticut Yankee. She was blonde, blue-eyed, Twiggy-thin, and a top radio advertising salesperson for Y-106 FM in Orlando. Like Jay's, her two earlier marriages had ended in divorce. They had met the previous summer in a restaurant at the Kahler, a downtown hotel that Helmsley had acquired and begun to refurbish as the new Harley of Orlando, the latest addition to his hotel empire. Mimi said she was instantly attracted to the stranger who introduced himself with a bottle of Dom Perignon.

"Jay was six-foot-two, weighed 205 pounds, with dark brown eyes—the longest lashes you've seen in your life and luscious full eyebrows." So charming was he "that I didn't even notice he was bald." Within months, they were married. Missing from the wedding party, however, was Jay's father, Leo Panzirer. "Jay was getting married so often," he recalls, "that I just didn't want to be affiliated. How many times does a guy get married?" The elder Panzirer said he had remained in close touch with Jay "in certain situations," but the relationship was strained. "I told him he was doing so many stupid things. He was pretty well spoiled." Mimi insists, however, that father and son had broken all ties approximately seven years earlier when Jay was hospitalized in Los Angeles for his second heart attack. "Jay said his father refused to sign a document taking responsibility for Jay's expenses. And it hurt Jay badly. He never got over it and they never spoke again." But Harry and Leona offered lavish congratulations as the newlyweds set out for a London honeymoon.

Unbeknownst to Jay, a crisis was brewing back home in Orlando as he and Mimi strolled in the shadow of Big Ben. The first spark came when an auditor visited Deco during the honeymoon and noticed stacks of catalogs piled up in Jay's office. The freshly printed booklets contained descriptions of myriad furnishings and supplies that could be obtained through Deco. It became apparent that Jay had prepared the catalogs to win purchase orders from companies outside the Helmsley empire, such as the nationwide Best Western Hotel chain. Under ordinary circumstances, such an expansion effort might be applauded, but Helmsley had previously vetoed the idea, insisting that Jay restrict Deco's services to hotels and office buildings owned or managed by the tycoon. "Mr. Helmsley felt there was enough to worry about in his own properties," recalls Milton Meckler, who reported to Jay as vice president of Deco. Another factor, Meckler said, was Helmsley's dubious regard for Jay's entrepreneurial abilities. "When Jay worked for Deco in California, he had a lot of accounts receivable—customers who turned out to be credit risks. And Mr. Helmsley didn't want to worry again about someone else's credit. He'd have to chase them." Despite Helmsley's prohibition, "Jay went ahead anyway," hiring extra salesmen, printing the catalogs, and negotiating secretly with Best Western. It was a brazen act of defiance, but Meckler said Jay's motive was almost understandable. "He felt overshadowed by his mother and it frustrated him. He wanted to show what he could do for Deco, really on his own, without anybody directing him." The plan backfired miserably.

"Leona called Jay in London," Mimi recalls. "And Jay was furious to be interrupted on his honeymoon, and angrier still that Harry was doing an audit behind his back." Instead of returning home to Florida, Mimi said she and Jay "went immediately to the Park Lane" in New York. "We went into the Helmsleys' den and Jay attempted to explain his Best Western plan and Harry just exploded. He was furious. He looked at Leona and looked at Jay and said, 'One more time and you're both out on your ass!' And that's the only vulgar word Harry ever used in front of me." Although there was no evidence that Leona had been involved in the catalog project, in threatening to remove both her and Jay from his business affairs, Helmsley apparently assumed she had been aware of her son's activities. As a safeguard against untoward future surprises, Helmsley appointed a trusted aide, Gerald Schlosser, to monitor Jay's affairs in Florida. For several months, Meckler recalls, Schlosser reviewed Deco procedures and had to approve all transactions. "Every purchase order and every letter was copied to him; he was looking over Jay's shoulder." In effect, Jay's wings had been clipped, and he resented his constant "shadow." Meckler said Jay concealed the real reason for Schlosser's presence. "Jay told the whole Deco crew that his mother and Harry were concerned about his health and wanted him to have someone work closely with him" to ease the work load.

In reality, Meckler said, Leona's own treatment of Jay seemed anything but healthful. "She used to blast him on the telephone almost every other day of the week. He'd walk out of the office and we'd say, 'You just had it!' and he couldn't comment because he was flushed and red as a beet. He was totally frustrated and aggravated and I think he feared her. He may have loved her and respected her, but he feared her too. She ran him into the ground. She embarrassed him in front of people. She told him he was no good and incompetent just like everyone else."

Despite the abuse, Meckler said, Jay had an excellent incentive to remain in the family business. As president of Deco, "Jay's regular salary was $250,000 to $275,000 a year." In addition, "He was getting a consultant's fee of $12,500 a month," for a total compensation of over $400,000 a year. Not to mention other perks such as free rent and furnishings. There were also the advantages of Florida sunshine and nearby golf courses. Tooling around town in his powder-blue El Dorado, Jay definitely qualified as a big fish in the Orlando pond. Nevertheless, he chafed at the punished-schoolboy treatment he had received during the catalog snafu.

"He was so upset he wanted to quit," Mimi said. "He told me, 'I have the contacts to open my own purchasing company. We're not going to starve. I want to get away from these people.' Jay always called his mother the 'barracuda,' and said he wanted to escape the barracuda."

"Jay, you're 38," Mimi countered. "You've had two heart attacks; who's going to hire you? This is the best game in town. You only have to see Harry and Leona twice a month and you can play the game." Her arguments prevailed, and Jay stayed aboard. Tensions with his mother, however, continued unabated. "Leona loved Jay," Mimi said, "and he loved her," but it was an uneasy alliance because of her mercurial personality. Mimi said Jay picked 'barracuda' as his mother's nickname because of her aggressiveness and distrust of others. "As a child, she told Jay that no one will ever love you for yourself; they'll only love you for your money." Indeed, it seemed to be Leona's own credo. "You have to be a friend to have a friend," Mimi said, "and Leona has nothing to give. There's nothing there, so she doesn't understand friendship. The only two things she cared about were Harry and Jay."

"Leona's *raison d'être* was that the only person Harry or Jay should depend on was Leona. She has a *tremendous* need to be needed. You can't survive without being needed, but it was a compulsion with Leona. I think she is an extraordinarily insecure human being and can only achieve satisfaction by having people need her and depend on her." Inevitably, Mimi said, Leona attempted to push her, the new wife, aside. The first occasion came when Leona invited Jay to vacation with her in Cozumel, but suggested that Mimi stay at home. "Jay was mad. He called her in Palm Beach and told me to listen on the extension. 'My wife comes first! You will not destroy my marriage! Is that perfectly clear?' " The lecture seemed to do the trick. "Our relationship became very warm," Mimi said. "If Leona saw a pair of shoes she liked, she bought them and sent them to me. And I did the same for her—one of every color. We shared very personal things like good friends would do. We talked several days a week on the phone, exchanged recipes and tips on hair conditioners because chlorine from swimming was murder on her hair. We sent makeup back and forth." Sometimes Leona would give Mimi financial advice. "She told me when I purchased clothes in New York to make sure I shipped them back to Florida. That way, I would avoid paying sales tax."

Leona's business dealings with her son increased exponentially as the individual Harley hotels were renovated and construction progressed on the Harley and Palace hotels in New York. More and more she was becoming an adviser and decisionmaker in the hotel operation. The rising Manhattan hotels, at least six months away from completion, had already thrust Harry and Leona prominently into the limelight. In a lengthy February 3, 1980, profile in the *Times*, Leona described her business role as a "troubleshooter" for Harry's far-flung projects. Leona noted that she kept a small office in her Park Lane Hotel and was currently busy with such diverse chores as decorating Park Lane rooms and monitoring progress at a Florida construction site. Another major responsibility, she said, was keeping tabs on the refurbishing of two arched walkways that sliced through the Helmsley Building on Park Avenue, linking Forty-fifth Street to Forty-sixth. The arcades, used by thousands of pedestrians each hour, would have red carpets and a Helmsley Hotel information center. And henceforth they would be known as the Helmsley Walk, in further homage to Harry. "I think it would be a great idea if somebody wrote a song called 'The Helmsley Walk,' " Leona joked. After all, she told the reporter, "He's an honorable man. Good looking, cute, a good sense of humor and tremendously romantic and he's my friend. Every morning I get up and turn to him and I say, 'Today is a good day because I'm with you.' "

A month later, on March 3, the *Post* gave its readers the lowdown on Harry's latest birthday party, celebrated by Barbara Walters, Bess Myerson and a host of luminaries. "When the 200 guests entered the ballroom every seat at the tables seemed to be taken, but this was only one of Lee Helmsley's tricks. The smiling faces, all of Harry, were cardboard masks mounted on sticks." A phalanx of security men stood at attention in tuxedos, keeping a protective eye on the heavily bejeweled guests. As the guests sat patiently, the Helmsleys made their grand entrance in a swirling blur to the strains of "I'm Just Wild About Harry." As always, food and wine were lavish. Leona's Miami advertising counselor, Joyce Beber, and her husband, Chuck, found themselves on the invitation list beginning that year. Chuck recalls that before dinner at each of the annual parties, guests gorged themselves on twenty pounds of caviar upstairs in Leona's apartment. "It was served by a fellow in white gloves. He took it out of four- or five-pound tins and would spoon it on your toast. He would just slop it on by the ladleful! The thing is that people don't usually serve caviar that way." Barry Gray, a New York radio personality who occasionally attended the parties, said it was "just incredible how extravagant and lush they were. Everybody eating too much good food. I just thought the costs were obscene," especially the party favors, given to guests in goody bags as they left. "One time I got a Cartier silver picture frame which now sits on my wife's desk. Another year, I got a music box that played 'Wild About Harry.' You're talking about bags that cost a hundred dollars each! It was not in very good taste." As hosts, the Helmsleys might have been short on savoir-faire, but not on party spirit. "Harry always seemed wide-eyed about Leona's parties," Gray recalls, "the noisemakers and balloons. He looked like he had opened his eyes to something he'd never seen before." Beber said Leona seemed to have met many of her celebrity guests through Phyllis Wagner, wife of former New York mayor Robert Wagner and widow of the late Random House publisher Bennett Cerf. Indeed, said Beber, "Leona adopted Phyllis as her social mentor. She was always grateful because Phyllis introduced her to Frank Sinatra." The Sinatras and Wagners forged a tighter bond with the Helmsleys by purchasing a small number of shares in the Palace Hotel.

Big parties notwithstanding, Leona and Harry otherwise had a fairly narrow social orbit. Blanche Slauson recalls that at one "Wild About Harry" affair, Harry scanned the roomful of plutocrats and movie stars and confided to her: "Most of them are business associates. You and Cid are our only close friends." And even with the Slausons, the Helmsleys were growing distant, too preoccupied with their hotels for frequent socializing.

"Before, I could call Lee and get her instantly, so I knew she needed that friendship," Blanche said. "After a while, it was harder to get through to her. She was becoming powerful. There was a change; I didn't think she was as friendly. She wasn't quite the same nice person. She became harder and harder, almost masculine, and started to use more four-letter words. I saw it and felt it."

One of Leona's greatest concerns was publicizing Harry's newly acquired chain of Harley hotels. To spread the word nationwide, she hired Joyce Beber, whose agency had done such an effective job of advertising the Palace condominium in Miami. Beber and one of her account executives, Tad Distler, were summoned to Leona's Palm Beach penthouse that March to discuss possible ad themes. Giving the hotels an identity was crucial, Distler recalls, "because here was a chain they had named Harley," identical to the brand name of a well-known motorcycle. Everyone agreed that a spokesperson was needed to project the image of a classy, comfortable hotel chain. Distler said he and Beber drew up a list of celebrity candidates "and Leona negated them all." Finally, Beber suggested, "Why don't we use you as the spokesperson, Mrs. Helmsley? You could represent the woman's touch in a hotel chain."

Beber had been reluctant to make the suggestion earlier, Distler recalls, "because Leona had been stabbed years before and we were concerned that her security would be compromised if we made her a public spokesman." Leona had no such qualms, however, and immediately shouted to Harry in an adjoining room. "They want me to be the spokesperson. What do you think?"

"Why sure, if you want to" was Helmsley's casual reply. It was settled, which was no surprise to Beber. From past exposure to the Helmsleys, the ad woman said she had noticed a predictable pattern. "Mrs. Helmsley was shrewd. She always deferred to Harry at meetings. When we suggested anything, she would say, 'Well, I have to ask Harry.' " It was a strictly procedural process, Beber said. "Harry knew that she was going to get to do what she wanted to do, but she made him feel so important to her that there was no refusing her anything."

In the meantime, Leona asked Beber to take on yet another advertising project. "Look, we're looking at advertising agencies for our new hotel in New York, the Palace." Beber accepted the offer and set out to devise slogans for both the Harley chain and the Palace.

As Helmsley entrusted Leona with more and more business decisions, relatives noticed, the couple seemed to thrill in their joint endeavors.

"Harry and Leona liked each other and spent a great deal of time together isolated from everyone else," Mimi Panzirer said. "Harry didn't go out for tennis or golf; he was with her. They shut everyone in the world out entirely, even in a crowded room." Indeed, Leona's sisters, Sandra and Sylvia, were excluded from her social orbit. Mimi found it curious that Leona never mentioned their childhood days, or virtually anything of the past. "Her earlier history was never discussed, never told, never mentioned. I don't know why." The sisters were seldom mentioned, much less seen. "One of Leona's expressions," Mimi said, "was that the only reason her sisters ever came sucking around is because they smelled money." But Joe Lubin kept in close contact with Sylvia—the plump eldest sister—after his romance with Leona ended almost two decades earlier. Lubin said he hired her as a telex operator in the mid-1970s after her husband died. Within four or five years, however, Sylvia lost part of one foot because of diabetes and was confined to a wheelchair. Lubin said Sylvia complained to him that Leona virtually ignored her while she was in the hospital for the amputation. "Sylvia was hurt, but she wasn't the type to be bitter. We avoided talking about Leona." A close relative said Sylvia was financially strapped as a widow and Leona extended only minimal assistance. "She offered to send her on a trip to Japan once and Sylvia didn't want to go. But most of the time Leona didn't do diddly for her." And when Leona did help, she lorded it over her. "It was like, 'Don't get out of line or you won't get any help next time.' " On one such occasion, "Sylvia told her to go take a leap. She was a very proud woman."

Leona remained in close contact, however, with Alvin

Rosenthal, her balding, rotund younger brother. In fact, following a heart attack, Rosenthal quit his teaching job and joined the Helmsley organization. One of his important assignments in 1979-1980 was to assist his nephew, Jay Panzirer, with the installation of furnishings and equipment in the rising Palace. "I think she wanted to help Alvin," the relative said, "after his heart attack. She felt it was the right thing to do." Yet she gave Alvin the same constant verbal battering that Jay endured. "For Leona, there's no difference between a relative and an employee when it comes to business. I've seen her belittle Alvin at meetings: 'You idiot! Why did you do it this way? I told you not to!' He takes the screaming because, number one, he wants the job, and he also knows that she can't hold a grudge against him too long." No doubt, in her own way, Leona had a soft spot for her grown-up "baby brother." Jay Panzirer, by contrast, could hardly abide Alvin. "The last person on earth Jay would ever associate with was Alvin," Mimi said. "He called Alvin 'the toad,' and wanted to give him a Baccarat frog, which Jay thought looked exactly like him."

To monitor his own serious heart condition, Jay endured a three-day battery of physical tests every six months at his doctor's office in Brookline, Massachusetts. In addition, his blood triglyceride and cholesterol levels were monitored every month in Orlando. He was put on a low-fat diet of veal, fish and poultry and given strict orders to quit smoking, Mimi said, "but went ahead and smoked two packs a day." Although doctors warned him his next heart attack could be fatal, "it didn't bother him. He would swim every day. He was in great shape." His three Staten Island children would come to Orlando once or twice a year, and occasionally join young Walter for a romp at Disney World. "And Jay would lug them around and have the best time of all. He was full of life. He called me five or six times every day except Saturday, when he played golf, and was always giving me presents—the kind that sparkle."

Jay's mother, then nearing 60, had the same vitality, boosted after a hypnotist helped her quit smoking. "On a good day with a tailwind," Mimi joked, "Leona could have safely passed for 45." Mimi and Jay occasionally studied snapshots taken of Leona over a decade earlier, and marveled at her resistance to the aging process. Indeed, her looks seemed to have *improved* considerably since her marriage to Harry in 1972. Of course, she had lost twenty pounds as her wedding vow, and kept the matronly excess off in the intervening years. The biggest change, however, was in her face. "When she married Harry," Mimi said, "she wasn't as attractive and seductive. She doesn't look like the same person." Features seemed to have been slightly shifted, or sculpted, into a more appealing combination. The eyes appeared to have been uplifted, into an almond shape. Her cheekbones, already prominent, seemed more so. The lips seemed fuller, and the throat better defined. It was a new look, and as hard to explain as walking into an empty room and wondering, "What's not here?"

"She looks fabulous," Mimi said, "and how she arrived at that is none of my business." Human nature being what it is, however, the issue was still raised. Leona would respond, Mimi said, by denying having ever been helped by plastic surgery "or any surgical procedures of any kind." Yet Leona freely admitted her devotion to a prominent Manhattan dermatologist named Norman Orentreich. Instead of using a scalpel, Dr. Orentreich is an acknowledged master at eliminating skin flaws and wrinkles with injections of silicone. He has practiced his skill on thousands of patients for decades, and none was more grateful than Leona. Many a time, Mimi said, Leona exclaimed, "Norman has the hands of an angel!" Just below the skin, he injects microdroplets of clear, oily silicone with fine needles. Before results are noticed, a chain reaction must take place: the body recognizes the silicone as a foreign substance and walls it off in tiny cysts by collagen, a protein. When the cysts lift the skin—*voilà!*, the wrinkle is smoothed away. Orentreich could also be depended upon to burn or strip away age spots. So pleased was Leona with Orentreich's results that she constantly steered family, friends and employees to his door at Seventy-second St. and Fifth Avenue. When Leona noticed an age spot on Blanche Slauson's hand, for instance, she insisted that Orentreich be seen right away. Blanche complied during her next trip to Manhattan but lost heart as soon as the burning procedure began. "I got up and ran out," she recalls, preferring to wear her liver spot proudly to the grave.

Leona, by contrast, was determined to look her best not only here and now but in the afterlife as well! Accordingly, Mimi said, Leona and Harry erected a magnificent mausoleum for themselves around 1977 at Woodlawn Cemetery in the Bronx. There, not far from the remains of earlier tycoons such as F. W. Woolworth and J. C. Penney, the Helmsleys built their future resting place in pink marble. "Leona said the mausoleum had to be in pink because it was her flattering color. Pink complements her skin tones. And they were not to be interred; their crypts are aboveground. She couldn't bear the thought of being underground." There would be no way to prevent their prized skyscrapers from passing into other hands. But memories would endure. On the walls, Mimi recalls, they hung framed photographs of the Empire State Building, the Helmsley Building, the Park Lane Hotel, and other favorites. All the preparations and monuments to self made Jay howl. "He used to say, 'When you're dead, you're dead. Toes up are toes up.' "

For months, Sarah Lee had been wrestling with a major design problem: a huge chandelier was needed to light the two-story grand foyer of the Palace. The marble expanse, located just inside the doors of the Madison Avenue courtyard, had been created from gutted interiors of the two houses in the center section of the Villard complex. It was here that the modern hotel tower rising to the east would meet the sublimely preserved interiors of the Villard-Reid wing. Age was the least common denominator in the mix. A faithful marriage of old and modern could only work if the new grand foyer had the look and feel of the nineteenth-century mansion. Mrs. Lee had taken care of other design elements. A brass staircase on the left would lead upstairs to the oval-shaped Versailles Ballroom, located in the new tower. By ascending a sister staircase to the right, and walking through the new Le Trianon dining room, one could enter the historic Gold Room and other parts of the Villard-Reid wing. A third staircase, located in the center of the grand foyer, would descend to the main registration lobby.

The chandelier dilemma was solved unexpectedly one day when a frail-looking man of about 80 entered Mrs. Lee's office with a proposal. The old-timer explained that he was a lighting man of considerable experience and wanted to make his "last masterpiece" for the Palace. "His name was Mr. Smith," Mrs. Lee recalls, "and he told me his first job was with one of the great banks of Wall Street. 'And my last job,' he said, 'is going to be with you.' " It was quite a sales pitch, and Mrs. Lee gave him the commission after he sketched a ten-foot-high, eight-foot-wide asymmetrical chandelier whose sparkle would be visible through the windows to passing Madison Avenue traffic. He brought her samples of his crystals, some of which were quite heavy and carved with fruit and flowers. "He put them down on my desk so I could admire them, and undid the tissue papers. They were his treasures. He got them from all over Europe. He had had them in his trunk for years." Finally, when his labor of love was finished, he presented it to the Helmsleys. Unexpectedly, Leona rejected the chandelier, saying it was "too thin" and needed hundreds more crystals.

Crestfallen, the old master phoned Mrs. Lee with the bad news. "You'd better come down here," he said. "I can't handle this lady. I told her the arms aren't strong enough for that much extra weight. I told her the design was carefully worked out. It is perfect. I am the king of chandeliers."

But Leona, the hotel troubleshooter, was unfazed. "I want more crystals!"

"Madam," he implored, "the arms will fall down. They're not strong enough!"

"Well, then, use guy wires!" she demanded quite seriously, to his utter horror.

As a result, Mrs. Lee said, "that's what she did to that glorious chandelier. You can see these terrible strings that hang down" in order to support the overload of crystals. The "last masterpiece" was ruined in Mr. Smith's eyes, and never again did Mrs. Lee hear from the old craftsman.

When books for the third-floor library came up for discussion, Leona issued another controversial decree. Instead of filling Whitelaw Reid's old bookcases with real volumes, she insisted that leather-trimmed boxes disguised as books be used instead. Her logic, Mrs. Lee explained, "was that real books would collect dust, and nobody could dust that many books in a hotel." The decorator argued vociferously against the brainstorm. "I told her, 'You just can't have fake! We're doing the hotel so real!'" Unswayed, Leona insisted, "They'll look real" while allowing the room to be kept immaculately clean.

Despite their stylistic debates, Mrs. Lee said Leona was often downright affectionate as the job progressed. "If I was in a restaurant, she and Harry would send me wine across the room." One day, Mrs. Helmsley became quite concerned about the decorator's huffing and puffing while climbing stairs. "She saw that I was out of breath and said she wanted to get me back in shape. She told me, 'I can build you up and make you stronger. Think what I've done for Harry! I can do as much for you. I want you to come and exercise at the pool with Harry and me.' I mean, that was very sweet of her."

Harry J. Scanlan, a former Helmsley aide chosen to supervise construction of the Palace and the Harley, said Leona's taste might have been questioned on occasion, but she was on target with a thousand other design elements that bear her imprint. As a vice president of Helmsley Enterprises, the holding company for all of Helmsley's personal and corporate assets, Scanlan worked closely with the boss's wife from start to finish. "She was involved with almost every design decision, much more than anyone could possibly realize," he recalls. "When I was doing mundane things like getting steel, she was choosing colors and putting the woman's touch on every corner of the Palace. It's the little things that interested her. In the hotel business you're selling a dream for hundreds of dollars a night. She wanted it to feel like a fairyland."

Decorating the hotel guest rooms, no mean chore, was Leona's main focus, he said. In fact, "She helped design most of the furnishings for all the rooms. She would call in a chairmaker and say, 'Change these legs to so-and-so; I want this kind of fabric for this kind of wear.'" She called for elaborately carved rococo headboards. Soft pastel color schemes of mint green or pale apricot and beige were of her choosing. Simultaneously, Scanlan said, she showed great ingenuity in decorating the far smaller rooms at the Harley Hotel. "She wanted the furniture to have the same design, quality and effect as the Palace, so she shrank the scale. Instead of a sixty-inch dresser, it might become fifty. Instead of being eighteen inches deep, it became fifteen. Instead of being two feet wide, a chair might be eighteen inches. To my eye, the furniture and the smaller rooms looked every bit as grand as the Palace."

At construction meetings, Scanlan recalls, Leona made many key decisions concerning the public areas of the hotel. "You'll never see any ice or snow in the courtyard because of Mrs. Helmsley." Before the pink granite and marble slabs were laid, "She called our engineers together and insisted that we put heaters underground so that the snow would melt. That way, ladies in slippers and gowns wouldn't get wet." A special drainage system without any hill or mound was incorporated into the scheme. "Everything's invisible." For the grand foyer's ceiling, Leona wanted rosettes. Accordingly, craftsmen located original rosettes in another section of the Villard Houses and duplicated them. In the elevator lobbies, Leona wanted three-dimensional plasterwork and got it.

Leona's love of pink led to a fortuitous design change, Scanlan said. Not until clear plastic covers had already been installed on recessed lights in the restaurants, lobbies and other newly constructed public areas of the hotel did Leona take notice. Upon observing their yellow glow one day, "She suggested that the covers be changed to pink because a woman's skin looks better in pink. We're talking about replacing hundreds and hundreds of covers! It was a big added expense." But once the change was made, the interior became a warm, inviting cocoon and Scanlan recognized it as a major improvement fully in keeping with Leona's fairyland vision. And when the time came to choose a wall covering for the elegant Le Trianon restaurant, Leona picked one of the most romantic, but expensive, fabrics possible: an apricot-and-silver brocade made in Italy.

Harry also enjoyed selecting materials and exercised veto power at design meetings, where architects and decorators reviewed plans and batted around ideas. Among those who huddled together were Leona; James W. Rhodes, architect in charge of the Villard renovation; Mrs. Lee; and executives from the Rambusch Decorating Co. of Manhattan, whose craftsmen painstakingly repaired the original lighting fixtures of the Villard-Reid wing and restored its marble, glass and wood surfaces. "A lot of it was technical work," Mrs. Lee said, "sitting down and looking at a blueprint and revising floor plans no telling how many times." Helmsley, the sober tycoon, relished the artistic tumult. "He enjoyed being there with us," Mrs. Lee recalls. "He never once raised his voice. He told little jokes. He was very jolly. And I was never worried about showing him anything, because if it was good he loved it. He was not an animated man, but his eyes were bright and shiny." Another surprise, given Helmsley's reputation as a tightwad, was his willingness to wildly exceed the budget when quality was at stake. For instance, there was the time Mrs. Lee's son, Todd, designed a pair of glass-and-bronze awnings for the Fiftieth and Fifty-first Street side entrances to the hotel tower. Helmsley took one look at Todd's drawing and said, "That's just what I want!" An afterthought later, he asked, "Sarah, is this in the budget?" She held her breath and confessed, "No, the budget is ridiculous. It's fifty thousand dollars. These are a hundred thousand without light or heat." Mr. Helmsley remained silent, "and everyone at the table looked appalled. Then, almost in a whisper, he said: 'I'll take two.' "

Helmsley's budget-be-damned attitude was most definitely out of character. Yet never before in his fifty-five-year career had he been quite so enthralled about a project. Improvement after improvement, cost overruns soared into the millions with little objection. "Harry spared no expense because he was excited all the time," Scanlan said. "Everybody has a creative urge. Everybody is an architect of some kind in their hearts. And he saw something of high aesthetic value. His wife was excited. They were excited together. They were creating something of lasting importance, and had been involved together from the beginning."

It may have been their joint creation, but Leona wanted her share of credit for building Manhattan's newest and tallest hotel. When her talents were overlooked by the experts, particularly by Sarah Lee, she brayed loudly. One memorable issue was Leona's desire to set aside a major portion of the fourth floor of the Palace for high-priced boutiques. Mrs. Lee, a former vice president of Lord & Taylor, wanted to ensure that only the most prestigious merchants be offered leases. Her worst fear was Leona's taste. "I was afraid she was going to install her furrier. I didn't think she had the sensitivity I did." To preempt any wrong choices, Mrs. Lee went to Leona's office at the Park Lane with a proposal. "Mrs. Helmsley," she said, "Neiman-Marcus doesn't have a store in New York. They should be in the Palace. I've already talked to Stanley Marcus on the phone and he's coming to see you because he should take over the whole floor." When Leona's face became flushed, Mrs. Lee realized her goof. By taking charge of the matter so independently, she had impugned Leona's own decision-making ability. Because a visitor was in the office, Leona told Mrs. Lee: "I'll see you in the hall!"

In private, Leona confessed her feeling of hurt over the unintended insult: "I love you and respect you and I want you to love and respect me back," she told the decorator. It was a terrible scene, Mrs. Lee recalls, "because she grabbed me tightly by the arm and tore my dress. She didn't mean to, but she tore it down to the elbow.

"I was so shocked. I grabbed myself together and said, 'Mrs. Helmsley, you have to deserve my love and respect.' And I went home to change."

Respect came, however, on June 10, 1980, when Harry publicly announced he was giving Leona a major promotion. No longer would she be an untitled "troubleshooter." He appointed her president and chief operating officer of Helmsley Hotels, his entire shooting match of approximately thirty nationwide hotels. He would continue as chairman. Among the hotels were seven in Manhattan: the soon-to-open Palace and Harley, the St. Moritz, Park Lane, Carlton House, Windsor and Middletowne. "I'm going to personalize the hotel business," Leona told the *Daily News* immediately after taking charge. "I'm printing comment cards for all the hotels so the guests can call me direct to complain. I want to refurbish most of the properties as well. Salary? I don't want to discuss that, but now Harry works me forty-eight hours a day instead of twenty-four." She added: "The good thing is that when we get out of bed each morning we can have a meeting of the board of directors immediately."

Within two weeks, Leona visited the Terminal Tower in Cleveland to give a pep talk to executives at the national headquarters of her Harley hotel chain. She also introduced herself and Harry to the *Plain-Dealer*. "We are the largest independent realty company in the nation and we think we are the largest independent hotel chain in the U.S." As for the Harleys, she added: "We do not like to call them motels—they are hotels and we are going to make our chain the best in the nation." Big-time respect, bordering on homage, came the following month in a lengthy profile in the *New York Times*. "Leona Helmsley: Power Becomes Her" was the headline of the July 22 close-up. Four columns of type, wrapped around a six-inch photo of Leona's smiling face, gave thousands of New Yorkers their first close look at Harry Helmsley's wife. As the female president of a national hotel empire, overnight she had become a fascinating public figure.

"She is," the *Times* gushed, "because of her new job and the man she is married to, one of the most powerful real estate women in the city, the country, and perhaps the world." The world!

Why the promotion? "It was Harry's idea," Leona explained. "He thinks I work hard, he thinks I deserve it, he thinks I'm good." She made it clear, however, that Harry would remain the decision-maker in the family. "I'm bright, but he's *brilliant*, and he has a much better batting average than I do. I will suggest, but he decides. His word is final. That's why we get along."

The *Times* then recounted Leona's life story, a mixture of fact and fiction to rival any Hollywood tale. Among the omitted milestones were Joe Lubin, Leona's former husband, and three of her four grandchildren. She also catalogued her current blessings, including the Park Lane penthouse, with its swimming pool, collection of pink jade, paintings by Pissarro and Dufy, and dozens of mounted plaques and awards, "Do you want to see my best award?" she said, leading the reporter to her hallway. "Here it is." She opened a large silver box and took out a fading piece of paper. " 'It's my marriage license,' she said, beaming."

Eight

Milton Meckler was horrified. For a solid year, truckloads of televisions, dressers, beds, lighting fixtures and fabrics of every kind had been stockpiled in New York. Now, in the summer of 1980, as they were being installed in the soon-to-open Palace, he added up his tally sheet and discovered the full extent of the damage. Almost $2 million worth of hotel furnishings and supplies had vanished into thin air. Meckler, vice president of Deco Purchasing and Jay Panzirer's top aide, knew all along that pilferage had been chipping away at inventory. But not until he compared his complete list of purchase invoices with goods on hand did he grasp the true scope. He checked and rechecked his calculations. It was staggering.

Since early that year, Meckler had traveled from Florida to New York every month for meetings concerning installation of furnishings at the Palace site. By March, he had begun to complain at virtually every meeting about the troubling pattern of losses. Deco would order goods from its Florida headquarters, and manufacturers from around the country would ship them to the Palace, where they would be warehoused on the lower floors of the hotel as well as in its basement and underground garage. Then, without explanation, truckloads of goods would disappear, requiring Deco to make costly reorders. As the problem continued, losses skyrocketed. Meckler says the same executives attended the installation meetings and took no action in the face of his repeated warnings. Alvin Rosenthal, representing his sister, Leona, was in charge. Harry Scanlan, Harry Helmsley's on-site manager for the Palace construction, also called the shots. On hand as well was Jerry Goodman, head of a Brooklyn firm, F & D Associates, hired to transport, assemble, and install the goods.

At the meetings, Meckler recalls, "Goodman or Scanlan would bring up that we need more of this or that." Meckler would then check his Deco records and say, "They were already delivered." When reminded of the continuing pilferage, he said,

"Alvin always played the whole thing down. He would tell me I was wrong. He would fume and scream that I didn't know what I was talking about. I was just hustled off and waved away and told it was none of my business." Undeterred, month after month, Meckler continued to complain. "I was the rebel in the group and was trying to bring up the fact that we were being ripped off by someone, somehow. Alvin would scream and I'd show him the records. Everybody else would raise their eyebrows, but nothing was done. It was a sick joke after a while because so much was missing."

Executives at the installation meetings were all intimidated by Rosenthal, Meckler said. "He's very hardnosed and aggressive, and has a volatile temper that exploded regularly. We called him Garbage Mouth because of his spitting and cursing. He wanted everyone to know he was Alvin Rosenthal, Leona Helmsley's brother, and that he was in a power position." In frustration, Meckler said he turned to Jay Panzirer for help. "I said to Jay, 'This is a kind of wild affair. Alvin's your uncle. I'm unhappy with the relationship going on between him and Goodman. He's signing off on this and okaying that. I think he's being ripped off or I think there's more to it.' "

Jay, in turn, would urge Meckler to forget about it. "He's my uncle. I wouldn't advise you to get too heavy." Panzirer did authorize him, however, to inform the Helmsleys of the unending pilferage. "So I kept documenting it in memos and sent copies of everything to Jay's mother, and to Harry also." Surprisingly, Meckler said, "I never got any response from Mr. or Mrs. Helmsley," and the problem went unchecked even after Leona became president of the hotel empire in June.

Finally, at one of the last installation meetings in July or August, Meckler said he brought along a tally sheet. For three months beforehand, he had been pulling together documents for the presentation. "I did a complete recap, and I was flabbergasted. I never expected it to come to two million dollars. This was not stuff you can carry in your pocket, either. Linens by the ton; hundreds of lamps and bedroom sets; a hundred and twenty Zenith color televisions, all twenty-five-inch models with custom-made cabinets, worth a thousand dollars each. We had to rush to get Zenith to make us another special batch. We had to replace a lot of silver from Reed & Barton."

Confronted with the hard data, long after the horse was out of the corral, the executives grew worried. Al Young, head of the Insurance Division of Helmsley-Spear Inc., had been invited, and was the most worried of all. "The thefts had continued over a period of five or six months, and Al Young thought the insurance company would buck it," Meckler said. "He wanted to know why they were never brought up before. How could you submit a claim and say, 'We forgot to tell you, but two million dollars' worth of stuff has been missing for quite a while?' " Also worrisome was the failure to notify legal authorities. "Scanlan was pissed about that," Meckler said. "He wanted to know why Alvin Rosenthal hadn't reported it to the police." Rosenthal's reply, Meckler recalls was, "We were worried about bad publicity. We didn't want adverse publicity."

Goodman accuses Meckler of exaggerating the pilferage. "Only a few things turned up missing," he said. "How much I don't know, but it wasn't in the millions. Very few people realize how much furniture a million dollars means. If I say a million is missing, in reality it could be just two hundred and fifty dollars' worth." He said he reported directly to Rosenthal and received nothing but praise for a job well done. Any items that disappeared, he speculated, were probably stolen by construction workers at the Palace. "We didn't come off being the culprit. The only heat I took was the usual heat I would take if ten dollars' worth was missing."

Scanlan, however, verified that "Two million dollars is a pretty accurate estimate" of the loss. "We were all upset about it and did our best to stop it. We put extra security on it." Al Young said he has only a dim recollection of the controversy, but remembers that the loss was uninsurable. "No monies were ever collected because it must have taken place over a long period of time," and indeed, without police reports, all insurance claims would have been automatically rejected. The pilferage scenario remains a mystery. Who got the missing merchandise? Why didn't Harry, Leona or Jay intervene? Harry's failure to stem the losses, despite what Meckler said were repeated written advisories, was especially puzzling. As general partner of the Palace, he was responsible for all cost overruns. Therefore, Scanlan said, "the entire two million dollars had to come out of Mr. Helmsley's pocket."

By August, the $2 million was the least of Scanlan's worries. Cost overruns, he knew, would leap into double digits because of the lavish Villard renovations and maddening construction delays. One of the biggest snags was the aluminum-and-glass façade—the "skin"—of the tall hotel tower. The company hired to fasten it into place was hopelessly bogged down with assignments at two other Manhattan hotels and fell eight months behind schedule on the Palace. Meanwhile, Helmsley would continue to pay an interest rate of 20 to 21 percent on his $50 million construction loan. The hotel was scheduled to be completely finished by December, four months away. At the current snail's pace of construction, however, the following summer was a more likely date. And each extra month's delay meant over $800,000 in unanticipated interest. Once again, as general partner, Harry would have to bear the entire expense. The Palace was hemorrhaging money at an alarming rate. Helmsley remained perfectly cool, nonetheless. "He was calm under pressure," Scanlan recalls. "He's a man of great patience and resiliency. He simply recognized that everyone was working seven days a week, as hard as they could. And therefore, what more could he ask?"

Sarah Lee was busily arranging flowers for the grand opening of the Palace when she was summoned to the front desk for a telephone call. The caller introduced herself as a *Daily News* reporter and asked, "Mrs. Lee, did you know you've been fired?"

"No, you're wrong," the decorator replied. "I'm busy, very busy."

"You're not invited to tomorrow's opening party either," the reporter said.

"I can't believe this! What are you talking about?" Mrs. Lee demanded.

"We have no reason to make up anything this terrible," the reporter answered. "It shouldn't be our job to tell you, but we just spoke to Mrs. Helmsley and she asked us to call you."

"That's not true!" Mrs. Lee protested, stunned beyond belief.

But, alas, it was indeed true. After almost three years of tireless creativity at the Palace, she was being thrown overboard at its very moment of birth. "It was a heartbreak," Mrs. Lee recalls. "I was so proud of the hotel. I worked with all these artists and they believed it was my masterpiece. When you work so hard on a project, and get so involved, you're in it for the rest of your life."

The next morning, the *Daily News* described the firing as the conclusion of a long rivalry between two women "on a burgundy-carpeted battlefield." Leona expressed no remorse. "Look, let's just say Sarah Lee and I don't have any love for each other," she told the reporter. The exact cause for the firing was ambiguous. But specifically, Leona alleged that Mrs. Lee had taken on too many outside decorating jobs. She also alleged that Mrs. Lee had fallen on her face earlier in preparing color schemes for the Palace bedrooms. The *News* said Leona thought Mrs. Lee's color suggestions were "too bright, too obvious. So she made her husband a proposition he couldn't refuse: an audition. She decorated three bedrooms, and Sarah Lee decorated three bedrooms, and Harry could choose. He chose. Sarah Lee was kicked downstairs."

Leona's newspaper account was pure fabrication, Mrs. Lee insists. "There never was a decorating showdown. I was never hired to decorate the bedrooms! In fact, the first thing Mr. Helmsley told me when he hired me was, 'She wants to do the bedrooms.' I asked him who 'she' was. And he said, 'My wife, don't you know her?' " The real reason for the firing, Mrs. Lee said, was more clear-cut. "The hotel was virtually finished, and she simply didn't need me anymore. She was through with me. She wanted the credit all for herself."

Indeed, only days before the firing, Leona stole Mrs. Lee's thunder when a crew from WCBS-TV came to film the hotel's Old World craftsmanship. "Mrs. Helmsley heard they were coming to interview me and forbade me to go on. She said *she* would be on the program and no one else!" From a helicopter, cameraman John Tomlin zoomed in on the Palace while reporter Bill O'Reilly described its glories to hundreds of thousands of viewers. Harry and Leona, hand in hand, took the TV crew for a personal tour of the hotel. Dressed in a ruffled pink blouse and black slacks, Leona ushered her media guests into the glorious Gold Room, where laborers were applying more gold leaf to the walls and ceilings.

"You saw what happened to the price of gold once I did all this," Harry quipped.

"Went up," Leona affirmed, flinging her arm skyward in a classic model pose.

O'Reilly wondered out loud just how much the Palace would be worth when finished.

"One hundred million dollars," Harry confided after some hesitation.

"Over that!" Leona interjected.

"Over that," Harry admitted.

The foursome then repaired, at Leona's insistence, for a view of different splendors—those of her Park Lane penthouse.

First, Leona showed off her swimming pool, noting, "We do

approximately half a mile a day. He swims twice a day; I swim once." Next, through a corridor from the pool area they went outside to the roof, where Leona showed them her "greenhouse." She and Harry had built the glass-enclosed structure several years before, not just for plants but for extra living space. Besides its superb view of Manhattan, it boasted a piano, a fireplace and furnishings more casual than those in the main living area below.

When they returned to the main living area, Tomlin recalls, Leona seemed proudest not of her swimming pool or living room with its Central Park view. "She wanted us to shoot her bathroom! She was more interested in showing us her bathroom than [she was in showing] the craftsmen at the Palace."

Next, Leona flung open the door to her walk-in closet and displayed her finery with the gusto of a hostess opening door No. 1 on *Let's Make a Deal*. Layers of shelves bulged with shoes, mostly in neutral shades of tan, brown and beige. Just how many pairs were there?

"Thousands," said Leona. "But every woman does today."

"This looks like Bloomingdale's," O'Reilly exclaimed when his eye landed on half a dozen shelves of sweaters.

"In case I need a special color," Leona explained.

Separate closets overflowed with casual wear, gowns and cocktail dresses. And how many dresses were there, the reporter asked.

"Three hundred dresses," Leona estimated proudly.

It obviously took lots of dough to live this lifestyle. "How much are you worth?" O'Reilly asked Harry.

"Yeah, tell me," Leona edged in.

"I don't know," the tycoon answered. "It's a matter of who's doing the counting."

"Would you be a billionaire?"

"No, no," Harry replied. "But so far we eat regularly. Don't we, darling?"

"Most of the time," Leona averred with a straight face.

The apartment tour was apparently great fun for the Helmsleys. It was poor entertainment, however, for Sarah Lee, who had been yanked not only from the limelight but from her job. To the decorator's chagrin, Harry refused to stand up for her when Leona unveiled the chopping block. "It would have been just impossible for him to cross her. He has this feeling about himself that he's an old, old man and that she's a very sexy, vigorous woman. And I think she has this equation going, and he just doesn't want to make her mad at him for any reason whatsoever! He just loves to have her idolize him. She sits at a meeting and looks at him like he's God. He doesn't want to lose her or the adoration." Helmsley, the courtly gentleman, failed to even say goodbye, much less send a card or letter of thanks for the decorator's thousand days of work.

The gates of the Villard Houses swung open on the evening of September 12, 1980 for the grand opening of the Helmsley Palace.

To help them celebrate, Harry and Leona invited two hundred notables for a first peek at their masterpiece. Out-of-towners invited for the black-tie gala found their way easily enough, thanks to a searchlight that pierced the sky over the city's tallest hotel. Through the courtyard, over a strip of red carpet, swept Governor Hugh Carey, Mayor Ed Koch, Terence Cardinal Cooke, Dina Merrill and Cliff Robertson, Douglas Fairbanks Jr., John and Mary Lindsay, and plutocrats of the highest rank. As they entered the grand foyer and gazed up at the overloaded crystal chandelier, the guests could look forward to a lavish feast and the first ball of the season. Leona, splashed with diamonds and wearing a strapless silver lace dress, welcomed all upstairs. Cocktails were hoisted, and television crews gave the rest of humanity a close look at the sumptuously restored rooms in the Villard-Reid wing. By 9 P.M., everyone crossed the grand foyer for dinner in the Versailles Ballroom, decorated so skillfully by Sarah Lee that only the keenest observers realized they had entered the modern section of the hotel.

The oval-shaped ballroom was a royal sight. A score of tables, graced with white tablecloths and tall candelabra, glistened with hotel silver and gold-band china. And waiters stood tall, well prepared for their first trial. For hours the previous evening they had practiced, pouring and repouring colored water instead of real wine. Water had also been used as they practiced soup-ladling. Far greater preparations had taken place in the hotel kitchen. Weeks in advance, Leona and her social mentor, Phyllis Wagner, had tested recipe after recipe. "They wanted the menu kept very American," recalls Carl Hofer, the former executive manager of the hotel. "The chef would prepare a dish and they would approve or disapprove." After much trial and error, their choices included American sturgeon caviar and tournedos Rossini, lobster, smoked salmon, liver pâté, and a duck brochette with orange sauce.

When Harry and Leona entered the ballroom, the band announced their arrival with "New York, New York" and a rendition of "I'm Just Wild About Harry." Little did the partygoers know, Hofer said, that the rest of the hotel was controlled chaos. Because of construction delays, only floors ten through twenty-three were ready for customers. In fact, the top twenty floors of the fifty-one-story hotel still had no façade; in lieu of windows, plywood was strapped to construction beams to keep out the rain. Piles of dirt and building materials created roadblocks throughout service areas of the hotel, forcing housekeepers and waiters to tread carefully. Even as the ball progressed, "fire alarms were going off about every hour," Hofer said, activated by ambient construction dust. Yet, in spite of all the hardships, Leona's soirée went on until past midnight without a hitch. She bade good night to her last guest knowing the Palace debut was a triumph.

In gratitude, Leona instructed waiters to bring out more champagne for a staff party. "At about one A.M. she called us all together on the ground floor and toasted everyone," Hofer recalls. "She hugged us for fifteen minutes. She was very happy and very emotional about us. She told us what a wonderful job we did. It was so tender, like she was talking to her closest children. Almost in tears, she told us, 'I'll never forget you.' "

A few days later, the *New York Times* bestowed its imprimatur on the Palace. The public areas of the hotel, particularly the restored Villard-Reid wing, were pronounced a "triumph" by *Times* architecture critic Ada Louise Huxtable. "The original interiors of the Villard Houses," she wrote, "are magnificent and these rooms have been superlatively restored. Careful cleaning and painstaking repairs have revealed the dazzling beauty of inlaid marbles, mosaics, frescoes, elaborately carved woods, art glass and art work by Tiffany, LaFarge, St. Gaudens and a galaxy of others." The restoration, she reported, had added an estimated $10 million to the Palace's price tag. Huxtable had only one major complaint: the "monumentally unfortunate" black aluminum exterior of the new hotel tower, rising directly behind the Villard Houses. "The soaring façade is a curtain wall of unforgivable, consummate mediocrity; somehow the lesson of quality got lost on the way up those 51 floors." Little matter to the comfort-conscious guest. Back inside, Huxtable lavished praise on the guest rooms themselves, which "pamper outrageously with apricot velvets and gold-and-silver baroque trim." She noted they had been designed by

Leona, "who has kept a passionately watchful eye on everything."

The *Times* accolade was a tonic for Harry, Mimi Panzirer recalls. At 71, he was no longer a bashful mogul; he was a toasted hotelier. "He needed and courted and wanted the publicity," she said. "He had made it big years before and was justifiably proud of his accomplishments. He wanted more recognition than an occasional two lines on page four in the *Wall Street Journal*." He wanted something his first wife, Eve, could never give him: "the glitz and the glitter. He wanted to showboat." The only problem, Mimi said, "was that Harry didn't have the personality to showboat. He needed Leona to showboat for him. She saw the need and fulfilled it."

Lester Belmuth was sitting in his Atlantic City office in late summer of 1980 when his secretary announced over the intercom: "Leona Helmsley is on the phone and would like to speak to you."

"Oh my God!" the design consultant replied, taken aback that the proprietress of the Helmsley Palace and president of the Helmsley hotel empire was calling him—a complete stranger.

The 62-year-old designer heard a deep, husky salutation: "You Brooklyn Romeo, how the hell are you!" it said.

"Pardon me? Just a minute," Belmuth replied, bewildered.

He put the mystery caller on hold and rang his secretary on the intercom: "Which line is *Mrs. Helmsley* on?" he asked.

"The line you're already on!" the secretary replied indignantly.

He returned to the phone. "Mrs. Helmsley, this is Lester Belmuth."

"I know who the hell you are! I'd like to get together with you and talk about old days," the voice continued.

"But Mrs. Helmsley, I don't believe we know each other," Belmuth replied.

"Les, this is Leona Roberts! Do you remember me—do you remember me from Bensonhurst?" she asked.

Leona Roberts—his old Brooklyn sweetheart! Had she become Leona Helmsley? It was almost unbelievable! Belmuth had lost touch with his former girlfriend in 1938 when she was but 18 years old—forty-two years earlier—and had never made the connection.

"Remember when we used to ride in your Hupmobile with the top down?" Leona asked, for further identification. "How the hell have you been?"

The pair traipsed down Memory Lane for fifteen minutes on the telephone. Mrs. Helmsley then explained that she had tracked Belmuth down after she received a promotional letter from Belmuth Design Group Ltd. and recognized his name on the letterhead.

Belmuth's company specializes in design and installation of furnishings for casinos, hotel rooms and restaurants. He routinely sends such promotional letters to hotels to drum up business, and one had landed on Leona's desk. The timing was favorable. Now that Leona's Palace was open, she had turned to the New York Harley, rising on East Forty-second Street. Someone was needed to handle the upcoming installation of furnishings in the midtown hotel. There could be no repeat of the disastrous Palace installation. Mrs. Helmsley inquired whether Belmuth might be interested in the job. He expressed interest and agreed to meet at her office to discuss particulars.

Belmuth kept his appointment and was pleasantly surprised when he laid eyes on "Leona Roberts" again. "She had the same face, the same figure, the same hair" and looked at least ten years younger than her actual age. As in the old days, he noticed that "She was beautifully dressed, like a model. Her appearance was always exemplary." Belmuth gave her a kiss on the cheek and couldn't help but continue to admire how well Leona had preserved her looks. It was a business meeting, however, so Belmuth cut short his meditation. After a brief discussion with Leona and several of her executives, he agreed to handle the installation. Deco would order the goods and instruct manufacturers to ship them to warehouses in New York. Belmuth would keep a close watch on inventory and ensure that all goods reached the Harley before its grand opening early the following year.

During the meeting, however, Belmuth noticed certain changes in the demeanor of the soft teenager he once knew. "She was arrogant and domineering, the way she talked to people. She was the boss. 'Do things my way!' It was not the girl I knew." The gentle voice of yore that never complained about anything was also gone. Instead, Leona's larynx was now a Gatling gun of ratatat profanities. The invective was especially intimidating because it spewed from a set of vocal cords roughened by a past three-pack-a-day cigarette habit. "Oh, boy, oh boy, you can bet your life it was completely sailor's language. I was absolutely shocked.

"I was in the infantry in World War II and we had two drill sergeants. One was a very nice guy who could bawl you out without using any of those words. The other couldn't drill without using heavy language. This is how it was with Leona. She had to use that language. In my wildest dreams, I could not visualize this woman behaving this way. It was hard for me to imagine how she had become so aggressive. I have never had a friend change that dramatically."

"There are no tissues in the ladies' room!" Leona bellowed after inspecting facilities in the grand foyer of her newly opened Palace.

"I'll take care of it, Mrs. Helmsley," replied Wolfgang Haenisch, as straight-faced as any general manager could be in the face of such an emergency.

"Who's in charge of that rest room?" demanded Leona.

"Anna Marie Veres, the housekeeper," Haenisch replied.

"Fire her!"

"But Mrs. Helmsley," Haenisch implored, "she has worked for months in the basement, like a slave, just to prepare for opening the hotel." As top manager of the Palace, he had to protect his employees, especially such a valued department head as Veres, who supervised a housekeeping staff of 250. "No, I just can't fire her."

"Fire her!" Leona demanded.

"I can't," Haenisch replied, risking his own job in the process.

"You're a pussycat; you're too weak," she charged, and mercifully dropped the matter. It was a close call for the housekeeper, who no doubt kept closer tabs afterward on powder room provisions.

By October, with the Palace just a month old, such extreme demands by Leona were already cracking the morale of the very staff members she had cradled so appreciatively on opening night. Haenisch, a former executive vice president of Sheraton International, was the most disillusioned of all. He had nursed grand dreams for the Palace since he beat out five hundred other applicants for the general manager's post in September 1979, a full year before opening day. "I traveled the world, picking up ideas from other hotels in Europe and the Far East," he recalls. "I selected the finest things: operating equipment, place settings and menu covers. I considered it the top hotel job in the world. The Palace had all the tools, every ingredient, to be number one in the world. It was a mixture of the old and the brand-new, in the most sophisticated location. Even if you had the money, you couldn't copy the marble and carving of its historic public rooms."

Yet there it was, staring him in the face! An unreckoned force named Leona, battering his fantasy lifeless even as the first paying guests checked in at the registration desk. It was such a turnaround. In the planning stages, months before the hotel opened, he said, Leona was patient and attentive. "She listened to me very closely. I had green lights for all the things I wanted to do." Then, once the hotel rolled into operation, Leona's real management style surfaced. She had become president of Helmsley Hotels only three months earlier, almost overnight, "and didn't know a thing about the business. She wasn't used to running the big show. And now, without experience, she had to prove to the world she was doing a good job, that she's a great president. But she didn't have the most important ingredient of a successful hotelier: the ability to motivate people. So she began to run the hotel by fear."

Hotel employees, as members of Local 6 of the Hotel and Motel Trades Council of the AFL-CIO, could only be fired with just cause. Leona fired them in droves anyway, without any pretense of due process, recalls Carl Hofer, who was hired as Haenisch's executive assistant manager. "If a customer complained that a waiter gave bad service, she would call me up and say, 'Fire him!' She wouldn't give them a hearing. Her mind was always made up very clearly. There would be no chance to defend yourself or even explain." Rather than carry out Mrs. Helmsley's orders, Hofer said he spared many employees "by changing their names. I'd tell her the guy had been replaced by So-and-so and is not with us anymore." Even those who were fired summarily were often able to return to work, however, after appealing their cases to labor mediators. "So what!" Leona would comment when notified that her ax had been stayed.

Employees of Leona's out-of-town Harley Hotels, by contrast, had no union protection. Bill Dowling, hired in 1980 as Leona's marketing adviser for the Palace and the Harley chain, recalls hearing details of a particularly memorable case. One day, he said, "Mrs. Helmsley received a comment card that had been filled out two months earlier by a guest at the Harley of Orlando. The guest registered a complaint about the hotel's engineering department, so Mrs. Helmsley picked up the phone and called the hotel and asked for Engineering. When she got someone from the department on the phone, she started questioning him about the complaint. At the end, she said, 'This is inexcusable and you're fired!' "

"But Mrs. Helmsley," the worker protested, "I'm not the one who did that. I wasn't even on duty. That was my day off."

"I'm sure you're a very nice person," Leona replied, "but I never go back on my decisions. You're fired anyway!"

Dowling said the manager of the Orlando hotel phoned him later that day with more details of the firing, as well as a confession that the engineer would be kept secretly on the job. "Any time the Helmsleys come down, he hid the fellow."

Indeed, overtaken with indignation, Leona sometimes targeted the wrong prey. Bob Young, a free-lance photographer, said he was shooting the hotel's elegant third-floor library in October when Leona rushed in and accosted two men seated at a table. "Who are you?! What are you doing here?" she demanded, as if she expected them to hop to their duties forthwith.

"What's it to you, lady?" one of the men shot back.

"I'm Leona Helmsley; I own the hotel!"

"But we're guests," they informed her.

Without a hint of apology, Young recalls, Leona muttered: "Oh, whatever," and walked away.

In mid-December, Harry and Leona threw their annual Christmas party for several hundred employees of Helmsley-Spear Inc. The affair, as usual, was held in the Lincoln Building, headquarters of Helmsley's giant property management firm. This year the guest list included an outsider named Alicia Heatherton, a face from Leona's earlier days as a broker at Pease & Elliman. Fifteen years had passed since Heatherton worked as a secretary for Marvin Kratter, developer of the St. Tropez condominium tower. And Leona, who had sold Kratter's apartments like hotcakes, had not forgotten their weekends on duty together in the condo sales office.

Heatherton had long since left New York and real estate. But Leona had invited her to the party in hopes of luring her back into the business. Specifically, there was a job opening at the Palace, and Heatherton was a leading candidate. At the time, Leona needed a manager to market long-term leases of large suites on several upper floors of the Palace. A male candidate had been hired earlier at a steep salary but had been dismissed.

"So she wanted to give me the job at half his salary," Heatherton said. "Leona still had to be top dog," just like the old days, "and nobody—particularly no female—was going to compete with her. That's why she wanted to give me a pittance of a salary. Everybody had to be lower than her—in personality, in money and everything else."

Although offended by the diminished salary offer, Heatherton was tempted by the glamour. "I visualized myself riding around in a limousine and handling apartments in this grand hotel. It was enticing." She agreed to mull it over and to meet Leona a few days later.

Heatherton arrived at the Palace in good spirits but became depressed as soon as a male housekeeper escorted her and Leona upstairs. "We walked through these apartments," Heatherton said, "and if *anything* was out of place, Leona just went through the wall! If a picture frame was one millimeter off center, or the lampshade was crooked, she laced this housekeeper up one wall and down the other. She was so nasty to him, basically accusing him of having no brains. You just don't treat people that way." New surprises came after the tour when Heatherton returned to Leona's office. Without warning, Leona launched into an unflattering critique of Heatherton's dress and overall appearance. Then Mrs. Helmsley laid down the program. "She went through this whole thing," Heatherton recalls. "I should go to her beauty parlor, I should do all these fashion and cosmetic things that she does. She wanted to make me more stunning, to make me over in the image of Leona." Heatherton was outraged by the unsolicited self-improvement program. "It was very, very demeaning because I have always been very professional in my business life. I dressed professionally; I carried myself professionally." Heatherton assumed that Leona had advanced to a new ego plateau. "She was flying high; she was the president of the Helmsley hotels and was running the Palace, the biggest and most expensive place in Manhattan. So she must have felt she could tell anybody whatever she felt like." No job, Heatherton decided then and there, was worth the kind of abuse she had witnessed upstairs, nor a Leona "makeover."

The irony, Heatherton said, was that Leona expected her to finance the makeover on half the income of the previous job-holder. "So I said, Can we do this makeover on my paycheck or yours, Leona?" '

"You'll have to do it on yours, of course," Leona replied.

Leona with her first husband, Leo Panzirer, ca. 1948, when she was twenty-eight.

Leona with her family in the late 1940s. Left to right: Alvin, Leona, Sandra, Ida, Sylvia.

Leona and her second husband, Joe Lubin,
in the early 1950s.

Eve Helmsley at the Park Lane Hotel.

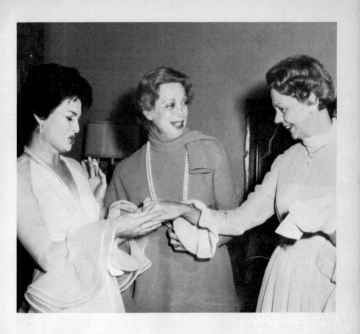

(*Opposite*) Harry and Leona on their wedding
day, April 8, 1972. (*Above*) Leona compares
rings with sister-in-law Terry Helmsley after
marrying Harry. Her sister Sandra is
in between. *(Both photos: Fred Marcus)*

The Helmsleys with their best friends, Blanche
and Cidney Slauson. *Mort Kaye Studios*

Dunnellen Hall. Copyright by the *New York Post*

9 ♣

Helmsley Palace

♣
6

Two of the thirty-six poses on Leona's famous playing cards. The top card shows the real Leona one reader called a "zaftig madam." The bottom card shows Leona slimmed down by the Scitex machine's trick photography.

Q ♠

Helmsley Palace

It's the only Palace
in the world
where the Queen stands guard.

The Queen inside her Palace: in the Gold
Room of her hotel.

Leona weeps after unveiling Jay's memorial bust. *Philip Eschbach*

(*Opposite*) Jay and Mimi Panzirer on their wedding day, January 12, 1980.

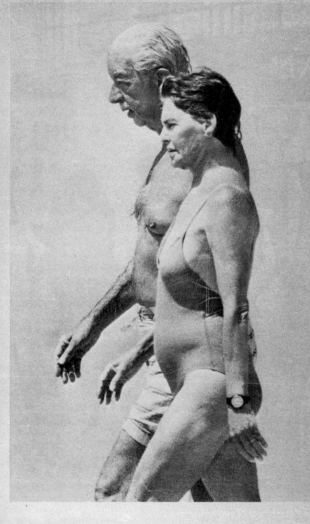

As the scandal in New York broke in December 1986, the Helmsleys hid out in Barbados. *Sygma*

Leona flashes a brave smile after the Helmsleys' arraignment on 188 state charges, April 14, 1988. *AP/Wide World*

That did it. "Who do you think you are, pulling me down this way?" Heatherton yelled. "I've gotten by just fine for forty-seven years. I don't need you telling me to make myself over for your clients!" Heatherton picked herself up and escaped after a sarcastic "No thank you, Leona." Instead of a limo and New York glamour, she moved to Las Vegas and happily settled for a night job counting markers at Caesar's Palace.

Holidays for the Helmsleys were no longer spent alone, once Jay Panzirer married Mimi in early 1980. Jay's previous two wives had rarely rolled out the welcome mat for his mother, Mimi said, a fact which had limited Leona's contact with her four grandchildren. Leona made little effort of her own to bridge the distance. "She sent no cards, no presents, nothing. So the kids never missed her because they never had a relationship with her." Mimi said she changed things, however, by arranging holiday family reunions. Jay's first wife, Myrna, agreed to send Craig, David and Meegan to the Panzirer home in Maitland, Florida, for Christmas. And Ruth, Jay's second wife, would allow little Walter to join his three siblings for the get-together, attended by Harry and Leona. For Thanksgiving, a few of the grandchildren would join Jay and Mimi for turkey at the Helmsleys' Palm Beach penthouse. In the summer, Walter would spend an entire month in Maitland, giving Leona an extra visit or two with her youngest grandchild. And "Wally," as the preschooler was fondly called by everyone, would spend at least one summer weekend in New York with the Helmsleys.

"The children were now a family unit with grandparents," Mimi recalls. One cardinal rule always prevailed, however: "The kids were forbidden to call Leona and Harry grandparents. They had to call Leona 'Lee' and Harry 'Harry.'" Joyce Beber recalls seeing a framed picture of Walter the first time she visited Leona's Palm Beach apartment in 1979. "Isn't he cute? How old is he?" Beber asked. And Mrs. Helmsley replied, "That's our little boy." Beber said Leona was wearing shorts and a T-shirt and had youthful, muscle-toned legs. "So I thought to myself, 'Mr. Helmsley is a really old man who married a younger woman.' I thought she was in her forties and had a young son."

At the holiday get-togethers, presents were exchanged, in a roundabout way. "Harry and Leona would have me go out and buy the kids Christmas and birthday presents and sign them, 'Lee and Harry,'" Mimi remembers. "And sometimes I might be reimbursed." For the sake of holiday spirit, Mimi shopped for the grandparents, albeit resentfully. "They wouldn't even go a block from the Park Lane to F. A. O. Schwarz and pick out a stuffed animal. It was too much trouble." Enthusiasm might be lacking, but any attentions were a vast improvement on the Helmsleys' past record as grandparents. "If Craig had done some particular project in school, Harry and Leona would admire his accomplishments. If David was learning to slam dunk, Harry would watch him. Jay and I and Wally went to Sea World with Harry and Leona. I don't think they enjoyed it, but they made the effort."

Walter, as the baby and the namesake of Harry's deceased brother, naturally got special treatment. "When he was three years old," Mimi said, "she gave him big teddy bears and a toy Starship Enterprise. 'Harry and LeeLee,' as he would call them, would play with him and the Starship and he just loved it. So Walter got along with Leona. She liked him because he was three and looked like her—the same dark eyes, dark hair and full lips." In fact, said Mimi, Leona wanted Jay to sue Ruth for custody of the child, "but Jay would have no part of it." Elaine Silverstein, Beber's advertising partner, recalls that Leona doted on Wally, "who would come visit in his gray flannel pants and navy blue Brooks Brothers blazer," but she rarely mentioned the other three grandkids. "It's bizarre, isn't it? She didn't want to acknowledge them because they were *old* grandchildren."

By 1981, Craig, the eldest at 13, left his mother's home in Staten Island and came to live with the Panzirers in Florida. "Jay apparently made the decision to bring him to Maitland," Silverstein said, "because Craig's mother had remarried and there were tensions in the home. And Mimi and he got along pretty well. Mimi was nice to him."

Getting Craig to Florida may have required outside help, according to Milton Meckler. The former Deco vice president recalls having breakfast with Jay at the Park Lane Hotel one morning when a slim, nattily attired fellow of medium height and with black hair walked up to their table and exchanged greetings with Panzirer. When the man left, Jay told Meckler: "That was Frank Turco, my good friend. He's an auditor at Bush Terminal." Helmsley employees often described the industrial park as "Siberia" because of its remote location on the Brooklyn waterfront, Meckler said, "and Turco had been put in Siberia for making mistakes." Panzirer then told Meckler, "If you ever want a guy's arm broken, Frank Turco is the guy to take care of it." The odd thing, Meckler said, which kept him from taking the remark too seriously, "was that Jay liked to give the air of being 'connected' " to tough characters. "And [Jay] said Turco was instrumental in getting his son to Florida from New York. Somehow, Turco had gotten Craig to Florida without going through a major legal process," possibly by slipping the lad a prepaid airplane ticket.

Turco eventually was shifted from Bush Terminal to an office in the Graybar Building, where he became the New York liaison for Deco Purchasing. After frequent trips to Florida, an observer remarked, "Turco and Jay became close friends. They ran around together and Turco was always under instructions from Mrs. Helmsley to look after Jay, to make sure he didn't get into too much trouble."

At 3:30 P.M. on February 18, 1981, Leona finally got in her forty winks. Grand-opening ceremonies for her new Harley Hotel on East Forty-second Street had kept her in motion since early morning. Only an hour earlier, Mayor Koch, Governor Carey, and two hundred other guests had departed after a festive luncheon in the forty-one-story hotel. The meal was a smashing success. "Your hotel is helping put the magic back into the Street of Dreams," Koch had declared in his toast to Harry and Leona. But the day was still young. Leona had invited another group of guests to the hotel for a 6 o'clock cocktail party, and her nap had refreshed her for the second wave of partygoers. She got up, slipped into a two-piece business suit and headed downstairs to supervise party preparations. Her inspection was cut short, however, at 4:35 P.M., when fire alarms were triggered by thick black smoke billowing up the sides of the brick and bronze-glass tower. The first of seventy-five firefighters arrived and made sure that hotel switchboard operators instructed guests to stay in their rooms.

In the lobby, fire captains huddled around a folding table, studying the floor plan of the $80 million tower. As smoke poured into the halls and elevator shafts, firefighters lugged heavy hoses upstairs in search of flames. Leona grabbed the hotel general manager, Mark Flaherty, and received a full rundown on the crisis. The location of the fire appeared to be on the third floor, but its severity was still unknown. A tangled mass of employees and guests, meanwhile, gathered in front of the registration desk.

Unexpectedly amid the confusion, Flaherty recalls, Leona took decisive action.

"Break out the champagne!," she ordered a headwaiter standing nearby. "Free drinks for everybody!"

"Flaherty," she commanded, "strike up the orchestra! But remember, Flaherty, tell them not to play 'Nearer, My God, to Thee.' That's what was played on the *Titanic*!"

Accordingly, a pianist in tuxedo battled with the sirens off to the side of the lobby in Harry's New York Bar as waitresses in crimson jackets uncorked bottles of white wine and champagne.

The sight of Leona "dressed for a cocktail party, while making order out of chaos" was one Flaherty will not soon forget. "You've seen emergencies where one person will emerge and take charge. That's what she did, and we had two hundred and fifty people in the lobby. Her adrenalin was pumping and it just took over. She turned a chaotic situation into a lively party. There was a force field surrounding her. She was emitting electricity. She did a remarkable job.

"It was certainly peculiar," Flaherty added, "because days before, if she saw a light bulb out she would go crazy. But here she was in a real crisis, as calm as could be and giving directions to everyone." Firefighters, meanwhile, traced the blaze to an auxiliary power generator in a 20-by-20-foot room on the third floor. "They got there just in time," Flaherty said, "because three drums of fuel were stored nearby. If the fire had reached them, a good chunk of the building would have blown out."

Harry Helmsley, who had been working at his nearby office in the Lincoln Building when the fire started, was equally calm when he arrived. "Honey," he told Leona after the danger had passed, "it's the hottest opening in town. But you really didn't have to go to such lengths." Luckily, there were no serious injuries, although fourteen guests and firefighters were treated at midtown hospitals for smoke inhalation. A month later, the cause of the mysterious fire was revealed when police arrested Jackie Morales, a 19-year-old hotel security guard, as he tried to set another blaze in the Harley. Morales admitted he had set both blazes in hopes of being hailed as a hero when he reached the flames first and put them out. Instead, he was sentenced to a maximum of eight years in prison for causing $1 million in damage to Leona's newborn hostelry.

Just as the Helmsley Palace had opened five months earlier

in an incomplete state, only 250 of the Harley's 793 rooms were ready for its grand opening. All were occupied, thanks to introductory rates of $76 to $116 for singles and $88 to $128 for doubles—20 percent off the official rack rate. Uptown at the Palace, by contrast, the official rate for a single was $150, up to $200 for a double. Because of poor occupancy, however, Harry and Leona were forced to take lodgers for only $95 a night.

The Harley, with its lackluster location near Grand Central Terminal, was geared for humbler, mid-level executives. Yet, Flaherty recalls, "Mrs. Helmsley had no thought of sparing any expense" to make it comfortable. "Her view of every property under her command is that they should all look like they came out of *House Beautiful*—the kitchen and the back areas of the hotel as well." For example, he cited the time one hotel executive recommended that guest rooms have only half-drapes to maximize the effectiveness of air conditioners in the window area. "She wouldn't have any part of it! She insisted on fully lined drapes because she didn't want a motel look. And she was absolutely right."

She also insisted that each Harley be equipped with the same twenty-five-inch, remote-control color televisions found at the Palace. "The glass and silver, everything that went into the hotel, was first class. Waiters and bellmen opened the hotel in white gloves. All the personnel wore fresh carnations every day. And at her direction, we had an abundance of fresh flowers delivered every day to the front desk."

Yet for all her graceful touches, Leona's role was perhaps secondary to that of an exceptionally capable behind-the-scenes expert. Flaherty recalls that virtually every amenity at the Palace and Harley was approved beforehand by Geoffrey Lerigo, a former general manager of the Park Lane and St. Moritz hotels who had just been given expanded responsibilities. Harry Helmsley had promoted the British hotelier to executive vice president of Helmsley Hotels, with oversight of the Park Lane, St. Moritz, Palace and Harley hotels. Leona's brother, Alvin Rosenthal, was given oversight of Harry's other three Manhattan hotels, all smaller, residential-type operations—the Carlton House (where Rosenthal and his wife, Susan, resided), the Windsor, and the Middletowne. Leona, of course, made the final decisions as president of Harry's hotel portfolio: the seven in New York and approximately two dozen others in the nationwide Harley chain (the number constantly fluctuated as

Harry bought or sold hotels). But in New York, at least, she delegated considerable authority to Lerigo and her brother.

In matters of taste, Flaherty said, nobody was held in higher esteem than Lerigo, a gray-haired, bespectacled man of about 50, standing about five feet eight, with a penchant for Bentleys and three-piece suits. "I've seen him in Mrs. Helmsley's office when they would set up china, glassware and silverware selections. In a very cultured voice he would make his recommendations and she would defer to him." Similarly, Lerigo would evaluate the quality of soaps, lotions and linens chosen for rooms. "He has worked all over the world and speaks with authority on European and Far Eastern hotels," Flaherty said. As a manager, Lerigo's skills were even more crucial. "He has extremely good rapport with managers and department heads of the hotels and forever counsels them how to preserve the integrity of the hotels." Lerigo, far more than Leona, "is the key ingredient for Helmsley's hotels. He's the cement. He makes the engines turn over and keeps them oiled so the ship stays on course. Without Jeff Lerigo it would all fall apart. It would be impossible for Mrs. Helmsley to operate without someone as stable and knowledgeable as Jeff around." Indeed, of Helmsley's entire roster of top aides, none was held in higher esteem than Lerigo and none but he could hope for ironclad job security. He was Harry's own Cardinal Richelieu, devising policy and practicing diplomacy in the shadows while allowing the Helmsleys—particularly Leona—to take full credit for his statecraft.

Lester Belmuth, Leona's old boyfriend, had done as near-perfect a job as possible. Under his supervision, according to Milton Meckler, less than $10,000 in merchandise was lost or stolen during the installation of furnishings at the Harley Hotel. The loss was infinitesimal compared with the $2 million in pilferage suffered during the Palace installation.

As his reward, Leona asked Belmuth to stay on as a Helmsley contractor. His next assignment was to inspect six Harley hotels undergoing renovations in the Midwest—including ones in Grand Rapids and Cincinnati.

Belmuth inspected the hotels and reported back to Mr. and Mrs. Helmsley with terrible news. They were a shambles.

"I visited all the hotels and saw that the work was being done wrong. It was the same in every hotel," he recalled. Perhaps millions of dollars "were being thrown out the window" by sloppy installation of carpeting, wall covering and furniture. "People were installing vinyl on the walls improperly, then tearing it down, throwing it away and starting all over again. Supervisors weren't on the job. Vanloads of furniture were buckling while left outside in the heat." Equally as bad, scores of hotel rooms were out of order because of the botched spruce-ups, costing the Harley chain enormous amounts of lost income.

Belmuth had been hired to do an honest survey and felt obliged "to put the fault right where it lies." And the fault was squarely on the shoulders of Jay Panzirer. As head of Deco Purchasing, the Florida-based Helmsley subsidiary which supplied all hotel furnishings and materials, Leona's son was responsible for ensuring proper delivery and installation.

"He was just incompetent," Belmuth said, adding that Panzirer spent much of his time playing golf in the Florida sunshine and throwing endless parties. "It was wine, women and song" all the time.

In a meeting with the Helmsleys, Belmuth reported that Panzirer had been nowhere in sight, and nobody was paying attention to the renovations.

"If he was my son," Belmuth said point blank, "he wouldn't be in charge of furnishing the Harleys."

Without batting an eyelash, Belmuth said, Mrs. Helmsley simply "laughed off the whole thing."

A month later, Belmuth said, he phoned Mrs. Helmsley to see what other projects she might need to have completed. Her secretary, however, stopped Belmuth dead in his tracks, telling him: "You're not going to get any more work." He realized immediately that Mrs. Helmsley's earlier laugh belied her anger at his frank comments about Panzirer's performance. "From that point on," Belmuth added, "she never talked to me again."

Belmuth concluded that Mrs. Helmsley "has a bitter need" to prove to her husband and the general public "that she's every bit as good a businessperson as Harry." And Belmuth had gone and exposed the incompetence of her son, Panzirer, whom she personally had selected as top officer of Deco. His performance reflected miserably on Leona, at a time when she was intent on proving her own managerial prowess.

Many of Leona's top aides became familiar with Panzirer's party lifestyle and how it compromised his job performance. But unlike Belmuth, they kept their jobs by keeping their own counsel. According to Bill Dowling, Leona's former hotel marketing adviser, nobody loved the ladies quite as fervently or as often as did Leona's married son. His enthusiasms created never-ending difficulties at the Orlando Harley, Dowling said. "Every time we hired a good-looking secretary in the sales department or the manager's office in Orlando, Jay would always take them to lunch and try to impress her with his importance, and then try to nail her. Some would start having an affair with Jay, and whenever we found out we fired the secretary because it was detrimental." Meckler verified the account. "Everyone in the Harley knew who Jay was: Jay was a ladies' man." And Leona was well aware of the situation. "Mrs. Helmsley knew that Jay played the social field even though he was married." In fact, she sometimes discussed the extracurricular activity point blank with Meckler and the need to avert any untoward publicity. "She would bring up the fact that I was friends with Jay, and implied that she appreciated my covering up for him."

Despite Jay's serious health problems, Meckler said, he "didn't look like a guy with a bad heart. He was a good six-three, muscular, and knew his way around town. He was a well-liked guy. He was an easy spender when it came to going out or buying drinks. He was not cheap in any fashion. He was definitely a sport." Meckler said Jay enjoyed posing as the owner of Deco. He also boasted wildly of having played center for the Washington Redskins, although team archives show no record of Panzirer's having so much as set foot in their training camp.

A former banquet employee at the Orlando Harley recalls having amiably refused many of Panzirer's amorous overtures. "Jay would ask me to go out. He hit on me four or five times, and I turned him down every time." With other employees, she said, he often got more cooperation. "He had a key and a room in the hotel set aside; he would bring his girls there." Despite her lack of interest in romance, the ex-employee said she truly liked Panzirer and enjoyed lunching with him at least once a month. Amazingly, for over a year the employee remained totally unaware that Leona Helmsley was Jay's mother. "I just assumed that Jay owned Deco, and since we had to buy from Deco that he and Leona had cut a deal—that they were just two people doing business together. Jay never offered that he was her son. He never once mentioned that she was his mother." In fact, she said Jay would sit impassively during the many occasions she cursed his mother's name. "I would tell Jay that the bitch was here last week and did this or did that. If I was really angry over someone she had fired, I'd say, 'You know what that bitch did the last time she was in?' I'd say, 'She's lucky she married an old man with money.' And all he'd ever say was 'That's a shame.'"

Leona, because of her Florida connections, visited the Orlando Harley far more often than any other hotel in the nationwide Harley chain. And someone was fired on practically every occasion, the banquet employee said. "It was so sad. Every time she came to town someone knew they were getting the ax, and she'd come month after month. We used to say, 'The bitch is here.' We also called her the Wicked Witch of the West. She thought she was the queen and we were all her slaves, that we were lucky to be getting paychecks. It's a game where she owns hotels and plays games with people's lives. She has no feeling for the consequences to people." To protect themselves, the employee said, "We had someone in the control tower at Orlando Executive Airport let us know when the Helmsleys had arrived" in their private jet. "When we got the call, we would have bellmen painting the curbs because she couldn't stand tire tracks on the curb. The Helmsleys would arrive and immediately Leona would let everyone know she was there. The general manager would greet them and it would never fail. There would always be something wrong! Then she'd say, 'Harry, you look tired. Why don't you go to your room and lie down?' You see, Leona was always a few steps off her throne when Harry was around. If she wanted to yell at you, she'd send him away first. And then Harry would leave, and it would be like Jekyll and Hyde. The smile would disappear and she'd start screaming and telling managers that they dared call themselves managers! 'You're idiots and you don't belong in the Helmsley organization!'"

Harry, by contrast, was loved by the 250 staff members. "He has unbelievable knowledge," the employee said, "and would share it with anyone. If you asked him a question, he'd give you an answer, and explain how he came up with the answer. He's the type of man you would want to be grandfather to your children. He was funny. He would tell jokes and little anecdotes, until Leona walked into the room. And then he'd just clam up! He doted on her and worshiped the ground she walked on. He never disagreed with her." The banquet employee narrowly escaped Leona's ax one morning at 8 A.M. "Without any warning whatsoever," she recalls, "Leona called me into the hotel general manager's office and totally ripped me apart. She called me a Southern lackey. She asked me if I had grown up in the sticks. She accused me of jumping a few beds to get my job." After being tongue-lashed for fifteen minutes, the employee summoned up enough courage to ask, "Mrs. Helmsley, what is the problem?"

"The problem," Leona howled, "is there are no eggs in the kitchen. The guests had no eggs!"

"That's the food and beverage director's responsibility," the employee replied. Nevertheless, Leona turned summarily to the general manager and ordered, "Terminate her." He pretended to execute the order, but quietly instructed the employee to return to work two days later and keep a low profile upon Leona's next visit.

Not until after she finally quit the Harley did the employee learn that Mrs. Helmsley was Jay's mother. "And when I did, I had to assume that Jay would just as soon not be Leona Helmsley's son. We had been having lunches for a year, and I had bad-mouthed her almost every time. If he loved his mother, I'd have been terminated on the spot."

Similarly, even as Leona spent more time with Jay's family and brought him ever closer into her business affairs, she seemed none too eager to advertise him as her son. Joyce Beber said Leona seldom spoke about Jay in public and actually discouraged him from making references to her. "She never wanted Jay to say that he was her son. Mrs. Helmsley said she and Harry tried to keep most people from knowing about Jay because of security reasons; she thought he could get kidnaped or something." Beber assumed another motive. "I thought she wanted to avoid being associated with Jay because of his age. He looked too old. He was bald. He had a beard. He was fortyish but looked even older. How could she pose as fifty and have a forty-year-old son? That's tough, just like Craig was too old to be an accepted grandchild. Age was always a very big thing with her."

Mother and son might have repaired their longtime rift eight years earlier, but apparently they had never gotten down to the business of becoming friends. As in childhood Jay could scarcely communicate with her. Blanche Slauson recalls that Leona and Jay exchanged few words the many times she observed them together. "Jay simply ignored her. He didn't seem to love her or not to love her. I never saw them speak together, in my home or at parties." Yet there was no public hint of animosity. "He was there and she was there," Blanche said, "and that was it." Deep down, however, Blanche said, "I felt that Lee really loved Jay. I think she was mad for him. But maybe she just didn't know how to show her love."

There was no such ambivalence in Harry's attitude toward Jay. "Harry didn't seem to like Jay or find him very interesting," Joyce Beber observes. "When Jay was around, Harry would be cordial, but it was like an annoyance. You could tell by his manner. He never had a real conversation with Jay. They would talk only about business."

In truth, Helmsley had ample reason for being so aloof. Not only had Jay defied the tycoon the previous year by printing Deco catalogs to drum up sales to Best Western and other outside accounts. According to Meckler, Helmsley became absolutely livid after learning of far bolder liberties taken later by his stepson. The cauldron boiled over when Joseph Licari, top financial officer of Helmsley Enterprises, performed a routine audit of Deco and uncovered several questionable Deco credit card charges signed by Panzirer. On one, Meckler said, "Jay rented a jet for four or five thousand dollars and flew Mimi to New York one weekend." That was bad enough. But Helmsley exploded when Licari informed him that Jay had charged Deco for a $10,000 table with a custom-carved Monopoly board top. It was the very same conversation piece, Harry realized, that Jay had recently given him as a birthday present. Instead of standard Monopoly addresses, the board had been hand-inset with Helmsley properties. A novel idea, no doubt, but hardly a personal sentiment under the circumstances. With a salary of almost $400,000 from the Helmsley treasury, Meckler says, "Harry thought Jay had enough to support himself without having to charge all these things."

Nine

By the spring of 1981, decorators and architects had completed the last of the offices in Leona's executive compound on the fifth floor of the Palace. Through a set of reception doors was the horseshoe-shaped stronghold, with Leona's feminine pink office toward the rear of the nearest prong. Visitors gained entry only after being screened by a security guard and a bank of receptionists at the center. Leona's senior executives, including Bill Dowling, worked in separate quarters along the far prong of the horseshoe. There was no shortcut to Leona; to reach her, they had to walk around the horseshoe and be announced by a receptionist, like any outside visitor. With the completion of the command center, Leona had a comfortable home base in the Palace. A small office adjoining hers was set aside for Harry, so that he could stretch out or review paperwork during his brief daily visits to the hotel. A routine set in. He would leave his Helmsley-Spear office in the Lincoln Building by 4 or 4:30 P.M. and be driven to the Palace by a chauffeur. For a half hour or so, he might discuss events of the day with Lerigo and Leona or decide hotel matters. Then he and Leona often repaired downstairs to the vaulted Gold Room for afternoon tea and finger sandwiches. A waitress would roll a portable lace-covered cart to their table and pour from a silver urn as a harpist played on the balcony above. It was a pleasant ritual, for which hotel guests willingly paid $8. Or instead, the Helmsleys might have a quick cocktail and call out requests to the piano player in the dark-paneled Harry's New York Bar at the Fifty-first Street entrance to the hotel. The cholesterol-conscious couple would watch, but not join in, as guests sampled such foods as beef Wellington with truffle sauce, at $17.50, or chili topped with sour cream, for $5.95. Finally, by 6 P.M., they would be driven back home to the Park Lane. After Harry's swim, they would often dine—American continental, with a French twist—in the hotel's second-floor Park Room overlooking Central Park. Following this, they often stopped for a nightcap in the adjoining Harry's Bar, smaller than that of the Palace, but having the same masculine feel, piano and $4 drinks. There they were not averse to chatting amiably with customers, particularly favorites like actors Mike Connors ("Mannix"), Hume Cronyn and Jessica Tandy. After a good night's sleep, Harry would have his morning swim, breakfast sensibly with Leona, and shove off to Helmsley-Spear by 9 A.M. Leona, in less of a hurry, might supplement her morning swim with a round of stretches and rowing exercises. Then, as she sat in a barber-type chair, the hair stylist would blow-dry her hair and help apply her makeup. At 11 A.M., the chauffeur would be waiting downstairs in the hotel carport to drive Leona to the Palace.

To be sure, Leona's was a grand lifestyle. By March, six months after the Palace opened, hotel managers noticed her efforts to make it even grander. Carl Hofer, the former executive assistant manager, cites that month as the beginning of Leona's first entourage. "On the way downstairs from her office," Hofer noticed, "she would start collecting any manager that she came across. 'Please come with me,' she would say. Within a couple of minutes, she'd have ten people tiptoeing behind her." Then, as the tour proceeded through the hotel corridors, Leona would call the individual members of the entourage to task. "She'd be pointing and screaming: 'That light bulb's dead, replace it!' Or 'Get rid of those flowers!'" Instead of relying on her general manager, Wolfgang Haenisch, or on Hofer, the assistant manager, to supervise and discipline the staff, increasingly she took things more completely into her own hands. "She would scream or bawl out whoever was there. She was totally out of control and had no idea of her own chain of command." It was unusual behavior indeed, Hofer said, for a hotel president to become so personally involved with employees, thereby undermining the authority and morale of Haenisch and department heads. "It was ego. At this point, she realized that the Palace was *her* Palace. Forget the Harley and all the other hotels. The Palace was it! It was her own Waldorf Astoria." Indeed, Hofer recalls, Leona invited the senior aides of Baron Hilton, owner of the Waldorf, for a tour of her new hotel and treated them like Motel Six flunkies. "She had them look at a few suites and said, 'So guys, let me show you how to run a hotel!' She meant it. She wasn't kidding. She wanted to let them know the Palace was the best, and I was so embarrassed."

Barely seven months after the Palace's grand opening, Wolfgang Haenisch was fed up. To be sure, there were some good memories to add to the pleasure he had taken in shopping the world to find the best of everything for the Palace. Just last November, Harry and Leona had thrown a dinner dance for Haenisch and his bride at the Palace. But within days of the party Leona began to blame him for everything real or imagined that went wrong at the hotel. By April, "I had had enough." He tendered his resignation to Lerigo and returned to Germany, where he began collecting castles for his own hotel empire, "Haenisch Castles," in the state of Baden-Württemberg.

Leona immediately declared Haenisch dead and forgotten. Hofer had been at a convention in Chicago when Haenisch left. When he returned to work, he said Leona called him into her office and demanded to know, "Where were you last week?"

"At a hotel show in Chicago."

"Who told you to go there?" she demanded.

"Wolfgang Haenisch."

"*Who* is Wolfgang Haenisch?" she snarled.

"The guy who killed himself opening your hotel," replied Hofer, so frustrated himself that he was willing to risk the consequences of sarcasm.

"Don't get smart with me," Leona shot back, letting the comment pass unpunished.

The following month, in its May 11 issue, *Business Week* noted Haenisch's resignation, adding that "Leona Helmsley is reportedly ruling with an iron hand. ..." The bad publicity was followed a week later by a report in the *Daily News* that both the Palace and Harley were off to a bad financial start, each having lost $1 million a month during the first three months of the year. As few as 40 percent of the rooms were taken, one expert estimated. But the Helmsley hotels were not suffering alone. Donald Trump's newly opened 1,347-room Grand Hyatt, adjacent to Grand Central Terminal, was faring no better because of the city's continuing economic slump. Helmsley shrugged off his $6 million loss for the first quarter, philosophizing that when the hotel business is good "it's very, very good, but when it's bad, it's terrible." Privately, however, the situation must have given the developer a few troubled thoughts. The operating losses of the two new hotels, combined with phenomenal construction cost overruns at the still unfinished Palace, added up to tens of millions of dollars in red ink.

A major factor in the low occupancy rates was Leona herself, according to Mal Seymourian, who served as marketing director of the Palace during its first year of operation. Instead of letting him do his job, he said Leona went ahead and decided marketing strategy on her own, losing tens of thousands of potential customers in the process. Standard policy in most hotels is to provide complimentary rooms to travel agents, potential volume customers or first-time corporate accounts in order to win their patronage and customer referrals over the long term. But with Leona, he said, "comps were not allowed." Everyone, with no exceptions, had to pay to sleep under her roof. The policy, Seymourian said, effectively prevented the hotel from promoting itself. The restriction was especially damaging with foreign clients, he said, "because normally you want to invite them to look over your hotel in hopes they'll switch over from one of our competitors. They're traveling a great distance and are probably comfortable with their present hotel. We're asking them to change, and take a chance." Few, however, would be interested in making the comparison test without the inducement of a free room. Leona also spurned Seymourian's suggestion that volume customers be given preferred availability—the ability to get rooms during the 100 to 120 nights a year when the city's hotels were booked to the hilt. The policy would have been a major selling point to corporations that must do business in New York during the busy holiday and convention seasons. Most frustrating of all, Seymourian said, was Leona's inability to stick to a coherent price strategy. "She had no one policy. Instead, she would change prices erratically [from] week to week." Consequently, he could not offer corporate customers guaranteed prices. "I'd go out and establish a corporate rate with large companies and she'd make it invalid, destroying our credibility." As a result of the seesaw pricing, he said, "major companies withdrew immediately." Among those who took their business elsewhere were the R. J. Reynolds Co. and the Condé Nast publishing group. "We lost at least ten thousand room nights a year," he estimated, for a loss of at least $1.2 million in potential revenue. Seymourian, who had worked at the Plaza Hotel for five years prior to joining the Palace, was simply nonplused by Leona's refusal to accept time-proven sales techniques. "She's a very bright woman, but there's something about her that's totally erratic or nonrational."

Another complaint came from Mark Flaherty, the former general manager of the Harley, who said his hotel was unable to offer comps or discounts. Complicating the occupancy problem was the lack of a well-orchestrated advertising campaign. As timing would have it, Leona had fired the Beber Silverstein & Partners ad agency in February, the same month the Harley opened, apparently to save money. Instead of continuing to rely on the Florida-based firm, she decided it made more sense to hire her own in-house advertising talent. But not until late April, on the brink of the crucial summer advertising season, did Leona finally fill the void. She hired Jane Maas, a seasoned Manhattan pro, to put together a campaign for all the hotels in the Helmsley realm. Although Maas was now in-house talent, the accommodations Leona provided her were almost a mile away, in a spartan cubbyhole of the Graybar Building.

After the two had gotten to know each other, Leona suggested that Maas follow her detailed formula for a sexier image. "Leona told me I had reached an age where I shouldn't have a haircut like a Marine recruit, like a lawnmower, like a butch.

She said it's not flattering; let it be longer. It's too bright red; subdue it. Stop wearing pants; you're a feminine woman." Obediently, Maas let her hair grow and then changed herself into a honey blonde. "The first time I came back from having my hair done, I looked totally different." On seeing the new look, Maas said, Leona approved. "She said, 'Did you see the way Harry smiled, the way I transformed you?' To this day, I have retained my changed image. The only time I wear pants is in the country. Leona was my Pygmalion."

Getting down to business, Maas decided to make Mrs. Helmsley the focal point of advertisements promoting the "magic" of tour package weekends at all the hotels. The ad splash for the Harley Hotel fell apart, however, when Leona unexpectedly rejected the work of Paul Elson, a professional photographer who shot the Manhattan hotel from every conceivable angle. In her later book, *Adventures of an Advertising Woman*, Maas described Leona's reaction upon seeing the best of Elson's eight hundred photographs. Mrs. Helmsley immediately focused on one of a hotel bedroom, with a wife showing her husband the results of a shopping spree at boutiques near the Harley. "That bedroom was a mess," Leona snorted. "It looked cluttered. I like bedrooms *without* people." With no further discussion allowed, she refused to pay Elson's fee, instructing Maas: "Tell him to sue me. Tell him to stand in line."

Elson accepted the challenge and collected approximately $10,000 from Leona, including interest and court costs, when the judge praised Elson's photography at the end of a two-year court battle, Elson says he fought long and hard "because I knew my work was good and I was not going to let this onerous woman treat me in a patently unfair way." Mrs. Helmsley's behavior was pure schoolyard bully, he alleges. "She was trying to take advantage of me just because I was a small fry—because she thought she could just run right over me. She has this attitude that the world owes her a certain type of obeisance." Elson said the strangest thing about the Harley experience was the hotel's refusal to give complimentary rooms to him and his small crew during their three days of shooting the hotel. Indeed, when he checked in at the registration desk, "they insisted that I give my credit card and pay my expenses up front, and that I would be reimbursed at a later date." Never before in his career, having shot over 150 hotels worldwide, had he encountered such a policy. "When you are working for a Hilton, or Marriott, or any hotel, they never charge. Everything is comped out." He concluded that Leona "was just a complete novice, or just doesn't care what the industry standards are." In any case, because of Leona's veto of Elson's work, the Harley hotel remained without a coherent advertising campaign, and occupancy rates remained in the doldrums. Through the summer, Flaherty recalls, "occupancy could run down to 25 or 30 percent," and barely hit 50 percent Monday to Thursday. But at the Palace, according to Seymourian, occupancy rates briefly shot up to almost 90 percent, helped by temporary price reductions. "We went from 30 percent occupancy to 90 percent in less than a year," he said, "but in the long term the erratic pricing was bound to damage occupancy levels."

Whatever the future held for the Palace, Carl Hofer was now beyond caring. By July, the assistant manager quietly circulated his résumé and was offered a job at an exclusive hotel in New York's Westchester County. "Mrs. Helmsley found out while I was on vacation in Vienna," he said, and preempted his resignation by firing him the second he returned to the Palace. Hofer said his vacation itself was no doubt as odious to Mrs. Helmsley as the implied insult of voluntarily leaving her employ. "She hated people to take vacations," he said. "As long as you killed yourself and worked twenty-four hours a day, you were okay. But the moment you took one day off, you were dead. If you were gone, even with authorization, and she needed you that day, you were in trouble." Haenisch's replacement as general manager, Michael Schweiger, accosted him with the news: "I'm sorry to tell you, but Mrs. Helmsley learned you were interviewing for other jobs. And she wants you out of this hotel in one hour!"

"Absolutely not," Hofer replied. "I certainly don't run like a dog. I will leave tomorrow after I have time to collect my things. I'll leave with dignity. I have not raped anyone. I have not killed anybody."

Gerald Kadish played the telephone message back a third time just to make sure he had heard correctly. "Hello. This is Harry Helmsley. Will you please call me during the week at this number....I look forward to hearing from you."

"Here is a living legend calling me out of the blue," Kadish thought to himself that midsummer of 1981. He dialed the number and was put through.

"I am interested in hiring you to help run my Harley hotel chain," Helmsley said. "Can you meet me at my office in the

Helmsley Palace next week?"

Kadish informed the mogul that he appreciated the fanfare, but he had no interest in relocating to New York. At the age of 42, the recently divorced hotel consultant wanted to spend more time with his college-age son, and had moved to Cape Cod to be near him. The ocean breezes and youthful lifestyle suited them both just fine.

"I'd like to meet you anyway," Helmsley insisted. "I would like for you to come to New York and just visit. Just so we can meet."

"I'm honored," Kadish replied in his Boston clip. "I'd certainly like to do that; I'd love to do that."

The following Wednesday, Helmsley ushered the tanned and lean six-foot-tall guest to his office on the fifth floor.

"We talked awhile," Kadish recalls, "and then I repeated that I wasn't particularly interested in the job, but it was a privilege chatting with him.

"I heard about your wife," Kadish added for extra clarification. "I hear she is difficult, to say the least, and this is not something I want to pursue as a job."

"But you've never met my wife. She's a really nice person. She's tough, but fair. You'd like her. I'd like you to meet her." Helmsley called Leona on the intercom, and a few minutes later, Kadish said, "In she came, like a breeze. Very cheerful, flowing, and beautifully dressed. She rushed over to Harry and kissed him on the forehead, checked his tie. And then she looked over at me."

"Lee, this is Jerry," Helmsley said. "He's been with Howard Johnson. I've been talking to him about the position."

"What makes you think you can do the job?" she asked.

"Firstly, I'm not looking for a job," Kadish answered. "But if I was, I could do an outstanding job of turning things around for you."

"What makes you think you can get along with me?" asked Leona.

"You could probably get along with me," said Kadish. "I could understand you. I've been married to two very difficult women."

Leona laughed and then confided: "You know the Harleys are having major problems. We're not making money."

"That's par for the course, and I could handle it," Kadish said, already taking Leona's bait.

Very deliberately, she then gave Kadish a complete lookover, up and down, starting with his shoes, his trousers, cufflinks, monogrammed shirt and jewelry. She studied his tie, his face and his salt-and-pepper hair. Then she looked at Harry and smiled. "I like him. Hire him."

"Okay," said Harry. "I'll take care of the details."

"That was interesting," Kadish said, after Leona had stepped away.

"Well, how much do you want?"

"I'm not sure I want anything. I'm not sure I'm interested."

"I'd like for you to think about it," Helmsley said. "This would be a wonderful situation. Come back and see me next week."

When he returned to Cape Cod, Kadish recalls, "I began thinking that it would be a challenge." A major factor in his turnaround was Leona herself—how she had instantly read him like a book and broken down his disinterest.

"She knew instinctively how to get me: that the way to do it was to challenge my competence. She behaved like an attractive woman, not just a business executive. She held very strong eye contact. She really knew how to gain your attention and soften you up just by her very gaze. Anybody would have been enamored with her way of handling herself."

Kadish took the job. For a $60,000 salary, he was hired as a vice president of the Harley Hotels chain, and expected that he could turn around the money-losing chain as he had done for other hotel groups in the past. He would work closely with Chet Kusek, vice president of operations for the chain. The headquarters of the hotel group was in Cleveland, but the real decisions were made in New York by the Helmsleys and would be funneled to Ohio by Kusek and Kadish. When he arrived in Manhattan, Kadish expected the Helmsleys to put him up at the new Palace or New York Harley for a month or so, until he could find an apartment. To his surprise, Helmsley insisted that he stay instead at the Helmsley Windsor on West Fifty-eighth Street, a sixteen-story hotel with a small lobby, antiquated rooms and no food and beverage operations. "It was not elegant or first class in any way," Kadish said. Even more surprising than his modest accommodations was Harry's insistence that "We have to charge you something. How about five hundred a month?"

More disappointment came the next day when he was steered to a shoebox of an office in the Graybar Building and told he would have to get by without a secretary. In meetings with the

Helmsleys, Kadish soon learned that Harry made all the financial decisions because "Leona never looked at financial statements or numbers; she didn't know how to read them. She certainly didn't understand them." He said most hoteliers constantly monitor a half-dozen key statistics to assure profitability: occupancy, average daily rate per room sold, gross sales, food costs, labor costs, net and gross operating profits. "She never observed them, never took notice of them. She had no idea about finances except that Harry would tell her, 'We're losing money.'" In all other areas, Leona ran the show. Rather than actually visiting her far-flung Harleys, however, she would make decisions mainly on the basis of guest comment cards left in each of the chain's 3,500 hotel rooms. The cards were pre-addressed to Mrs. Helmsley. Her secretaries would read and answer the complimentary cards; negative ones would be routed to Leona's desk. "She would fire employees over guest complaints even if the guests were wrong," said Kadish. "She would totally dehumanize the presumed offender. Or she would simply call up the hotel and say, 'I want that person fired.' Her favorite expression was, 'I don't want that person in my checkbook.' " Because the hotels weren't unionized, employees bit the dust without recourse.

Kadish also learned that the chain was losing approximately $3 million a year, and Leona held operations v.p. Kusek responsible. "She put him through a meat grinder that was merciless. Leona would say, 'What kind of guy is this? I'm getting terrible, terrible guest complaints. My motels are filthy, my employees are surly.' " She would also rail about continuing losses, even as the disorganized shipments of furnishings by her son, Panzirer, added millions to renovation costs of the hotels. A showdown came in early fall, when Kadish and Kusek were summoned to Leona's office. "She walked in loaded for bear," Kadish said, and confronted Kusek.

"You stupid! You stupid! Harry tells me you're losing more and more money. And my staff is poorly trained!" With veins bulging from her neck like drawstrings, Leona repeated the refrain without letup. "Kusek finally reached a point where he couldn't take it anymore," Kadish said. "He turned beet red and stood up like a perfect gentleman and said, 'I'm sorry, Mrs. Helmsley, but I must leave now.' Then he turned his back to leave her office and began to walk down the long hallway." Leona chased him, "and screamed like a madwoman, at the top of her lungs for everyone to hear: 'You can't walk out on me!

You can't turn your back on me!'" But Kusek kept walking and never returned. Helmsley then promoted Kadish to executive vice president, making him second to Leona in command of the chain.

But Leona warned him: "If you last six months, that will be a long time. Nobody lasts that long with me." Kadish had already seen enough firings to take the warning seriously. "She was proud of it in a sort of sick way. She felt she was so powerful and so omnipotent that nobody could survive her. She really felt that in that period of time, people would have done all they could do for her and then she could spit them up or flick them off. She had a deep disrespect for everybody because she was so much better in her own view. The mere fact that anybody was in need enough to be in her employ and therefore be beholden to her by accepting her paychecks made them unworthy of her respect. They were just hired hands—'idiots' she would call them. Everyone was an idiot, even Jeff Lerigo." In truth, Kadish said, "I think she had a need really to kill. When she was firing someone, she was killing that person. Getting them out of the way. Ruining them. She just didn't care. And she had a need to kill on almost a daily basis—to get somebody every day. Inside New York, she had to behave to the union people. But outside New York, anything goes. It could be a housekeeper, cook, chef, banquet person, salesperson."

Early on, Kadish added, he decided that Leona "respects nobody but Harry—not anyone or anybody. Everyone else was shit, even if it was a Rockefeller. She said she had been at a party with Laurance Rockefeller, her friend, and he was a shit. Bob Tisch was an idiot, a complete idiot. He doesn't know how to talk or anything. Trump was a young squirt—a brash whippersnapper. He didn't know what he was doing; he didn't have good taste."

Yet for all her frightful behavior, Leona was able to maintain control and project a powerfully alluring public image. "She could do it because she is an actress par excellence. She could be sitting here right now being a miserable bitch and giving someone a terrible time. But as soon as she walked out the door, if there were television cameras, the smile would come on, the charm and sexuality exuded, and she performed! A whole different personality. She could be flirtatious, a meek child, a father image, doting, creative, affectionate." The same star quality kept many key aides in thrall, however badly they were treated or how many tirades they had witnessed. "She was amazing," Kadish said. "She made me love her when I should have hated her. When she complimented me with that smile, 'You're a wonderful guy,' I would have done anything for her. I'm addicted to powerful, aggressive women, and she was a challenge. I was determined to please her."

Doing so was no easy matter because she demanded total devotion. In fact, Kadish said, Leona discouraged him from dating. "I was fine as long as I was a single guy and a workaholic and had no personal life. But when she heard I was reconciling with my ex-wife, she started treating me very shabbily because, after all, how could I divert my attention and focus from my job and her? Family life and spouses get in the way. You're supposed to be totally beholden and available to the job and to Leona."

To stem the flow of red ink, Kadish brought in cost controls, restaffed the hotels and supervised continuation of the chain's two-year-old renovation program. "Everything was done in a homey atmosphere. Most Harley lobbies have a fireplace and piano in the lobby, with lots of flowers, very nice background music and complimentary fresh fruit, coffees and teas." Crystal chandeliers were installed. Parking lots were repaved and roofs replaced. Gradually, the collection of motor inns was being transformed into more upscale, if not exactly first-class, hotels. Throughout the project, he said, Mrs. Helmsley accused contractors and vendors of shortchanging her. "She always suspected and thought that everyone was screwing her. There wasn't one honest person out there. That's the way she looks at people and life, generally. Everybody was bad, everyone was out to screw each other, and especially to rip her off. She used to say, 'I'm so wealthy and beautiful that everyone wants to screw me.' "

Yet if anyone was being ripped off, it was Harry Helmsley himself, whose money was being spent. And of all the participants in the renovation, none cost Helmsley more than Leona's son. "Jay ripped off Harry for millions and millions," Kadish said, through incompetence and fraudulent charges. Panzirer's home expenses, for instance, were routinely charged off to the Harley chain. "We would get charged for all types of supplies, furniture, dog food, fertilizer, dozens of cases of Dom Perignon champagne, wine, cigarettes, cleaning the house and doing the landscaping." Whenever Kadish questioned the personal expenses, Panzirer would invoke his mother's name. "My mother's aware of it, and you don't question her." Constantly,

Panzirer would deliver far more Deco furnishings to various hotels than were ordered, and then force the Harley chain to pay for the surplus goods. It was the same problem that Lester Belmuth had reported to Mrs. Helmsley the year before. "In a two-hundred-room hotel," Kadish said, "the furnishings and equipment would arrive for a three-hundred-room hotel and most of it would be the wrong stuff anyway. He was ordering the hell out of vinyl wall covering, enough to do the hotels twice. I would complain, 'First, we got too much; second, we got the wrong stuff.'" And Jay would pull rank, saying, "You're questioning me! This is my decision. I have authority over you." The Harley chain would then eat the expense and Panzirer would sometimes remove the paid-for surplus goods to warehouses under his control. When the time came for the Harley chain to place new orders, Kadish said, it never knew whether it was repurchasing the same goods that Panzirer had carted off at an earlier date. There was also the suspicion that Panzirer might be selling the paid-for, surplus goods on the open market, Kadish said, because Panzirer "bragged that he handled other accounts" outside the Helmsley realm. A great cause for concern, Kadish said, was Deco's refusal to submit printed invoices for items sold to the Harley chain. Instead, Deco would transmit bills electronically to the chain's Cleveland office. "We didn't know what the hell the charges were for," Kadish said. "We couldn't question them. Jay could literally charge what he wanted. It would have been suicidal to question Jay, because if someone was on his trail he would bad-mouth that person to his mother. He had conversations with his mother every day. You didn't rile him. If anything, you told him how wonderful he was." Because Helmsley owned both Deco and the Harley chain outright, theoretically any unjustified charges to the hotels would be offset by an equivalent financial windfall to Deco. In effect, Helmsley would suffer no loss because money would simply be shifted from pocket A to pocket B. That would not be the case, however, if Panzirer was acting in his own interest rather than Helmsley's.

Indeed, in at least one known instance, Panzirer secretly made a side deal to benefit himself. By 1981, he had bought a partnership interest in an Orlando firm, Contract Drapery, which manufactured draperies for Deco. Deco, in turn, would sell the goods to Helmsley's hotels, providing Panzirer with a sideline income. In effect, Panzirer became a secret middleman, in utter defiance of Helmsley's orders to steer clear of outside entanglements. Charles Edgin, the principal owner of Contract Drapery, verifies that "Jay owned 20 percent of the company. We were business associates." But he had nothing else to say on the matter.

Although the drapery deal was hush-hush, Panzirer did confide his secret ownership interest to Meckler. After hearing the disclosure over lunch at a Steak and Ale restaurant near Deco, Meckler said he pointedly warned Leona's son of the potential adverse consequences. "I told him, 'You're kinda sticking your neck out, Jay. I don't think Harry would care for this.' " Jay shrugged off the danger, saying, "Don't worry about it. It's no problem." Meckler said he couldn't understand how, "with Jay's salary," he would risk upsetting the apple cart for a few extra bucks.

Kadish said Leona was even more concerned than Jay about financial security, despite her vast wealth. "She had this tremendous complex about her future, about what would happen if Harry died. The fear was that Harry's investors and partners would somehow screw her out of whatever Harry left, that she would have no friends, and that she would have no income because it would be taken away. She knew she was getting old. She feared she would lose all her position and stature without Harry, and therefore she was ultra-concerned about providing for her own security and for Jay's future." Many a time, Kadish said, Leona worried out loud: "What happens when Harry goes? I hope I go first." Kadish assumed, therefore, that Leona's steadfast efforts to improve Jay's financial status were motivated in large part by a desire to calm her own long-term financial worries.

One of Helmsley's former close aides recalls a tense meeting with Leona's son earlier that spring concerning another questionable business affair. The aide said he was dispatched to Deco headquarters in Maitland to review Deco's records. While they were going through records together, he said Panzirer informed him that Deco was planning to bill the New York Harley for furnishings, fixtures and equipment ("FFE") which had actually been installed in the Palace. The aide said Panzirer broached the matter during a discussion of massive cost overruns at the Palace. Theoretically, Helmsley would benefit because, as general partner of the Palace, he was responsible for every penny of cost overruns. But at the Harley, cost overruns would be jointly shared by Helmsley and his construction partner, the Metropolitan Life Insurance Co., each of whom held a

50 percent stake in the new hotel. In effect, for every dollar of Palace expenses shifted to the Harley, Helmsley would only have to pay fifty cents. Unwittingly, Metropolitan Life would pay the other half dollar.

The financial switcheroo would have been possible because Deco supplied all FFE items—light fixtures, furnishings and amenities such as drapes, valances, sconces and carpeting—to both hotels. The aide recalls that Panzirer's exact words concerning the Palace overrun were: "Don't worry. We're going to shed the FFE cost between the hotels."

"That's crazy," the aide replied, and demanded a look at more Deco paperwork. Immediately, he said, Panzirer picked up the phone and called his mother to protest the interference. "He called his mother then and there," and Leona demanded to speak to the aide. He said she told him point blank: "You are not to inquire about any costs! You are not to review any financial statements or accounting information."

When the aide returned to New York, he said he briefed Helmsley thoroughly on the whole affair. In addition, he said he informed Helmsley that Panzirer, through Deco, had billed the St. Moritz hotel for repairs to his Maitland swimming pool. "I told him these were exorbitant cost allocations and might raise questions among investors in the hotels." After briefing Helmsley, the aide recalls that "Mr. Helmsley said nothing, except that he would talk to Mr. [Harry] Scanlan," the Helmsley Enterprises vice president in charge of both construction projects.

Shortly after this, he said Mrs. Helmsley confronted him about the briefing. "What are you doing going to my husband?"

"I'm here to protect the interests of all concerned," he replied.

"You have no right to question appropriations," she said, and then forbade him ever to handle Palace or Harley matters in the future.

Scanlan, who is now retired in Virginia, insists: "There was never a billing to the Harley for stuff delivered to the Palace. Nothing was ever switched to the Harley. It never, never happened. I never heard it from Mr. Helmsley and it never was done. Each of the hotels was handled completely separately."

In yet another situation, a former senior executive of the Helmsley Palace recalls having received several highly questionable Deco invoices for large shipments of silver flatware delivered to the hotel. Under standard billing procedures, he said, the Palace would send a requisition order to Deco whenever it needed merchandise. Deco, in turn, would contact a manufacturer, which would route the goods to the Palace and forward its bill to Deco. On at least three occasions the billing procedure went awry, and duplicate invoices from Minners Associates, a Manhattan china and silverware distributor, were inadvertently forwarded directly to the Palace. Later, when Deco forwarded its bills to the Palace, the Palace executive compared them with the duplicate copies that had landed on his desk.

"Comparing them side by side," he said the quantities of merchandise purchased matched. And Deco's standard purchasing fee of 15 to 20 percent was tacked on to Minners's wholesale price, as would be expected. What was wrong, he said, was that Deco had misrepresented Minners's wholesale price. "The three bills, I remember clearly, were jacked up an extra 30 percent. Each one was increased an average of three hundred or four hundred thousand dollars." If so, any padded cost would have come directly out of Helmsley's pocket, since it would have increased the hotel's cost overrun. Although Panzirer supervised Deco's billings, it was unclear who might have benefited by inflating the invoice information. The hotel executive kept his observations to himself, however, because Deco was one of Leona's touchiest subjects. "Purchases made before the hotel opened were in the millions," he said. "Deco's commissions alone were in the millions." And Mrs. Helmsley gave strict orders that nothing, not even an emergency purchase, could be obtained except through Deco. "Deco was the holiest thing in the world to her. You couldn't buy a cup outside of Deco. It was always 'Deco, Deco, Deco.' She would be furious, she would scream, she would go through the roof when you didn't use Deco. 'If that happens one more time, you're fired!'" In the final weeks before any hotel opens, he said, "you have to make decisions a hundred times a day. You need things. You have to have it fast. But she would insist, 'Get it from Florida, or else!'"

Despite her newfound prominence, by the fall of 1981, Leona was unable to round up enough friends to fill her table at charity dances. Instead, employees like Bill Dowling would find themselves on her command-appearance invitation list. He and his wife were dutifully present at one such affair that season when an attractive woman walked up to Mrs. Helmsley.

"Leona, you don't mind if I dance with your Harry just one

dance?"

"Yes, I do mind," she replied. "Nobody dances with Harry but me!"

"Leona, you're so funny. You're so cute," the woman responded, and took Harry by the hand onto the dance floor.

A few dances later, she returned Harry to the table and said, "Thank you, Leona, for letting me dance with Harry."

"You bitch!" Leona screamed for all the world to hear. "Don't you ever touch my Harry again! I'm the only one who's allowed to dance with him. You biiiitch! You biiiitch! You biiiiitch!"

Time and time again, Dowling saw examples of Leona's possessiveness—indeed domination—over her husband. Not long before, Harry had summoned his Palace investors to the hotel for a board meeting. En route from the Lincoln Building he was to stop off at Julia's dress shop in the Graybar Building and pick up Leona. She was running late, however, and was nowhere to be seen when Helmsley dropped in. Unable to keep his investors waiting, he left without Leona and continued to the Palace. "Harry was in the middle of the meeting with investors," Harry Dowling recalls, "and she walked in and slammed the big heavy doors and read him the riot act. 'How dare you come up here without me! How dare you leave me behind!' In front of these investors, she totally humiliated him. His only meek reply was, 'You were late.'"

But the first sign Dowling had of Leona's real control over Harry took place the prior year at Leona's Park Lane office, before the Palace opened. As Dowling and Leona discussed marketing of the Harley chain, Harry quietly entered at 5 P.M. and sat in a chair opposite her desk. Abruptly, Dowling said, "She interrupted me and screamed to him: 'Harry, stop picking your face!'" In a trice, Dowling said, "Harry's hands flew away from his face like a boy scolded. He sat up in his chair and didn't say a word of rebuttal to her. And throughout the next year of watching them together I saw more and more of that treatment. Like a mother scolding a child, and him accepting it. It seemed to be progressive. I was aware of it happening more and more."

By late 1981, he said, Leona's grip was virtually complete. One day around Thanksgiving, Dowling explained, he gave Helmsley a month's advance notice that he would be leaving his marketing post at the Palace and Harley hotels in order to pursue a more lucrative account in Bermuda. "I said now that the Palace was open and doing well, I had done my job and I couldn't afford to stay involved with him anymore. And he said he understood that money is money and told me he knew Leona would miss me."

Word filtered back to Dowling that instead, Leona was furious. "And as a result," he said, "she didn't come to work for the next couple of weeks. I assumed she didn't want to see me until I was out of there." Then, he continued, "Harry called me in and said, 'This is becoming a problem. She's so upset with you leaving, she won't come in. Maybe you should come report to me in the Lincoln Building and avoid a confrontation.' "

On the holiday weekend, thinking the coast was clear, Dowling said he slipped into his old office at the Palace to do some paperwork. "I heard a noise, and looked up and saw someone was fooling with my doorknob, trying to get in the office." When he got up to open the door, he found himself face to face with Leona, with Harry behind her. In a fierce verbal assault, he said she vowed: "No one walks out on me! I'll get you! I'll destroy your business career!" Harry, meanwhile, refused to intervene on his behalf. "He was looking at me and turned his eyes down towards the floor and just followed her out like a puppy dog." Rather than phone himself, Helmsley instructed one of his attorneys to contact Dowling. "The lawyer said for me not to worry, that Harry would see to it that no harm came to me."

Dowling says Leona could read people "like a book, and knew how to play them. She almost has X-ray vision. She can almost see through them. She can spot their fatal flaw, their weakness. She's such an incredibly powerful person, one on one with people, that she can intimidate anyone. She can play them along for months and months and then, when she's tired of them, she'll take their fatal weakness and use it to try to destroy them." Dowling, spoilsport that he was, had jumped one unexpected step ahead of the X-ray.

Jane Maas the blonde was far happier than Jane Maas the redhead. For that she could thank Leona. But the advertising agent's relationship with Mrs. Helmsley had gone steadily downhill the rest of the year. First, there was a pay dispute. For a brochure on the New York Harley, Leona insisted: "No professional models." To get the job done, Maas went ahead quietly and hired unemployed actors, students and friends to pose for a very nominal twenty-five dollars a day. When Leona found out, she extended her ban to "nonmodel models," thereby leaving Maas to pay the fees. Another source of friction, according to Maas's memoir, was Leona's somewhat condescending attitude. "You call this a real estate ad?" Leona asked after receiving one Maas proposal. "My little grandson can write a better ad than this. Now, you just go back and do this ad over again, five hundred times if you have to, but you get back here to me before this day is over with an ad I can accept." After just seven months as Leona's in-house agent, Maas bade an amicable farewell to her Pygmalion.

In February 1982, Leona caused a crisis at Beber Silverstein & Partners by the simple act of inviting Joyce Beber to lunch. The significance of the gesture was all too obvious: Leona wanted her back.

"No way!" Elaine Silverstein advised her partner, still resentful that Leona had fired the Miami agency the previous year and had taken her very sweet time paying their balance due. Staff media director Myer Berlow said, "What have we got to lose? Let's just have lunch with her."

"I'm afraid that if I have lunch with her she'll talk us back," Beber replied.

The trio flew to New York for the deciding meal at Le Trianon. "It took Mrs. Helmsley about fifteen minutes," Beber confesses, "and I was won over." Leona's opening gambit was the decisive factor. "She asked us, 'Supposing I give you all the hotels?'" In their earlier dealings, Beber explained, "We handled advertising only for the Palace, the New York Harley, and a little bit for the Harley chain. Now she's also giving us the Park Lane and the St. Moritz. Everything they own!" Beber said the biggest sucker for Leona's charms was Berlow. "I mean, he was just fawning all over her, and he's not that kind of guy. She was so charismatic and charming and fun and funny, telling us, 'I never should have let you go. You were so wonderful. You did great advertising. We want you back to do it again.'" Leona then escorted the threesome upstairs to Harry's office and announced, "The kids are back!" As a goodwill gesture, the Helmsleys then offered to fly the advertising crew back to Miami in a very special aircraft. Just months before, Harry and Leona had traded in their compact Sabreliner for a giant BAC 1-11 commercial jet capable of seating one hundred people comfortably. All but a dozen of the seats had been removed, to make room for the Helmsleys' queen-size bedroom, fully stocked bar, built-in backgammon tables, and cabinets for their bone china and crystal stemware. Nor were the stereo system and Big Band album collection to be left behind! For the extra leg room alone, no doubt, it was $5 million well spent. When they landed several hours later, Helmsley confessed a bit of guilt over the extravagance.

"The one thing that embarrasses me," he said, "is when people greet me on the tarmac and say, 'When are the rest of the passengers coming off?'"

Jay Panzirer walked straight to the telephone after leaving his doctor's office in Boston. Without wasting a moment, he phoned his stockbroker in Florida with instructions to transfer his entire portfolio into a joint account with his wife, Mimi. Panzirer then made another long-distance call. "Please put aside Friday night," he asked Michael Mennello, an Orlando gift store owner who was one of his very best friends. "I'm flying in lobster for a party," he explained, and insisted that Mennello and his wife, Marilyn, attend.

A few nights later, on Friday, March 26, the Mennellos arrived for a most unusual party. Panzirer steered them into the kitchen, where two or three other guests were helping Mimi uncrate thirty pounds of live, seaweed-covered lobster. After they were boiled everyone sat for a festive meal. Dom Perignon was served. Then came a succession of fine wines: first, a Piesporter. Next, a dry, red Lafite Rothschild, which Jay loved but everyone else spurned. Finally came an unexpected announcement.

"I am so happy to be alive and have friends at the table," Jay told them all. "But my time is limited." Mennello said Panzirer then explained that his doctor had examined him earlier in the week and told him that his heart was shot. It was only a matter of time before another short circuit, another electrical misfire, would occur. The next heart attack would probably come soon, the doctor informed him, and would almost certainly be fatal. Now, on this cool Florida night, Panzirer had called his best friends together for a last meal.

"He toasted his wife," Mennello said, "and told us he had made provisions for her. He was making a new will and had changed his stocks over to Mimi's name. He said he was so happy to be down here in Orlando. He liked New York, but he really loved Orlando. He said he and Mimi loved to enjoy the high style in New York with the Helmsleys, but Orlando was much better. It was a wonderful way of living with no competition in business. He was working for his mother. He had a wonderful home. And he loved his golf. He was able to play tennis twice a week. And he had treasured friends whom he loved very dearly." The announcement was a shock to everyone, but especially to Craig, Panzirer's eldest son, who left the table with tears running down his cheeks. Panzirer then noted that Craig's future was assured: Leona had set up a trust fund three years earlier in the youth's name. He indicated that his other three children, living in Staten Island and California, would also be taken care of.

The Mennellos returned Panzirer's toasts, trying not to seem overly alarmed. But as they drove home at 11 P.M., tears formed in the corners of their own eyes. Only five days later, at approximately 4 P.M. on March 31, Gerald Kadish received a phone call at the Helmsley Palace from a manager of the Orlando Harley: "Mr. Kadish, we just put Jay in an ambulance." Kadish said the manager explained that Panzirer had come to the hotel around lunchtime and taken an unidentified woman upstairs to his reserved room. "They had room service, wine, booze and more booze," Kadish said.

Then the front desk received a phone call from the woman, who implored, "Please send help!" A group of hotel employees rushed upstairs. "Jay had his pants down. He was on the floor, hunched over in a pile of his own vomit and secretions of all kinds. They called the ambulance, but nobody could revive him." Meanwhile, Kadish said, "the woman disappeared."

Panzirer was rushed to the emergency room of Lucerne General Hospital, but ventricular fibrillations had already done their damage. Upon arrival, at precisely 3:57 P.M., he was pronounced dead.

Ten

Gerald Kadish was reluctant to tell Leona of her son's death for fear that in days to come she would blame the messenger for the message. Instead, he asked a secretary to interrupt a conference that Leona was conducting at that moment in the Palace. Without giving any details, the secretary informed Mrs.

Helmsley that Kadish needed to speak with her right away. A few seconds later, Kadish skirted the hard facts as best he could.

"Mrs. Helmsley," he told her, "I just got a call from Orlando, and Jay is at the hospital. He is not doing well. You might want to talk to someone there."

For a brief moment, Leona seemed to freeze. Then she seized command, informing Harry at his office in the Lincoln Building. Because their BAC 1-11 was being serviced out-of-state, the Helmsleys booked the first available commercial flight to Orlando that Wednesday afternoon.

In the meantime, Mimi Panzirer, Milton Meckler, Jay's top aide, and Jay Panzirer's executive secretary, Doris Le Cours, clung together outside the Florida emergency room hoping for a miracle. A doctor emerged through the swinging door, however, and announced, "We did our best. But we couldn't bring him back."

"Mimi burst into tears, Doris did. I did, too," Meckler said. "The staff fed Valiums to all three of us to calm us down." Despite her grief, Mimi insisted on notifying Harry and Leona immediately, reaching them in the limo en route to their flight. Mimi delivered the final word: "Jay is gone."

There was a dead silence at the other end of the phone. Then Harry picked up the receiver and calmly told Mimi that their plane would be arriving at Orlando Executive Airport at approximately 8 P.M. In the interim, Meckler drove Mimi to her home in Maitland, where Craig had just returned from school. "Mimi took him into the living room and told him his father had died," and the sandy-haired youth soaked his stepmother's shoulder in tears. Meckler excused himself at 7 P.M. and drove Mimi's white Cadillac to the airport to meet the Helmsleys. Leona walked off the plane, he recalls, "and she was hysterical when she saw me at the gate. She was on Harry's arm. She was in tears. She was devastated—a mother's devastation." Meckler drove the Helmsleys directly to the Panzirer home, "and Mimi and Leona gave each other a long, long hug at the door." Meckler was well aware that the two women had had their occasional scraps in the past, "but for that instant, all negative feelings were wiped out." Harry, Leona, Craig and Mimi spent a good while alone and then Mrs. Helmsley asked to use the telephone to call the manager of the Orlando Harley.

"She was on the phone with him for an hour in a separate room," Meckler recalls. "She wanted to know if the hotel staff acted promptly. 'Did you get the emergency squad quickly?' "

Meckler said Leona pressed for a fuller accounting of her son's death and warned the manager to give her "the entire story, from soup to nuts. He was told that it was his job if he didn't give her all the true details." Only then was Leona informed about Jay's female companion, and was told that the woman was a sales representative for a furniture company. After more prying, Leona was given the name of Jay's paramour. She hung up the phone and came to Meckler with the details. "She was very upset," he recalls, "but wasn't in total shock about the woman." After all, for several years Leona had relied on Meckler to keep Jay's philandering out of the spotlight. Now, when discussing the final tryst, he said Leona acknowledged: "I expected as much." Nevertheless, she vowed vengeance against the woman. "I'm going to get all the details, and then I'm going after her!"

Keeping the sordid details from everyone else, Leona rejoined Mimi and Craig in the living room and turned to the sad chore of making funeral plans. Arrangements were set for a funeral service the following day, Thursday, at the Congregation of Liberal Judaism in Orlando, with a eulogy by Jay's rabbi, Larry Halpern. The body would then be flown to New York aboard the BAC 1-11 for a funeral service Friday afternoon in Manhattan. Entombment would follow in the Helmsleys' mausoleum at Woodlawn Cemetery in the Bronx, the pink monument which Jay had ridiculed so often.

Thursday, on a cool and cloudy afternoon, Mimi was allowed into a side room of the Orlando synagogue, where she saw Jay one last time before the bronze casket was sealed. "I brought the collar stays that he always wore," Mimi recalls, "and put them in for him. I put his wedding ring, a plain gold band, on his finger." She kissed him goodbye and followed behind as his casket was wheeled into the sanctuary. Leona, in a dark dress and clutching Harry, wept loudly in the front row as rabbi Halpern conducted the brief ceremony. Moments later, Craig, Mimi, Harry and Leona headed by limousine for Orlando Executive Airport, where the BAC 1-11 had arrived to ferry them to New York. A dozen friends and employees, including Meckler and his wife, were invited to accompany the family. An emotional delay came, however, when cargo handlers were unable to fit Jay's casket into the plane. After much confusion, Leona entrusted Jay's casket to Eastern Airlines, and the BAC 1-11 took to the sky.

Once the group was airborne, spirits seemed to lighten.

Meckler said Helmsley was particularly relaxed, and obviously relished playing host aboard his luxury jet. "He walked around serving us candy and packaged fancy cookies even though he had a steward who could have done it." Meckler said he and several other passengers joked privately about the $125 crystal wine glasses and bone china that Leona and Harry had stocked aboard the aircraft, supplied free of charge by Deco. "We didn't want to break anything. They were quite expensive."

Limousines were waiting when the plane landed at Teterboro Airport in suburban Bergen County, New Jersey. When they reached the Park Lane Hotel, Mimi noticed that Jeff Lerigo, the invisible diplomat of the Helmsley hotel empire, "did a very kind thing for me. He made sure that I was given a different suite than the one Jay and I always stayed in on the forty-sixth floor." Craig was given his own room down the hall so that he need not return to his mother's home on Staten Island. That evening, Mimi, Craig and the rest of the Florida contingent were invited to Leona's penthouse for dinner.

While attending to guests, Leona and Harry wrestled with another unexpected problem. "No synagogue in New York would conduct Jay's funeral because Leona didn't belong to any temple," Mimi recalls. Finally, the Helmsleys won over the Orthodox rabbi of the Park East Synagogue on East Sixty-seventh Street. There was apparently some negotiating, Meckler recalls. "The rabbi came up himself to the penthouse." However, while he agreed to handle the ceremony, the rabbi insisted that a bronze coffin was inappropriate for the austere service and that Jay would have to be transferred to a wooden casket. The objection was overcome after Mimi insisted equally loudly that it was out of the question. "I absolutely refused," she said. "Jay was in his final resting place and I wasn't going to have him juggled around!"

Word went out quickly. The next morning, Friday, more than a thousand mourners took their seats in the synagogue. Little did they know, Mimi said, that a spirited contest was underway between the Orthodox rabbi and Halpern, the Panzirer family's Liberal rabbi from Orlando. "Park East wouldn't give Halpern his robes," Mimi said, "and told him he couldn't deliver the eulogy." Halpern ignored the restrictions and stepped forward to give the same eulogy he had delivered in Orlando the day before. "Short of knocking rabbi Halpern off the podium," Mimi said, "there was nothing they could do about it." After the service, only a few cars were allowed to proceed to the cemetery. Jay's father, Leo Panzirer, obviously had every right to join the funeral cortege, but he quietly disappeared with his wife, Zelda.

By 3 P.M. family and friends returned to Leona's penthouse to commence sitting shiva, the traditional seven-day Jewish mourning period. As they entered the apartment, guests dipped their hands in a basin of water to wash the sorrow away and affirm that life must go on. Meckler said Leona was visibly cheered by the presence of her four grandchildren, particularly young Wally. The mourners had a meal together before going their separate ways.

On Saturday, Meckler said, Leona invited Mimi to accompany her and Harry to West Palm Beach, so they could continue sitting shiva in more private surroundings. Surprisingly, he said, Mimi declined the offer and decided instead to return to Orlando that afternoon on a special flight Harry had arranged for Meckler, Le Cours and the rest of the Floridians.

Even more curious than Mimi's decision to skip shiva, he recalls, was her behavior once the BAC 1-11 headed south. "She called me up to the front of the plane and announced that she was planning to take over Deco. Like a queen in waiting, she told me, 'Sit down, Milt…' "

"Jay liked you a lot," Mimi continued. "You've done a good job. And now I'll probably be taking over and getting involved." Meckler said the announcement was a shock because Mimi had had little or no experience in the purchasing business, and yet was "sitting there passing judgment on me after I had been Jay's right-hand man for several years." He said Mimi then suggested that Deco was Jay's company and she was his rightful heir. Stunned, Meckler said he demurred. "Are you sure, Mimi? Because I believe Harry owns 100 percent of the company." He said she responded quite confidently, "No, Jay had an agreement that he could buy Deco for a dollar at any time." It was the first Meckler had heard of any such arrangement. Even if it were true, what evidence was there that Jay had actually exercised the option to purchase Deco? "Mimi was saying it was her company," Meckler recalls. "You could see that she was planning to become the Queen of Orlando!"

The following afternoon, on Sunday, Meckler went to check his mail at Deco headquarters in Maitland. As he sat in his office, he looked up to see Mimi unexpectedly enter the building with Jay's secretary, Doris Le Cours. Following close behind the two women was a close friend of the Panzirer family:

Charles Edgin, principal owner of Contract Drapery, the firm in which Jay had secretly become a partner in defiance of Meckler's earlier warning. Meckler said the threesome immediately headed for Jay's office "and closed the door behind them." The visitors stayed for several hours. At one point, he said, Edgin came outside and said, "Mimi doesn't want you to come into Jay's office until things are straightened out." Meckler made no objection but recalls, "I didn't like the atmosphere. It was definitely a power play by Mimi, who shouldn't have been in there exercising power. But I let it go." When he left the office, he said the visitors were still busy with their unexplained mission.

The next morning, Meckler said, Harry Helmsley called him at work just to check on things. Meckler told the tycoon about Mimi's claims regarding Deco ownership and about her visit to Jay's office. "I'm confused," Meckler said.

Helmsley's fury was instantaneous, Meckler recalls. "It's the first time I've heard Mr. Helmsley so angry. He questioned me as to what they did in the office." Meckler explained that the door was closed, but he speculated that files were examined and that Mimi might have had plans to bring her friend Edgin into Deco because he already owned a purchasing firm of his own.

"Mimi has nothing to do with the business," Helmsley fumed. He verified that Jay never had any ownership interest in Deco, despite what Mimi might have been led to believe by her husband. "You're in charge," Harry affirmed. "I don't want her involved!" To ensure that no uncertainty remained, Helmsley pledged, "I'll be down there. I'll get it straight with her. She will not be in the office anymore." When Leona got word of the incident, she was even more upset. "Mimi's skipping the shiva and running to Jay's desk to scrounge through his things set Leona's firecracker off," Meckler said. "She was right. It didn't seem like the time to go worrying about possessions. Mrs. Helmsley thought it was a time to mourn."

That week, however, Leona proved that she could also be distracted from mourning. Obituaries in the New York and Florida newspapers were based on a sanitized account of Jay's death issued by Leona's spokeswoman, Frances Friedman of the Howard Rubenstein public relations firm. It stated that Panzirer had collapsed while conducting a business meeting at the Orlando Harley. The papers also reported that Jay was 42, two years over his real age. When Mrs. Helmsley learned of that mistake, Joyce Beber recalls, "She went berserk. I mean, that upset her as much as Jay's death, if not more! How could she pass for a 50-year-old woman if she had a son that was 42? She just went crazy and blamed it on Fran Friedman, who had sent out the press release." From that moment on, Beber said, "Mrs. Helmsley could barely look at Fran. She would tell her, 'You're dumb. You're stupid.'" Sure enough, Beber said, Friedman was soon taken off the Helmsley account. "It was shocking, because Fran had spent every day with her for several years. She had invested herself in Leona, and Leona just threw her away."

Mimi's doings in Jay's office, meanwhile, remained a burning issue. By the second week in April, Harry and Leona dispatched Frank Turco, Jay's old friend and the New York liaison for Deco, to Maitland to investigate. A major question was whether important documents had been taken from the building. Turco brought along two aides who seldom left his side, Vincent Sclafani and Neil Petruzzi, a pair of husky, middle-aged former New York City policemen who still wore their firearms: Sclafani on his ankle, Petruzzi on the hip. Unlike Turco, who was partial to jewelry and flashy ensembles such as maroon shirts and white ties, Sclafani and Petruzzi stuck to inconspicuous dark suits. Even to Meckler, who was still upset over Mimi's power play, the armed trio seemed to be overkill for the job of investigating a willowy 33-year-old widow.

Turco's first move was to take temporary charge of Jay's office and draw some attention to his arrival. "It was a very dramatic introduction," Meckler said. "Frank opened his briefcase and there was a thirty-eight inside. He did little things like that." After getting his bearings, Turco assembled the Deco staff and announced that the Helmsleys had designated Meckler to step into Jay's shoes as executive vice president of the company. (Meckler's pay would be approximately $100,000, only a fourth of Jay's salary.)

Next, Turco summoned Doris Le Cours to Deco at 6 A.M. for an explanation of Mimi's visit to Jay's office. Meckler was astounded when he walked into the office at 8 A.M. and saw Turco and his investigative team interrogating the secretary. "They had Doris in the hot seat," he said. "And she was frightened to death. They wanted to know about the entry into Jay's desk, and which papers were missing. They were giving her the third degree about this break-in situation. Doris was really crying about it."

Meckler demanded an explanation from Turco: "What in the world is going on?"

"We called Doris last night," Turco replied. "She's not a criminal. We just have some questions to ask her." Le Cours disclosed that she had used her key to open Jay's desk for Mimi and Edgin and that they had carried away some files. After further research, the team learned that on April 6, Mimi had emptied a safe deposit box she held jointly with Jay at Southeast First National Bank in Maitland. In turn, Mimi opened another box in her own name at another bank. When the Helmsleys were informed of these developments, their anger at Mimi intensified.

Mrs. Helmsley had been peeved with Mimi for over a year anyway, Meckler said, because Mimi had instructed Le Cours "to give Jay as few telephone calls as possible from his mother." The daily telephone tongue-lashings were no boon to Jay's health, and Mimi knew it. Her rush to the safe deposit box during shiva only fueled Leona's rage further, Meckler said. "Mrs. Helmsley claimed that Mimi had stuffed her pocketbooks, with cash pouring out." In any case, because the box was used jointly by the Panzirers, Mimi had every legal right to handle its contents. But Leona could not be mollified by such logic.

Gerald Kadish recalls that Mrs. Helmsley bitterly complained "that Mimi cleaned out the box before anyone could see what was in it." Jay's financial affairs were muddied by the fact that he had prepared a draft of his will but died without having signed it. As a result, under Florida law, Mimi was automatically entitled to half her husband's estate, with Jay's four children sharing the other half. Therefore, Myrna and Ruth, the mothers of Jay's children, presumably had far greater reason than Leona to scrutinize Mimi's handling of the estate.

A few days after Turco's investigative crew arrived on the scene, Helmsley made good on his promise to visit Deco personally for a look-see. He brought Leona with him. The tycoon inspected mounds of documents and discovered that Jay had advanced over $20,000 in Deco funds to a company named Contract Drapery. Inquiries were made, and Meckler then disclosed all the details of Jay's involvement in Charles Edgin's firm. Upon hearing of his secret partnership, mild-mannered Harry blew his stack.

"I warned Jay!" Helmsley shouted. "I told him not to get involved in outside business! And he did it anyway. And he didn't use his own money. He invested Deco money in a private company!" Meckler said Helmsley paced up and down Jay's office "yelling and screaming about it. He just went ape over it." Then, unexpectedly, Meckler said Helmsley lowered his voice and opened his eyes brightly like a kid on Christmas morning.

"Jay had a brand-new leather attaché case in his office," Meckler explained, "and Harry spotted it. He was absolutely joyous over the fact and showed it to Leona. It calmed him down. He was overjoyed that he had found it! I remember standing there and shaking my head in disbelief that he could get so excited over a Samsonite slim-line briefcase. This was a *free* attaché case that he could take home with him." Yet, try as he might, Helmsley was unable to open its combination lock.

"How do you do this?" he asked Meckler.

"I don't know the combination, Mr. Helmsley, but I'm sure if you contact the manufacturer they can find out a way to open it."

"Yeah, that's a good idea," Harry said enthusiastically. Meckler was amazed. "That attaché case, pure leather, might have been worth three hundred dollars. What could three hundred dollars mean to Harry Helmsley? He could have just picked up the phone and told Samsonite. 'Send me a leather attaché case and put my initials on it.' They'd have been glad to do it. In fact, they'd probably have given him one free of charge just to say that Harry Helmsley uses their case. Yet this just thrilled him!"

The finders-keepers diversion lasted just a few minutes, however, and Helmsley regained his train of thought. Jay's earlier charge-card purchases and his Deco catalog scheme had been bad enough. But the Contract Drapery deal with Edgin meant Jay had truly double-crossed Harry by using Deco funds for his own personal gain. Harry was so disgusted with Jay and the whole series of secret deals that he informed Meckler he was thinking of closing Deco down.

"I think we have a good organization here," Meckler replied, and gave a good enough pep talk to calm the atmosphere. But Helmsley was still scowling when he left the office. During the meeting, Meckler sensed that Leona was worried about her husband's reaction to the latest revelation. Leona still seemed quite concerned when she returned to Meckler's office a short while after Harry's tirade. She lamented all the problems Jay had gotten into and told Meckler that at one point Harry was so angry he was on the verge of divorcing her "because of the things Jay had done, and because Harry felt she had covered for Jay when he ran into these problems." Meckler said Mrs. Helmsley then made a play for his allegiance. "She told me, 'You were a good friend of Jay's. You saved him a couple of times when Harry almost threw him out. And now we have this thing [Contract Drapery] to contend with.' " Leona assured Meckler, "If you do a good job, you'll never have another care for the rest of your life."

Mrs. Helmsley then revealed her plans to punish Mimi for breaking into Jay's desk and a host of other misdeeds, most of which seemed absolutely groundless to Meckler. "She blamed Mimi for Jay's death. She felt Mimi had brought marijuana and cocaine into his life. She said Mimi didn't cook him breakfast in the morning and made him eat at Sambo's, up the block. She said her overall goal was to get Mimi and ruin her. And her level of determination was 100 percent." By contrast, Meckler said he never saw any hint that Jay or Mimi used drugs. As for Sambo's, "Jay just happened to like it. He would just go eat there." To be sure, Jay had vices—particularly drinking, smoking and partying—which were strictly forbidden by his doctors. Evidence was ample, however, that he indulged himself without Mimi's prodding, and often without her knowledge. Regardless, Meckler said, Mrs. Helmsley kept up the revenge talk: "She killed my son and we're going to get her." Simultaneously, to Meckler's surprise, Leona renounced her earlier vow to punish the saleswoman who had shared Jay's hotel room the afternoon of his fatal heart attack. "To heck with it," she told Meckler. "It's foolish to go after her. I can't bring Jay back." In effect, Leona had decided to switch targets. There was no doubt in Meckler's mind as to what was really going on. "It was all a guilt trip in Mrs. Helmsley's own head. She had her own guilt just spilling out on Mimi Panzirer. Her own conscience bothered her about the way she abused her son on the telephone and the way she had treated him and embarrassed him in front of people. She chose Mimi as a scapegoat."

Kadish agrees completely with Meckler's scapegoat theory. He recalls that Mrs. Helmsley went into deep mourning and openly reproached herself for Jay's early demise. "She grieved very deeply and very sincerely. She would say, 'No mother should have to endure a child's death. God should have taken me and not him. I don't want to live anymore.' She would want me to sit opposite her in her office and she would go into a crying jag, saying how terrible the loss was and regretting that as a mother she didn't spend more time with him, that she didn't really raise him, all those punishing things." Kadish said he tried to play the role of cheerleader. "I told her, 'You still have a life to live. You have a wonderful life. Get on with it and enjoy it.' But she wouldn't, couldn't. She became morbid and more miserable, more embittered." Apparently unable to shoulder her own misery, Kadish said Leona "went into a complete tailspin and embarked on this terrible vendetta against Jay's widow."

Leona made her first move on April 23 by filing a claim in Circuit Court of Orange County, Florida, demanding that Jay's estate repay a $100,000 loan Mrs. Helmsley had advanced her son a year earlier. Jay had used the funds to buy a partial share of Helmsley Palace stock and Mrs. Helmsley now wanted satisfaction of the debt. As evidence of the loan, Leona produced a demand note for $100,000, signed by Panzirer and payable to his mother. Mimi, the personal representative of Jay's estate, responded by hiring her own lawyer to challenge the claim. On April 28, the outlines of a true vendetta emerged when Leona's lawyers sent Mimi a letter ordering her and Craig to vacate their Maitland home by 6 P.M. on June 15. They also demanded that Mimi surrender its furnishings, right down to Jay's used Zenith video cassette recorder, a unicorn tapestry and a backgammon table. Because the house and furnishings were bought and owned by Deco, Mimi knew she faced tough sledding. By now, she also knew that Leona was after her. "The woman wanted to push me over the edge, either to insanity, to blow my brains out, or to run down the street begging. She wanted me to crack." Perhaps forgetting the Helmsleys' anger over her search of Jay's office (she says she took only photos and love letters, not files), and her emptying of the jointly held safe deposit box, Mimi said she had no earthly idea why Leona had targeted her. "Before, our relationship was very warm, even loving. The change was like a bolt of lightning. Maybe she and Harry felt I had something that they wanted. Maybe they thought I had stock certificates that showed the actual ownership of Deco. Maybe they thought I had incriminating papers about Deco or Helmsley Enterprises. Or maybe it was just jealousy: I was 33, and Leona wasn't." The strangest thing, Mimi said, was Leona's insensitivity to her own grandchild, Craig, who would also have to be thrown on the street. "Craig couldn't understand it," she recalls. "He kept asking, 'Why, why,

why?' "

Leona ordered Meckler, as her chief executive at Deco, to coordinate with her Florida lawyers to make sure the eviction proceeded as planned. "It was given to me as a job," Meckler recalls, "and I didn't feel great about it at all." He too was confused by Leona's callousness toward Craig, a ninth grader at Maitland Junior High School, and the other grandchildren, whose inheritances would also diminish if Leona prevailed in her financial claims on their father's estate. "Her grandchildren didn't seem to be her prime worry. She did like the little one, Wally, but I didn't see any closeness for the others." Nor did Harry seem overly concerned about Craig's dilemma, Meckler said. "I don't think it bothered Harry in the slightest. Certainly, the whole family relationship was strange. But who was I to question it?" Meckler said Leona phoned him almost every day, not only to discuss the eviction, but to broach ideas for new ways to hurt Mimi. "She'd say, 'There's another thing I could go after her for!' She wanted to know what was going on. Every day she put the pressure on. 'Are we doing this? Are we doing that?'"

Mimi said the Helmsleys hired private detectives to harass her as soon as the eviction letter was sent. "They parked in a van in front of my home. They also had limos parking across the street with their windows blackened. It was out of a Grade B movie. Obviously, she and Harry had been staying up late watching 1940-era movies. It cost them a lot of money. And it was Harry's money. I think he was a full and willing participant, and probably the brains behind the whole thing."

Meckler verifies that Harry was an active player. Yet, although Helmsley was angry at Mimi for rifling Jay's Deco papers, Meckler said the tycoon appeared to support the vendetta less out of spite than from a simple desire to assist his wife. In discussions, "Harry would join in with his thoughts, but no in the same tone as Mrs. Helmsley. You didn't hear that heavy yelling or screaming coming out. He would just discuss it like anybody discussing normal lawsuits."

A less complicated motive for evicting Mimi was plain frugality. The costs of investigating Mimi's visit to Jay's office and her overall affairs were adding up, and Helmsley didn't want to continue paying her rent even as Turco's bloodhounds pursued her. "One of the first things Harry wanted to do, even before Mimi moved out," Meckler said, "was shut off the gas to her swimming pool. He wanted to save the cost of heating it, so we went ahead and killed those expenses right off."

Helmsley appeared at Mimi's door in early May and confronted her personally. "He demanded [that I accept] a hundred thousand dollars for the partial share of stock Jay owned in the Palace Hotel," she recalls. Realizing it was worth perhaps twice that much because of appreciation, Mimi refused. "I told him I couldn't because I had already listed it" as the major component of Jay's estate.

"You shouldn't have done that!" Helmsley protested, aware that once the Palace share was included in the estate, it was up for grabs by Jay's creditors as well as his heirs. "That was a family matter. It was a stupid thing to do!" Mimi said Harry then stopped his lecture. "He caught himself. He rarely yells or screams. That's not his style."

It was now Mimi's turn to complain. "Why are you evicting us from this house?"

"I have to sell it," Helmsley replied.

"Why?"

"Because I need the money."

At that moment, Mimi says, "I realized I was in the presence of true evil. Truly a man with no conscience, with no vestige of human feeling. A nonhuman. That's when I realized that money was his god." She pleaded for time. "Can't we stay at least until Craig finishes the school year?" That much, a few extra months, Helmsley would agree to. But with a proviso. She would have to let his investigators take an inventory of every last article in the house.

"Bring anyone you want," Mimi said. "But if you bring Frank Turco, I'll call 911."

Money problems of a far higher scale were weighing on Harry that spring. Although cash flow from the Empire State Building and other investments remained stupendous, the Palace was flooded with red ink. All the loving touches and gold leaf in the historic rooms ended up costing $9 million, almost four times the original budget of $2.3 million. The budget was also shot in the modern hotel tower, where an extra $12 million was spent for equipment and furnishings (including, presumably, the $2 million worth of furniture that vanished). Similarly, construction delays and increased interest rates on the construction loan had added another $4.85 million in cost overruns. Adding to the cash drain was the problem of a dismal 40 to 50 percent occupancy rate, which created operating losses of over $8 million in the hotel's first year. Harry Helmsley added it all up and realized that his $73 million dream hotel was at least $31 million over budget. It was a sobering statistic because he would have to pay every extra penny. That was the deal he struck with his limited partners as construction began. The investors—who included Jack C. Massey (founder of Hospital Corporation of America), corporations and wealthy foreigners—put up $23 million with the understanding that they would be guaranteed roughly half the hotel's profits. Helmsley would receive all remaining profits for putting the deal together, using his good credit to raise $50 million in construction loans from banks. As general partner, Helmsley agreed to absorb all cost overruns. In a rare predicament, he would now be forced to dig into his own pockets. Rather than dig too deeply, however, Helmsley had devised a scheme a year earlier, when the overruns were first tabulated. In May 1981, Helmsley had advised his investors in writing that he intended to cover $19.4 million worth of overruns by taking out a second mortgage on the hotel for that amount. In effect, he was attempting to shift the liability to his partners because the interest that would have to be paid on the second mortgage would cut into their profits. The proposal was nothing less than a bold effort to change the rules of the game in midstream. By definition, limited partners have only limited financial risk. Helmsley was now insisting, not asking, that they be good sports and share his cost overrun burden. The investors refused to be buffaloed. Seven of them, who together put up about half the original $23 million partnership contribution, banded together and rejected the proposal outright. And now that Helmsley had aroused their curiosity, the investors also demanded to inspect the hotel books to see how all the additional costs had come about in the first place. When Harry refused to produce all the requested documentation, the investor group filed suit in Manhattan Supreme Court on May 28, 1982 against Helmsley, Deco, Helmsley Hotels and another Helmsley subsidiary. They condemned his attempt to strap them with a second mortgage. Furthermore, they accused him of shaving their profits by making "sweetheart deals" between the hotel and companies Helmsley controlled. For instance, Deco's 20 percent commission on hotel furnishings (twice the industry standard) was described as "unduly favorable to Deco and unfair to the Palace partnership." Helmsley had completely underestimated his partners' fighting spirit. Rather than slug it out in the courts, however, he and the partners agreed to put the entire dispute in the hands of a three-member panel of the American Arbitration Association. The panel's decision might be a year down the road, but at least it would be final and binding.

In the meantime, Harry and Leona turned their attention to the New York Harley, whose occupancy rate was even worse than that of the Palace. On an average night, only 20 to 25 percent of its rooms were taken. Joyce Beber came to the rescue with a brilliant advertising campaign. She recalls that the theme dawned on her unexpectedly after months of observing Leona's personal involvement with guests and their creature comforts. "I would watch her read comment cards from guests at all her hotels, and she would get ideas instinctively on how to run the hotel." Beber said she didn't give it much thought at first. "I just thought this was a very good thing for a hotel president to do. And I saw her continuing to do it. Then she picked up the telephone one day and called someone in Kansas who had complained about his stay at one of the hotels in the Harley chain. And she told him: 'I'm sorry the air conditioning in your room was noisy.' And the person didn't know who she was, but appreciated the call." At that moment, Beber's brainstorm began to emerge. "I thought, 'There's something going on here. There is this responsiveness. There's a real person, not an anonymous sale.'"

As a first step, Beber suggested that Mrs. Helmsley redo the comment cards. "Let's make them personal. You really do read them!" Leona agreed. "So we changed the comment cards at all the hotels. We put Mrs. Helmsley's picture on them. Cards for the New York Harley carried Leona's special message: 'I really do read every comment card. I really do know what you expect at the New York Harley.'" Beber's ad concept for the hotel took fuller shape as she continued to observe Leona in action. "Mrs. Helmsley would sit there and she would complain, 'These towels are too small! These cups are like Dixie cups!' And I thought, 'Wow, what a campaign!'"

Leona's concern for her guests and their contentment became the focus of a major print campaign that summer for the New York Harley. Instead of a single full-page ad per publication, Beber had the idea of running three smaller ads in a row, all in the upper right-hand corners of successive pages. Each was one-third of a page and featured Leona, the smiling proprietress, examining a different luxurious amenity. One of the first ads proclaimed Leona's towel fetish, under the headline: "I won't settle for skimpy towels. Why should you?" The body copy of the ad was pure Leona, direct and breezy: "You don't have to put up with a hotel that doles out a few small and quickly waterlogged towels. For the same price, you can stay at the Harley, New York's newest hotel. I make sure you get a stack of thick, warm towels, big enough for the widest waist...." In another ad, Leona proclaimed: "I couldn't get along without a phone in the bath. Why should you?" "I couldn't get along without a magnifying mirror," read another. "Why should you?"

The "Why should you?" campaign was the stuff of dreams. Within months, Beber says, the occupancy rate at the New York Harley skyrocketed from 25 percent to 70 percent. "That ad campaign worked the way you fantasize an advertising campaign should work." Nobody was more thrilled at the response than Harry Helmsley. "As the occupancy rose," Beber said, "he started raising his prices accordingly. They started at eighty dollars, and as the campaign worked, he said. 'Let's raise it to ninety.' Then, 'Let's go to a hundred and ten.' Then, 'Let's go to one twenty-five.' I began to see the real estate astuteness of Harry Helmsley. The man knew to the second when to raise it another notch! He was always looking at the numbers and juggling the figures."

Tad Distler, Joyce Beber's supervisor for the Helmsley account, said over $1 million was budgeted for the remainder of the year "to advertise this one hotel." Ads ran week after week in the *New York Times Magazine*, *New York* magazine, *The New Yorker*, *Business Week*, the *Washington Dossier*, and the in-flight magazines of Eastern, Pan Am, TWA and United Airlines. The total audience—or "reach"—was in the tens of millions, Distler says. "The *New York Times Magazine* alone reaches a million and a half households every Sunday, multiplied by two point five people per household. That's substantial reach." Reaching readers was important, but capturing their attention was the real paydirt. "Using three ads in a row proved a very effective way to gain attention rapidly." A survey of ads in *Business Week* showed the New York Harley ads finished first, second and third as the most memorable small ads to run in the magazine that year.

Now on a creative roll, the Beber Silverstein firm came up with an even more audacious campaign for the Helmsley Palace. In full-page color ads in the same prestigious publications,

Leona was formally introduced as the Queen of the Helmsley Palace. Not as president, but as a resplendent queen! "The Only Palace in the World Where the Queen Stands Guard" became the unforgettable slogan for the flagship of her hotel empire.

The ad experts wanted to capitalize on America's fascination with celebrity and royalty, so the queen theme became a play on magic. "Americans are tremendous star worshipers," Elaine Silverstein explains. "We treat movie stars as royalty. And we have a great fascination for real royalty. We hoped people would look at Leona the Queen the way they looked at Jackie Onassis and Elizabeth Taylor as royalty. Glamorous. Larger than life. More money than they'll ever have with her thousand-room palace that she's keeping immaculate for me. The magic made it possible for anyone with two hundred and fifty dollars a night to go and be a royal guest at the Palace."

Beber and Silverstein sensed that Leona was a natural for the role because of her innate charisma and dramatic ability. "This was an actress waiting for her role. We explained it to her. We put an identifiable name on it—the wealth and power, the president of the hotels. And she became something that Bill Marriott or Conrad Hilton could never be. It was a reflection of her own persona."

Distler helped create a series of three large ads of the vigilant Queen fussing over her Palace. In one, Leona is shown admiring a vase of tulips and Peruvian lilies on a table in the Madison Room, the elegant drawing room in the Villard-Reid wing. He recalls that she wore "a gold gown, very low cut, with her bosom greatly exposed." Later, upon examining the revealing photo, Distler suggested: "Shouldn't we retouch your dress a bit, Mrs. Helmsley, so there's not so much cleavage?"

Harry scuttled the idea pronto by interjecting, "It looks great. Leave it!"

In another shot taken in the Palace kitchen, wearing the same gown, Leona playfully holds a spoon under her chin while two chefs stand by. The third ad was to be photographed during afternoon tea in the Gold Room. Distler said Leona showed up wearing an equally low-cut red chiffon dress, with ruby-and-diamond earrings and bracelets. Unwisely, the agency had hired a male model to sit and pose as a grateful guest when Leona greeted his table. When Leona realized the arrangement, Distler recalls, "She started screaming that she wouldn't pay for models." She calmed down when Distler quietly slipped into the model's place and posed—looking up adoringly at the Queen—

for no extra charge. Never again did Distler even attempt to hire professional models. Instead, he said he would recruit people wandering around the hotel, be they guests or employees.

"You there!" he would say. "The Queen wants you to be a model!" Staff never refused, he said. "They trembled in their boots and said, 'If I have to, I have to.'" The Gold Room ad ran in the *Times Magazine*, complete with the "Queen stands guard" slogan.

The obvious goal of the Palace campaign was to woo new customers. In years to come, however, Leona would confide that the timing of the high-profile exercise, so soon after Jay's death, was no accident. "I believed in very little after his death—only Harry," she told *New Woman* magazine, "and Harry gave me a reason to live. He gave me work and put me in a limelight that blinded my grief, temporarily."

"Harry is all I have left," Leona would often tell Gerald Kadish in the months following Jay's death. Sometimes, after a bit more thought, her spirits would brighten. "There's also Wally," she added, speaking of her five-year-old grandson who had moved to California with his mother, Ruth. Wally, the grandchild who looked most like Jay and Leona, was special, but so far away. To remedy the situation, an invitation was extended. The Helmsleys would purchase and furnish a comfortable home for Ruth and Walter if they would only move back to the East Coast, close to Leona. The invitation was accepted, and preparations commenced.

Leona wasted no time informing Milton Meckler, the head of Deco. "Ruth and Wally are coming!" she exclaimed that June. "She told me Harry was excited, too," Meckler recalls, "which was surprising because Harry's not fond of kids. But he seemed to enjoy Walter, maybe because he was at such a cute age." Meckler was notified that Wally and Jay's second wife would be moving into a luxurious two-story condominium the Helmsleys had acquired in suburban North Hills, Long Island, less than an hour's drive from Manhattan.

Meckler said Leona instructed him to order approximately $120,000 worth of furnishings through Deco, and to ship them free of charge to the Long Island apartment. In effect, Deco would be forced to "eat" the $120,000 expense, just as the firm had once absorbed the costs of furnishing Jay Panzirer's home in Florida. There was a difference this time, however. Although many of Jay's chargeoffs, such as food and Dom Perignon, had been completely out of line, his home furnishings and free rent arguably qualified as legitimate company benefits. Ruth Panzirer, however, had no connection whatsoever with Deco, yet was receiving valuable financial benefits through Leona's arrangement. And every Deco dollar spent on her condo cut into the purchasing firm's profits.

Jay's third wife, Mimi, found herself in less enviable circumstances. By June 15, she and Craig had vacated their Maitland home in Florida. They moved in with Mimi's mother in nearby Casselberry, but were forbidden by the Helmsleys to keep the furniture from their former home. Instead, Leona instructed Meckler to ship it all to Ruth's new condo. By July, Meckler says, a moving van arrived, loaded up $80,000 worth of Jay and Mimi's erstwhile goods, and headed north for storage in Long Island.

To make matters worse, Ruth joined in Leona's legal battle against Mimi on July 8 by filing suit in Orange County Circuit Court. In papers prepared by Leona's Orlando lawyer, Robert L. Young, Ruth argued that Mimi had refused to pay $3,900 that Jay allegedly had owed her from overdue alimony payments. The very same day, Harry Helmsley increased the heat by suing Mimi for reimbursement of $1,419.66 paid to a Manhattan funeral chapel for Jay's expenses. Deco also filed suit that week demanding that Mimi reimburse the purchasing firm for Jay's last payment of $37,500. The money was merely a "loan or advance of salary to Mr. Panzirer for services not yet rendered," alleged the suit, filed by Meckler on Leona's behalf.

Her guns still blazing, Leona filed another suit against Mimi on July 26, demanding the return of an $18,000 topaz and diamond-studded ring. Leona alleged she had lent Mimi the ring to wear at Harry's most recent birthday party and Mimi wrongfully held on to it. Mimi answered the complaint by informing the court that the ring was never a loan, but a gift from Leona on the occasion of Craig's bar mitzvah. In one last blow, Leona and Ruth filed a motion to prevent Mimi from using or controlling $68,000 worth of stock that Jay had kept in an Orlando money market account supervised by a branch of the company now known as Shearson/American Express. It was the same stock that Panzirer had been so worried about after the visit to his Boston doctor only days before his death. He had picked up the phone immediately after hearing his dismal prognosis and instructed an Orlando broker to transfer the stock into a joint account with Mimi. Because the broker had failed to do so until after Jay died, Leona and Ruth asked the court to freeze the funds until it could be determined whether the assets belonged to Mimi or to Jay's estate.

Mimi, Leona soon learned, was a tough Irish lass unwilling to roll over and die. "I didn't know where the line was to quit," she recalls. "It wasn't in my upbringing. My lawyers told me my chances going in against Leona were 'pissing in the wind' because her money could buy her just about any kind of justice she wanted." But Mimi girded herself for a bloody war and responded to each and every one of the lawsuits.

As Jay's widow huddled with her Orlando lawyers, work was continuing apace on the Long Island condominium. In addition to all the furnishings, Leona embarked upon a major renovation of the sprawling, ranch-style apartment. She and Turco lined up masons, carpenters, electricians and other craftsmen, most of whom regularly performed work for the Helmsleys' many commercial properties. An outdoor patio of slate and brick was laid. Flowerboxes were installed around the perimeter of the home. Enormous closets and built-in furniture were constructed for its three bedrooms and four bathrooms. Hi-hat lights were installed everywhere. A heavy crystal chandelier was hung from one of the cathedral ceilings. Rolls of magnificent silk wallpaper were stretched into place.

Leona designated a Helmsley-Spear engineer, Steve Fitzmaurice, to coordinate the construction project on company time. Approximately $100,000 worth of renovations were completed by late August. Fitzmaurice recalls that the Helmsleys came for an inspection and expressed delight with the job. "Leona kissed me. Harry shook my hand and said, 'You've done a wonderful job.' " Nevertheless, Fitzmaurice found himself in their bad graces shortly thereafter when Ruth and Wally had moved in. He explained that Leona became distressed at hearing that the condo's dishwasher was leaving spots on the dishes. Harry laughed off the sudden crisis, suggesting: "Try Cascade!" But action had to be taken. Fitzmaurice ordered a replacement and summoned a plumber to install it. Afterward, the plumber asked if he could cart off the old machine. "Here I was in the middle of Long Island with a rental car and a three-hundred-pound dishwasher," Fitzmaurice recalls, "so I told him, 'Okay. Take it.' It was either that or call the salvage service to come take it."

A few days later, Leona summoned Fitzmaurice to her office. "Who the hell do think you are?" she yelled. "You stole my dishwasher!"

Leona then questioned Fitzmaurice about a bill she had received from a landscaping company for laying the outdoor patio. He said he had reminded her that the bill was overdue and should be paid because the job had been completed satisfactorily. Just a week or two earlier, in fact, Leona had sung its praises.

"What kind of a kickback are you getting on this job?" she demanded to know. The allegation startled the engineer. "I was floored. I couldn't believe it."

"You're entirely overpaid!" she continued. "I could have gotten the job done at half the price with a kiss! I don't want to see you again. Get out of my sight. This is it! Get out of here!"

Paralyzed, Fitzmaurice stood quietly as the tirade continued. "She ripped my heart out. Her strategy was to degrade my worth and humiliate me." The next day, he was officially fired, with no explanation given. "I still wake up at night and wonder why." He speculated that Leona was upset because she "just didn't want to pay the landscaper," and he had spoken up for the company.

Indeed, the electrician for the condo renovation recalls that Mrs. Helmsley refused to pay his $30,000 bill, expecting him to donate his services. He had been hired to rewire the condo on the personal recommendation of Harry Helmsley's senior vice president in charge of engineering, Jeremiah McCarthy. "And naturally," the electrician said, "I assumed the Helmsleys could well afford to pay me." When the electrician continued to press for payment, he said Frank Turco telephoned him with an ultimatum. Unless he forgave the bill, Turco would make sure that the electrician's friend, Jeremiah McCarthy, was fired from his senior Helmsley-Spear post. He said he took Turco's threat seriously because of his close relationship with Mrs. Helmsley. "I would take Turco seriously any time. I thought, yes, he'll fire him." Rather than risk seeing McCarthy axed, the electrician said, "I sent a letter absolving the Helmsleys of the debt."

One former Helmsley-Spear executive involved with the condo fixup claims that superiors informed him that other contractors would be paid, but not by the Helmsleys. Instead, they would receive checks drawn on the Graybar Building, the Helmsley Building, and other Helmsley business properties. "Turco took care of the money matters," the executive said. If the condo expenses were indeed charged to the buildings, serious violations of state and federal tax laws would have taken place. Falsifying business records, including the creation of fake invoices, is a first-degree felony in the state of New York. Presumably, there would have been a great temptation to then declare such fraudulent business expenditures as legitimate tax deductions. Each such false declaration would constitute felony tax evasion under both federal and state statutes. Would the Helmsleys, with a net worth of $750 million, stoop to such illegal penny-saving? It made no sense. But neither did Leona's decision to stiff the electrician.

Leona's vendetta against Mimi reached the courtroom the first week in September, when Orange County Chief Circuit Judge W. Rogers Turner opened a probate hearing to decide the ownership of Jay Panzirer's $68,000 Shearson money market account. Depositions taken earlier by both sides were introduced into evidence and witnesses testified on key events just prior to, and in the weeks following, Panzirer's death. The court learned that Jay had indeed phoned his broker several days before his death and instructed him to switch the Shearson funds into a joint account with Mimi. Panzirer was asked to put the request in writing, in the form of a notarized authorization letter. One day before Jay's death, the broker received the signed form. The broker failed to switch the funds into the joint account, however, until the following week, after hearing that Jay had died. His delay in acting created a dispute: Although the switch was made, was it legally binding, given the fact that it was not executed until after Jay's death?

An unexpected drama came when Leona's attorneys produced a handwriting expert, June C. Ross, who said that Jay's signature on the authorization form was a forgery. "Two different hands have done the writing on these documents," she testified under oath. Relying on her professional judgment, Judge Turner declared: "Apparently there is some cloud over the validity of those signatures." He ordered Mimi, as personal representative of her husband's estate, to post a bond that would equal the funds in dispute. The Orlando *Sentinel* reported the juicy developments on page one, under the headline: "Wife gained by forgery, expert says." The lead paragraph reported: "Faked signatures of deceased hotel heir J. Robert Panzirer allowed his wife access to more than $67,000 in money market funds, a Winter Park handwriting expert testified Tuesday." It was damaging publicity indeed for Mimi. The implication was that Leona Helmsley's daughter-in-law had pulled a fast one. As soon as the newspaper hit the stands, Meckler phoned Leona long distance with the details.

"I told her what happened, that there was a big write-up in the *Sentinel*," he recalls. "And she was hysterically happy. She was absolutely crying in happiness that there was great newspaper coverage, which is what she wanted."

To keep the pressure on, Leona summoned Meckler and her Florida lawyers to New York one weekend for hard-nosed strategy sessions. Leona, Harry, Young and another lawyer gathered in the Helmsleys' solarium high atop the Park Lane Hotel. Things started out peacefully, Meckler recalls.

"Leona took me into a little kitchen in this glass house, which had a microwave oven. We were going to have a snack. She said, 'Do you want to see how well I cook?' " Instead of donning her apron, Leona phoned room service "and they brought up trays and trays of lox and bagels and hors d'oeuvres." At the sight of Leona's "cooking" Meckler broke out laughing, and she popped a few of the snacks into the microwave. The mood changed when discussions got under way.

"Mrs. Helmsley was totally in control and it was total fire and brimstone," Meckler said. Whenever the lawyers insisted, "We can't do this and we can only do that," Leona would rail at their cautious approach. "No, I want this done! She destroyed my son and I want this done. I want her! I want her!"

When Harry spoke up for the lawyers, Leona would instantly overrule her husband. "Harry, shut up! Don't mix in! This is what *I* want to do, and this is what *I'm* going to do!" And Helmsley would back off, Meckler recalls. "She was absolutely screaming. You could have heard it across the rooftops that surround the Park Lane." Strategy sessions continued on a regular basis thereafter, Meckler said. Sometimes Harry and Leona would land their BAC 1-11 at Orlando Executive Airport specifically for that purpose. "They would fly in from Palm Beach and we would meet them on the plane sitting in the runway for a couple of hours." Once the tarmac talks were completed, "the Helmsleys would fly off." Even Leona's attorneys were apparently astounded by her determination to wreak vengeance. "They were getting a good fee," Meckler says. "But even they felt it was ridiculous." The potential financial gain to Leona just wasn't worth all the trouble. Jay's entire estate was worth barely $200,000, Meckler explained, "and Leona's attorney fees were already approaching $90,000. So, was it a vendetta?

You bet it was."

By November, barely two months after settling into their new Long Island condo, Ruth Panzirer and young Wally pulled up stakes and moved to California. Leona's noble experiment, to bring her youngest grandson closer into her life, had failed. She had tried hard to be an attentive grandmother. But she had clung too tightly, Tad Distler recalls, and lost him as a result. "Leona would drag Ruth and Wally with her, or make them appear whenever she wanted them," he says, "and basically was setting out to control their lives." Milton Meckler was more shocked than anyone by the news, having spent so many hours helping to furnish the condo for Ruth's and Wally's comfort. During lunch with Leona at Le Trianon, he says, the Queen explained matter-of-factly that she had received a hand-delivered letter from Ruth. "She said the note was short and simple. Ruth told her, 'I've left. I can't live this way.' "

Jay was dead, but Leona had an idea for keeping his memory alive. Panzirer had been an active member of the Central Florida chapter of the American Heart Association. So why not raise funds to build a new headquarters for the chapter and have it named after Jay? She discussed her idea with Shelburn Wilkes, executive director of the chapter, and won his strong encouragement. Leona insisted, however, on approving the architectural plans for the Orlando structure, which would replace two rundown houses used by the heart chapter at Marks Street and Highland Avenue. A design by a Miami architect was accepted. It would cost approximately $300,000 to build a 3,200-square-foot center, to house the group's executive offices and offer space for educational classes, cardiopulmonary resuscitation training, and other vital services. Construction would be of stucco, glass and brick, with a travertine marble façade.

Instead of writing a check to finance the Jay R. Panzirer Memorial Heart Center, Leona went public. She sent out letters on her own stationery and on American Heart Association letterhead soliciting funds from friends and business associates. One of the first checks that came in, Milton Meckler recalls, was a $5,000 contribution from Donald Trump. "I remember it clearly, because at the time, Mrs. Helmsley wasn't talking to Trump. I think they had had a fight, and she said his buildings were like garbage." Meckler said he phoned Leona with news of Trump's generosity and she replied blithely: "Oh, I see he wants to make up." Blanche Slauson, Leona's Palm Beach friend, was astounded when she received her solicitation in the mail. "It was a form letter from Leona asking for contributions. And Lee didn't even say a word about how much *she* was going to give." The letter informed Blanche that a fund-raising event, the Jay R. Panzirer Memorial Golf Tournament, would be held Saturday, February 5, at the Errol Estate course in Orlando. Tickets were $200 and would entitle her to a day of golf as well as the opportunity to attend a banquet that evening at the Orlando Harley. The last paragraph of the letter, Blanche said, was in shockingly poor taste. "It said something like, 'By the way, you can stay at my hotel in Orlando.' But she didn't say to stay as her guest! So here she was asking for contributions for a building she could have paid for on her own, and at the same time she was touting her hotel." Other residents of the Palm Beach Towers condo received the form letter, Blanche said, "and we all thought it was very gauche. Everyone at the pool said so." Nevertheless, she said, "Most of the people here are from New York and have business dealings with the Helmsleys, so they sent contributions." But Blanche absolutely refused. "I didn't answer the letter because I thought it was in dreadful taste. I figured, if she wants to build a memorial to her son, let her build it. She has a lot of money. She has no right to ask her friends. I mean, I thought that was terrible nerve!"

Food suppliers and vendors of every kind to Leona's hotels were also approached, but much more vigorously than her society friends. Tad Distler recalls, "One of Mrs. Helmsley's big things was to get all the vendors to contribute. I heard her so many times on the telephone: 'It's my son! We give you millions in business. You are only making a five-thousand-dollar donation. I want more!' And this went on and on. I mean, she had lists of contributors and how much they were giving. She called up each and every one and squeezed them for more donations after they had already pledged." Louis Hautzig, then the general manager of the New York Harley, recalls that Leona also used Turco to apply pressure. "Turco had to call up all the vendors and tell them to contribute to that memorial 'or we don't buy from you.' If they didn't put up the money, they were finished." Hautzig said managers at all the Helmsley hotels were pressured to collect "anywhere from ten to a hundred dollars" from employees. "We asked everybody to pay. And it personally cost me a hundred dollars."

Optima Press Inc., the firm responsible for printing all of the menus, brochures and other materials for the Helmsley hotel empire, was pressured to donate its services. Leslie Schwartz, owner of the Manhattan firm, confirms that he agreed to print ten thousand color programs for the golf tournament at no cost. "This was a very elaborate job with gold pages and color photographs." The programs were an important fund-raising tool because vendors were asked to purchase ads, which were inserted in the booklets. Schwartz said he reluctantly agreed to swallow the forty-thousand-dollar printing cost. "It would be a very big expense for anybody," but he complied because the Helmsley account "was over half my business."

John Drohan, owner of the oldest poultry supply house in New York, recalls that one of Leona's aides ordered his firm to donate $5,000 worth of chicken for the golf tournament. "A threat was implied," he said, "that if we wanted to continue to sell to the hotels, this is what we should do." It was a most unusual request. "We've been asked to contribute to other charities before. Sure, we'll buy tables at a banquet. But we've never been told, 'If you don't contribute, that's it!' " Drohan said he refused to part with his birds. "I thought to hell with the Helmsleys because I didn't need their business that badly."

Rod Ortiz, a former food and beverage employee at the Helmsley Palace, recalls that higher-ups instructed him to boycott the Drohan firm for not playing ball. "Mrs. Helmsley sent word to me not to buy from Drohan because he didn't give anything to her party." Moreover, Ortiz said he was ordered to approach a Manhattan seafood company, M. Slavin & Son, for free merchandise. "I was told to get so much from this guy and that Mrs. Helmsley wouldn't pay. It was like a gratuity." Unlike Drohan, Ortiz said, the seafood company readily agreed to cooperate. "They donated about two thousand dollars' worth of shrimp and king crabmeat." Barry Slavin says he cannot recall the incident but adds: "I sell fish and I get paid for what I sell."

Sam Solasz, a Manhattan meat supplier, says he sacrificed his account with the Helmsley Palace rather than submit to demands for free beef for the golf tournament. The 60-year-old executive, a survivor of the Treblinka death camp, said Leona's project didn't sound like a charitable event to him. "I escaped Treblinka by jumping the gate when I was 14 years old and running three kilometers. It taught me that the real meaning of charity is helping people, like the priests who work to get kids off drugs." He said he wasn't about to be shaken down by one of the country's wealthiest women. "I didn't have time for her nonsense. So what! I lose one customer and pick up two more."

Meckler said more and more contributions were needed as time went on because Leona kept suggesting expensive changes in the original design of the heart center. For instance, she commissioned a noted sculptor, Granville Carter, to create a $17,500 bronze bust of Jay, which would be placed on a pedestal in the entrance lobby. Then, after more thought, she decreed that it be plated with 24 karat gold at an additional cost of $21,000.

February 5 rolled around. A large entourage of relatives and business aides accompanied Leona and Harry to Orlando, and everyone took rooms at the Orlando Harley. The golf tournament was held on a bright, sunny afternoon, and good food, much of it from New York vendors, was enjoyed by all. A free car offered to the first player to hit a hole-in-one went unclaimed.

That evening, guests attended Leona's Grand and Gala Champagne Banquet, held in the Eola Ballroom of the Orlando Harley. A special appearance was made by singer Carol Channing. Prizes, including a Zenith large-screen forty-five-inch rear projection TV, were raffled off. Sitting across from Meckler was Leona's sister Sandra. Meckler became concerned "because she wouldn't speak to me all evening." Finally, one of Leona's secretaries clued him in: "It's because you're smoking. She's allergic." When he apologized, Sandra verified, "My eyes get red. Smoke gives me convulsions." Later in the evening, Meckler informed Leona that he had apologized to her sister.

"No apologies necessary," Leona replied. "She shouldn't be here eating with us in public if you can't smoke."

"But Mrs. Helmsley," he countered, "she had tears rolling down her face."

"Smoke!" Leona advised. "Blow it in her eyes. She shouldn't be in public!"

Meckler's biggest surprise came weeks after the successful tournament when a stack of invoices landed on his desk. He scanned them carefully and was astounded to discover that Leona had skimmed the memorial contributions to cover her own hotel accommodations at the Harley that weekend, as well as the rooms, liquor, food and entertainment of her entourage! Even for her own son's memorial weekend, the no-comp rule applied. No such thing as a free room. Meckler said $12,504 was taken from the heart chapter contributions to pay the Orlando Harley. Among the charges was one for $1,283.47 to reimburse the hotel for Harry and Leona's three suites; expenses of $190 for Leona's brother, Alvin Rosenthal; and $809.84 for Frank Turco.

Leona also docked the memorial fund $29,400 for two hundred heart-shaped gift lockets which she had privately ordered from Cartier. Meckler said his wife still has hers, a 14 karat gold keepsake with a diamond chip. In all, over 10 percent of the $400,000 in collections went for Leona's personal expenses, for those of her entourage, and for the cost of Jay's bronze bust. One thing still weighs on Meckler's mind. "If only Donald Trump knew how his five thousand dollars was spent."

Eleven

Blanche Slauson bolted upright from her sun-nap one afternoon in late February when Leona announced herself unexpectedly at the Palm Beach Towers swimming pool.

"I didn't get your check!" Leona said to her best friend.

"You did so!" Blanche replied. In fact, Blanche had mailed a check just a week earlier to one of Leona's charities, Boys Town of Italy. She took action after receiving a letter in the mail, signed by Leona, asking for donations to a March 24 charity ball at the Waldorf for the organization.

"Well, I didn't get it!" Leona insisted.

"But I know I sent it, Lee. I sent it for Boys Town."

"To hell with Boys Town!" Leona fired back. "I don't care about them!"

Then it became clear. Blanche realized she was catching hell for having failed to send a check to Leona's *favorite* fundraiser: the Jay R. Panzirer Memorial Golf Tournament. But she was too upset to dignify the scolding with an answer.

"It was shocking to me," Blanche recalls. "Lee's name was on the Boys Town solicitation. She was the one asking for money. She didn't give a darn about Boys Town. She was angry that I hadn't sent money to her! It was terrible nerve." Even before the poolside incident, Blanche had become resentful. In early February, she explains, "I had emergency open-heart surgery in Miami and got a shoebox of cards and gifts and flowers from friends, even friends I hadn't seen in thirty years." Although Leona did leave a telephone message at the hospital, "she didn't send a card. She was one person I thought would have filled my room with flowers—not one flower. And I couldn't understand that." Indeed, Blanche had not heard from Leona until this moment. "I had just returned from the hospital that weekend. I had lost a lot of weight and wasn't well. And the first thing she says to me is, 'I didn't get your check!' "

From that moment, Blanche says, "We never spoke again. We would sort of go past each other and say 'hello.' " Soon, even the forced hellos stopped, and their boisterous ten-year friendship came to an end. "The funniest part of it," Blanche adds, "is that Harry and I remained good friends and he stopped one day to talk to me."

"Haaaarrrrrry!" Leona's voice interrupted from the distance. "In the pool—now!"

"And from that time on," Blanche said, "Lee never let Cid and me talk to Harry. It's a terrible thing, because he's a wonderful guy who is sort of in a shell when she's around. But he won't talk to us when she's nearby. He won't come near us." Never again would Blanche and Leona stroll arm-in-arm under the Royal Palms and mangos. Nor would the Helmsleys and Slausons sing "I'm Just Wild About Harry" together in the wee hours of the morning, or cheer opposing greyhounds, or share carrot sticks at the movies. At a time when Leona presumably needed friendship the most, it died.

On March 24, as scheduled, Leona received the Boys Town of Italy International Humanitarian Award at the "Return to Renaissance" ball held in the Waldorf. She came dressed for the occasion in a low-cut Italian peasant's costume, laced in the front, with billowing sleeves. Joyce Beber, who attended the gala, says Leona's greatest thrill that evening actually came when Carol Channing made a speech from the dais.

"When Carol got up," Beber recalls, "her whole speech was a takeoff on the 'Why should you?' campaign we had just started for the New York Harley."

"Leona wouldn't settle for anything less than generous contributions," Channing said. "Why should you?"

"Leona wouldn't settle for anything less than the best for these boys. Why should you?" The audience was familiar with the ad campaign, Beber said, "and everyone clapped and chanted. Leona couldn't get over that everyone recognized the campaign. She called me aside and said, 'Look at this. Everyone knows about it. It's successful. Thank you.' When she stood up, she got an ovation. She felt like more of a celebrity than

Carol Channing. She was thrilled. That was the moment she realized she was a queen."

Reality intruded in April, however, when the Queen and Harry found themselves on the losing end of several key battles in their continuing war against Mimi. On April 18, an Orlando probate judge ruled that Harry had no grounds to force Mimi to reimburse him for $1,419 the tycoon had voluntarily paid for Jay's funeral expenses the year before. Another judge, meanwhile, ruled against Leona's motion that Mimi be forced to place the $18,000 topaz-and-diamond ring in escrow. Although Leona could have continued to pursue return of the ring, which she had described in court papers as a mere loan to her former daughter-in-law, Mimi claims her mother-in-law let the issue drop because there was incontrovertible proof her claim was a lie. "Leona gave me the ring in 1981 at Craig's bar mitzvah," Mimi said, "and news photographers took a picture of it and identified it as Mrs. Helmsley's *gift* to her daughter-in-law." By suing for return of the ring, Mimi said, "Leona proved beyond a doubt that she is capable of fraud and deception. And since Harry backed her, or never raised an objection, I'd have to find him also culpable. It showed a large chunk of their character." In a third rebuff to Leona that spring, a different judge ruled there was no merit to Deco's claim against Mimi for recovery of Jay Panzirer's last paycheck of $37,500. Deco's argument that the check was a salary advance rather than actual earned income failed to sway Circuit Judge Bernard Muszynski. Rather than accept his verdict, however, Deco filed an immediate appeal to the Fifth District Court of Appeal of Florida.

Mimi stepped aside as personal representative of Jay's estate, meanwhile, and an Orlando lawyer, Harold A. Ward III, was appointed by the court to manage Panzirer's assets. Nevertheless, Mimi recalls, Leona and Turco found new ways to torment her. The most brutal example, Mimi said, came when Turco demanded the right to buy Jay's jewelry from the estate, rather than see the sentimental items remain in Mimi's hands. "Without my knowledge," she said, "Frank Turco got virtually all the jewelry my husband owned." According to court records, Turco and his wife, Rosemary, paid the estate $450 for a 20 karat gold neck chain, $450 for an 18 karat gold vest pocket chain, $600 for a gold pocket watch and $2,000 for one of Jay's rings. "After a while," Mimi said, "you just become sick. It's stomach-turning. Leona, who's still weeping and crying about the loss of her son, saw to it that his jewelry didn't go to his family, but to a hired flunky."

Turco was well rewarded for his loyalty. Seemingly overnight, he became known throughout the Helmsley empire as Leona's personal troubleshooter. In addition to his role as Deco's New York liaison, Leona appointed the accountant Chief of Financial Services for Helmsley Hotels, in charge of internal audits for her New York hotels. Along with Sclafani and Petruzzi, his armed mates, Turco was assigned to visit the out-of-town hotels and critique their day-to-day operations. Mark Flaherty, who left the New York Harley to become general manager of the St. Moritz Hotel, recalls that Turco and his crew "would come into the St. Moritz and go over petty cash and other checks. If they found anything detrimental, they would report it to Mrs. Helmsley." Leona's choice of Turco to perform internal audits was surprising, Flaherty said, "because he was not trained or educated in the hotel business." Although an accountant, "Turco was not familiar with hotel audits. It would be like picking some guy off the street and asking him to give you a medical exam."

Turco relished his power, Meckler recalls. "He became her heavy hammer for the hotels and right into the Helmsley-Spear structure." In no time, Turco was sassing top Helmsley-Spear executives. At first, Meckler said, Helmsley's top aides questioned Turco's authority. "They'd ask, 'Does this order come from Mr. Helmsley?' And Turco would make it very clear where his power came from. He'd say, 'This is from the Madam! You may work for Harry Helmsley, but I work for the Madam. You want to fight that?' And nobody ever fought that. You would not take the chance on fighting that because it would be sudden death if you went to Mr. Helmsley and complained directly about his wife."

Gerald Kadish said he was forced to give Turco carte blanche to investigate any aspect of the Harley Hotels operation. Although Leona's ads claimed she personally inspected the far-flung hotels, Kadish said she actually entrusted the job to Turco. "He became her spy and henchman. And he built an almost vigilante kind of staff." In addition to Sclafani and Petruzzi, "Turco had four or five guys on the road doing various studies and spy work. It was a terrible, terrible scene. They would check into all the hotels across the country and write reports on how the hotels were and what the employees were doing or not doing. They came up with almost nothing, but they magnified it into big things. They'd say they woke up at two in the morning and found a door unlocked. Mrs. Helmsley would be informed and she'd find out who was responsible and fire them. Real crapola." Kadish said Turco took to heart Mrs. Helmsley's own belief "that everyone has something you can get them on. So he became like a traffic cop, who's got to hand out a certain number of tickets. He had to assassinate a certain number of people to maintain his credibility. He would get her to believe someone was dishonest or doing a bad job and she would fire them. Most of his victims were hotel managers, comptrollers, and food and beverage directors."

Kadish said Harry had little personal regard for Turco, yet raised no objection to his meteoric rise to power. "Harry thought he was a scumbag, but pretty much just let him do Leona's dirty work." Kadish once asked the tycoon how he could tolerate such rough company. "He sort of smirked, and told me, 'You can't be just a nice guy and achieve what I've achieved here.' It was very apparent that he maintains this image of being a nice guy and being soft and gentle, a pussycat kind of guy. But he has a real strong organization and Turco followed that organization of getting things done."

With Turco as her "heavy hammer," Meckler said Leona relied less and less on Harry to fine-tune the empire according to her vision. Nor did she need Harry to discipline recalcitrant executives. "Frank was her way of isolating the guys she didn't want, and that weakened Harry terrifically." Indeed, Turco became so confident of his power that he could stroll unannounced into Harry's office at the Lincoln Building at any moment. Helmsley was further weakened, Kadish adds, by Leona's continual pampering. "In business meetings, she would comb and primp his hair, showing whoever the audience was that she was in love with him." Kadish never doubted the love was real. But the stroking also seemed "part of her game, making him totally beholden to her. It got to the point where he wouldn't do normal things without her presence or involvement. Things like choosing what to wear, or making any sort of travel or business plans, doing anything at all related to the hotels. He wouldn't so much as have a haircut or manicure without her supervision or approval. He was therefore under her spell in a way, and he loved it. He enjoyed someone caring that much about him, giving that much concern and love. I never saw any signs of him rejecting it at all. The more he allowed it and reveled in it, and she knew it, the more she had him. She would say things like, 'Harry, how could you get along without me?' Or, 'Harry, you're a genius.' She would always use the word 'genius' to him and about him." By mid-1983, Kadish claims, "Harry literally could not make a move without her."

Louis Hautzig, then general manager of the New York Harley, recalls that Leona used the stick as well as the carrot to get her way with Harry. "She would be very attentive, giving him a pill to help him, or watching his diet. 'Don't eat these sandwiches. They're getting you too fat.' And the next thing, she would hit him over the head with something. She'd say, 'Harry, you're interfering!' Or, 'Get rid of this!' Or 'I want you to do this' and 'I want you to do that!' " She apparently also wielded a powerful sex cudgel. On one occasion, Hautzig said he heard Leona threaten: "And if you don't do what I say, you are not going to sleep with me tonight!' " Hautzig said he was appalled that Harry stood by so meekly while Leona fired executives without cause and unleashed Turco on hotel employees. "Mr. Helmsley could have cut it off right from the beginning and not tolerated it. He had no gumption whatsoever. He was a wimp first class. If I didn't know any better, I would say she bewitched him."

The sexual equation was obvious to Helmsley's inner circle. At 74 he still had a bounce in his step that had not been there during his earlier marriage. One of Helmsley's closest former aides said he walked unannounced into Helmsley's office at the Lincoln Building one afternoon that year to behold the Helmsleys frolicking half clothed on Harry's desk. Embarrassed beyond words, he muttered, "Excuse me," and walked off. After waiting a prudent spell, the executive returned to Harry's corner office and immediately noticed a sartorial problem. "I turned to him and said, 'Mr. Helmsley, you have a stain on your pants and you can't go to luncheon like that. And believe me, it doesn't wash off too easily.' " A week or so later, the executive said, "Mrs. Helmsley gave me hell. She warned me in no uncertain terms, 'Don't you ever step foot in my husband's office again without being announced!' "

Lois Barnett was relaxing at home when the phone rang one evening early that spring.

"I saw your ad in *Avenue* magazine," the caller said, "and I'm interested in the cute little country house."

Barnett, a Westchester County real estate agent who specializes in sales of country estates, was all ears after the caller identified herself as Leona Helmsley.

"I want a little hideaway in the country," Leona explained. "A little house to come to and relax on the weekends. Tell me about the one in your ad."

"It's small and private," Barnett replied. "It's a frame one-story house with four bedrooms, covered with ivy. It's in Bedford, on a hill with twenty-four acres and a little cottage and a fifteen-by-thirty-foot pool. It has tremendous charm. The price is six hundred thousand." Barnett assured her, "You'll love Bedford. It's real country, not manicured. We have dirt roads by choice. Dirt roads keep the traffic out. Lots of horses up here; sometimes more horses than people." Barnett then gave a detailed description of every room in the house.

"It sounds lovely," Leona said. "A lovely private country feeling."

"Tell me a little more about what you are looking for," Barnett asked.

Leona then explained that a maid, a bodyguard and perhaps a driver would stay with her on the weekends. "And a pool is very important. We swim every day."

"Well, I really don't think this house is large enough for you," Barnett advised. "But there is this other house, much grander scale. Six bedrooms and two levels. Walls of fieldstone and fireplaces. A lot of glass overlooking a lake. Wonderful cedar decks all over. Thirteen acres. A tennis court and larger pool. It's not far away, in Pound Ridge, and it's going for one million three hundred thousand."

For an hour and a half, Barnett recalls, Leona kept up the questions.

"She was very upbeat, very flamboyant. Very aware of what she liked and didn't like and one smart woman. And like anyone buying their first country house, she was excited. She was buying a dream."

Before hanging up, Leona said, "Let me talk it over with my husband." Two weeks later, Harry and Leona inspected the Pound Ridge property and pronounced it a beauty. "Mrs. Helmsley loved the lines, the proportions. She described how she was going to redecorate it." Although the Helmsleys bid on the property, they asked Barnett to show them other houses just to satisfy themselves that they had made the right choice. She took them through about ten other Westchester homes, "and every one intrigued them." Just for the hell of it, Barnett then decided to show the Helmsleys a house ten times more expensive than most of the others. In no way could it qualify as "a little hideaway." They drove ten miles south to the "back country" of Greenwich, Connecticut, the estate area. This is a landscape of velvet lawns, corrals, and mansions populated by many of America's wealthiest families. The Helmsleys' limousine paused before a four-foot-high fieldstone wall that was topped by an unsightly three-foot-high chain link fence at 521 Round Hill Road.

Beyond the wall, all that could be seen was the skirt of a steeply rising forested hill. Only when the limousine moved forward, through a spiked wrought-iron gate, did they catch their first glimpse of Dunnellen Hall. It was perched 100 yards away on the verdant hilltop, and seemed a block long. In a courtyard just below the crest of hill and home, sparrows splashed about a gurgling fountain. A 1,000-foot-long asphalt driveway cut a semicircle through the front lawn, looping from the spiked front gate to a twin at the far end of the wall.

Barnett and the Helmsleys hiked up to the three-story Jacobean mansion whose roofline danced with fretted English Renaissance scrollwork. The back lawn, they could see, was an undulating downslope with all the quiet beauty of Central Park's Sheep Meadow, and it was vastly larger than the mansion's front lawn.

When they stepped across the threshold, they could see that the mansion was built for keeps, with thick limestone walls and marble floors. It was basically a very long house, without true wings. Three horizontal sections came together not in a straight line, but in a modified zigzag. A magnificent staircase with ornamental wrought-iron rails and marble stairs was centrally located in the rear of the mansion.

"The expression on Mrs. Helmsley's face when we walked into the house was priceless," Barnett recalls. "It was exhilaration. From that point on, it all got better because the house is glamorous." They paused in a drawing room with silk brocade walls, a teak floor and molded-plaster ceilings. No less impressive was the dining room, with its carved oak paneling, marble floors and fireplace. Also on the ground floor was a handsome library, dominated by a fifteenth-century carved-stone mantel and a large bay window overlooking a terrace.

In the basement, a dramatic passageway and sixteenth-century French cathedral doors led to the refrigerated wine cellar. Over 5,000 bottles, the Helmsleys were informed, could be stored at a constant temperature of 54 degrees. The second floor had seven bedrooms, including a master suite with two baths and a dressing room. "Mrs. Helmsley was oohing and aahing over one of the bathrooms," Barnett said, "because it was exquisite. Everything, including the shower walls, was lined in pink onyx." Harry took one look at the bathroom and announced, "Oh no, this is my bathroom!" From the master bedroom, they admired the back lawn and could see the blue waters of Long Island Sound and the bay-indented shores of Long Island, New York, beyond. Also on the second floor, off to the left and separated by a set of locked doors, was a servants' wing with seven bedrooms and two baths.

From the downstairs breakfast room, they walked to the back terrace and admired a small swimming pool close to the house. On a lower plateau of the back lawn was a second, much larger swimming pool. "Oh look, Harry!" Leona exclaimed when she spotted the ninety-foot-long pool, surrounded by a flagstone terrace. "We can have one pool to entertain and one for ourselves." The tour continued on the front lawn, where the Helmsleys were shown the elegant brick gatehouse, a home in itself with two separate apartments for security staff or domestic help. The apartments were separated by a six-car garage, and each had its own kitchen, breakfast room, living room, bedroom and bath. The Dunnellen Hall estate, it was obvious, was an American manor; like the Helmsley Palace, it reflected the baronial lifestyle of an earlier age. Leona and Harry's earlier fascination, the house in Pound Ridge, was instantly forgotten. "They knew right away they wanted Dunnellen Hall," Barnett said. "They wouldn't have been happy anywhere else. They couldn't have lived their lifestyle anywhere else. They wouldn't have fit." With little dickering, Harry agreed to pay $8 million for the mansion and its 26 acres, and another $3 million for its furnishings. The entire sum would be paid in cash by mid-June, within forty-five days, to Indian shipping magnate Ravi Tikkoo. It would be a tidy profit for Tikkoo, who had bought the estate for $3 million in 1974. At $11 million, the Helmsleys' "little hideaway" would be the second most expensive home ever purchased in the United States. But Barnett said Leona, an experienced real estate saleswoman in her own right, had no worries about the price tag. "She kept telling Mr. Helmsley, 'I *know* this is a good investment. I *know* we're paying right!'" Unable to contain her excitement, Leona trumpeted the good news through the executive corridors of the Palace. In his nearly two years with the Harley chain, Gerald Kadish had never seen his boss display such unbridled enthusiasm. "She was like a little girl, flighty and feisty, and actually bouncing around her office—jumping and skipping."

"You're really happy and excited about this," Kadish observed out loud. "This is wonderful."

"You must understand," Leona replied. "This is my first house!"

"What do you mean, your first house?"

"Well, you know," Leona explained, "my whole life, I've always lived in apartments or condominiums or hotels. This is my first real house. It has a lawn and landscaping and a big driveway."

A hideaway only thirty-five miles away, Leona added, would give Harry more time to relax. The Palm Beach penthouse would still be used on occasional weekends, but a Greenwich estate could be used every week. Instead of the hassles of driving to and from airports and flights in uncertain weather, the Helmsleys' driver could deliver them to their new retreat at a moment's notice. "Harry wanted to slow down," Kadish said. "He was of the opinion that other people should help run the business." A lifetime workaholic like Helmsley, however, needed a little nudge toward the lounge chair. Leona's newest project, Kadish said, was effective persuasion. "Mrs. Helmsley truly wanted to keep him healthy, and the house was as much for his benefit as her own. The mansion was another way of keeping him alive as long as possible."

To finance the mansion, Kadish said Helmsley instructed him to sell the Harley of Sarasota. At the last minute, however, the deal collapsed because of potential zoning problems. "The local preservationists in Sarasota," Kadish recalls, "made it clear they wouldn't allow the intended buyer to alter any part of the hotel, as the buyer had planned, so Mr. Helmsley had to back away." Leona was furious at the unexpected snag. "She was really pissed at me," Kadish recalls, "because I didn't come forth with the money needed to close on her house." The cash-flow emergency was solved at the eleventh hour, he said, when Harry ordered his chief financial officer, Joe Licari, to raise the funds.

On June 24, the *Greenwich Time* announced: "The man who owns most of the Empire State Building now owns a little bit of Greenwich—a costly little bit." The newspaper noted that Harry Helmsley had already moved into his furnished estate, and intended to adopt a new lifestyle. "The 74-year-old developer said that he had plans to stay in his Park Avenue home during his work week—that is, from Tuesdays to Thursdays—and spend the rest of his time in Greenwich. He particularly likes swimming, which he'll be able to do easily in one of the estate's two pools." Ironically, the newspaper added, Helmsley's "uptown competitor, Donald Trump," had also scooped up a Greenwich estate that very week, paying $3.5 million for a place on Long Island Sound directly across from the exclusive Indian Harbor Yacht Club. Trump reportedly bought the mansion, the article said, "after his wife, Ivana, scoured the area in a helicopter."

Right away, Leona set out to upgrade her country house. A team of carpenters from a Bronx firm, Commercial Cabinet Corp., worked evenings and weekends to install a butcher block kitchen table, enlarge closets and refinish doors as quickly as possible. To spruce up marble floors and columns at the Greenwich estate, Leona hired Remco Maintenance Corp., a Manhattan firm that routinely cared for dozens of Harry Helmsley's office buildings.

Décor became a major priority. Although she and Harry had spent $3 million for Tikkoo's furniture, they did so only for the convenience of moving right in. Many of the rugs and fabrics were of garish floral design, and a good percentage of the "antiques" were obvious reproductions. Leona dispatched her Manhattan interior designer, Joe Catania, to England to select real McCoys as replacements. He spent over $1 million on fine English tables, dressers and rugs. When the merchandise arrived, he recalls, "We moved some of Tikkoo's stuff to the Helmsleys' hotels and donated some to Father [Bruce] Ritter," the founder of Covenant House, a Manhattan shelter for runaway teenagers. Leona's little hideaway was becoming enormously expensive. Even everyday expenses were of an unimaginably higher caliber. Like any other homeowners, the billionaire Helmsleys gritted their teeth and prayed for grace when they received their first utility bill. When they peeked into the opened envelope, however, a $3,000 charge smacked them right between the eyes. The couple, who enjoyed free utilities in their sprawling Park Lane Hotel penthouse, were thunderstruck. First thing the following day, according to an eyewitness, Mrs. Helmsley came into work "screaming and ranting and raving because she was positive the electric company was overcharging her. She screeched to her secretary, 'Get me the president of Connecticut Light and Power!'"

When a top CL&P executive came on the phone, Mrs. Helmsley let him have it. "Just because my name is Helmsley doesn't mean you can overcharge me! I've never seen anything so absurd in my life—three thousand dollars for electricity is ridiculous!"

The CL&P executive must have held on for dear life as the Queen completed the cycle of her rage—refrain after refrain of purple prose.

Finally, in conclusion, Leona let loose with a full head of steam: "I'll only pay half!" she vowed, and slammed the telephone down.

"It was typical Leona," the office eyewitness said. "She felt she was above paying for anything. Her name was Helmsley, so therefore she shouldn't be charged—the same as the Duke and Duchess of Windsor, who never paid for anything." In all likelihood, Mr. Helmsley eventually picked up the tab and spared his wife from seeing more CL&P correspondence. As the owner of New York's largest private real estate portfolio, he would know the inevitability of taxes and utility bills.

Like any good home economist, Leona did discover ways, however, of paring her household budget. According to Milton Meckler, when she decided more furnishings were needed at Dunnellen Hall, rather than buying exclusively from expensive European dealers she began ordering hundreds of thousands of dollars' worth of fine goods from Deco—at absolutely no cost. On a daily basis, Meckler recalls, Leona and Frank Turco both placed orders through his Florida purchasing firm "for sofas, dining chairs, custom-made draperies at $125 to $175 a yard, chandeliers, appliances, carpeting, linens" and every imaginable amenity for the mansion. "Deco became Mrs. Helmsley's own little store. If she needed anything, we'd have to expedite it. Everything was a priority," Meckler said, and Leona intended to pay for none of the merchandise. Deco would simply have to "eat" the cost of the merchandise, just as it had done years before with shipments to Jay Panzirer. Meckler said he was upset about the continuing "freebies" trend because the costs were cutting deeply into Deco's annual profits.

"I'd be on the phone with Mrs. Helmsley or Turco four or five times a day. I made sure I was in the office bright and early because normally I'd start getting calls from them by 8:30 A.M. It was the most important thing in her life. You just couldn't mess up." Meckler said at least half his working day was devoted to the mansion decorating campaign and occasional shipments of free goods to Leona's penthouse apartments at the Park Lane and Palm Beach Towers. He said Leona and Turco would want to know: "Are the goods rolling?" or "How is it proceeding?" In addition to the incessant phone calls, he said, "Deco had to keep Mrs. Helmsley informed as to progress by mail almost every day of the week. Then I'd get memos in return from Mrs. Helmsley." At first, Meckler said he winced at the truly costly orders. "I'd say to myself, 'Look how expensive!' But then after a point I wouldn't even notice. It became old hat." Outdoor items were also popular with the Queen. A white golf cart was ordered to help the Helmsleys negotiate their Greenwich acreage. Another object that really caught Leona's fancy, Meckler says, "was a motor she spotted on an overseas trip that creates waves in a swimming pool. We found her one, and she'd switch it on and swim against the current" in her ninety-foot pool. He joked with his Deco staff about the dangers of the $3,000 device. "I hope she doesn't accidentally throw it into reverse," Meckler quipped, "or she'll go right down the drain!"

But it was the smaller pool, on the back lawn just outside the breakfast room, that seems to have captivated the Helmsleys more than any other amenity on the estate. They were aware that Tikkoo, Dunnellen Hall's previous owner, had intended to enclose the pool so it could be used during the long Connecticut winters. For more information, they contacted Tikkoo's former architect, Henry Loheac of Westchester County. Loheac informed Harry and Leona that Tikkoo had planned to build a simple boxlike enclosure, but scrapped the idea after suffering financial reverses. On the spot, Loheac said, "Mr. Helmsley asked me to finish what Tikkoo started, and to do it as cheaply as possible. He couldn't have cared less what it looked like. All he wanted was a functional shelter to keep the rain off his head." Leona objected to Harry's simple vision, however. "She wanted to go fancy," Loheac says. "She wanted a quality pool enclosure that she could show to her friends. Something that looked expensive." After analyzing a half-dozen models built by Loheac, a compromise between Harry's frugality and Leona's aesthetics was reached. The Helmsleys obtained a building permit that spring for a rectangular one-story enclosure measuring 108 feet by 63 feet. To match the Jacobean mansion, it would be constructed of red brick and limestone and would be attached to the house at the breakfast room. Privately, Helmsley budgeted the project at $600,000, although the value listed on the permit was only $100,000. For security reasons, Loheac said, Leona vetoed his recommendation of skylights. The pool enclosure would be divided into two living areas. From the mansion's breakfast room one would walk directly into the first section, a small 500-square-foot room with a series of floor-to-ceiling windows looking across the back lawn to Long Island Sound. It would be known as the sun room. Through glass doors at the far end of the sun room, one would enter the pool area itself, a far larger space with the rectangular swimming pool as its centerpiece.

Natural light would flood down because one of its side walls would be built almost entirely of glass, parallel to a nearby brick wall of the servants' wing. Shrubs would be planted in the three-foot gap between the glass wall and servants' wall, giving the appearance of an enclosed greenhouse open to the sky. A roof of prefabricated concrete slabs laid on steel would keep the rain off Harry's head, but certainly win no design awards.

As project coordinator, Helmsley hired Carlos Olivieri, an engineer who had played a supervisory role in construction of the New York Harley. One of Olivieri's first moves was to award a $102,000 contract to a Scarsdale contractor, Mike DiSisto, to excavate the poolside area and build a concrete foundation. Not until DiSisto's painstaking job was completed the following spring could the steel supports and brick walls be erected. In the meantime, there would be no winter swims at Dunnellen Hall.

New York might have its Broadway lights, the Empire State Building and the Statue of Liberty, but nowhere on its vaunted shores could the weary traveler hope to find a five-diamond hotel. Not even the legendary Plaza or Waldorf was accorded highest ranking in the *TourBook*, the annual travel guide published for thirty million members of the American Automobile Association. In late 1983, however, Leona made the grade. AAA had evaluated fifteen thousand hotels during the year on its scale of one to five diamonds, and only forty-four in the United States were recognized as "renowned for marked superiority of guest facilities, services and overall atmosphere." For a hotelier, the five-diamond designation was as special as an Academy Award. Leona's excitement was unbounded when she learned that the Helmsley Palace was the only New York hotel on the exalted list. Her own Renaissance dollhouse was in the fine company of such landmarks as The Greenbrier at White Sulfur Springs, West Virginia; Salishan Lodge in Gleneden Beach, Oregon; The Broadmoor in Colorado Springs; and the Alameda Palace in Kansas City.

As a reward to her thousand employees for their role in capturing the honor, the Queen of the Palace decided a souvenir pin was in order. As luck would have it, Leona's sister Sandra worked part-time in Atlanta as a designer of costume jewelry.

"Let's hire Sandra to do it," Leona told Joyce Beber during a discussion of the souvenir project. "You know she's talented. It will make her feel good. She could use the money." Sandra accepted the assignment, Beber said, but at terms that offered her only a token profit. She designed a horizontal pin studded with five sparkling cubic zirconium stones; to the uninitiated eye, the costume jewels would pass for diamonds. Leona enthusiastically accepted the design but became alarmed on learning that each pin would cost almost fifty dollars to manufacture. Her kindly feeling toward her sister curdled.

"Sandra's fucking up!" Leona complained to Beber. "She said she's giving me the pins at the lowest possible cost, but I'm not so sure. I could have gotten them cheaper somewhere else!"

Leona's sudden suspicion came as no surprise, recalls Beber's advertising partner, Elaine Silverstein. "Mrs. Helmsley was the most distrustful person I've ever seen in my life. She felt that nobody, not even a relative, could be a purely honest person." And from experience, Beber was quite familiar with one of Leona's strangest, and most predictable, behavior patterns. "If Mrs. Helmsley does you a favor, and you accept it, you eventually pay a very heavy price for it!" At first, Leona might have the best of intentions, "but she is not really a person for sharing. She is incapable of really giving or sharing, so eventually she gets very angry that she gave you something. She gets in a rage against you." And in Leona's mind, "She considered she had done Sandra a favor by letting her design the costume jewelry." The sisters remained in contact, Beber said, but their on-again-off-again relationship was strained by the pin project.

On November 18, the pins sparked laughter in a gossip tidbit on the *Post*'s widely read Page Six. It noted that 950 Palace staffers had received a sparkling souvenir, "but the honor had strings attached." Before being pinned, "the lucky many" were required to sign waivers stipulating that they wear the pin "on the job at all times, that they turn in the pin when they leave the hotel's employ, repair it if damaged *and* fork over $50 if they lose it. 'Nice token of appreciation,' sniffed one disgruntled staffer."

Under the glare of publicity, Leona admitted the waivers were a goof and promptly removed all the strings. "Harry and I have given these pins with a full heart and thankfulness," she assured the gossip editors.

One of Leona's close aides suggested that the five-diamond award was too great an honor to enjoy privately. "What a wonderful basis for an ad," he suggested. "It's your employees' award. Why not have a big group of them standing on the stairs, with you congratulating them?" Forthwith, Leona passed the idea along to Beber Silverstein, but with key revisions. Instead of congratulating her employees, as suggested, the ad heaped praise on the Queen. Two rows of uniformed employees stood stiffly at attention on the staircase while Leona, at front center, proudly modeled *her* five-diamond pin. The glory was all Leona's. Black employees got the least recognition of all, recalls Tad Distler, Beber Silverstein's account supervisor. Twenty employees had to be chosen to stand behind Leona in the ad, and he said the Queen objected "to one or two people we had chosen who were of dark complexion. She said, 'I don't want them in it!' " As it turned out, a black maid was placed in the background; all the remaining nineteen staffers were white. Leona's exclusion of blacks from her advertising was a constant problem, Distler said. "We always had to be careful about sneaking a black in."

Harry and Leona's high spirits over the five-diamond honor were interrupted the following month. "Hotel's Limited Partners Win Arbitrators' Award" was the page-one headline in the Dec. 14, 1983 issue of the *New York Law Journal*. The article reported that an arbitration panel had ruled against Harry Helmsley in his long financial battle with limited partners of the Helmsley Palace. In fact, after twenty days of hearings, the arbitrators had practically skinned Helmsley alive for his treatment of the investors during and after construction of the hotel. The panel ordered Helmsley to stop trying to strap the partners with a $20 million second mortgage to defray mammoth cost overruns that were his own liability. The arbitrators didn't limit their sights, however, to that original issue. After examining hotel financial records, they ordered Harry to refund to the partners $605,000 in excessive commissions charged by Deco Purchasing for hotel furnishings. They ruled that Deco's 20 percent commission was excessive and slashed it to 5 percent, thereby also saving the hotel an estimated $2.8 million on future Deco commissions. In yet another blow, the panel ruled that Helmsley, often through sweetheart deals with his own subsidiaries, had improperly increased the hotel's operating expenses by a projected $6.2 million. For instance, instead of supplying telephones, computers, room refrigerators and televisions as part of a finished hotel, Helmsley had billed the hotel $65,000 a month for lease of the equipment. Those expenses, too, had to be returned because they had enriched Helmsley, while reducing the hotel profits of the investors. All in all, the limited partners had saved themselves $30 million, including the cost of the second mortgage, by daring to fight their general partner. "Helmsley was beaten and got a goose egg," recalls Gerald J. Fields, the lawyer for the limited partners. "It was a case of enormous overreaching by a general partner who thought he could get away with it. But he didn't because he had substantial limited partners who stood up and said, 'You ain't getting away with it.' "

The arbitrators' ruling, confirmed by the State Supreme Court, amounted to a virtual declaration that Helmsley had stolen from his partners. The case was far too abstruse and narrowly reported in the mainstream media, however, to greatly harm the Helmsleys' public image. Leona's crown was untarnished, and with each new queen ad Beber noticed that Leona increasingly took the role to heart. "She laughed about it, about how she wasn't a *real* queen, but she actually began to become more imperious. As she became a national celebrity through the advertising, she came to think more about her national persona. And like many public figures, she began to believe her own press." Even without ads, temptations to the ego were great. For one thing, Beber said "The hotel business was completely different from Leona's earlier career as a real estate broker. Real estate is quieter. Nobody's waiting on you. But as owner and president of the Palace, she suddenly had legions of service people to accommodate her, to make her comfortable. If she wants tea and crumpets, the food manager comes, and the maître d', and the waiter, and they all stand around to make sure it's right. You have the power of a queen, and you're royalty."

Ad shoots, moreover, were regal affairs. To set the mood for her poses, Leona would often bring along a pianist to play her favorite Julio Iglesias songs. A hairdresser, makeup person and maid were on hand. And someone was always present to take care of the Queen's jewelry, which was stored in vaults in the Palace and Park Lane.

Jewelry was one of Leona's greatest loves. She did much of her shopping at Van Cleef & Arpels, on Fifth Avenue. For convenience, the Queen would also summon jewelers to the Palace. One day, Distler said, a Parisian jeweler came calling with his wares. "Her office looked like Aladdin's cave. There was jewelry dripping from the mantelpiece and all over the sofa. And she was playing with this immense yellow diamond, just a loose stone." Harry walked in as Leona was admiring the rock and commented, "That's pretty."

"Yeah, you like it?" Leona asked.

"Yes, do you want it?"

"I think it would be wonderful," she cooed.

"How much is it?" Harry asked the Parisian.

"Madame has already got me down to the lowest price possible," the jeweler replied. "It's a million eighty."

"If you want it, dear," said Harry, "let's get it." Distler said Leona had the stone set and eventually wore it to the grand opening of Maxim's New York restaurant. It seemed paradoxical to Distler that Leona would gleefully spend over $1 million on a stone, yet protest for days if a bicycle messenger was paid $5.95 to drop off advertising proofs at the *New York Times*. "Any time she saw a messenger charge, she'd go bananas. She thought it was an outrageous expense. She'd scream, 'Five ninety-five to the *Times*! You should have mailed it, or brought it over yourself.' " He concluded that Leona was "psychologically incapable of comprehending what a million is," maybe because of her background. "All she knows is it's nice to have lots of them. Big numbers are abstract. But if the jeweler had asked her to pay ten dollars and fifty cents, she'd have bargained it down to six dollars." Leona's lack of financial insight was tolerable, Distler said, only because Harry handled important money matters for the hotels. "Her forte was the décor, uniforms, the food." Above all, "her purpose was to be the gracious, smiling hostess of the Palace and Harley chain." So striking were the ads, particularly the three-in-a-row ads for the New York Harley, that fans from around the country wrote hundreds of letters a week to the coddled Queen. A San Francisco housewife wrote an adoring letter that concluded, "Let's go shopping next time you're in town." Fraternities at Columbia

University and as far away as Ohio loved the campy poses of Leona swathed in fur and gold lamé. "They'd live for Sunday morning," Distler recalls, "to see what she was wearing" in the latest *Times* spread. "They'd call and say, 'Can you send us some posters?' " One of the Queen's most prized letters came from an inmate at Sing Sing. "He had a mad crush on her and could hardly wait to get out and marry her and love her." Leona split her sides laughing, Joyce Beber says. "It carried on for pages, and she thought it was so flattering. She joked, 'Aw, he's got at least eighteen more years before he can stay at the Palace, and by then the rates will be too high.' " Yet, like every letter, it was answered either by the Queen herself or secretaries assigned specifically to guest correspondence.

Some of Leona's mail, however, was less than flattering. The Queen actually changed her dress code, Distler says, after receiving a hailstorm of letters criticizing her low-cut gowns. "She got a lot of bad letters saying she looked like a cow with so much bosom showing." The final straw was one that accused her of looking like "the zaftig madam of a Middle European whorehouse." That's when she changed her wardrobe, Distler said. "She decided she wanted to be slim and svelte instead of a full-figured woman." Despite Harry's protests, "she never showed bosom again." And frankly, at 63, Leona was falling victim to middle-age spread. Henceforth she wore fairly high-cut dresses for ad shoots and insisted that all her photographs be retouched to remove wrinkles from her face and avoirdupois from her torso. "Artists would actually paint the changes she wanted," Distler says. Major surgery was performed, for instance, on a Helmsley Palace ad of Leona dressed for dinner in a gold lamé top and black velvet dress. "We took lots off the waist. We very definitely shaved off the right side of the gold lamé, bosom and all. We slimmed down her cheeks, shaved off the neck and pizzazzed the teeth to make them sparkle." The final result was "a woman who looked thirty-five or forty years old."

From two decades before, when she was a secret grandmother at Pease & Elliman, and earlier, youthfulness was everything to Leona. And now, while millions of *Times* readers marveled at how wonderful the Queen looked, Distler said Leona marveled the most of all. Every weekend she did the crossword puzzle in the *New York Times Magazine* and could see as many as four flattering photos of herself in one issue. "She got the feeling that she actually looked younger in real life, that she *was* younger." At that point, Distler says, "the queen thing began to seriously affect her. That's when her ego really began to escalate. She was beginning to think she really was a supreme being." Beber says Leona stuck to an ambitious "self-improvement program" to keep herself an attractive queen. "Every aspect of her body was her persona, and would be subject to self-improvement—better health, better beauty, even a better vocabulary. When she learned a word, she would use it ten times the next day. It was sort of touching because she was like a child, trying to figure it out." If Leona looked in the mirror and saw microscopic lines, Beber recalls, she would phone her dermatologist, Dr. Orentreich, for another silicone injection. "She didn't need an appointment. She just called and said, 'Norman, I'm on my way!'" Elaine Silverstein recalls the time Leona cried out, "Oh, I have a freckle on my hand!" and rushed over to have it removed by dermabrasion. Leona visited the doctor's office virtually every week, Beber says, and even convinced Harry to undergo the wrinkle-removing silicone treatments. The tycoon went too seldom, however, to derive lasting benefit. "Silicone is subtle," Beber explained. "You don't go just once or twice, you have to keep going." Although Leona never informed the media of her debt to Orentreich, surprisingly, she made no bones about it off-camera. "She constantly recommended him to people. It was Jewish mothering at a certain level. In a good-natured way, she would say: 'You're an emergency! You have to see Orentreich!'" The Queen's teeth were also under constant upgrade. "They were the bane of her existence," Silverstein says. "She has caps in front"—plastic over her real teeth—"and they never suited her. She was forever changing them. We'd show her her photographs and she'd say, 'The teeth aren't right!'" During one six-month stretch, Distler says, "She was going to the dentist almost every Tuesday, Wednesday and Thursday." A close former aide to Leona recalls that she changed dentists constantly to achieve the right appearance "and spent about twenty-five thousand dollars a year" in the elusive quest.

The package might not be perfect, but Leona was well able to relish her celebrity. Joe Catania, her former interior designer, recalls an incident where Leona (in a reversal of the Andy Warhol adage) tried to forfeit her fame but failed after 15 minutes. "We were strolling down Fifth Avenue without her security man and I told her, 'You cannot be Leona Helmsley and walk through the street without your bodyguard, or we'll have trouble. You have to do what Marilyn Monroe used to do. You have to pretend you're just another ordinary individual. You have to blend in with the crowd.' " Leona accepted the challenge, threading her way soberly through the crowded sidewalk. "And nobody bothered her." When the pair reached Botticelli shoestore, Catania recalls, "I poked my head in and they said, 'Sorry, we're closed.' " Without even thinking, Leona switched her charisma back on, poked her own head in the boutique and asked sweetly, "Even for meeeeee?"

"And the moment she did," Catania adds, "they said, 'Come right in, Mrs. Helmsley.' "

Lee West, a liquor salesman for Peerless Importers, Inc. of Brooklyn, was told to report ASAP to Frank Turco's second-floor office in the Graybar Building. West, who already supplied booze to the Park Lane, St. Moritz and New York Harley, had no idea why he was wanted. But he hoped the meeting held promise of expanded business with Helmsley Hotels. When West arrived, he was greeted by Turco and his two inseparable aides, Vince Sclafani and Neil Petruzzi. West, a streetwise jazz drummer on his off hours, quickly sized up the trio. Sclafani and Petruzzi, wearing cheap suits and packing guns, were good-natured subordinates. "They looked like they could break bricks with their hands, but weren't looking to shove anyone's head down the toilet." Turco, thin and frail by comparison, was sporting a tailored suit and custom-made shirt. "He ran the show; everyone else was quiet. He went into an Edward G. Robinson pose, a poor imitation of a tough guy. A caricature of an Italian hood."

Turco demanded to know if West was paying kickbacks to his three Helmsley hotel accounts. "No," West assured him.

"Are you sure? Think hard."

"No, I don't give my salary away," West insisted.

"Well," Turco asked, "what could you do for us if we also gave you all the business at the Helmsley Palace?"

Surprised by the quick change in moral atmosphere, West stumbled for a reply.

"I'll tell you what I've been offered," Turco said. "One salesman offered me a Jaguar. One offered my family a trip to Europe."

West managed a smile and thought to himself, "What is this fucker looking for?"

"What will *you* do for me?" Turco continued.

"I have a four-year-old Volkswagen," West quipped, trying to introduce some levity into the tense situation. "How about I lend it to you every other Sunday?"

Nobody laughed.

"What will you do for me?" Turco repeated.

"I won't give you any kickbacks," West made clear, "but how about if I teach you how to keep from getting raped by your food and beverage suppliers?"

"What kind of shit is that!" Turco shouted, jumping out of his chair.

"I just don't give money. But I can come up with ideas to save you thousands of dollars."

Turco calmed down and asked for an explanation.

West then suggested that the four Helmsley hotels in question could collectively save $100,000 a year by buying only through him. "For instance," West suggested, "you should eliminate Gordon's gin and vodka and replace it with Gilby's. You'll save six to nine dollars a case, without sacrificing quality. Another thing—you're not buying properly. When you buy four cases, you get no discount. If you buy ten cases, you save two dollars a case. No more small orders."

West sensed that his sales pitch hit home. "It went right. I felt I was now something to them." Turco said that he would talk it over with Mrs. Helmsley. Weeks later, in late December, West said Turco informed him that "Mrs. Helmsley okayed everything." Starting January 1, he would coordinate all liquor purchases for the four Helmsley hotels.

Just before New Year's, however, West said Turco pulled the rug out from underneath him.

"He called me to his office," West recalls, "and told me I would have to pay a kickback after all. From my five percent sales commission, I would have to kick back two points. I was angry and fucking shocked."

"Are you serious!" West demanded. "I only get five percent. If two goes to you, and two goes to taxes, I'm left with only one percent. Instead of making five dollars, I'm stuck with one dollar. In all these weeks, you've never mentioned kickbacks."

"Unless it's done this way, Mrs. Helmsley will not do business," Turco said. "Everybody pays to do business with us. Nothing comes into this hotel unless we get a piece of it. Even you, Lee, who I like."

West said he reluctantly agreed to sacrifice the two points—equivalent to 40 percent of his commission earnings—rather than lose the accounts altogether. "If I walked away, I made nothing." The policy took effect that January. On the tenth of each month, West said he would cash his commission checks "and take them their share in cash. They never had to wait. I'd usually give it to Petruzzi in an envelope. If he wasn't there, I'd give it to Vinnie [Sclafani]."

After several months, West said he complained to Petruzzi that the paltry earnings "were killing me." Petruzzi intervened with Turco, West said, and the kickback was halved to 1 percent of gross sales. "It was a big help. I was giving them over one thousand dollars a month. It gave me an extra hundred or hundred and fifty a week to play with."

West said he never knew whether his payoffs actually went to Leona, or whether Turco and company kept them for themselves. It just seemed so strange that the billionaire Queen would need to seek kickbacks from vendors. "I can't relate to people that rich. You'd think there would be a point where you'd realize you have more money than you'll ever need forever and ever." On one occasion, West said he asked Turco, "Who's actually getting my money?"

"Oh, it goes to the Missus," Turco insisted. "We don't touch it. We put it in an envelope, the same envelope you give us, and it goes up to her apartment at the Park Lane—either there or to Greenwich, wherever she's around."

West said he became friendly with Sclafani and Petruzzi and often shot the breeze with them while making his dropoffs. "I really liked them. I would bring cake up to their office and they'd make coffee." West said he also asked them, "Who gets the money?" and was told, "Mrs. Helmsley."

During one memorable visit to the Graybar office, West recalls that Petruzzi boasted: "I want you to hear an order," and then placed a phone call. "I want a million light bulbs," Petruzzi said, as West laughed hysterically in the background.

"What do you do with a million light bulbs?" West asked afterward.

"I have twenty-five hotels throughout the country."

A thought flashed through West's mind. "If Mrs. Helmsley is getting my liquor kickbacks, that's a thousand dollars a month. But if it's from all the hotels, that's a lot. If it's also from flowers, meat, produce, the beer man, the guy who sells air conditioners, and anybody who sells to them, then that's a fortune."

Indeed, Milton Meckler says that Turco enjoyed veto power

over vendors selected by Deco to supply the Helmsley's hotels and office buildings. "Any major deal, we'd have to send the vendor up to Frank's office in New York." Vendors frequently reported back to Meckler that Turco had tried to shake them down. On one occasion, Meckler recalls watching as Turco tried to wrest kickbacks from a linen supplier at Deco's office in Orlando. Meckler said Turco told the businessman, "If you want to be a preferred vendor, we'll have to work something out where there's enough money left over for us."

Meckler said the vendor flashed him a pained look and asked, "Milton, is he asking what I think he's asking?"

"No, he's just kidding you," Meckler said. "Frank, you are kidding, aren't you?"

"No, no, no. You know I'm not kidding," Turco replied.

Meckler said he dismissed the visiting vendor and warned Turco, "Don't ever do that in my office! I don't know what you do in New York; I don't wanna know about it."

When Meckler once asked Turco who received such kickbacks, he said Turco replied: "Her Highness. She *loves* kickbacks!"

Because the Helmsleys had appointed Turco an executive officer of many Helmsley subsidiaries, Meckler said he had countless ways of obtaining goods and cash. As chief of Hospitality Services, the subsidiary that provided administrative support to the various hotels, Meckler said Turco used a particularly bold method involving Bush Terminal, the Brooklyn industrial park where Deco warehoused financial records and surplus merchandise. Deco's fixed monthly rent for the warehouse space was approximately $4,000. Instead of paying Bush Terminal directly, however, Deco would mail a payment to Hospitality Services, which would then forward its own rental check to the industrial park. Occasionally, Meckler said, Hospitality Services would bill Deco $30,000 to $40,000, instead of the customary $4,000 rental fee. "Suddenly, we'd get an exorbitant bill for storing merchandise that didn't even exist!" Meckler said he always called Turco after receiving the crazy invoices and demanded an explanation.

"Don't ask any questions, just send us a check," Turco would reply. Meckler said he obeyed, assuming the excess rent payments never reached Bush Terminal but were pocketed by either Turco or Leona. He claims Turco pulled the scam several times over a period of about three years.

Leona apparently also received plums in the form of free services. "Paulie," a former driver for Manhattan Limousine Ltd., claims the company provided the billionaire Helmsleys with free use of a limousine and driver for several years. "They get about a hundred and fifty thousand dollars' worth of free service a year," he said. "It's there for them twenty-four hours." When their assigned driver is sick or absent, Paulie said, other drivers tremble in fear that Harry and Leona will commandeer their services. "They're bastards to drive," he said. "They never give you a compliment and they never take a dime out of their pocket to tip a driver. They're bloodsuckers, just cheap bastards. You drive them to Greenwich, to their great parties, you'd think they could say, 'Thanks, here's twenty dollars.'" Although a skinflint, Harry at least greets drivers with a civil hello. But Leona, Paulie said, couldn't be bothered. "The way she just walks into the car and holds you in disdain! She pressures you like a bone. 'Where's your hat!' If you told her your name, she would still call you 'driver.' If you make a wrong turn, she'll say, 'Don't you know where you're going?' 'Go to this lane!' 'Get in that lane!' 'Go slower!' 'Go faster!'"

Another driver, "Ed," says Leona's previous limo company, Celebrity Limousine Service, dropped the Helmsley account because Leona abused the drivers and demanded too many freebies. For instance, he recalls that for one of Leona's first parties at Dunnellen Hall she demanded that a half dozen limousines remain on call—gratis—at the estate to accommodate her guests. "She wouldn't let the drivers off the estate," he said. "She didn't feed us. She wouldn't let us have coffee. She wouldn't let us go to the bathroom." Finally, at 11 P.M., he said, "Mrs. Helmsley told us, 'Go into town and get something to eat. Be back in a half hour.'" Ed said he went without food because the terms were hopeless. "It takes fifteen minutes to get into town."

At a later date, Ed recalls, he had the misfortune of being first in line outside the Palace marquee when Leona's regular driver, Albert, was missing. "Mr. and Mrs. Helmsley walked outside and she was shouting, 'Where's Albert?'"

"Albert's off as far as I know," Ed said as the Helmsleys hovered over him.

"Don't you lie to me!" the Queen bellowed as she and Harry hopped into his back seat. "How dare you lie to me! I'm going to get you fired!"

Job or no job, it was one indignity too many for the chauffeur to tolerate.

"Mrs. Helmsley," he said, "I'll tell you what. You want me to give you the keys to the car, you take the keys to the car. You want another driver, you get another driver. You want to get me fired, get me fired. I don't give a damn. But don't you *ever* open your mouth to me that way again. Who do you think you are! Because you have money, you're gonna talk down to me and make me feel like dirt? No way! I don't need you and I don't need your money."

Through the rear-view mirror, Ed could see Harry smirking, visibly enjoying the sound of his wife getting a rare dose of her own medicine. All the way to Greenwich, the driver says, "Mr. Helmsley spoke to me. He was kidding with me all the way after I spoke to her that way. She hates it when anyone talks to her husband. She hated it. She just sat in the back of the car and kept her mouth shut."

Leona treated her pilots little better than the chauffeurs. For instance, Tad Distler recalls the time her two copilots and steward were fired for living beyond the Queen's means on a trip with the Helmsleys to Hawaii. He said he was in Leona's office weeks after the trip "when the pilots' expense reports came in. She went into an apoplectic fit because the three of them did not share a room. And the three of them had rented a car and put it on their expenses, and each spent thirty-five or forty dollars a day on meals. The ranting, raving and screaming! 'Get those pilots on the phone.' And she blessed them out individually for not sharing a room. These are grown men in responsible positions, making seventy thousand dollars a year, and she expected them to share a room, and to eat for fifteen dollars a day, and she didn't expect them to have a car. 'Well, Harry and I don't even have a car!' " Distler said Leona fired all three men, thereby putting her aircraft in mothballs for six full months "because no new pilots were to be found. She'd tell people, 'We can't go anywhere; the plane's undergoing maintenance.' "

Joyce Beber was amazed by Leona's contempt for the pilots, who held her very life in their hands. "It was ridiculous. Here she was with bone china and crystal, foxtrotting in the air with Harry, and she wouldn't let the pilots rent two cars when they landed. Here were these mammoth billionaires; nothing was good enough for each other. But for everyone else, they could sweat it out."

Twelve

Spring of 1984 had sprung and Leona was growing impatient with progress on her Greenwich pool enclosure. So she summoned Henry Loheac, its architect, and a half-dozen participating subcontractors to the Helmsley Palace for an announcement. Everybody was standing in the fifth floor conference room near Leona's office when she strolled in with Harry. Without ado, Leona said, "I'm unhappy with how things are going." She disclosed that Carlos Olivieri had been fired as general contractor and replaced by La Strada General Contracting Corp. of Queens. Henceforth, subcontractors would report to Frank Ferrante, a La Strada construction manager. Loheac recalls that Leona then clipped his wings. "She told me she was the architect," he recalls. "From now on, I would do nothing without her approval. I couldn't make any changes in drawings without conferring with her. It was clear she was going to make all the decisions." What a professional insult! "It would be like me going to the dentist and tell him how to work on my teeth," Loheac says. "But she decided she could do it better. She was going to play designer."

With the return of good weather, work resumed apace on the pool enclosure. Leona, at Ferrante's urging, announced a major change in plans. "She decided she wanted to build a room under the pool for the pool equipment," Loheac recalls. At the time, a cellar underneath the mansion's breakfast room had been used to house the pool circulation pump and related equipment. "Ferrante's theory was that the Helmsleys didn't need to hear noise from the equipment during breakfast, so it should be moved." Easier said than done, however. The foundation for the pool enclosure was to have been a simple concrete slab on dirt. Now, after excavation for a room underneath, an expensive structural-steel deck would have to replace the slab. The work proceeded, although the Helmsleys failed to notify the town building department of the design change, thereby apparently avoiding an increase in their property taxes. By summer, Loheac said, the foundation was completed and structural supports were bolted in place above ground to support the roof of the pool enclosure.

As a lark one afternoon, he recalls that Harry and Leona climbed up a rickety construction ladder to walk on the concrete-plank roof. That's when the revelation came.

"Look at this!" Leona exclaimed, gazing at the distant shoreline of Long Island Sound. "Harry, look at the view I've found! It's wonderful."

"Mrs. Helmsley was in a self-congratulatory mood," Loheac says. "She was the designer, and she had made this wonderful coup! She had discovered the view. 'Look how innovative I am. Look how wonderful I am.'" By contrast, "She said all the rest of us were incompetent because we never found it." Leona's discovery necessitated yet another major design change. "She decided she wanted to use the roof." In the original blueprints, there were no stairs of any kind to the roof. "Now, she wanted us to design a fancy three-foot-wide staircase, covered with brick and limestone and given a finished look to match the exterior of the pool house." Finally, as a third major design change, Leona ordered that the concrete roof deck be yanked out and replaced with a more attractive surface. No longer would the roof be just a functional shelter to keep the rain off Harry's head. "She suddenly saw a vision that this roof would make a wonderful place for dancing. She wanted a dance floor to show off the view to all her guests." The open-air dance floor would be the most unusual ballroom in all of Greenwich. Guests would commune with Jupiter and Mars while swirling to Big Band sounds. A debate arose between Harry and Leona, Loheac said. "Mrs. Helmsley wanted us to refinish the roof deck with marble, but Mr. Helmsley wanted to use imitation marble made of plastic."

"An imitation plastic is all we need," declared the cost-conscious king of the manor.

Leona won out, however, and heavy travertine marble blocks were ordered. Just as Leona's idea for a country house had grown to palatial scale, so had her pool enclosure. "Anything worth doing is worth doing to excess" was Leona's motto, according to ad adviser Elaine Silverstein.

She continued her policy of stiffing contractors, as she had done with the electrician and other contractors previously at Ruth Panzirer's condo in Long Island. Loheac said he had to practically get on his knees to receive even partial payment of his architect fees. "I worked six months at a time without receiving a cent," he says. "It was the Helmsleys' way of operating, and it took me a long time to realize what was going on. The only way to get paid was to say, 'I'm stopping.' You had to say, 'I can't work anymore without being paid.'" From the start, Loheac was instructed to submit his bills to Jeremiah McCarthy, head of engineering for Helmsley-Spear. "I sent them to McCarthy," he says, "and they weren't paid." In frustration, Loheac protested to Harry that McCarthy wasn't following through. When approached, Loheac said Helmsley "was always a gentleman and well mannered," but gave him the royal runaround. "He'd say, 'Oh, McCarthy's not the one. Send your bills to Frank Turco.'" And when Turco failed to forward payment, Harry would tell Loheac, "Why did you send it to Turco? Why didn't you send it directly to me?" And sure enough, Harry would also fail to pay up. "It was a game that Mr. Helmsley was playing. He was sharp. He knew what he was doing and condoned it." Finally, Loheac said Frank Turco issued him a check for approximately $30,000 to cover six months' worth of unpaid architect fees. Loheac noticed that it was not a personal check signed by Harry or Leona. "It was a check from the Graybar Building."

If Harry and Leona knew Graybar funds were being used to pay for their mansion spruce-up, thereby reducing the Graybar's profits, they were also cheating Lawrence Wien, Harry's closest partner for thirty-five years, out of his fair share of profits.

Later payments from Turco were equally curious, Loheac says. "I don't think I received one check that said, 'Mr. or Mrs. Harry Helmsley.'" Instead, he said checks came from a smorgasbord of their corporations and commercial properties. "With Turco, you didn't know who would pay you." In addition to the Graybar Building, he said Turco liked to issue checks drawn on Hospitality Services.

For all his remuneration woes, Loheac was among the luckier contractors. At least he received partial payment. Many others received nothing. Months before, Commercial Cabinet Corp. had to file suit in State Supreme Court, Manhattan, after the Helmsleys ignored its bill of $12,055 for closet work and other carpentry. Commercial's lawyer, Barry LePatner, told the *Post*'s Page Six that his client sent Leona the bill and her response was, "I'll send them ten percent." Litigation is the last resort, the lawyer added, "but if somebody slaps you in the face and says go to hell, you have no choice."

The company hired to repair the mansion's marble and pillars, Remco Maintenance Corp., filed suit in the same court in July 1984 after the Helmsleys ignored its $147,000 invoice. It alleged that Mrs. Helmsley personally ordered Remco to "withdraw the invoices for [her] Connecticut residence" or lose its lucrative metal maintenance contracts with dozens of Helmsley commercial properties. The threat was ominous because Remco derived a good portion of its revenue from Helmsley accounts, including the Lincoln Building, Graybar Building, Helmsley Building, and most of Harry and Leona's Manhattan hotels. Nevertheless, Remco refused to work free of charge on the Greenwich mansion. Sure enough, the suit alleged, every Helmsley property canceled its contract and inflicted worse pain by refusing to pay Remco's outstanding invoices. But that was just for starters. As further punishment, Remco alleged that Leona then pirated four of its employees in order to create a competing maintenance company under her own wing. Remco demanded $30 million in damages from Leona and her turncoat commercial properties for "wanton, willful, malicious and intentional" actions.

Leona did not personally establish the competing company. She turned to Jay Nichtberger, a private painting contractor with contracts on dozens of Helmsley-Spear buildings. Nichtberger said Leona had phoned him with a startling ultimatum a few months earlier, in February, the month Remco slapped the Queen with its $147,000 bill. "She called me and insisted that I open a metal maintenance company." Nichtberger explained that he knew nothing whatsoever about the business, and couldn't hope to compete with Remco's fleet of trucks and hundreds of employees.

"It doesn't matter," Leona insisted. "I hate this Remco," she said. "They screwed me. And therefore you must open the company."

"I can't do this," Nichtberger pleaded.

"Do it, or get the hell out of painting," she fired back.

Nichtberger said he finally agreed to open the firm rather than have Leona cancel his estimated $1 million to $2 million worth of annual painting business with Helmsley properties.

Demands grew heavier, however, when Frank Turco summoned Nichtberger to his office in the Graybar Building. Alvin Rosenthal, Leona's brother, was waiting with Turco when Nichtberger arrived. Turco got down to brass tacks quickly, insisting not only that Nichtberger open the rival firm, but that

297

he put one of Leona's in-laws on its payroll. Leona's eldest sister, Sylvia, had died about a year earlier after a long struggle with diabetes. Now Sylvia's daughter, Frances, was in a tight financial bind. Her husband, a 60-year-old Long Island businessman named Lee Becker, was out of a job. Leona, who had barely tolerated Sylvia during her lifetime, rallied to Frances's aid.

"How much are you going to pay Mrs. Helmsley's nephew?" Turco asked Nichtberger.

"What am I gonna pay a guy that doesn't know anything?" Nichtberger asked in protest. "That is just more money coming out of my pocket."

"You better pay him seven hundred fifty [a week]," Turco replied. "That's what I believe the Queen wants."

Nichtberger recalls that Turco made a quick phone call and then clarified himself: "Jay, you will pay him [Becker] a thousand dollars."

For emphasis, Nichtberger said, Rosenthal repeated Turco's order: "You'll pay one thousand dollars."

Terms changed once more when Leona sent word that Becker had to be made a 50 percent partner in the new firm. Nichtberger agreed. He said he then borrowed $200,000, bought two trucks, hired several workers, and opened Hillco Metal Maintenance Company at 1775 Broadway. "It was a big investment," Nichtberger recalls, "but my main concern was to keep the [Helmsley] painting work." And despite his inexperience in the metal maintenance field, he said, "I thought there was a good chance I'd build a real live company." His staff quickly grew to more than a dozen sprayers and refinishers, who polished the brass and weatherproofed metal on the Empire State Building and other Helmsley skyscrapers. Although still too small to threaten Remco, Hillco had taken away its Helmsley accounts and was inching toward profitability. Within a year or two, Nichtberger planned to recoup his entire investment. "The company was off and running" in August, he recalls, when Leona ordered him to meet her at Dunnellen Hall. He rushed to Greenwich and hiked down the back lawn, where he found the Queen lounging in her robe beside the large pool. Harry and Turco were seated nearby. He said Leona, still dripping wet from her swim, lambasted him totally without warning.

"You're a crook! You're a liar!"

"Mrs. Helmsley, please," Nichtberger pleaded. "I am not. Show me what I've done wrong."

He said Leona then explained she had learned he had paid himself $1,000 a week from Hillco revenues.

"What are you talking about me taking money?" Nichtberger replied. "It's my money. I'm funding this company. I've already put hundreds of thousands of dollars into this company." He added, "Every time I gave your nephew a thousand dollars, I wrote out a check for myself for a thousand dollars." Nichtberger then explained that in order to preserve Hillco's cash flow, he actually never cashed his own checks. He had written them merely to document that he was a full partner with Becker and entitled to half the profits in the event the firm hit its stride.

Deaf to his appeals, he said, the Queen barked out a series of orders.

"There are three things you *will* do and it's not up for discussion. You will close down the company [Hillco]. You will give my nephew, Lee Becker, fifty thousand dollars. And you will transfer the company over to him and he'll operate the company under a different name."

Sign over the company to Becker! Give him fifty grand! Stunned, Nichtberger said he turned to Harry for support. "Harry was right there reading the *New York Times,* and he lifted his head and said:

"Lee, Lee! Jay is innocent in this matter!"

"You fucking old moron jerk!" Leona answered her husband. "If you lift your head from that newspaper again, you're in real trouble!"

Nichtberger said he was astonished by the exchange. "I had been up to the mansion before and heard her refer to Harry in derogatory terms, but never like that." Even more appalling was Helmsley's meek response. "Harry Helmsley, the biggest billionaire in the city, just put his head down. It was absolutely stunning."

Nichtberger said he then appealed to Turco. "Frank, please, you're a bookkeeper. Look at this goddamned bank statement. What am I doing wrong? Look, here's the checks from February to August, and I never cashed one!" His protests were to no avail.

Rather than lose millions of dollars' worth of potential painting business with the Helmsley empire, Nichtberger said he caved in once again to Leona's demands. "I didn't know whether to call it extortion," he says, "but I signed over Hillco to Becker. They wouldn't pay me ten cents." To comply with Leona's second demand, he said he took out a personal loan of

$50,000 "as a parting gesture." Altogether, he had gone into hock for $250,000 to satisfy Leona's escalating demands. Still, he held hopes of recouping the money within a year from continuing painting contracts with the Helmsleys. Thanks to Nichtberger's capital, he says Leona's niece, Frances, and her husband now had a company of their own. Becker renamed it Beacon Metal Maintenance Inc. and moved its offices to Long Island City, Queens. Asked for his response to Nichtberger's account of how he acquired Beacon, Lee Becker refused to comment.

Another family member, Alvin Rosenthal, also continued to enjoy Leona's beneficence, in great part because of his willingness to endure her frequent scoldings. The Queen's baby brother remained in-house manager of the Carlton House and supervised operations of the Middletowne and Windsor hotels in midtown Manhattan. And Alvin's wife, Susan, held a comfortable post as Leona's "Inspectress," responsible for monitoring the tidiness of rooms in the Manhattan hotels. Gerald Kadish, former head of the Harley hotel chain, recalls that Alvin had his fingers in many other Helmsley pies. At one point, when Harry was toying with the idea of selling the entire Harley chain for $100 million, Kadish said Alvin tried to wangle a piece of the sales commission. "I was attempting to sell the chain for Harry," Kadish recalls, "and Alvin horned in on it. He was really into it and told me that *he* would make the arrangements." Later, a group of prospective buyers notified Kadish that they had been approached independently by Alvin. "These guys told me, 'Oh, we're going to have to take care of him [Alvin], you know.' " Harry kept the chain, however, because the group refused to meet the asking price.

Although Leona was willing to help Alvin and her niece, Frances Becker, she was less comforting to her sister Sandra that summer of 1984. A relative recalls that Leona was "cold as ice" when informed that Sandra's husband, Jerry Kaufman, had died of leukemia in Atlanta. "Will you come?" Leona was asked.

"I'm not coming," she replied. "Jerry was nothing to me."

"But Sandra could use your support," the relative insisted, reminding Leona that Kaufman had been one of the very few guests at her wedding to Harry twelve years earlier.

"She'll get by," Leona replied, and left it at that.

Lee West wasn't starving. Although he had to kick back 20

percent of his sales commissions to Frank Turco (and, presumably, the Queen), the liquor salesman had enjoyed a profitable year as sales coordinator for the Palace and three other Helmsley hotels in Manhattan. But around Thanksgiving, he recalls, he was jolted by a phone call from Turco. "Come up," Turco said. "I want to talk to you."

West was prepared for the worst when he reached the Graybar Building office.

"You and your company made a lot of money this year," Turco said right off.

"Probably," replied West, "but I really straightened things out for you, didn't I?"

"Yeah, we're happy with your work. The Missus is happy. Now we'd like your company to do something for us. We'd like you to lease a suite at the Carlton House," the Madison Avenue hotel managed by Leona's brother, Alvin Rosenthal.

"What would my company need with a suite at the Carlton House?" West wondered out loud.

"Well, we're trying to build up occupancy in the hotel," Turco explained, "and if this guy takes a suite for a year, and that guy takes one for a year, we'll have some good business going for us."

"It's not up to me," West said, amazed by the grandiosity of Turco's latest kickback demand.

West said he relayed the news to Antonio ("Nino") Maggliocco, son of the owner of Peerless Importers.

"Carlton House, it's a crap joint!" Maggliocco exclaimed. "What do I need it for?"

"I agree, you don't," said West, who added: "By the way, the price is fifty-five thousand to be paid up front to the hotel."

After more thought, West said Maggliocco agreed to play ball, but on different terms.

"Tell them," Maggliocco said, "that I'll take a room at the Palace or the Park Lane, because that I can use. That's nice. I have people coming from Europe all the time. They could stay there. Not at the Carlton House."

West, surprised that Maggliocco would agree to anything, reported back to Turco.

"Frank, they can't use the Carlton House. It's not fancy enough. But they'll do the Palace or the Park Lane. They can use it for entertaining."

"No!" Turco retorted. "Those hotels I have no trouble selling. I sell out every night. I need the Carlton House."

"Let me get back to you," West said, and then informed Maggliocco of the rebuff.

"You know, Lee," Maggliocco responded, "I don't like blackmail. And that's what this fuck is doing! Tell him to stick it in his ass. I know you're gonna lose money, and I'm gonna lose money, but I'll sleep better."

Like a little emissary, West beat a path back to Turco's door.

"No," West said, "Nino will only consider the Palace or the Park Lane."

"Fuck it!" Turco angrily shouted, and notified West on the spot that his last day of business with the Helmsleys would be New Year's Eve. "You're out! I'll find someone else who will take the room."

"Just like that?" West protested. "You really mean out?"

"On January first, we'll find someone else to do your work and that's it. After December, you can't ever go into the hotels, not even to use the john. We don't want to hear your name. I don't want to see you anymore."

In fact, Peerless lost about 80 percent of its Helmsley business. Never had the salesman encountered such stiff demands and sudden punishment. Kickbacks, West says, are as common as dirt in the business world. "In that respect, the Helmsley organization is no different than any other business. It's just the way business is done. But the Helmsleys are more vicious. I mean, if you don't pay, you don't live! You don't survive!"

Joyce Beber verifies that occupancy at the Carlton House was a big concern to Leona, and that the Queen mentioned that renting to vendors might be a good way of filling the empty rooms. "Mrs. Helmsley would say, 'Maybe some of our suppliers would want to rent there.'"

After losing the majority of his income because of the Carlton House scenario, West licked his wounds and found new accounts. Despite Turco's warning, he continues to visit the Helmsley Palace. "I sneak inside to use the johns, because they're clean."

Leona Helmsley had a houseful of television sets to divert her from all the construction turmoil at the mansion. The lady of 521 Round Hill Road was never more than a few paces from *Wheel of Fortune* and *Jeopardy!*—her two favorite programs.

In early 1986, Mrs. Helmsley ordered her top purchasing officer, Milton Meckler, to sever all ties with Zenith, her previous home brand. Meckler said Zenith had fallen into the Queen's bad graces because of service problems at one hotel. His job now was to solicit bids from other companies, whose televisions would gradually replace the aging Zeniths in thousands of hotel rooms scattered from Florida to Ohio.

He immediately took bids for the first of the replacements, 600 new sets, and specified that they be nineteen-inch table models with built-in clock radios. RCA came in with the low bid and Meckler received a phone call from an RCA sales representative. "This guy was really mystified, agitated and shocked," Meckler recalled, "because he had gotten a call from Turco. Turco told him RCA had been selected as far as the hotel deal went, but that as part of the deal Mrs. Helmsley was to receive three free television sets. And the sets had to be delivered to Dunnellen Hall."

"Who is Frank Turco?" the sales rep asked, taken aback by the demand that he cough up three free TVs or lose out on a $200,000 deal. "Is he putting me on?" And why the hell did Leona Helmsley need this kind of handout?

Meckler gave the RCA man a quick rundown on doing business with Leona. First of all, the Queen required freebies, regardless of her vast wealth.

Secondly, "you don't ever fight with Frank Turco or you're going to lose the contract altogether."

"But what does she mean, she wants three TVs?" the still incredulous salesman demanded.

"Don't get upset," Meckler replied in his acquired Florida drawl. "I'll contact Frank and get back to you."

Moments later, Meckler reached Turco by telephone and went to bat for the RCA victim-to-be. "Frank, what's going on? You've got to be kidding me. You're pressuring this guy for three televisions that are worth three hundred and thirty dollars apiece. We're talking about a drop under a thousand dollars."

"That's what Mrs. Helmsley wants!" Turco replied, holding his ground. "Tell him that's the deal, that's it or there's no deal. This is what she wants!"

"Okay, Frank, whatever you want," Meckler replied.

With a fatalistic sigh, he got the RCA salesman on the phone and explained the preordained reality: "This is what she wants, and that's the deal."

"How am I going to explain this to my boss?" the salesman complained. "Do you really mean we'll lose the order?"

"I can't explain the woman," said Meckler. "That's just what she wants."

The salesman gave in and said that three nineteen-inch RCAs, with built-in radios, would be sent to Dunnellen Hall. Meckler reported the exciting news to Mrs. Helmsley. "I got you those three televisions."

"Couldn't you get me more?" she demanded.

After five years of serving the Queen, even Meckler could not quite comprehend her ways. "Why would someone whose husband controls a five-billion-dollar fortune go to such great pains for a couple of hundred dollars worth of free merchandise? We're talking strange."

Nonetheless, one of Meckler's prime duties was to satisfy the Queen's insatiable freebie habit.

Regardless of how successful he was in getting "the goods," they could never arrive fast enough at Dunnellen Hall or in ample enough quantity to satisfy the Queen. If Meckler failed to produce, or advised against pressuring a reluctant supplier, she would deliver an ear-shattering salvo over the hot line. " 'I'm Leona Helmsley and I can do whatever I want to!' She said it all the time. Vendors were told they could not be vendors unless they donated."

The daily calls became a predictable script for Meckler, and he would always brace himself for the grand finale. "They would usually start out with her saying 'Well, you're an imbecile, aren't you?' And then she'd repeat, 'You're an imbecile, aren't you?' "

Meckler would defend himself after each and every refrain by replying, "No, I'm not!" Then the Queen would continue her usual refrain, "You're a dope, aren't you?"

"No, I'm not!"

"Yes, you are." Back and forth.

Finally, Mrs. Helmsley would scream, "You're irritating me! I'm going to pull you through the telephone!" On that cue, Meckler always held the receiver a safe distance away as Mrs. Helmsley hurled her phone down in the purchasing kingpin's ear.

Suppliers of every description caved in and delivered free merchandise right to the Queen's door, Meckler said. "Nobody would argue because they didn't want to lose her business account. They didn't like the idea of giving her the items, but they did it."

Mrs. Helmsley, he said, felt it was an *honor* for them that she was willing to accept their merchandise. She said that to me many times. "I'm Leona Helmsley. Just think, they can walk around and say, 'Mrs. Helmsley has my merchandise!' "

Rather than send her staff to a Greenwich supermarket, the Queen would order hotel vendors to dispatch special deliveries from Manhattan on an instant's notice. No item was too small or insignificant. Meckler said one Manhattan distributor, Allied Paper Products Co., made constant deliveries of toilet paper and cleaning supplies to the estate. "Supplies got there immediately," he said. "We never reached the point where she was out of toilet paper, God forbid. I wouldn't have liked to be at the other end of the telephone if she did." On one occasion Mrs. Helmsley wanted several cases of toothbrushes—the same generic, hard-bristled brushes left for guests in her hotel bathrooms. "They cost maybe four or five cents each and were probably made in Taiwan."

When delivery trucks pulled up to Dunnellen Hall's winding red driveway with their complimentary cargoes, Meckler said, they sometimes were stopped just inside the swinging wrought-iron gates. Merchandise had to be hand-carried up the hill. Or freebies would be taken from the truck and loaded onto Mrs. Helmsley's white golf cart for the remaining 100-yard voyage to the mansion. It was assumed that the Queen instituted the procedure for fear that delivery vehicles might leak oil onto the spotless drive. Meckler pulled up to the gates one afternoon with a trunkload of carpet samples. "She wanted to see them for possible renovation of some hotels, and they were heavy. The guard told me, 'Don't drive into the driveway.' So I asked, 'Where do I drive?' And he said, 'Don't! Walk it! So I walked them to the house, and luckily I didn't get a hernia."

Even when vendors followed Leona's dictates to the letter, million-dollar accounts could still go down the drain for arbitrary reasons.

For example, soon after the Helmsleys bought the mansion, Harry Helmsley woke up one morning with a backache. "She called me about it and said it was the bed that did the whole thing," Meckler recounted. He called the Simmons mattress company to notify them of the crisis "and they were flabbergasted" that blame had been ascribed to one of their mattresses. "They got their engineers together and actually made him a special king-sized box mattress unit, and delivered it to him within a couple of weeks."

The backache persisted, however, and Mrs. Helmsley declared war against the mattress firm. "Throw them out," she ordered. "They're no good. They've been cheating me all these years, anyway." Meckler had no reason to believe any of the charges, but solicited new bids. The Queen personally chose Sealy mattresses for her future hotel needs.

Often, Leona would ask for samples of products with no apparent intention of purchasing the real thing. "I would tell the company she wants to look at a sample, and we're going to buy it for all the hotels, but it would be strictly a come-on pitch," Meckler says. "And most vendors, particularly a big supplier, would go for it most of the time. And even if they never got the account, she wouldn't give the merchandise back."

Companies already supplying the hotels frequently would send Mrs. Helmsley samples of new items in hopes of widening their product line. "I had one guy from New Jersey who sent in a thousand dollars' worth of terrycloth bathrobes. She didn't need them for the hotels but wanted bathrobes for Dunnellen Hall. So she asked me, 'Can I keep these?' And I asked her, 'Do you really want those robes?' And she said, 'Yes, I like them but I don't want to buy them.' So I promised to talk to the salesman."

Meckler said the salesman agreed to donate the robes "because he had a lot of business with Mrs. Helmsley's hotels and didn't want to risk angering her." Meckler added, "This was done regularly with all kinds of items."

Another one of the Queen's favorite pastimes, Meckler said, was ordering merchandise, using it, and then refusing to pay on the grounds that it was defective. A classic example, he said, was a New York company that installed carpeting inside the mansion's newly built pool enclosure. "It was a multicolored carpet right off the pool area, and this company installed the whole shot. The company's accountant called me up many, many times and said, 'How come we're not being paid for it?' And I had to say, 'As far as Mrs. Helmsley is concerned, the carpet wasn't like it should be.' "

Tad Distler, the Queen's ad man, said he once overheard her ordering a meat company to replace four hundred pounds of "bad veal" that had been shipped to Dunnellen Hall.

"She was ranting and raving that the veal that they had sent to the country house was awful, and that she hated it, and she hated them, and that they had better replace it all. And while they were at it, they had better also send forty pounds for her airplane." Distler said he had no doubt it was a ploy "to get more free veal." He said she routinely demanded—and received—free provisions from hotel food suppliers. "She considered it her due because they supplied the hotels; therefore, she should get her share."

On another occasion, he said he overheard this seemingly contradictory demand by the Queen to M. Slavin and Sons, the Manhattan fish distributor: "Your stuff is rotten, no good! I want more!"

Distler said Mrs. Helmsley then informed the company that she had eaten a bad piece of their fish in the Helmsley Palace dining room. "It stinks!" she fumed. "Come and replace it. And by the way, I need some for the freezer in Dunnellen Hall."

The Queen's love of getting something for nothing or less than cost was not only at the expense of outside suppliers— Helmsley hotel partners came in for their share.

A half-dozen security guards worked rotating shifts at Dunnellen Hall to protect the Queen round the clock, and their services were apparently charged off to commercial properties. Tony Champa, a former payroll officer for security personnel of Helmsley Hotels, recalls that he was ordered to use St. Moritz and Park Lane funds to pay guards at "the Farm," a popular nickname for the Greenwich mansion. "From the St. Moritz we had three men, and from the Park Lane we had a minimum of three. We started each one off at three hundred fifty-five a week, plus meals." He said the Park Lane also paid the $68,000 salary of Edward Brady, who had doubled for many years as Leona's top bodyguard and chief of corporate security for the Helmsleys. Brady, a retired New York City detective who stood about five foot ten, was a compact bundle of dynamite who would often explode at chauffeurs or anyone else who annoyed the Queen. In addition, the Park Lane paid a second bodyguard "who stayed at the Farm twenty-four hours a day, seven days a week." Overtime for everyone began after forty hours, Champa said, "so you're talking big bucks," possibly $250,000 a year. By shifting the charges to the hotels, the Helmsleys enjoyed free security. But their partners presumably were unaware that their share of profits was being reduced in order to subsidize the Helmsleys' country lifestyle.

Harry had taken on partners in 1981 when he purchased a bankrupt company named Investing Funding Corporation. In order to buy the outfit at a fire-sale price, Helmsley was required to merge the troubled firm's assets with several of his own healthy investments—including the Park Lane Hotel and his Brown, Harris, Stevens real estate brokerage firm. The larger, reorganized company was christened Realesco Equities

Corp., with Helmsley owning 78 percent of the stock and bank creditors of the original firm retaining 22 percent. Therefore, any mansion chargeoffs to the Park Lane would have sliced the profits of the Realesco partners.

According to Tony Champa, the Park Lane and St. Moritz supplied Leona with astounding streams of spending money. Instead of going to the bank, he said Leona would retrieve bundles of cash right from the lobby cash registers several days a week. "The St. Moritz was the biggest one," Champa said. "She'd call from the Helmsley Palace to the security man at the St. Moritz or Park Lane and ask them to get her fifteen hundred at a time. It was always cash. My security man would just go to the front desk and get whatever she asked for. She did it three times a week, easy." Occasionally, Champa said, "she would also use the Windsor" on West Fifty-eighth Street, "but it was usually under a thousand dollars there because that was a smaller hotel." Upon receipt of the cash, Champa said, Leona would initial a small white slip. "She'd sign it with a big 'L' and the security man would bring it back" so the donating cashier could account for the missing money at the end of the day. From knowledge of Leona's other questionable chargeoffs, Champa said he assumed the Queen never reimbursed the hotels. "Everything up at the Farm was being charged to some other hotel or one of the properties in New York." All things considered, Champa was grateful for the Farm because it kept the Queen away from the Park Lane on weekends, thereby restoring calm to the hotel staff. While in Manhattan, Champa explained, Leona caused many a royal ruckus. "She can drink like a fish. She'd get bombed to the gills and lose her keys. I should have a record of the number of times we had to call the locksmith at 3 A.M. to change the lock—to take the cylinder out so she and Harry could get in the apartment." Harry liked a drink or two, "but never made an ass of himself." From two years of supervision at the Park Lane, Champa said he could find no fault, save one, with Mr. Helmsley. "He would never stand up for anybody that worked for him" once Leona singled the employee out for punishment. "He has no gumption at all." For instance, Champa recalled that the Helmsleys' chauffeur was thrown in jail one evening. "He got into a fight and the police locked him up." When the Park Lane security staff tried to intervene to have him released, Champa said Leona ordered: "Leave him there. Just let him stay there till morning." Although Harry seemed concerned for his driver, he knew better than to argue the prisoner's case. He just said, "All right, dear," and left the driver in the slammer. "He's a real wimp," Champa says. "Really, it's sad."

Champa's own day of reckoning came after he suffered a stroke in early 1984. He said Ed Brady quietly returned him to his security post at the Park Lane five months later, despite his paralyzed arm. Then, as fate would have it, Leona eventually lost her keys again. "She got locked out of her apartment and one of the security men said, 'Well, maybe Mr. Champa has got a key.' " After some inquiry, Leona was reminded of Champa's stroke and continued employment. "That's when I was fired," Champa says. "She told Brady to get rid of me because she was not running a charity ward."

Thirteen

"Queen Leona—mistress of, watchdog of, every elegant touch at her Palace."

With those words, Mike Wallace introduced Leona Helmsley to thirty-three million viewers of *60 Minutes* on the evening of January 27, 1985. "And like most queens," Wallace assured his TV audience, "she's used to getting her own way." To prove his thesis, *60 Minutes* trailed Leona through the Palace as she disciplined her troops. "I want the engineer up here," she snapped at one minion after noticing leak stains on the ceiling of one of the public rooms. "I want him in the ceiling and I want to know whether it's still continuing or if it has dried out. Loud and clear?"

"Honest to Pete," Wallace said. "You run the hotels, or you're just the figurehead?"

"My foot!" Leona protested. "I run them."

The hotel tour completed, Wallace dashed off to Greenwich for a sightsee of the mansion with Harry and Leona. He noticed one thing right off the bat. "Leona Helmsley, tough business-woman, turns into the little woman where Harry Helmsley is concerned."

"He's brilliant," Leona explained. "He's funny, and he's gorgeous."

"Aside from that, I am nothing," Harry humbly chipped in.

Leona, the frustrated female Charlie Chaplin, shifted into high camp by extolling Harry's physiognomy.

"Here, look at the shape of the head, you could just see the brain; it just sits there. I'm very serious now. Beautiful head, darling. I love it,"

"Darling, as long as you're convinced, let the rest of the world go by," Harry replied appreciatively.

Wallace and Leona then dived into the freebie Deco golf cart for a tour of the back meadow. "I have sheep," Leona confided.

"How many sheep?"

"We only have four. . . . One is Bo, one is Peep, one is Baa, one is Baa-Baa. Come here, Bo! Come here, Peep! Here, Bo! It's your mother!"

"I think this is the only individual I have ever seen ignore you altogether," Wallace remarked when Bo stood impassive.

"Wait till I take the grass away."

The still unfinished pool enclosure was the next stop on the mansion tour.

"On the top we're going to have, of course, a dance floor," said Harry.

Just how much money was it costing to build the enclosure? "Not a penny less than a million dollars," Wallace speculated.

"You're just about right," Harry affirmed.

"But it's got special things," said Leona.

For a last peek at the Helmsleys' rarefied lifestyle, Wallace visited their Park Lane penthouse. He marveled at the view from their wraparound rooftop terrace.

"Oh, my! How much of this do you Helmsleys own?" asked Wallace, pointing down to the isle of Manhattan.

"Well," said Leona, "I would say that Harry owns about two hundred buildings. He stands here and he says, I'm taking inventory. I own this, I own this, I own this, and that one, and that one and that one."

With trademark boldness, Wallace had to ask Leona: "Did you marry Harry at all for his money?"

"No, Harry Helmsley married me for my money," Leona said. "I gave him one million dollars that I had put away for myself because I was never getting married. . . . That I had earned, all right, as a broker. I was the best in the field. That's why he went after me, see."

Now, as president of Harry's hotel empire, Leona told Wallace she works for free. "I don't get paid. . . . He gives me titles, no money!"

"Why should I pay for something when I can get it for nothing?" Harry explained, laughing.

Leona's flippant mood changed when Wallace mentioned that her son, Jay, had died suddenly two years earlier. "All the success, all the fulfillment of life with Harry is forgotten in a flash of pain," Wallace said after watching Leona burst into tears. When she regained her composure seconds later, he noted: "And then the steel reasserts itself."

The *60 Minutes* segment won rave reviews in the Helmsley household. Leona came off as a tough, but glamorous, celebrity. Also a billionaire homebody, doting wife, actress. And Harry, always so dishwater dull in print, projected a semblance of wit and personality seldom glimpsed in public. Beyond a doubt, Joyce Beber says, the national broadcast "was the pinnacle of Mrs. Helmsley's career. She loved it! She videotaped it and showed it when people came to visit her at the Park Lane and in Palm Beach. She'd take it out and say, 'You wanna see something? Look at this! Isn't it great!' She took it out at every possible opportunity. She would play it and replay it. She showed it to me five times."

Things had worked out so well. It was hard to imagine that Leona's top aides initially had warned her against being interviewed by Wallace, an interrogator with a renowned appetite for the jugular. "I didn't want her to do it," one former aide recalls. "My God! *60 Minutes*! To go in front of Mike Wallace! He'd crucify her." Instead, Wallace seemed charmed by, and sympathetic to, the Queen. One reason for their chemistry, the former aide said, was a common bond. "Mrs. Helmsley told me that Wallace had talked to her about her son like a man who had lost his own son." Indeed, the television personality's teenage son, Peter, fell to his death in 1962 while hiking on a cliff near Corinth.

Also of importance was Leona's chemistry with Grace Diekhaus, CBS field producer for the *60 Minutes* segment. Diekhaus supervised filming at the Helmsley Palace during a two-week period in September 1984. At first, Leona's former aide recalls, "We were intimidated by this horsy, totally-in-charge woman from *60 Minutes*. But in no time, the aide said, "Mrs. Helmsley had Grace charmed, wrapped around her finger. Suddenly, this formidable woman is being led around by Leona and yes-yessing Leona. It went from Diekhaus saying, 'We're going to want you to do this tomorrow, Mrs. Helmsley' to 'Do you think it would be okay if we did this, Lee?' It wasn't Mrs. Helmsley anymore, but Lee! Leona became her friend."

Another one of Leona's former aides said the Queen used a time-proven method, the makeover, to curry favor with the CBS producer. "Leona was taking over on Diekhaus by saying, 'You should look like this. You should fix your hair; you should get a little more blonde in there. I want your hair cut by *my* hair cutter.' " The next day, "Diekhaus had done it! She actually went to Leona's hairdresser. She seemed more blonde." When Leona's aide admired the new look, she said Diekhaus sheepishly replied, "Yeah, Lee insisted, and I like it."

"And then Leona wanted to redo Diekhaus's clothes," the aide recalls. "She told her she should dress more feminine, more sexy. She wanted her makeup artist to do her. It seemed very social, back and forth. She had Diekhaus where she wanted her." Although the program candidly described Leona's unpopularity with the Palace staff, the aide criticized Diekhaus and Wallace for stopping short of the mark. "It turned out that these were hardly investigative reporters. If they had done their job, they would have had some idea of the wrath of employees all over the place. There was tremendous dissension and anger at the time inside the organization. Grace was exposed to it, but I think she didn't want to see it. So it turned out to be a puff piece on the Helmsleys." Once again, the aide said, Leona had worked her media magic. "She was marvelous with the press. It was no accident that when she got these profiles, every one of them turned into a eulogy. She had this bad, terrible side to her. Yet, when she wanted to turn it on, she also had an irresistible charm. She was a sorceress."

The carefree luxury sketched by *60 Minutes* was a far cry from the daily strife that contractors witnessed and endured at Dunnellen Hall. Nicholas Vasileff, whose Greenwich nursery pruned hundreds of trees and planted gardens for the Helmsleys from April 1984 until January 1985, recalls that Leona "yelled and screamed every day. She wasn't happy. Swimming was the only time she relaxed." Her little weekend hideaway had simply become too complex a project. "She was trying to do too much," Vasileff said. "She had this big place and she wanted to show it off, and it got away from her. Anything would set her off. The first thing she did every day was go in the kitchen. If there was a speck of dirt it would set her off. Then she'd start outside. She'd reprimand the gardener."

Nor was Harry immune from the tongue-lashings, Vasileff said. "One moment she'd be delighted and the next she's yelling and screaming at him. When he came down the stairs, she'd get after him. She'd scream at him real bad, enough to make you cry. She'd tell him, 'You don't know what you're talking about! You stupid ass!' She'd humiliate him and he'd have to stand there while others watched." Helmsley would never fight back. "He knew better. She'd have ripped up the stairs and thrown them at him if he did." Silently, Helmsley would just "go mope off into the house and not speak to anybody."

The estate might have been purchased for Harry's benefit, to allow him to trim his Manhattan work week, but Vasileff said it seemed obvious that the still energetic tycoon had grown completely bored with life in the Greenwich backcountry. "Aside from swimming, which he enjoyed a great deal, he had nothing to do. He just walked around doing nothing, sitting on the outdoor terrace. You knew he just couldn't wait till Tuesday, to go back to Manhattan. He told me he'd rather be in New York than the country." The only real excitement Vasileff ever witnessed at Dunnellen Hall was Mike Wallace's visit four months before the CBS profile was aired. "Mrs. Helmsley was really up for it. She told me, 'You know Mike Wallace is going to be here. I'm going to be on *60 Minutes*.' " Leona then ordered him to manicure the grounds as they had never been manicured before. But the four sheep were a problem. Leona had graciously accepted them as a gift from an acquaintance, but she totally ignored the creatures. To keep them from roaming over the entire estate, Vasileff said he put up fences deep in the back meadow and then electrified the four-acre enclosure. His crew also mowed the two dozen acres, pruned trees, weeded, planted flowers and hung floral baskets for Wallace's imminent arrival. The day of the interview, Vasileff recalls, "Mrs. Helmsley was absolutely bubbly. For once, she was nice to everybody. 'How are you?... How are your children?' " He said CBS writers noticed the barricaded sheep and thought they would be great video. From Leona's charming introduction of her friends Bo, Pete, Baa and Baa-Baa, no one would have guessed that "it was the first time she went down to look at them." The day after the interview, Vasileff recalls, "we got rid of the sheep. They were given away to a farm in upstate New York."

Leona's constant improvements to the mansion and pool enclosure, meanwhile, continued apace. "Poor ole Harry saw all this money go down the drain," Vasileff says. "He saw it leaving his pocket." Yet it seemed as though the Helmsleys also knew how to economize, and in the most peculiar ways. Just as Loheac, the architect, had been paid by Frank Turco with a corporate check from the Graybar Building, Vasileff noticed that Turco was sending him corporate checks for his personal services to Harry and Leona. "I was being paid through the Harley of Enfield," a Connecticut hotel within the Harley chain. "Turco's role was to discuss finances and pay the bills."

Vasileff said he was surprised that the Helmsleys placed so much trust in Turco. In fact, he said, Turco privately boasted about feathering his own nest at the Helmsleys' expense. "Turco isn't smart," Vasileff said. "He'd tell me that he was trying to get as much as he could out of them. Isn't that stupid? Here's the finance officer telling me this." Vasileff said Turco was forever cozying up to contractors. "He'd say, 'Here I am, buddy.' He acted like 'I'm one of you guys.' " And Turco constantly boasted about a house he had just purchased in a well-to-do corner of East Hills, Long Island. "He was a nouveau riche," Vasileff said. "He tried to dress sharp, but something never went together. And he couldn't stop bragging about that house." One of Leona's top former aides recalls that Turco's home became a sore spot with the Queen when she attended his 1985 housewarming and saw familiar construction materials in its walls and floors. "She walked inside and saw that he had used marble and materials identical to hers at the mansion," and the aide said Leona immediately assumed that Turco had obtained the materials at her expense. Despite Leona's suspicions, Turco remained her troubleshooter at the Greenwich mansion and chief of financial services for Helmsley Hotels.

Much to Henry Loheac's chagrin, meanwhile, Leona continued to play architect for the pool enclosure. The walls and windows that Mike Wallace had seen no longer suited her. She ordered work crews to rip out a group of small rectangular windows in the pool area and replace them with a pair of expensive floor-to-ceiling bay windows jutting out into the back lawn. "The bay windows were all brick and limestone," Loheac said, and were built by a New Jersey firm, Bergen County Cut Stone Co., at a cost of $130,000. Once again Leona was going fancy, but in a maddeningly haphazard way. Joe Moliterno, an executive with the stone company, said the Helmsley job was among the strangest in his long career. "It's not unusual for a customer to make design changes. But you do it with an eraser; you erase lines on architectural drawings. This woman [Leona] would just knock down walls" and start over again.

For the mansion itself, crates of furnishings continued to arrive courtesy of Deco. Milton Meckler said that by January 1985, Deco had delivered $1.1 million worth of unbillable goods to Dunnellen Hall, making it difficult for the subsidiary to remain profitable. "Every month, Deco would issue a financial statement to Harry saying that X amount of merchandise was nonbillable." Unexpectedly, Meckler said, Helmsley's accountants alerted him that the backlog of Deco statements "might flag the IRS" that Harry had drained Deco in order to receive free personal goods. Uncle Sam would certainly take a dim view of such proceedings. To be on the safe side in case of a tax audit, Meckler said Helmsley immediately reimbursed Deco the $1.1 million.

Although redeemed, Helmsley apparently was unrepentant. Meckler said an elaborate scheme was devised whereby the Helmsleys could continue to receive free Deco goods without inviting IRS attention. Mrs. Helmsley, he explained, established a separate Deco checking account at a Manhattan bank. In reality, Meckler and other Deco officials had no control over the account. It was to be a piggy bank for Leona's own personal use, replenished by Deco when the Queen's balance dipped too low. Only three people—Leona; her secretary, Mary Ann DiMicco; and Turco—had check-signing ability. Deco would not deposit money directly into Leona's piggy bank, however. Instead, it would bill the various hotels for make-believe merchandise and filter the receipts back to Leona's Deco account in Manhattan. Because the money moved in a constant circle—from the hotels, to Deco, and then to Leona—Meckler jokingly nicknamed the scheme "the circle jerk." As usual, Meckler said, Frank Turco called the shots on Leona's behalf. "We would get monthly directives from Turco. 'Send out invoices to these hotels for these amounts.' " Interestingly, Meckler said Leona insisted "that we use the U.S. mails" for all correspondence. "She went crazy about people using Federal Express" because of the expense.

Meckler said he was amazed that the Helmsleys would go to such extremes to skirt taxes. "I used to scratch my head. It was a stupid procedure. The type of wealth they had, why look to avoid paying taxes? Why not just pay?"

On the steps of the Orange County Courthouse in early January, the Sheriff's Department put Mimi Panzirer's gleaming stainless steel DeLorean sports car up for auction. The moment was pure victory for Leona in her three-year-long vendetta against Jay's widow. Months earlier, the Fifth District Court of Appeal in Daytona had overturned the lower court decision that had granted Mimi the legal right to her late husband's final $37,500 payment from Deco. The appeals court sided with Deco in its claim that the check had been improperly cashed because Jay had died before actually earning the money. As a result of the revised legal logic, Mimi was now required to reimburse Deco the entire payment, plus $11,383 in accrued interest and court costs. Altogether, Mimi found herself almost $49,000 in debt to the Helmsley subsidiary. When no check arrived in the mail, Deco won a court order forcing Mimi to hand over her car to the sheriff. Any money raised at auction would be counted as partial satisfaction of the hefty debt. Not until that moment, Mimi recalls, did Leona's vendetta really hurt. "I didn't break until the sheriff showed up with a writ to get the car. Everything she had done to me until that point never hit me emotionally. If that woman wanted revenge, that was the closest she came to it." The gloom was only momentary, however. Fortunately for Mimi, she had remarried the previous year and her new husband, a local contractor, was the most determined bidder at the public auction. The sheriff forwarded Deco a check for $5,589 and Mimi was reunited with her streamlined auto. But she was still personally in hock to Deco for the balance of the $49,000. And Mimi could hope to recover only a fraction of Jay's estate because of an earlier circuit court ruling that upheld the validity of Leona's $100,000 promissory note from her son. Mimi's crushing debt was slashed on February 1, however, when the appeals court reversed an earlier ruling that had prevented Mimi from being awarded $51,000 from the disputed Shearson stock account. The lower court then ruled on the forgery issue, finding there was not sufficient evidence that the documents which had given Mimi ownership of stocks and money in her late husband's account had been forged. Leona's previous victory in the Shearson battle, which she had shouted so exultantly over the roof of the Park Lane, was thereby snatched away.

Later, after Jay's partial share of Palace stock was sold to actor Paul Newman for $175,000, the estate was finally apportioned and the long vendetta reached an end. The bulk of the $231,437 estate went to Leona M. Helmsley. Thanks to Jay's promissory note, plus accrued interest, she walked away with $147,704—which was 63 percent of her son's financial legacy. According to Milton Meckler, "Mrs. Helmsley spent more than that in legal fees" during the long vendetta, making her an actual net loser. In addition, Leona got to keep Jay's used Zenith video cassette recorder; his amateur painting of ballet dancers; his silver service for sixteen with Wild Rose pattern; and his backgammon table. Two local banks were next in line, taking $82,895 for loans they had extended to Jay. Mimi's share, $1,731.66 was immediately garnisheed by Deco as partial payment on her remaining personal debt to the subsidiary. By vendetta's end, her legal fees had soared to $60,000, eating up every penny she had recovered from the Shearson stock account. In effect, Leona had succeeded in preventing Mimi from receiving a penny of Jay's estate. Almost nothing remained for Jay's four children. Craig, David, Meegan and Walter: each got exactly $432.91

"That's the thing that really frosted me," Mimi says, "that Jay's children got such a pittance and Leona got so much. That's shocking. That's obscene." Rather than stew endlessly over the outcome, Mimi said she leaves it up to karma. "I believe in reincarnation. If you do evil things in your lifetime, you are doomed to come back again to live a human life. This is indeed a vale of tears and you get to do it over again. We've not seen the last of Leona Helmsley."

Joe Lubin couldn't get over it. She was like Big Brother. Everywhere he went, his former wife, Leona, gazed at him. When he opened an airline magazine at 40,000 feet, the Queen of the Palace smiled broadly. When he hurried through the bustling walkway beneath the Helmsley Building toward Grand Central Terminal, five giant Leonas smirked in mini-billboards for her various hotels. When he hunkered over the Sunday *Times,* there she was in triplicate and quadruplicate in the magazine and travel sections. And wouldn't you know, when he tuned in to *60 Minutes* there she was with a flock of sheep! Lubin had not seen Leona for over two years, since the funeral of her sister Sylvia, and she had been curt with him on that occasion. "Leave me alone!" Leona snapped when he tried to offer his condolences.

Now, sitting in his garment district office in early 1985, Lubin fell into a mischievous mood. He thought to himself, "I wonder what the Queen is doing today?" And was Her Majesty capable of shooting the breeze with a commoner such as himself, husband number two? To find out, he phoned the Helmsley Palace.

"My name is Joe Lubin," he told Leona's secretary. "May I speak to Mrs. Helmsley? It's a personal call." He couldn't get through to the Queen, but left a message. A short while later, his phone rang and it was Leona.

"Whaddaya want?" she snarled.

"I'm writing a book," Lubin said matter-of-factly. "I want you to know about it first."

"Whaddaya want?" she barked, apparently unappreciative of Lubin's stab at humor.

"I'm devoting a whole chapter to our sex life," he continued, as irreverent as ever.

"Whaddaya want?" she asked again, obviously impatient with the fun and games.

"Well, the main reason I'm calling is that I want the Empire State Building moved to Forty-eighth Street because I can't get any sun in my office!"

His eardrums rang as Leona slammed the phone down. So much for hijinks.

Another former spouse who could not escape Leona's ubiquitous capped teeth and airbrushed smile was Leona's first husband, Leo Panzirer. Suddenly, he recalls, "She was the queen of everything." Capturing the spotlight was one thing. Coping with it was a far different matter. Panzirer says the ads convinced him Leona had become "paranoid with power." The private satisfaction of her billions was inadequate. "She starts thinking she's *it*! And she wants everybody to *know* she's it. You got it? Does she believe she's it? You're goddamned right she does. Why all the ads? Very simple, she wants the world to know it! 'I'm the Queen. I do this and I do that. I wouldn't eat this, why should you?'"

"She was getting in the company of [former mayor] Robert Wagner and people of notoriety. Maybe she felt the only way she could fit into this category was to show she was as good as they are—or *higher* than they. Only problem was, she didn't have their background or education, or their experience in life." Through her work, she could redress the imbalance. Her ads and personal command of eight thousand employees in the nationwide hotel empire provided a status that even culture and education could not confer.

Although she was always regally clothed and coiffed, something was lacking in the Queen's wardrobe. Then, like a revelation, the missing element occurred to Leona. By 1985, she ordered the Beber Silverstein ad agency to photograph her with a tiara. When word got out, jewelers began arriving at the Palace in profusion. Sometimes accompanied by armed guards, they would be ushered into the Queen's sanctum. "They would have tiaras on red velvet and she would try them on. She was always trying them on," Joyce Beber recalls. "She loved them. They were an extension of the Queen image." But instead of buying the jeweled headbands, Beber says Leona "would borrow them for an ad, often with the promise she was going to buy it. She never did."

Meanwhile, the uncrowned Queen remained mindful of the guest who had unkindly described her bosomy "zaftig madam" appearance. In all ads, Leona insisted on looking youthful and slim. The task became greatly simplified that year, Tad Distler recalls, when he discovered a technological breakthrough in the field of trick photography. The name of the invention was Scitex, a special computer screen upon which Leona's features could be redrawn with utmost ease. "It's a wonderful invention," Distler says. "It's such fun to play with." A photo transparency is fed into the computer, he explained, which enables the computer operator to zoom in on any desired feature and retouch it through the use of a hand-held device. "You can fill the whole screen with an ear, or a nose, and get to work on it." A Scitex operator at a Miami production company would follow Distler's editing suggestions. "I was the one who knew best what the Queen wanted to look like, so I'd sit and direct him. We'd go over her whole persona. If there was redness in her left eye because of her contact lenses, I'd say, 'Take out some of the red.' If she was squinting, I'd say, 'Open her eyes up a bit.' Or I'd tell him, 'Bring in the waistline; carve it off on both sides about this much.... Make her neck thinner.... Shave some off her legs.' " After the editing session was over, generally in less than an hour, the machine would spit out a revised negative ready for the *New York Times* printer. It was a vast improvement over the costly, time-consuming old system, where artists would retouch photos by airbrush and mail them to Distler, having no idea whether the revisions would pass muster. And whereas the face was the main battleground of the airbrush artist, the Scitex put the Queen's entire body up for improvement.

Sometimes, however, Leona photographed well. Distler recalls the time he got back a half-dozen eight-by-ten shots taken at the New York hotels. "They were fabulous! The lighting was perfect and she looked wonderful." But when the royal adman showed the photos to the Queen, she became apoplectic.

"This one makes me look like a dumpy old woman," she protested, throwing the whole batch of pictures into the air. "It makes me look like a horrible old cow."

With no time to spare, Distler said he canceled a planned vacation to Greece and caught the first jet back to Miami. "I raced to the Scitex" and performed major cosmetic surgery on her entire body. He returned to Manhattan and entered the Queen's pink chamber with his handiwork, prepared for the worst.

" 'Oh, look,' the Queen said upon seeing the first photo. 'There's my Harry in the background!' She could find no fault. No wonder, I turned the 'dumpy old woman' into a thirty-year-old."

Yet in spite of the computer's flattering ways, the Queen often demanded more. Distler recalls one photo that failed to please.

"Nigger lips!" Leona shouted. "It looks like I've got nigger lips. I should be sitting there eating a watermelon." Since Distler knew the Queen's prejudices, the racial stereotype came as no shock. And although Distler considered the Queen's full lips a mark of beauty, he said he trimmed them down on the Scitex "and retouched the photo to death before Mrs. Helmsley thought it was all right." The Queen's obsession with her ads had become total, and surprised even her own ad advisers. "She became a publicity junkie," says Elaine Silverstein. Joyce Beber recalls "how pleased and touched" Leona was three years earlier when she made her photo debut as Queen of the Palace. "She was really thrilled with the ad campaign and how it was going." Now, after winning her third five-diamond award in a row from the American Automobile Association, the thrill was gone. Instead, the Queen simply took the mega-spotlight as her due. In earlier years, Beber said, Leona had been proud to see her ads framed and hanging among those of the agency's other famous clients. Now she wanted the entire spotlight for herself, as well as Beber's undivided attention. During one stopoff in Beber's office at the Palace, Leona grimaced at seeing actress Sophia Loren in an ad for Coty's Sophia perfume. And she demanded an explanation. "Who is this? Why do you have Coty?"

Pointing at Beber's ad for Steinway pianos, Leona sneered sarcastically: "What is Steinway?"

In spite of her swelling ego, the Queen continued to show flashes of her best asset: a sense of humor. "Without warning, she might go nuts and fire somebody and do awful things," Beber recalls, "but she could laugh at herself, and be funny and adorable. She was absolutely fun." For example, Beber said Leona insisted on poking fun at herself that year in an ad headlined, "Who said it's good to be the Queen?" Leona actually wrote much of the ad copy, Beber said. "It was really cute. Many of the lines came right out of her mouth. It described how hard she worked, about how she was a working queen, and how she toiled all day long." The signed message concluded with Leona's personal assurance: "It's not easy being the Queen.... But don't worry. I'm not abdicating." Typical of Leona's quick wit was the time Tad Distler inquired about her stiffness during a photo session: "Mrs. Helmsley, are you comfortable?" To which the billionaire Queen instantly replied, "No, but I make a living."

Despite a general upswing in occupancy at Manhattan hotels in 1985, the New York Harley was barely coasting along. By May, Metropolitan Life, Harry Helmsley's partner, decided to sell the tycoon its half interest in the four-year-old hotel on East Forty-second Street. Distler said one reason the insurance company bailed out was weariness with Leona's high-profile ads. "They didn't think the ads were effective anymore and they didn't want Mrs. Helmsley in them." But removing Leona would have been impossible, Distler said. "She would have complained bitterly and never would have allowed Harry to live it down. So Harry bought the hotel outright." In another hotel transaction weeks earlier, Helmsley and Lawrence Wien had sold the St. Moritz to Donald Trump for $71 million. Ready cash, therefore, might have encouraged Helmsley to proceed with the Harley buyout. A top former executive of the Harley insists, however, that Met Life actually started the wheels in motion after Leona continued to insist that the hotel buy furnishings from Deco at premium prices. He said she was also blamed for another key problem: chronic management turnover. "She's very loud, rude and abrasive. When Met Life was sitting in on audit, they complained that in the space of three years we had six general managers and that maybe the lack of continuity was why the hotel wasn't doing as well as expected."

At the time, he said, the hotel was barely breaking even, with occupancy in the dismal 50 to 60 percent range. Again, Leona was held responsible, for refusing to allow group discounts and other standard incentives to woo customers. "She wasn't aggressive enough. With more ambitious sales, we could have done 70 percent."

The finger pointing took place strictly behind doors, however, allowing the Helmsleys to put a happy face on the buyout. Harry told *Post* columnist Cindy Adams his first act would be to change the name of the hotel. "Harley sounds like a motorcycle," he explained, "and doesn't imply it's a Helmsley hotel." At a press conference later that year, Leona rechristened it the New York Helmsley. "I just named my favorite hotel for my favorite person, Harry," she said. "Who else?"

"I'm gonna get you, and I'm gonna get you soon!" Leona warned Joseph Licari, her husband's top financial officer. As Licari's face grew redder in his booth at Mindy's, the lobby restaurant of the New York Helmsley, Leona continued with her threat.

"You had no right to tell Harry!" the Queen fumed.

"Well, I work for Harry," Licari replied in self-defense. "I'm his financial adviser and vice president, and I have to tell him these things."

Milton Meckler, who had stopped at the booth to say hello to the Queen, accidentally walked into the tirade. Leona, always eager for an audience, motioned for him to stay put while she continued to chew Licari to bits.

"You had no right to tell Harry anything," Leona said. "You did the same thing with Jay. You exposed all his charge cards and made a big fuss about that."

Meckler had no idea what Licari had done this time to incur Leona's wrath, but he instantly understood the credit card reference. Meckler remembered well how Licari had spilled the beans on Jay Panzirer several years earlier, notifying Harry that Leona's son had charged personal expenses to his Deco credit card. Meckler also remembered how surprised Harry had been to learn that among the questionable charges was the carved Helmsley Monopoly table that Jay had given the tycoon as a birthday present. Now, in 1985, Meckler was tempted to shield his ears as Leona railed on.

"I'll never forget what you did to Jay," she continued. "I'm gonna get you!"

"Well, I've got to go back to work," the short, pudgy, 49-year-old financial adviser replied, no doubt knowing that it would be futile to make explanations.

"Remember!" Leona screamed at Licari as a final warning. "You don't sleep with Harry! I do!"

When Licari walked off, Meckler took his seat and sipped some coffee with the flushed Queen. Without letup, Meckler recalls, Leona cursed Licari's name and swore vengeance against him.

Licari had joined Helmsley's staff as an entry-level book-keeper in 1965 and worked his way up through the ranks of Helmsley Enterprises, the flagship holding company for all of Harry's far-flung personal assets. Now, as Harry's right-hand financial adviser, he served as corporate secretary for virtually every Helmsley subsidiary and kept his finger on the pulse of most transactions big and small. Licari's office on the fifty-third floor of the Lincoln Building was just a few paces from Harry's. Several times a day they would enter one another's office unannounced to direct the finances of Helmsley Enterprises, including its biggest subsidiary, Helmsley-Spear Inc.

Leona's dining room threat left little doubt, however, that Licari's days as adviser were numbered. "It wasn't until 1985," Licari recalls, that Leona developed a real itch to control the big boys at Helmsley headquarters. "She was mostly involved with hotels and advertising at that point," he says, "but she decided to veer into other facets of the business." Instead of extending her influence over Helmsley Enterprises slowly, like a lamb, Licari said she came on like a lioness even though she had no real handle on the business. "Leona's not a real estate investor," he explains. "She used to be a condominium broker, which is not the same thing as a real estate entrepreneur. She may understand the operations of a hotel," but buying and managing a national grab-bag of skyscrapers, shopping centers, warehouses and office parks required a different expertise altogether. Yet, just as Leona had hurtled into hotels with no background and ridden roughshod over her seasoned staff, she pulled rank instantly on Harry's lieutenants at Helmsley Enterprises. In earlier years, she had dabbled in affairs at Helmsley headquarters. Now, without bothering even to visit the Lincoln Building, she was wreaking absolute havoc. Licari said the boss's wife would just pick up the phone and summon him and other senior Helmsley aides to her fifth floor office in the Palace. A tongue-lashing could be predicted, often on the flimsiest of pretexts. "She shouts, and if you try to say something, she calls you a liar. And then if you say something else, you become a thief." Indeed, Leona's most frequent allegation was thievery. "She has this tremendous distrust of people, which is part of her personality. She accuses everyone of stealing; I mean everyone!" If executives proclaimed their innocence or suggested solutions to a perceived problem, he said Leona would shut them right up. "To think out loud or come up with ideas doesn't mean anything."

Tad Distler agrees that Leona changed her focus in 1985. He saw the reason as twofold: "Boredom and suspicion. She started to get bored with the hotels. And she felt there were too many people influencing Harry when she was not around. He was a mile away at his office on Forty-second Street doing his own thing, and she couldn't keep a total eye on him. So she decided to get more involved in his main real estate business." Almost immediately, the bloodbath began. "She started to fire people that were very close to Harry—his most trusted advisers for many years." Among her chief targets were the dozen senior vice presidents of Helmsley-Spear, who reported directly to Harry and his two top partners, Irving Schneider and Alvin Schwartz.

Jeremiah McCarthy, the senior v.p. in charge of engineering, was considered one of Harry's personal favorites. Still in his thirties and loaded with boyish enthusiasm, he had saved Helmsley millions of dollars by upgrading boiler and mechanical systems in such properties as Bush Terminal. McCarthy was known throughout Helmsley-Spear not only for his engineering prowess but for a pronounced independent streak. "Jerry's not the kind of guy to take much bull from anyone," recalls Steve Fitzmaurice, one of his former engineers. "He's not afraid of anybody or anything, including Mrs. Helmsley." For example, he recalls the often told story of how McCarthy dared to scold the Queen one afternoon when she fired a waiter in his presence at the Palace. "She didn't like her tuna fish sandwich," Fitzmaurice explained, "and told the waiter he was fired. Jerry spoke up and said, 'You can't do that to the guy! He didn't make the sandwich. Someone in the kitchen made it. He's probably got a wife and family.' " Either dazed by McCarthy's daring, or perhaps softened by his appeal, Leona relented, Fitzmaurice said, "and told the waiter to return to work."

Like many Helmsley-Spear employees, McCarthy had been drafted by the Helmsleys to supervise ongoing improvements to Dunnellen Hall. Inevitably, he would find himself at logger-heads with Leona. One fateful dispute involved Eugene Brennan, a Stanford contractor hired by McCarthy to do brickwork and masonry around the pools and barbecue pit. When the Helmsleys ignored Brennan's $13,000 bill, McCarthy pleaded with Harry, reminding him that the contractor had six kids to feed and had performed his job admirably. Won over, Helmsley authorized McCarthy to send Brennan a $10,000 Helmsley-Spear check as partial payment for the mansion job.

Although Harry had approved the payment in advance, Leona pitched a fit anyway, arguing that McCarthy should have secured her authorization as well. To set things straight, Brennan says Leona ordered McCarthy to reimburse Helmsley-Spear the full $10,000 out of his own pocket or be fired. "McCarthy was very upset," Brennan recalls. "He told me he had to take the money out of his own checking account and repay them. It was a strain on him, a real hassle. He probably had to borrow a few dollars from his friends."

Leona rampaged for days over the incident in her Palace lair. "She carried on something ferocious with McCarthy," Tad Distler recalls. "You would have thought he'd doubled the national debt." Distler overheard Leona excoriate the engineer over the telephone. "To save his job, she told McCarthy that he'd better come up with the $10,000 right away."

"How dare you spend it!" Leona shouted. "It's *my* money. You're spending *my* money. I didn't authorize that bill to be paid." At least a dozen times more, Distler says, Leona repeated the refrain. From that moment on, Distler says, "she was determined that she was going to get him, even though he was one of Harry's closest advisers, confidants and friends."

"You've got to get rid of him," Leona yelled at Harry over the phone the same day. "I don't care how close he is, you've got to get rid of him!" But for the time being, at least, Helmsley stood firmly behind his fair-haired engineer. Few other Helmsley executives enjoyed Harry's protection, however, once Leona decided their time was up. Even if they'd been condemned for the flimsiest of reasons, Helmsley virtually always went along with the program. "He'd rather stay married to her and tolerate her abuse of other people," Milton Meckler says. "I think her insensitivity finally transferred to him. If you're around her long enough, maybe it's catching. He's either heavily brainwashed, or he just doesn't want to hear her mouthing off to him."

Knowing that Leona's word was usually final, hardened real estate executives quaked in her presence in much the same way as Palace waiters, who approached the Queen with rattling teacups. The very mention of her name, Joyce Beber recalls, terrified Philip Blumenfeld, a Helmsley-Spear vice president in charge of Harry's Florida investments. "She treated Blumenfeld like a serf, as bad as a person can be treated, like he didn't exist." Leona constantly mispronounced his name, Beber said, to put him on edge and make him feel like a true peon. "One way to put you down was to forget your name. While Blumenfeld was standing in front of her, she'd scream: 'Blumenstein! ... Blumenfield! ... Blumenthal! What's your name!!?' " Then Leona would try her best to humiliate him further. "She'd say, 'What did you do this for, Blumenthal? How dare you have the *temerity* to order that furniture without my approval!' " ("Temerity" was possibly Leona's favorite word, Beber says. "Once she learned it, she used it a thousand times.") Leona hated Blumenfeld more than most, Beber speculates, not only because she smelled his fear, but because his vocabulary and Jewish background reminded the Queen of her own carefully concealed roots. "Blumenfeld was a very small ethnic kind of guy, who came from a poverty-stricken home. And he was proud of it. But Mrs. Helmsley has so much hatred for her past that all those things disgusted her. When she was with people like that she didn't like it."

During a get-together at Beber's Miami home one evening, Beber made the mistake of mentioning the Queen in Blumenfeld's presence. "He was holding a very expensive wine glass," Beber recalls, "and he was so tense talking about her that he crushed the glass." When Blumenfeld had departed, Beber's husband, a physician, cautioned her: "You should never mention Mrs. Helmsley's name in front of him. The man is so tense when you talk about her. Did you see the veins in his neck and the color in his face?"

A former top executive with Owners Maintenance Corp. says Leona made a determined effort in 1985 to run his office-cleaning subsidiary by remote control. "From that point on it was total turmoil. She'd call and rant and rave for nothing, convincing you she's boss and you're nothing." Leona would order OMC chieftains to her office "for meeting after meeting and insult after insult." Executives at other subsidiaries received similar drubbings, he said. "She was out to control the whole bucket of bolts—everything in real estate." Leona's main objective, the ex-aide speculates, was to eliminate all executives who had built up close ties to her husband over the years. By creating a power vacuum, he says, Leona hoped to expand her own personal control over Helmsley Enterprises. "Everybody who had a direct line to Harry, she went after. By eliminating these people, Harry would be left naked. There would be nobody to report to him except those she brought in herself as replacements. Once she put a hook on somebody, that's it. Harry didn't back up any of his people. She just had the run of the mill." How did she sway the tycoon, whose faculties remained scalpel sharp at age 76? "How do you control a man? You've got to control his ego. So she played him for a fool. I guess the man was ready for it. When you reach the heights and you're up in age, you go for that kind of stuff. She made Harry think she could see through people and that all these people were connivers, crooks, and overpaid. She did it by inflating his ego to a point where he believed it himself. And she was trained from the street to do it and she had the power of the mattress to do it. Don't forget this was an attractive woman. The mattress is a powerful arena."

After being summoned to Leona's office three times, the OMC executive said he saw the handwriting on the wall. "She was going to manipulate me into a corner where she would have control over OMC and everything else." Rather than wait for the Queen's ax to fall, he said he went to Harry in desperation and pleaded with him to curb Leona's meddling. "For an hour and a half," the ex-aide recalls, "I went through the whole gamut. I told Harry that the empire it took him fifty years to build up, she would destroy in five. I told him she was a manipulator who destroyed people. Your length of service to the company didn't mean anything. People who had been in high positions with him for twenty years she was trying to get rid of: attorneys, brokers, presidents of subsidiaries, vice presidents. They were all key people, prime movers, and they were leaving because of her constant interference and abuse and his inability to protect them." The executive complained to Helmsley that Leona and her attack dog, Frank Turco, could not care less about the long-term damage their bloodbath would inflict on Helmsley-Spear and Helmsley Enterprises. "They enjoyed putting pressure on people. When you play with people's emotions, that's cruelty—and they were. If she wanted to get rid of you, she'd just drop a hint to Turco and from that point on you were dead. Finished. Their personalities clicked because they were two of a kind. They enjoyed putting pressure on people. Your length of service meant nothing. If they wanted to get rid of you they would do it by firing you or making life miserable, by threatening in person. Someone who brought millions to the company, they'd call him an imbecile to his face." The executive recounted for Helmsley the endless times Leona had accused him of being a thief. "She accused everybody down the line of being a crook. That was her famous remark. 'You're a crook; you're stealing.' Ninety-nine percent of them weren't in a position to steal, but she accused them anyway. It's outrageous when you're in a top position, and have brought in millions, to be accused of petty theft."

The OMC executive concluded the appeal by telling Helmsley, his boss for over fifteen years: "If that's the way you're going to run your operation, I feel sorry for you." Helmsley kept a stone face through the meeting and made no effort to defend his wife. The former aide said he was devastated by Helmsley's silence. "He said nothing. 'Let me see. Let me see,' was all he could say. He probably said less to other people. So I got up and walked out." He said he then resigned in disgust and continues years afterward to ask himself: "How can a man watch this stuff happening to his friends and not have anything to say?"

In a 1981 *Daily News* interview, Leona boasted about being a power in her own right. "All I need is a mustache and glasses and I'll be Harry Helmsley," she quipped. By 1985, the joke was no laughing matter at Helmsley headquarters in the Lincoln Building, where Leona continued her purge.

Outright firings weren't required. A former top Helmsley-Spear construction executive says Leona often preferred to play cat with Harry's executive mice. "She's sneaky. She'd try to posture people into situations where their loyalty to Harry would be questioned, enough to get you fired. And there would be no way out. If she couldn't get you, she would somehow get you to get yourself." For example, the ex-aide said he was convinced that Leona tried to lay a trap for him after he complained to Harry about excessive Deco charges to the Palace. Shortly later, he said Leona repeatedly summoned him to her Park Lane penthouse while Harry was away at work. "She wanted me to come check an air conditioning duct" after it had already been fixed. "I knew better than to be caught in her penthouse alone. I didn't want to be put in a situation where my motives would be suspect. But she kept calling me over there. She kept calling and saying, 'I want you to come up here. I want to talk to you.' " The key to survival, he had learned from tracking the Queen's casualties, was to hide as far from her as possible. "It's a real experience to see her power in action," he says. "Her dynasty-type wealth gives her the power to squash you like an ant. When you see her exercising that power without any remorse, without any sense of conscience, you become a little fearful. And I'm a pretty big guy."

In frustration, he said he once approached Harry and told him: "I've seen so many people that your wife has indiscriminately fired, for no reason whatsoever. We've paid so many headhunter fees." Helmsley just stroked his silver mustache "and looked at me blankly. He tries to talk to her at times, but he doesn't want to fight with her. I think he's so blinded that he is unaware of how vicious she is."

Joyce Beber was amazed that Harry would stand lamely by and watch the slaughter of his former aides without so much as a raised eyebrow. One possible explanation for Helmsley's lack of loyalty, she speculates, was his "shallow emotional depth. So often, he never seemed to be affected by things one way or another." More than anything, however, she attributed it to selfishness. "In my opinion, he got to the point where he became truer to the essence of Harry Helmsley—a greedy, insatiable man who has met his match" in Leona. In earlier years, Beber says, the only difference between Harry and Leona "was that he kept his selfishness inside and she didn't. And now, with her encouragement, he was letting it out. It was easier to let her fire a colleague of thirty years than for him to go home to an angry wife. He didn't wish to inconvenience himself or his lifestyle. A man who was less self-centered would have stood up to her and had that fight after supper." Was it possible, moreover, that Harry had a mean streak of his own that fed on Leona's exploitation of others? The thought crossed Beber's mind one day when the purple-faced Queen was raging at an employee over the telephone. Harry was sitting right next to Leona, Beber says, egging her on every shrill step of the way. "He was telling her, 'Give it to him! Give it to him!' "

Just as Leona showed utter disregard for Harry's trusted employees, Beber said the Queen expressed contempt for his longtime business partners. "She had no use for them because they competed for Harry's time and his energy and she wanted it all. She always put down Lawrence Wien," the devoted partner whose syndication formula catapulted Harry to riches. "She said he would have been nothing without Harry, that he wanted to take too much credit."

Irving Schneider and Alvin Schwartz, Harry's top partners at Helmsley-Spear, were also mental midgets in Leona's book. "Harry made them what they are today," Leona would scoff. "Harry's everything. Harry's the genius that paved their way." Helmsley never protested when the Queen berated his confreres, Beber says, "maybe because he now had another partner—Leona. They were a team, their own entity, and there was never enough money or glory for themselves."

As partners were ignored or deprived of their fair share of profits, the bloodbath at Helmsley headquarters picked up steam by fall. In September, Leona finally put the screws to Jeremiah McCarthy after a series of continuing run-ins with the senior engineer. Reportedly, McCarthy was axed for refusing to obey direct orders from the Queen that he approve phony bills to shift Dunnellen Hall expenses to Helmsley commercial properties, including the Garden Bay Manor apartment complex in Queens.

Meanwhile, the Queen enlarged her own entourage in late October by adding a recent law school graduate, Martin Goldstein, as a personal aide. Milton Meckler recalls that Leona hired Goldstein—a tall bachelor in his early thirties—out of the blue after he sent her a devotional letter in the mail. "He had written her a letter saying he read so much about her, and he thought he would be a great asset to her. It was a good forceful move on his part, and she apparently gave him an interview." It was also good timing for the newcomer because Leona's executive secretary, Mary Ann DiMicco, resigned the following month. Immediately, Meckler says, Goldstein filled the vacuum "and became a power guy." The Queen turned to him constantly for advice, and much of the advice was pure gossip. "Whether it's true or false doesn't make any difference. He was instrumental in getting people fired. One day I was at Dunnellen Hall," Meckler recalled, "and he created two or three incidents. I heard him say to her, 'Did you hear this? Did you hear that?' and that would really get her going." Only seconds later, even as he sat next to Goldstein and the Helmsleys, Meckler said he was surprised to find himself squarely framed in Goldstein's cross hairs.

"Goldstein was talking about company cars, and it turned out Mrs. Helmsley didn't know that this employee or that employee had a company car. Well, then Goldstein brings up the subject of *my* company car."

The Queen, energized by Goldstein's prodding, then demanded an immediate explanation of why Meckler was entitled to a Cadillac. A company Cadillac!

"Mrs. Helmsley, that's in my contract," he replied defensively.

"What do you mean!" she cried. "I can change your contract!"

Thanks to Goldstein, Meckler found himself poised smack in the path of a funnel-shaped cloud. Mr. Helmsley, who saw the approaching whirlwind, moved as quickly as possible from his chair in the glass-enclosed pool area. "Harry couldn't stand it, and just walked out," Meckler recalled.

Meckler knew there was no way to argue with the Queen. "You don't get in an argument with Mrs. Helmsley if you want to live." It was far better to eat crow and hope that the dispute would eventually evaporate.

"I'm not going to get in an argument with you, Mrs. Helmsley," he said quietly, instead of reciting the fine print of his employment contract which clearly stipulated the Caddy.

His strategy worked. Mrs. Helmsley then left the room and returned a few minutes later. "She came back and put her hand on my back and said, 'I'll think about it, but we won't talk about it again until your contract's up.'"

"Fine," Meckler replied, grateful that the contretemps had passed.

Meckler said that Mrs. Helmsley felt that hotel employees, vendors and Helmsley Enterprises executives were stealing from her. She appreciated someone like Goldstein—someone who could point out hidden conspiracies. "He started out as a real flunky, and then you could see his power and commands coming in." Goldstein loved the Palace intrigue and the excitement of working alongside the Queen, Meckler adds. "He called me long distance many a morning, and his favorite comment would be, 'I wonder who she's gonna throw to the lions today.'" Meckler said Frank Turco quickly noticed Goldstein's rising star and was determined to shoot it down lest he be displaced as chief aide to the Queen. "Frank was out to knock him out of there because he was stepping into his territory. He had managed to get too close to her." Goldstein sensed the danger, Meckler says, and put Turco at the top of his list for the lion's den. Little escaped Goldstein's attention. "He would open Mrs.

Helmsley's mail," Meckler recalls. "I would mark my letters to her 'Personal' and then he would tell me about the letter before she even got it. And apparently it was all right with Mrs. Helmsley." To circumvent Leona's new secretary, Meckler says he sent all subsequent private correspondence directly to the Queen's Park Lane penthouse instead of to the Palace.

In December, another one of Harry's dozen senior vice presidents at Helmsley-Spear bit the dust. The victim this time was Ben Lafiosca, who had worked closely at Helmsley's side for seventeen years, most importantly as head of the cooperative conversion effort at his giant Parkchester housing complex in the Bronx. Lafiosca resigned after Leona ordered him to fire his son, Steven, who also worked at Parkchester. "She suddenly decided she didn't believe in nepotism," one former Helmsley aide recalls, although her own brother, Alvin Rosenthal, remained a highly visible employee. Lafiosca gave his son the gloomy holiday message and resigned only hours later.

The same month, Leona stunned everyone by erasing Turco's name from the royal flow chart. Perhaps encouraged by Goldstein, the Queen stripped him of his position as finance chief for Helmsley Hotels and closed down his spacious command post in the Graybar Building. After firing eight members of his staff, she moved Turco to drab quarters on the fifteenth floor of the Lincoln Building and assigned him the lowly task of supervising telephones and switchboards for Helmsley hotels and office buildings. It was a rude tumble indeed for the chief minister of state. No longer would he hire and fire heads of subsidiaries with a simple nod, dispatch investigation squads, or dictate kickback terms to vendors. Instead of the royal portfolio, he would carry a note pad and equipment catalog. And instead of his accustomed perks, Turco was required to route the simplest requests through proper channels. "He wanted to renovate his new office," one top former aide to Leona recalls, "and Mrs. Helmsley told him no. She kept him alive, but he lost everything. Basically, she castrated him. He was out of favor."

"Pick up extension 8500," shouted the telephone clerk on duty at the City Desk of the New York *Post*. "It's something about the Helmsleys."

A skeleton crew of only four reporters was on hand because the newspaper's Christmas party was in full swing at a nearby beer joint. The one most interested in real estate fielded the call.

"Are you interested in winning a Pulitzer Prize?" the anonymous tipster asked by way of greeting. "I'm serious. If you meet me tonight, I assure you you'll win a Pulitzer Prize."

"Good salesmanship," the reporter replied. "What's it all about?"

"It's about the Helmsleys. They're thieves," the caller announced in a tone of utter contempt. "Meet me tonight and I'll tell you the whole story."

"First, tell me a little more," the reporter answered, averse to wasting traveling time on a crank call.

"For instance, their mansion in Connecticut," the caller replied. "They're charging off millions of dollars worth of renovations to Uncle Sam."

"What kind of renovations?"

"They've built a brick-and-marble enclosure for their outdoor swimming pool, and it matches the house exactly. It's the finest that money can buy, and it didn't cost them a penny."

"Explain how they got it for free."

"Simple," the caller continued. "They dummied up a bunch of bills and sent them to the Graybar Building and the Helmsley Building for payment. The description of work supposedly done on the buildings was completely made up. And so were the prices."

Slightly confused, the reporter asked him to repeat the scenario.

"Okay. What they did is…they have contractors doing work at the mansion. Instead of paying the contractors, they have their office buildings pay them. So bills from the contractors are sent to the Graybar Building and the Helmsley Building for work actually performed on the mansion."

"If that's the case, how do you know the Helmsleys know about it?"

"Because their initials are written all over the fake invoices," the tipster said. "Leona Helmsley's initials are 'L.M.H.' and that's what's on a lot of dummy invoices. Harry Helmsley's initials are 'H.B.H.' and they're all over the place."

The caller, who refused to identify himself, then issued an ultimatum: "If you want to talk to me, you've got to come see me tonight. Tonight or no night."

All the subtle clues indicated that the tip was authentic. The caller was exceptionally attentive, unlike most crank callers, who are more interested in the sound of their own jangled voices. He also gave highly specific answers, the kind of detail that implied definite firsthand knowledge. And although he was obviously angry at the Helmsleys, he was cool and scientific in his presentation of the facts. Maybe an accountant.

"I'm out of town on business," he said, "so you'll have a long drive ahead of you. If you leave now, you should be here by midnight." He then gave the name and address of a hotel and instructed the reporter to meet him in the lobby bar.

Several hours later, a stranger rose from his barstool and greeted the reporter with a firm handshake. "I was serious," he said. "Tonight is the only night I could have seen you. So I'm glad you made it."

After identifying himself, the tipster assigned himself a code name, "Bill," for future reference. He explained that a whole-sale purge was in progress at Helmsley Enterprises and many of his friends had already been fired by Leona Helmsley in the past year. "She's wreaking havoc. She doesn't know her ass from a hole in the ground and she thinks she can run a five-billion dollar empire."

He described Mrs. Helmsley as "a cold, heartless, blood-thirsty bitch" who was bound to tear her husband's organization apart. He went on to disclose what he knew of the mansion billing scam, but admitted he was unfamiliar with many key elements. For instance, he didn't know who actually created the fake business invoices. He just knew they were fake. He didn't know whether the bogus invoices were submitted to the Helmsley office buildings with the knowledge of contractors working on the Greenwich mansion. But he swore "on a stack of Bibles" that the Helmsleys personally initialed the tainted invoices for perhaps "as much as five million dollars'" worth of renovation work on the mansion. Bill then opened his brief-case and removed a yellow legal pad. On it, he scribbled the names of at least four Helmsley office buildings. "Do some checking around," he said, "and you'll find that most of the money is buried in these buildings."

"Buried?" the reporter asked.

"I mean these are the buildings that got stuck for—that had to pay the fake invoices."

"Where are they? Where can I get my hands on the invoices?"

"Talk to the building managers," Bill advised, and then scribbled down the address of the mansion.

"Give me a list of all the contractors working on the renovation," the reporter said. "And can you get me a copy of the in-house phone directory at Helmsley Enterprises?"

"I'll try tomorrow."

"These employees who have been wiped out by Mrs. Helmsley," the reporter added. "I need all their names, every last one of them. And also their home phone numbers. They'll be golden. Tell me how everyone got fired—all the circumstances." A beer later, the reporter headed back for Manhattan, intrigued by the possibilities.

Without warning, Frank Turco received his *coup de grâce* in February 1986, while vacationing with his family at the Orlando Harley. "He was told never to return to work," a former aide to the Helmsleys recalls. "He was cut off and never allowed back." Like so many of Turco's own victims during his days of glory, he was cashiered on the flimsiest of pretexts. Mrs. Helmsley ditched him without a second thought, the aide said, after a staff member expressed mere suspicion that Turco was using his telecommunications expertise to tape employee phone calls. "So she figured he was taping her, too, and never spoke to him again in person or otherwise." Neither Turco's four years of service to the Queen nor his old friendship with her late son counted for anything.

By the time of Turco's departure, Milton Meckler said new business procedures were set up to allow the Helmsleys to continue furnishing Dunnellen Hall at no personal expense. For over a year, the "circle jerk" had worked like a charm. Through her special Deco checking account in New York, Meckler said Leona managed to spend over $1 million for truckloads of antiques, fine china and other luxury goods between November 1984 and early 1986. He said the Queen and Turco had sent written directives every month to Deco headquarters in Florida, ordering his subsidiary "to bill specific hotels in the Helmsley realm for furnishings actually delivered by Deco to Dunnellen Hall." A typical order from Leona might read: "Deco New York has now spent $150,000. Send out invoices to these hotels for these amounts." The name of the vendor would appear on the invoices, but the destination—the mansion—would be changed to make it appear as though the furnishings were installed in the hotels. When the hotels paid up, "the money would be filtered back to Deco's account in New York"—thus completing the circle and replenishing the piggy bank.

On February 14, the Helmsleys were able to refine the complicated scam that had been designed to conceal their private gain from the IRS. On that date they set up a Delaware corporation, the Five Twenty-One Corp. (named after the mansion's address at 521 Round Hill Road) and deeded Dunnellen Hall to their wholly owned new entity. The corporation was not a company in the usual sense, but an estate planning device. Title was put in Leona's name to free her from paying inheritance tax on the mansion upon Harry's death. The corporation was also a helpful accounting tool to handle expenses related to the estate. After creating the corporation, Meckler says, Leona virtually ignored the Deco checking account in New York and opened a new account under the Five Twenty-One Corp. name. It would become the Queen's new piggy bank. Meckler said Leona's secretary, Martin Goldstein, controlled the checkbook itself, and Donald Hesselburg, treasurer of Helmsley Enterprises, collected Deco's money, apparently for deposit into Leona's account. When funds in the piggy bank dwindled, Meckler explained, "Hesselbirg would call Deco and say, 'You owe the parent [Helmsley Enterprises] three hundred thousand dollars.' He would just say, 'You now owe the money.' You didn't ask any questions. Deco would then enter a debit that we owed the parent that amount. But we owed the money for nothing." He said Deco, in turn, would send Five Twenty-One Corp. a bill for the identical amount. But as soon as Five Twenty-One Corp. remitted its check, Meckler said Deco would shoot the funds to Hesselbirg instead of retaining them as payment for goods delivered to Dunnellen Hall. In effect, Meckler said, Deco was continually draining its own profits to replenish the piggy bank.

Frequently, he said, Goldstein was reluctant to dip into the piggy bank. Instead, "he would tell me to order a whole list of things and not send Mrs. Helmsley an invoice for it. He would always use the term, 'Eat it! Just eat it.' In other words, she won't be billed."

Another possible rationale for creating Five Twenty-One Corp. was a desire by the Helmsleys to escape personal responsibility for mounting debts related to improvements at the mansion. In typical fashion, the Helmsleys stopped paying outstanding bills once contractors finally completed the pool enclosure to meet Leona's artistic standards the previous summer. Among those left holding the bag was Sheldon Feinstein, whose stone company was unable to collect its balance due of $85,000. Landscaper Nicholas Vasileff went to Superior Court in Stamford on April 8 when the Helmsleys ignored his bill of

$15,000. He collected after a judge slapped a lien on the estate.

Leona's beloved pool enclosure might have improved her exercise regimen, but its country comfort in no way distracted her from affairs at Helmsley headquarters. In May, two more of Harry's closest aides departed Helmsley-Spear. Seymour Rabinowitz, Harry's in-house attorney for almost a decade, reportedly was forced out after repeated clashes with Leona. "I don't want Rabinowitz between me and the electric chair," Leona had often declaimed, well aware that his real specialty was cooperative and condominium conversions. Rather than take things personally, Rabinowitz still attributes Leona's past outbursts to bitterness over her son's early death. "It was a trauma and a blow. The grief hit her in the solar plexus and she was not the same person afterwards. She became angry more easily and it was harder to be evenhanded. Everything became either black or white; she couldn't compromise to gray." That month also marked the exit of Joe Licari, the highest financial officer in Harry's empire. Leona finally made good on her promise to "get" him for exposing Jay Panzirer's financial ways. Her pretext for dumping him was excessive car expenses. Like so many others, Licari pleaded with Harry for mercy. And like the rest, he was only whistling Dixie. "Let's say it was one of the six wonders of the world," Licari recalls. "I was there for twenty years and he just wished me luck. She had the final word. He believes what she's doing is right. It's hard to believe. It's something I'll take to the grave without ever understanding."

Fourteen

By laying waste to Harry's high command, the suspicious Queen steadily reduced the number of executives able to advise her husband. Another way Harry was protected from invidious influences was simply by his staying isolated on the farm. Thus, under Leona's wing at Dunnellen Hall, Harry Helmsley often pared his three-day work week to one or two days, and would sometimes skip visiting his office for weeks on end. His retreat from the concrete canyons was anything but comforting news to remaining aides, who found themselves increasingly at Leona's mercy. She could fire or discipline them with a mere phone call from Dunnellen Hall, and they'd have nobody to run to for help.

No doubt Harry had to fight boredom harder than ever once the renovation hubbub ended the previous year. Except for annual parties—a New Year's open house and a Fourth of July birthday bash for Leona—the mansion was a lonely place indeed.

"I don't think Mrs. Helmsley has one friend," recalls Juan Carlos Bedoya, a 22-year-old native of Colombia who worked as the Dunnellen Hall butler in 1986. "Nobody ever came to visit her. Nobody came into the house to see her except her managers or secretaries." Mr. Helmsley, however, had an occasional visitor. "One day a month or so, a friend will come see him and have dinner." But over all, the excitement of friends and family was rare in the household. Instead, Leona instituted a never changing daily regimen which kept the mansion staff in a constant yawn. "Every day is like the next, " Bedoya recalls. "The only thing that changes is the staff. Breakfast is the same. Lunch is the same. Dinner is the same. It was a boring house, every day the same. Every morning, first thing, the Helmsleys would jump into their indoor pool and swim for up to forty-five minutes. Sometimes she would swim first, and then Mr. Helmsley." Lucite tables and chairs, overstuffed aqua furniture, and rose-colored marbletop end tables made the pool area a zone for comfort as well as exercise. Leona would also use a small exercise room near her upstairs bedroom, equipped with barbells and a stationary bicycle. Then, at about 10 A.M., breakfast was served in the pool enclosure's sun room. As soon as the enclosure had been completed, the Helmsleys virtually abandoned the breakfast room and adopted the sun room as their cozy corner. Harry would have oatmeal or pancakes, with grapefruit juice. The Queen restricted herself to fruit, juice and strong black coffee. To cap the meal, Bedoya said, the couple would each down a dozen vitamins.

After breakfast, the billionaire lovebirds would take a stroll through their gardens and around the property, "and Mrs. Helmsley was watching to make sure everything had been done right." Thirty minutes or an hour later, Mrs. Helmsley would retire to her bedroom for her morning nap while Harry read the morning papers or dozed off outside on a metal lounge chair. In cold weather, he would stretch out in his upstairs library or the downstairs den.

At 2 P.M., after a long restful nap, Mrs. Helmsley would stroll to the kitchen and tell the chef what to prepare for lunch. An hour later, the Helmsleys would be waiting when the meal was carried on a sterling silver platter into the sun room. Afterward, it was time for another outdoor stroll. That done, Mrs. Helmsley typically would repair to her upstairs study or the sun room and play backgammon with her security guards, particularly her square-shouldered chief bodyguard, Ed Brady.

One observer noted that the Queen and Brady sometimes threw the dice and moved pieces about the backgammon board for up to eight hours at a stretch. It was amusing to watch the glittering Queen of the Helmsley Hotel empire—the ever watchful, fastidious Queen—while away endless hours hunkered over a backgammon table in blue jeans and tennis shoes. Like everything else, the game had to be played by the Queen's rules, the observer added. "She and Brady would play for money. When Brady won, he couldn't ask her to pay up. But when he *lost*, she demanded that he pay her immediately."

While the Queen rolled the dice, or caught up on hotel paperwork, Mr. Helmsley frequently would read in his upstairs office, Bedoya says.

The Helmsleys would nibble on appetizers in the late afternoon, and after 6 P.M. Leona would go downstairs and tell the chef what to prepare for dinner. Lobster, fish or veal and fresh vegetables—especially snow peas, carrots and baked eggplant—were standard evening fare. Mrs. Helmsley strictly controlled her husband's portions, to keep his weight down, and he would often complain about being shortchanged.

After dinner, Bedoya would bring drinks to the den on a silver tray with two napkins. "Mrs. Helmsley would always have Absolut vodka on the rocks, and sometimes drank five tall ones." Occasionally, he said she would consume a whole bottle "if she drank all night." Bedoya says he enjoyed it when that happened because "when Mrs. Helmsley is drunk, she's happy—laughing all the time! Everything's fine! She drinks Absolut like water. One-two-three, like downing beers." Mr. Helmsley enjoyed drinking tomato juice cocktails or a couple of Budweisers.

Yes, the mansion routine bored the six live-in staffers to tears. But Bedoya, a waiter, two maids, a house manager and a chef yawned on the run, for Leona was a bona-fide slave driver. Bedoya was expected to work six days a week from 7:30

A.M. until as late as 10 or 11 P.M. His pay would be $450 for work weeks that sometimes stretched to ninety hours. "She wanted everyone to work all the time. Every day the house had to be vacuumed and the pictures had to be cleaned. The marble floors and the tile floor in the kitchen had to be polished with a machine every day. She would inspect every room, every day. If she saw a spot or a wrinkle, she'd scream: 'This is wrong! This is dirty! Everything is dirty. You stupid!' " Not surprisingly, Bedoya says, "Nobody liked to work in the house. Some would stay two or three weeks and leave." In his six months of employment, from July to December 1986, Bedoya said he trained at least fifteen people as butlers to assist him and none of them stayed "because she screamed all the time."

He said Mrs. Helmsley was profoundly suspicious of employees, and speculated she made sure there was a steady turnover. "She doesn't want anyone to work very long because she doesn't want anyone to know much about what's going on inside the house. She likes you for two or three months, and then you're fired." The Queen, he said, imported many employees from St. Thomas and paid them a pittance. When she got tired of them, she'd fire them on the spot and procure others from the Virgin Islands. Other employees were recruited by Manhattan employment agencies. During his stay at the mansion, Bedoya says two or three gardeners from St. Thomas worked nonstop for only $200 a week. "They worked six days a week from 7 A.M. to 4 P.M. in the garden. After work, they would come in tired and Mrs. Helmsley wanted them to work *inside* the house until 7 P.M. She said, 'These people think this house is only for vacation. This house isn't for vacation. It's for work!' "

A young foreign student took a break from her studies that year to serve as Leona's personal maid at Dunnellen Hall. Maria (not her real name) confirms that Leona was a fearsome taskmaster. "She treated us like slaves, like we were in jail." Foreign-born workers had to endure especially brutal browbeatings. "She would warn me that I had no choice but to do as she said. And if we threatened to leave, she would say, 'If you leave me, I'll call Immigration—and then you won't be in the United States very long.' "

Bedoya says Leona's suspicion of employees was extreme. "Sometimes when you leave the house a security guard checks you. He checks your bags. Sometimes they frisk you. They go through your purse and your satchel. If you have a car, they check the car at the back gate."

Employees frequently would heighten the Queen's natural suspicions, the former maid says, by spreading gossip about each other. "And if Mrs. Helmsley liked the person who told her, she believed that person, and fired the other person." At the opposite extreme, Maria said, was Mrs. Helmsley's dread that employees would become too friendly with each other (a phobia that also caused great morale rifts in her hotel empire). "If she saw employees talking too much to each other, she fired you." As a result, staff meals could be cheerless. "When we all sat down for our half-hour lunch, nobody talked about anything because everybody was afraid to be fired. We'd just sit and eat, or talk about something outside the mansion—never anything important. At night, everybody would go to their rooms, or just watch TV, instead of talking to each other."

Employee togetherness was such a gnawing concern, the maid says, that Leona wouldn't allow more than one person to work on a floor at the same time. "I had to clean the second floor by myself—all of Mr. and Mrs. Helmsley's rooms—because she thought two people working together would steal."

The maid's routine never varied: washing Mr. and Mrs. Helmsley's clothes, cleaning and shining the marble in the two master bathrooms, dusting, mopping, sweeping and scrubbing the entire floor. "I had to clean all the time. She always used to say to me, 'Honey, when I'm not home nobody does anything. So when I'm home, I like to be served.' One day she said, 'If you work, I love you; if you don't work, I hate you! You have to work all the time for me to love you.' "

Cleaning Leona's clothes closets alone was a Herculean task. The problem was that the Queen was an obsessive consumer. There was no such thing as buying one dress or one pair of shoes. "When she likes a sweater, she buys twenty or twenty-four of the same kind, but in different colors," the maid said. Few, if any, were ever worn, but if one was needed at least the right color would be available. Nevertheless, the unused sweaters would have to be dusted and tidied on a daily basis. The same went for garments of every variety: dresses, pants, blouses and skirts—identical copies in every possible hue.

Even unopened packages of stockings—hundreds of cellophane bags stuffed into closets and drawers—had to be cleaned. "I had to take them out and dust them. She never used them. She just liked to have them." One former aide said Mrs. Helmsley sometimes would buy and "put up" like preserves "ten gross of stockings all in the same color. Do you know what a gross is?" the aide asked, in an attempt to underscore the enormity of such a stocking binge. "A gross is exactly a hundred and forty-four pairs." One day the Queen pointed with pride to a newly received truckload: "I just bought these!" she boasted, and then burst into laughter. "There was a mixup and I accidentally ordered twelve gross." Not twelve gross *in toto*, but twelve gross of each color! "There were three or four colors," the aide recalls, "and she had over a thousand pairs of each.

"There was this insatiable quality about Mrs. Helmsley," the aide said. "There was always a hunger for *more*—there was never enough of anything."

Especially red lipsticks. There could never, in one lifetime, be enough tubes of red lipstick to satisfy the Queen. On an astounding grand tour of the royal closets, the aide counted "twelve cases of lipstick, all in the same color—a fairly strong red. Can you imagine—there must have been hundreds of tubes to each case! That's over two thousand tubes! She couldn't possibly live long enough to wear so much lipstick! Even if she put lipstick on from morning till night—and while she slept— she could not use all those lipsticks!"

Leona's most prized possession, however, was Harry. With her only child dead at a relatively early age, and grandchildren rarely around to fill the void, she gave him her utmost concentration. Bedoya and Maria, who bitterly complained about being mistreated by the Queen, acknowledged their admiration for her devotion to her husband. The two employees, unlike contractors such as Jay Nichtberger and Nick Vasileff, never saw Leona upbraid her elderly husband. "Mrs. Helmsley was always so nice to Harry," Maria recalls. "She treated him like a baby," making sure he got enough rest, ate the right foods, and stayed physically fit with daily swims in the mansion pools.

Although the love seemed genuine, Maria couldn't understand why Mrs. Helmsley prevented all staff members from getting too close to him. During her year as Leona's personal maid, Maria recalls, "I never talked to him at all because Mrs. Helmsley was always over him. He had no chance to talk to anyone else. I had to assume that she was probably afraid to lose him, and that's why she always was sitting close to him and talking to him." Employees seldom heard even a peep from the quiet tycoon, who seemed to rattle about the house unnoticed. Much of the time he spent in his upstairs office, reviewing real estate documents or reading newspapers. He was also wont to sleep upright for hours on end in one of the burgundy club chairs in the downstairs den. And, of course, he spent long, scenic stretches with Mrs. Helmsley in their beloved sun room, looking out on their vast back meadow. Such a quiet, unassuming, peaceful man. You couldn't help but like him.

With infrequent company, there was little incentive for the Queen to trouble with makeup. At Dunnellen Hall, consequently, there could be seen an older, less glamorous Queen than the classic Leona showcased in the ubiquitous ads. "The truth," Maria says, "is that Mrs. Helmsley is an older woman and she looks a little wrinkled. Makeup can do anything for any woman. With it, she looks really beautiful—about 49 years old. Without it, she looks about 60," still younger than her real age.

When it was time to return to the city—typically on Tuesday morning—the Queen made great preparations. "She would take three or four hours to get ready, putting on her makeup and trying to find the right dress. With so much time and nothing to do in Connecticut, I guess she took it too seriously." Nothing pleased Maria's boss more than "when you said she was so beautiful. She was so proud of her looks that that would get a smile. She used to tell me how her family thought she was so beautiful. And how her mother thought she was so beautiful." Despite her lack of friends, Maria says, Leona boasted that she was the toast of Manhattan. "One day she told me, 'People in Manhattan love me so much! I'm the Queen! They kiss my hands when I go to my hotels!'" The claims made Maria wonder "whether Mrs. Helmsley's mind was working quite right."

Maria was often curious whether Mrs. Helmsley's various medications influenced her moods, particularly large doses of "hormones and pills for her skin." She said that Mrs. Helmsley "probably took the hormones to keep her skin from aging."

Cleanliness was a cardinal rule in the mansion; a speck of dirt would sent the Queen into a near delirium. "Mrs. Helmsley used to pass her hands over the furniture to make sure it was clean; if it was dirty she'd start screaming." Her demands could be more esoteric. For instance, Leona could not abide any fragrance in her clothes, Maria says, "so I'd have to wash them once with detergent and then wash them three or four more times without detergent to get out any soap smell."

In addition to the two master bathrooms, there were three other bathrooms in the Helmsleys' upstairs living area, "and believe it or not, she used all five in one day." Washing was endless because Leona would routinely use ten towels after a shower. Absolute perfection was demanded in each and every chore, and demands were often patently ludicrous. For instance, "If a sheet had a wrinkle, she would tell me to iron the sheet because she would have a hard time sleeping on it! Imagine, a wrinkle keeping you up all night! You have to be crazy to think like that! She was spoiled, but we would do anything to please her, because we were afraid of losing our jobs." Bedoya recalls that employees frequently were required to rise from their sleep in the middle of the night and herald the Helmsleys' arrival. "Everybody was supposed to get up and see her," Bedoya said. "The whole staff had to be awake and line up outside and just wait for her to arrive, say: 'Hello, how are you?' and go back to bed, and get up again at six-thirty."

Food was another major inconvenience, he said. "Mrs. Helmsley believes everybody should work for their food, and that if she pays three hundred dollars a week that's too much money." In fact, Bedoya says, the Helmsleys ate high on the hog while forcing employees to eat egregiously unbalanced meals. "When I started work there my weight was a hundred and forty-five pounds. When I left, I was down to one twenty-five. Everyone lost weight."

Safeway and A&P were alien concepts in the household. The word "supermarket" was virtually never uttered. Instead, the mansion's food—a dozen bags a week—would come straight from the pantry of the Park Lane Hotel. Every Tuesday, Bedoya said, "a security guard would bring a van from the hotel with food for Mrs. Helmsley. And he would also bring food for us, the employees." Typically, the Helmsleys would receive cartons of shrimp, lobster, veal, fish, fruit and fresh vegetables.

By comparison, "our food was like animal's food. The chef cooked something for her and something completely different for us. For lunch on Monday, we would have chicken with rice; for dinner we would have rice with vegetables, with no meat.

"On Tuesdays, we would have lasagne for lunch and dinner. Just lasagne—no vegetables, no salad. On Wednesdays, we had plain fish with rice—no vegetables. If we had vegetables, we, the staff, had to make them. If we had four people, the chef made four pieces of fish and rice. That's it."

The Helmsleys, who enjoyed vintage white and red wines with their evening meal and who kept cases of Dom Perignon champagne in their cellar, limited their employees to apple juice. "Apple juice was all we could drink, nothing else," Bedoya says. "We couldn't have any sodas because Mrs. Helmsley likes apple juice." In frustration, Bedoya says he once begged Mrs. Helmsley for something different to drink, "for sodas or something. And she said, 'That's all you have. That's it!' " To redress the food problem, he would sometimes make risky trips to Greenwich and return with sodas, vegetables, red beans and Spanish foods for the Latin employees. "Nobody was supposed to get out of the house," he says, "but I could go to the store if the chef needed something." Maria recalls that the staff had steak one evening and Mrs. Helmsley walked into the servants' own eat-in kitchen. "She started screaming at us while we were eating, and told us that steak was too much money for her to be paying for us." Another day, "Mrs. Helmsley looked into our refrigerator and said it was dirty. So she took all the food out and threw it away. We didn't have anything to eat that day except hot dogs. We didn't ask to go to the store, because she didn't allow anyone to leave the house." Even a married couple who worked at the mansion were discouraged from leaving the grounds, she said. "Mrs. Helmsley didn't allow them to go out to the show."

When the Helmsleys went on trips, the Park Lane would cancel its weekly food runs to the mansion. With no funds for grocery shopping, staff members would be left in the lurch. "When she was away, all we ate was rice and pizza because she didn't leave any food for us," Bedoya recalls. "She only took care of herself. She didn't care about the people who lived there." Mrs. Helmsley was unfazed by the food complaints, Maria says. "She would say she's giving us enough. She told us we had good food, and were 'living like people'! She said, 'You have good food, a good house, and a good room. So you are living like people.' "

Harry and Leona decided to celebrate their birthdays together that summer. No "Wild About Harry" bash had been held at the Park Lane Hotel in March for his 77th birthday, according to one former Helmsley aide, "because Leona finally got fed up with the whole production. She decided, 'To hell with it.' " Instead, Leona decided it would be easier to throw her annual July 4 birthday party two weeks early, on Saturday, June 21, and invite guests to Dunnellen Hall for a combined shindig. (Though it was none of their business, she would be 66.)

The party was only hours away and vital chores remained

undone. But help was on the horizon. Seven workers were being dispatched to Dunnellen Hall that morning from Owners Maintenance Corporation, the Helmsley subsidiary that specialized in cleaning office buildings. Before dawn, the workers had already gathered in front of the Graybar Building at 420 Lexington Avenue and were rolling toward Greenwich by 5:30 sharp. Within an hour their truck screeched to a halt inside the mansion gate.

The crew reported immediately to Mrs. Helmsley, and were dispatched forthwith to her back yard. Their orders were to manicure each hillock and hedgerow. Roses had to be cut for the house and weeds needed to be pulled. The thirsts of begonias, daisies and rhododendrons had to be slaked. There would be plenty of fresh air that day for the city workers, who found themselves transformed from an urban mop brigade to country field hands.

As the summer sun beat down on the men, they also helped set out two dozen round tables on the back lawn, each seating ten guests. A score of smaller marble-top tables were hauled out of the basement and taken to the dance floor atop the pool enclosure.

At 3 P.M., after eight hours of work, the OMC workers took time for a brown-bag lunch. They had been told to bring their own food, and unpacked their yeomen's assortment of bologna, salami and ham-and-cheese sandwiches. They finished their working-class meal and prepared to knock off by 5 P.M. They had been told they would spend the entire weekend on the estate, in the gatehouse apartments. Yet a few of the men had hoped for the chance of making a quick return trip to New York for the evening with friends and family. Their plans were dashed, however, when Mrs. Helmsley insisted at the last minute that they work the *entire* party, which might not end until the wee hours of the morning. They were needed, she said, for housework and cleanup after the last guests had departed. None protested. She was, after all, the boss's wife, and the party seemed of terrific importance to her.

Leona and Harry Helmsley were, of course, newcomers to the Greenwich "back country," whose society was divided into two groups: the Old Guard and the nouveau riche. The Helmsleys were quickly relegated to the nouveau category after buying their weekend estate in the summer of 1983. Several faux pas expedited their entry, including Harry's decision to attend a formal United Way banquet wearing an open-collared shirt. There was also the time the Helmsleys sent party invitations to board members of the toplofty Round Hill Club, complete with press releases about piano-playing Harry and his famous wife. It was a monumental gaffe and sorely hampered Leona's ambition to be accepted by the Old Guard.

"She wanted to conquer the Greenwich crowd; what drove her was getting accepted," said one longtime guest on the Helmsley party list. The Queen's annual birthday parties were a grand opportunity to expand her influence into this exalted social stratum. "She was like a crazy woman getting the party together," one helper recalled. "She wanted to show off the pool and dance floor so badly. Why else do people give house parties?"

Another motivation, perhaps, was the March 1986 cover story in *Town and Country* magazine, which had glorified the home of a competing hostess, Ivana Trump. The article had waxed euphoric over Mar-a- Lago, a 118-room Mediterranean-style mansion that Ivana was decorating for her husband, Donald, in Palm Beach. Donald and Ivana, aged 39 and 36, respectively, had just bought the coral-colored winter palace. It boasted no fewer than fifty-eight bedrooms, thirty-three baths, three bomb shelters and a nine-hole golf course.

The Helmsleys, aged 77 and 66, had their own retreat, of course, at the Palm Beach Towers condominium complex, but it paled by comparison with Mar-a-Lago. Instead of diving into their own pool, the Helmsleys had to take turns swimming laps with three hundred other apartment owners.

It was clear that in Palm Beach, Ivana—not Leona—was living the life of a queen. Leona, with a spouse $400 million richer, always seemed to be comparing herself with Donald Trump's wife. Ivana, after all, was also hotel queen, the overseer of fifteen hundred employees at Trump's Castle Hotel & Casino in Atlantic City. But she was a full generation younger than the age-conscious Queen of the Helmsley Palace. The media couldn't take their cameras off Ivana, "a stunning blonde" who had been an alternate for Czechoslovakia's women's Olympic ski team before immigrating to North America. Nor could Leona forget that Ivana's husband was virtually forty years younger than Harry, and was considered the modern-day "young buccaneer" of New York real estate. Harry was "the living legend," whereas Donald was the reigning heartthrob.

"Leona saw Ivana on the magazine cover, and then saw this

whole spread on her and Mar-a-Lago, and you could see that she was just burned about this," recalled Tad Distler. "Leona never made the cover, and rarely was mentioned even inside *Town and Country*, and it was something she really aspired to. She was so jealous! She criticized Ivana's clothes. There was a resentment that somehow the Helmsleys weren't up to the Trump caliber."

In Greenwich, where the Trumps and Helmsleys each owned weekend mansions, at least Leona could entertain on an equal footing. A host of celebrities had been invited to the birthday party, including, for courtesy's sake, Donald and Ivana.

The guest list for Leona and Harry's annual birthday parties, however, had been shrinking in recent years because of poor attendance, according to one former party staffer. "Mrs. Helmsley was disturbed to find that fewer and fewer of the social elite were returning. 'The Tisches aren't coming!' she would complain after receiving a negative RSVP. 'The Rockefellers aren't coming either!' " To ensure satisfactory attendance, key Helmsley executives were expected to make command appearances.

Despite the summer heat, guests had been instructed to wear jackets and party-best dresses. When they rang the front doorbell, Leona greeted them in a stunning pink chiffon garden dress. Pink was Leona's favorite color, and as usual, it irradiated her complexion. For other women her age, the strapless, ankle-length dress might have seemed too young. But thanks to her exquisite posture, Leona wore it perfectly.

Mrs. Helmsley led the guests from the front door into the grand foyer which cut through the width of the house and led directly to the back patio through French doors. The foyer's marble floor had been polished to such a gloss that, for caution's sake, a few women removed their high heels and negotiated the distance in stockinged feet. Many of the male guests, it was noticed, wore Old Guard uniforms: Kelly-green pants, pink jackets and the other pastel tones so popular among retirees in Palm Beach. It was clear to the visitors that the house itself was off limits, because its rooms had been sealed off with red velvet ropes. Mrs. Helmsley, so correctly portrayed in her ads as a cleanliness buff, did not want her two hundred guests muddying up the place. Rest rooms were made available, however, including the glorious downstairs powder room. The pale yellow chamber was truly fit for royalty, with silk-covered love seats, chandeliers and a porcelain cabinet filled with charming

Meissen figurines.

Guests mingled on the back terrace, sipping champagne and sampling hors d'oeuvres as twilight approached. Then they ventured down a stone stairway to the lower plateau of the garden. There, surrounded by a flagstone terrace and Grecian statuary, was the mansion's ninety-foot outdoor pool. It, like the smaller indoor pool, was always strictly off limits except to admire. Waiters, meanwhile, set out huge platters of whole lobsters on linen-covered banquet tables near the pool. The piles of lobster eclipsed everything in sight, even silver chafing dishes piled high with barbecued spareribs and chicken.

Food was served buffet style, with guests lining up single file. It was a sight, one guest recalled, "seeing Donald Trump, in his business suit, waiting at the end of the line with his plate—like an ordinary fella." Ivana, in a striking red gown, kept him company.

Although it was a birthday party, Leona preferred to downplay the anniversary aspect. No birthday cake was served, nor did guests sing "Happy Birthday" to the couple. Instead, the event was treated as a Fourth of July celebration. Fireworks would have been too jarring for such an elegant outdoor picnic. As a compromise, guests applauded as thousands of white balloons were released into the clouds before sunset. Everyone then ventured upstairs for a new peek at the rooftop ballroom. On arrival, they looked up to see a giant white arch, fashioned from thousands more balloons, floating magisterially from the dance floor. The Trumps applauded, as did Barbara Walters, actress Jane Powell and Kitty Carlisle Hart, among other notables.

"We went up over the pool," one guest recalled, "and on the rooftop in the fading light we could look down on the gardens and see Leona's twenty-eight-room mansion, and her twenty-six acres. For a poor Brooklyn girl like Leona, who hadn't grown up to the purple, it must have seemed like a fantasy. Suddenly, we were at Alice's tea party." Musicians struck up the beat, and Leona became a rosy blur as Harry whirled her around the travertine deck.

The OMC employees and Mrs. Helmsley's own house staff, meanwhile, couldn't take their eyes off the banquet table on the back lawn, burdened with leftovers from the sumptuous feast. The OMC crew had eaten nothing all day except their 3 o'clock cold cuts.

Finally one of the OMC contingent peeked discreetly into

the kitchen and asked if they could help themselves to dinner. He got a fast "No!" from the chef, who explained that everyone—house staff and OMC draftees—would have to curb their appetites. "Mrs. Helmsley wants everyone to wait until after the guests leave. Then you'll be able to eat."

The OMC employee couldn't believe his ears. "Until the guests leave! That might be five hours. We're hungry and there's *lots* of good food out there."

"Sorry," the chef said, "those are the orders."

Even employees from Mrs. Helmsley's hotels, who had been imported to prepare the food, were ordered to keep the all-day fast. "They had to go into the bathroom to eat a piece of cake," recalled a former mansion housekeeper. "They couldn't eat a thing, and neither could anyone who worked in the house."

Desperation grew. The OMC worker recalls that he considered sending a scout to Greenwich for any kind of fast food—Burger King, Wendy's, Pizza Hut, whatever. That plan fell through when the house manager grew suspicious and warned them not to leave the property. Hours went by, and many of the guests quietly slipped away from the ballroom and departed. By 1 A.M. the Helmsleys thanked the band and bade good night to the remaining partygoers.

But the visitors were not to go home with memories alone. As they streamed out the front door, Mrs. Helmsley pressed into each of their palms a special gift—a party favor to commemorate the evening. Every guest received a rectangular maroon box, adorned with the "Helmsley Hotels" crown.

Ripples of excitement! What could it be? Jewelry perchance? Something sterling?

Lo and behold, tucked inside the package was a deck of playing cards. One of the lucky recipients was Cindy Morris, who lived directly across the street from the Helmsleys. She took the special deck home and showed it to her kids. Her collegiate daughter Deven took one look at the party favor and hooted with laughter.

"Every other card was Leona, in ten different outfits!" Deven remembers. "What a funny thing to give out at your party. Cards with your pictures on them. Not conceited!" Deven tried to imagine the time and effort that must have gone into the curio: "It's like, God, can't you have anything else better to do?" The strange thing, she noticed straight off, was "that Harry only got on the kings! But he paid for it all!"

One person, however, seemed to be impressed with the

Helmsley playing cards. Later that year, Ivana Trump summoned an executive from Beber Silverstein advertising—who also handled the Trump account at the time—to Trump's Castle in Atlantic City. While at the casino, the Beber executive saw four decks of the "Harry and Leona" cards spread out on desks in the hotel's marketing department. "I asked, 'What do you intend to do with all these cards of Leona Helmsley?' " the executive recalled. "And Ivana's marketing people told me, 'Ivana wants us to make a set of cards with Donald and Ivana's picture.' " The Beber executive rolled his eyes and hurried by as quickly as possible, and at last word no Trump deck had been produced.

With cards distributed and guests now departed, every Helmsley employee—both imported and domestic—was desperate for the go-ahead to eat. "We had to wait until Mrs. Helmsley said it was okay," the OMC employee recalls. "A security guard was supposed to come tell us."

The security guard finally arrived, but without the signal. "He said other employees were cleaning up the tables outside and they were throwing everything out—the food was going into the garbage.

"We went to look," the OMC worker recalls, "and it was true. We couldn't believe it. Good food was being dumped into big plastic trash bags. Whole chickens, big tubs of salad, fifteen kinds of cakes and pies. It was enough food to feed a hundred and fifty people. She didn't want anyone to take any food home, so the manager ordered us to go help throw it away in plastic garbage bags. She didn't have any feelings. She treated us like shit." But the OMC crew members were too far gone, too drained by fatigue and hunger, to care any longer about official orders. The group skulked into the back yard like rats in the night and picked several platters clean. "I got a little salad and some beef," the OMC employee says.

Not until 3 A.M., exactly 21½ hours after they set out for Greenwich, did the OMC workers retire for the night to their outdoor cottage. Yard work continued the next day, and they were dismissed finally at 3 P.M. "Mrs. Helmsley didn't even tell us 'Thank you,' much less give us a tip," the OMC worker recalls. The crew returned to Manhattan within an hour, and were grateful to be breathing unfit air again and walking the gritty sidewalks. Even the endless little rows of mangled garbage cans seemed downright charming compared to their taste of country life.

Fifteen

Joyce Beber and Elaine Silverstein knew every facet of Leona's personality. There was the volcanic Queen; the sultry, sexy Leona who took such pride in her cleavage; the sentimental Leona who would cry the instant her deceased son's name was mentioned; the funny Leona who laughed loudest at her own impersonation of royalty. But "the girls" had never seen a *morbid* Leona until an evening in late October 1986. It happened as the Miami advertising partners shared a table with the Helmsleys at Harry's Bar in the lobby of the Palace. It was common, Beber recalls, for Mrs. Helmsley to strike up conversation with strangers at bars in her various hotels. "The guests at the hotels adored it. They recognized her, and she would say, 'Hello, are you enjoying your drink? How is your meal?' And she would always be very, very charming." This time the Queen "turned to a couple sitting at the next table and she picked up the guy's hand."

"You want me to read your fortune?"

"Yes, Mrs. Helmsley," replied the delighted guest.

"I see a line here," the Queen announced, "and it ends!"

"Well, what does it mean?" the man's girlfriend interjected.

"Death!" Leona announced with an air of finality.

The answer was delivered so coldly, Beber recalls, "It gave me the chills, because you just don't do that to a human being. You don't frighten another person like that. And I'd never seen her do anything like that before."

Harry Helmsley seemed equally surprised and reproved her: "What are you telling him that for!" Beber says Leona then "sort of took it back and told the man: 'I'm only kidding!' " Despite the clarification, the man and his girlfriend remained visibly upset as they continued their meal.

More warning lights flashed in the minds of Beber and Silverstein at the end of the evening when Leona told them: "You know, girls, you haven't been coming up as much as you used to. I'd love to spend more time with you. I miss you and I want you to come to Dunnellen Hall."

"And then Mrs. Helmsley looked at Harry," Beber recalls, "and she said: 'You know, our lives are going to change. We're not going to have many friends anymore.'"

Beber was stunned by this declaration, delivered out of the blue. "I had no idea what she was talking about. She was drinking a lot of vodka that night and she was going all over the place. And she repeated, 'People aren't gonna want to spend time with us.' "

"Why do you say that?" Beber demanded. "Of course people will want to spend time with you."

The soothing words were lost on the Queen, who seemed convinced of her own strange prophesy.

"We're not gonna have any friends anymore," she repeated. "So we want to be close to you. It would just be us and we'll spend more time together."

Then, just as inexplicably, Leona swore, "From now on, we're not gonna have any more parties."

No more parties! No more "I'm Just Wild About Harry" bashes, or July Fourth blowouts for Leona! It was unthinkable. Silverstein could make no sense of Leona's revelations and thought to herself: "Something is happening and Mrs. Helmsley doesn't know how to stop it. She's preparing herself for something."

Beber says the Queen then burst out laughing and predicted once more: "Other people won't want to be with us." Leona then strolled over to the piano and scolded the pianist for his choice of music. The mood turned around "and Mrs. Helmsley and Harry began singing nice songs. But I couldn't get over the things she had just said."

Although the evening's events were alarming, for months Beber had been noticing other clues that something was amiss. By late summer, she says, "I realized that Mrs. Helmsley's firings and fights with other people were getting closer together. She was angry almost every day," without her usual cooling-off periods. "The pressure of whatever was bothering her had to be immense." Beber said she mentioned it to Silverstein. "I told Elaine, 'Something's wrong. This woman is cracking up. The woman is getting nuttier. It's very distressful.'" And if the trend continued, Beber predicted, "One day soon, it's going to be our turn, because there's less and less reason for her to explode at everyone else.'" Only a week after Leona's fortune-telling incident at Harry's Bar, Beber's prediction came true.

"I knew Mrs. Helmsley was going to fire us," Beber says,

"when she called my Miami office" and asked for the agency's entire portfolio of advertisements for the Helmsley hotels. "She wanted all the ads that were in progress and those that had been retired" over the past seven years. "So I knew something was up. You don't ask for that unless something's wrong." The Queen's voice was another dead giveaway. "Usually, she was very warm and enthusiastic on the phone; this time she was calm and subdued."

The next day, even before Beber had a chance to ship the ads, Leona phoned again.

"I want you to get here tomorrow morning," the Queen demanded in a peevish tone. "Be here first thing, and I want you to bring a whole new [ad] campaign with you."

Beber says she was tempted to laugh at the ridiculous order because "There's no way I could do a whole new campaign overnight." Instead of saying so, however, she replied, "I'll have to think about it." The next day, when Beber failed to appear, the Queen called again.

"I'd prefer you not work for me any longer," Leona said matter-of-factly. "You betrayed me." The Queen explained she had learned that Beber was preparing an ad campaign for rival hotelier Donald Trump. Indeed, Beber had agreed to advertise Trump's latest project, a high-rise condominium in West Palm Beach named Trump Plaza.

"But we're not doing Trump's hotels," Beber protested. "We're just doing his condo in Florida." Besides, Leona had introduced Beber to Trump in the first place and encouraged him to use the agency. "Hire them," Leona had told the young developer. "They're wonderful."

Recommending Beber was one thing. Watching her actually follow through and obtaining sideline business from Trump was a far different matter. "It was a question of control," Beber speculates. "It was okay for her to say it. But when we did it on our own, it upset her very much."

"I'd prefer not having you anymore," Leona repeated, deaf to Beber's logic.

"That's your privilege," Beber replied, unwilling to plead further.

"I felt I wanted it to be over at that point," Beber recalls. "She had been getting so crazy with so many people—I had watched her humiliate so many—that I just didn't want to be exposed to it anymore." Five days later, on Halloween, the agency was officially fired.

When the *Post* heard rumors, Beber confirmed them by evoking her catchy ad campaign: "We couldn't please Leona for more than seven years, could you?" The paper noted that the Queen had spent $17 million on advertising over the past three years, much of it on changing the name of the New York Harley to the Helmsley. Although fired, Beber was determined to retain her Palace office down the hall from Leona for the remaining six months of its commercial lease. She needed it to serve other clients. While important, the Helmsley empire accounted for only half the agency's New York business and less than 10 percent of its $65 million national billings. Unable to evict Beber, the Queen rankled at the sight of her longtime media adviser. "She saw me in the hall once when I was coming out of my office," Beber recalls, "and put her finger in her mouth and gagged. It was such childish, immature, foolish behavior that I felt sorry for her." Of greater concern was Leona's refusal to pay the ad agency's outstanding bill. "She owed us a million dollars," Beber says, for hotel ads the agency had already placed in newspapers and magazines across the country. Only after waging a vigorous legal battle did Beber collect, settling out of court for the entire amount plus interest.

Was it a shock to be treated so coldly after such long service to the Queen? Beyond the initial surprise, not really, says Beber. She had watched Leona banish her only surviving sister, Sandra, for a far flimsier reason just a short while earlier. It had happened when a string of Sandra's costume pearls broke as the Queen tried them on. "Only Sandra could get them strung like this!" the Queen fumed. "Now I have to restring them!" At that point, Beber says, Leona "started to have a hate on Sandra. She complained, 'Sandra's always hanging on. She's always coming here. I don't have the time for her or her costume jewelry.' She didn't want Sandra around at all. She was persona non grata. You couldn't even mention her name anymore." Nor was Elaine Silverstein stunned by Leona's sudden disaffection. "If she can throw away a sister or her grandchildren, why should she have any warmth or regard for someone she pays? Her value system is so distorted—'I'm Leona Helmsley and have it all and you don't'—that she has lost all ability to trust anyone to like her, to care about her, to love her, or to be concerned about her except under the most stringent rules. She's just like the Red Queen in *Alice in Wonderland*. She makes the rules, and if you don't live by her rules, then off with your head."

"Leona Helmsley Accused of Sales Tax Fraud." The *New York Times* article of November 6 reported that Leona had failed to pay sales taxes on at least $485,000 worth of jewelry purchased over the years from Van Cleef & Arpels. The story caused more titters than shock waves, however, because Leona was only a peripheral figure in a shopping scandal. The real target was Claude Arpels, elderly owner of the swank Fifth Avenue store, who had been indicted the year before in a state crackdown on jewelers who routinely winked at the sales tax. Attorney General Robert Abrams had already prosecuted two other exclusive jewelers, Cartier and Bulgari, for pretending to mail purchases to out-of-state addresses. The pretense freed customers from paying sales taxes because goods shipped for use across state lines were tax-free. In reality, however, buyers would simply walk out of the store with their new jewelry, and an empty box would be sent to the given address. The "empty box scam" was an outrage, Abrams told another newspaper, because it allowed the rich to evade taxes while "middle-class and poor people pay sales taxes on virtually all their purchases." In a motion to dismiss the indictment, Arpels' lawyer blew Leona's cover, mentioning that she was one of many customers who took advantage of the popular scam. And depositions in a related civil case revealed that Leona had actually testified under immunity before the state grand jury about ten Van Cleef & Arpels purchases she had made between 1980 and 1984. In September 1980, for instance, she bought a $375,000 diamond necklace and an empty box was sent to her Palm Beach penthouse. In December 1981 she carried away a $105,000 platinum-and-diamond clip and another empty box was sent to Florida. According to court records, for those two purchases alone, the scam saved Leona $38,662 in New York state sales tax. But Leona insisted she had no idea any hanky panky had taken place. Her lawyer, Steven M. Hayes, told the *Post*: "When she paid Van Cleef & Arpels, Leona Helmsley believed that the price included sales tax." Hayes pointed out that Leona and Harry had donated $33 million to New York Hospital only months before so the private hospital could complete ongoing construction of a residence tower for its patients and staff. With such proven generosity, "Why would she try to evade $38,000 in sales taxes?"

A former member of Leona's inside circle says he privately scoffed at the lawyer's reference to the hospital donation because the Helmsleys had not contributed their personal funds. Instead, he claims they had pledged monies that had accumulated in the Harry B. Helmsley Foundation, a charitable foundation established decades earlier as a tax shield for the tycoon's mammoth income. "There are federal requirements that so much has to be given away periodically and it can't revert to personal use. It was money that Leona could never hope to get her hands on." (Laurance Rockefeller, a member of the hospital's board of governors, had persuaded the Helmsleys to make the donation, the former aide said, "And Mrs. Helmsley did it because of the magnitude. She bragged about it. It catapulted her and Harry to the top ranks of American benefactors. She liked that; she liked the superlatives: being the biggest, the richest and the best." Appropriately, the 519-unit apartment building at East Seventieth Street was named the Helmsley Medical Tower. Later, Leona peered up at the sign on the completed building and demanded a replacement. "She was furious," the aide says, "because the letters weren't big enough: 'I give $33 million, and that's the size sign they're going to give me!'")

No legal action was taken against Leona or any other beneficiaries of the empty-box scam. But the Queen detested the press coverage, which included the *Village Voice* headline: "Leona Helmsley Didn't Pay Sales Tax, Why Should You?" Her former aide recalls, "She thought it was totally unfair because she was pointed out and a lot of other people weren't mentioned." Leona was learning the down side of having such a toplofty profile. "Notoriety comes with the territory, no matter what I'm doing," Leona told one columnist when asked about the jewelry snafu. The media quickly shifted their focus to meatier diversions, however, including a vast city corruption scandal and a tangled love affair between former beauty queen Bess Myerson and a reportedly mob-connected sewer contractor.

But at the New York *Post* newsroom at 210 South Street, in a six-story stucco building overlooking the East River, the empty-box scam loomed large. The *Post* reporter who had been tipped off the previous December about strange doings at the Helmsleys' Greenwich estate read the clippings with special interest. Frustrated by uncooperative sources, he had dropped his Dunnellen Hall research nine months earlier, in February, and stashed his notes in a linen closet at home. Now, with Leona identified as a major league sales-tax scofflaw, the Byzantine tax-evasion tale that tipster "Bill" had outlined seemed even more plausible. After getting permission from his editors to revive the probe and to pursue it full time, the reporter returned to his original notes. With help from Bill, he had obtained a Helmsley Enterprises telephone directory, which became a valuable blueprint of the $5 billion Helmsley empire. Of greatest interest was the first page of Helmsley-Spear Inc., its largest subsidiary, which listed fifteen senior vice presidents. The booklet also identified scores of Helmsley-managed buildings, complete with the names and office telephone numbers of their respective managers. Helmsley subsidiaries and their officers were also enumerated, as were the names and managers of six Manhattan hotels and seventeen nationwide Harley hotels. Within a few days, the reporter had made contact with a dozen key executives, few of whom were willing to stay on the line for more than five seconds. It was the same problem that had stymied the reporter earlier in the year. All were terrified to discuss anything remotely concerning Leona Helmsley. And if they were familiar with the Greenwich renovation, they certainly weren't saying so. Several agreed, however, to provide home phone numbers of former executives who might be more willing to cooperate. And indeed, it was the departed honchos—many of them Leona's fresh kills—who were willing to talk. All they asked was to be guaranteed anonymity. Some jumped at the chance to recount their particular horror story. For hours on end, they described to the reporter how Leona had maneuvered them into a corner, or pulled the rug from underneath them. Time had not healed their wounds. Even those who had been fired two years earlier nursed an exquisite hatred. Reviling the Queen was catharsis. "I'm glad you called," said one Helmsley expatriate. "It kind of helps me get it all off my chest."

A breakthrough came when the reporter obtained a fascinating stack of invoices. It was a collection of bills—two inches thick and totaling almost $250,000—from a half-dozen contractors who had worked on the pool enclosure and other mansion improvements. Curiously, instead of being sent directly to Harry and Leona, the bills had been addressed to Helmsley-Spear, the Graybar Building, and the Helmsley Building for payment. The reporter immediately recalled Bill's tip that the Helmsleys' mansion expenses had been "buried" in at least four buildings.

The pile of documents also included Helmsley-Spear purchase orders. By comparing them to the invoices, the reporter could tell that the company purchase orders were used to authorize payment to contractors performing the Dunnellen Hall renovation. Indeed, the suspicious purchase orders had to be examples of the "dummied up" documents Bill had mentioned—the paperwork needed to shift the mansion expenses over to Harry's office buildings. And lo and behold, Harry's and Leona's handwritten initials ("H.B.H." and "L.M.H.") blanketed the dummy documents.

Among the documents was a letter from Audio Sound Productions Inc. of Hempstead, New York, dated Jan. 4, 1985. On its own letterhead, the company estimated how much it would cost to install a sophisticated stereo system "for the Dunnellen Hall breakfast room, pool and dance deck." But a photocopy of the document appeared to have been altered, perhaps with correction fluid, to blot out any reference to Dunnellen Hall. Typed in its place was a new caption: "Security/Audio System for 230 Park Avenue," the Helmsley Building. Leona's handwritten initials and notation "OK" filled the right-hand margin of the doctored copy. In effect, Leona's ballroom sound system had been transformed by a few drops of white-out into an office burglar alarm. Also among the documents was a check dated April 3, 1985, drawn on 230 Park Avenue and payable to Audio Sound, apparently as the deposit for the home stereo. Without delay, the reporter phoned the stereo company. Audio Sound president David Rosen answered.

"I'm interested in doing a story about the stereo system you installed at the Helmsley place in Greenwich," the reporter said. "Everybody's talking about it. It must be one helluva system."

"It's an outrageous system," Rosen confirmed, adding that it was perhaps his biggest project ever and had taken over two years to install. He said he had buried three thousand feet of speaker wire in underground pipes throughout different areas of the back lawn. "Speakers are planted in the ground. Not that you have to water them or anything like that," he quipped. "They have a canopy over them. They're sort of in the flower bed. And she goes out there with a wireless remote control and she can play anything she wants as far from the stereo as she wants. She can adjust the volume. She can turn on the tuner. She can change stations. She can turn on the tape deck if she wants to. From anywhere—the pool, the gazebo, the barbecue area, the south patio, the fountain. It's nice."

The reporter was feeling good about the interview. Rosen,

by confirming that his company had installed the stereo, had helped authenticate the invoice obtained by the *Post*. The reporter then asked the obvious follow-up question.

"Have you done any work at her office buildings?"

"We haven't yet," Rosen replied, "but there's talk about that."

Bingo! The document initialed by Leona, which identified the Audio Sound equipment as a Helmsley building security system, had truly earned its place in the dummy pile. For the first time, a verified scent of skulduggery was in the air.

Audio Sound, perhaps curious about the line of questioning, notified Leona right away. "Mrs. Helmsley was at the mansion," a former aide recalls, "and got a call from the stereo people. They told her the *Post* had called and asked a lot of questions." Although Leona pretended to shrug off the matter, the aide could sense she was worried. "We knew something was going to happen."

The reporter analyzed invoices from other mansion contractors, which seemed to have been dummied up in similar fashion. An authentic $513.50 invoice from Omni Service Corp., for example, clearly stated that air conditioning work was performed in "bedroom #11" at "Helmsley Residence, Conn." Yet a Helmsley-Spear work approval form from the dummy pile falsely identified the work site as "room #11" at "230 Park Ave./ The Helmsley Building." Among other documents in the dummy pile were a dozen invoices on the letterhead of LaStrada General Contracting Corp., the lead contractor for the Dunnellen Hall pool enclosure. Each invoice listed the work site as "Graybar Building/420 Lexington Ave." Curiously, they were all stamped "passed for payment" on August 15, 1984. The reporter added the dozen bills up and noticed that they came to exactly $50,000. The suspiciously round number indicated that the invoices were indeed dummies, created at one sitting to satisfy some different, larger debt. Highly technical office-building repairs were listed on the suspect invoices, such as: "Southeast Stairwell (17th, 18th and 19th Floors) Furnish and install new face brick on column in shaft due to installation of anchors for chilled water lines—$6,600." No doubt someone with construction experience had helped create the bogus descriptions. The reporter phoned the construction firm to see if it had actually worked at the Graybar Building, as the invoices said it did. LaStrada president Peter Guglielmi expressed surprise at the question.

"I don't think we did any work for their [Helmsleys'] office buildings" except for possible minor "patchwork."

Another Bingo! His answer left little doubt in the reporter's mind that the contractors' invoices were being altered within the Helmsley organization itself, without participation by the contractors.

Although the clues were pouring in, the mansion scam was still shrouded in mystery. Key questions remained. Who was the mastermind of the dummy-invoice procedures? Did Harry and Leona know they were initialing bogus invoices for payment? Who concocted the elaborate descriptions of office building repairs that appeared on the sham bills? Although this had the markings of a tax-evasion scam, was it? Having no access to IRS records, the *Post* had no way of knowing whether Helmsley-Spear, the Graybar Building, and the Helmsley Building actually reported their bogus expenses as deductions on year-end tax returns.

Another big worry: the invoices—both the real ones and the dummies—were mere photocopies. Although the reporter trusted his sources, he was unable to guarantee that they were faithful copies of actual financial records. Unless they could be authenticated, there was no way the *Post's* lawyers would allow them to be mentioned in any news article.

Almost at his wit's end, the reporter stumbled across a forgotten name in his notes of the previous year. Someone had mentioned that a Helmsley-Spear construction chief named John Struck had helped Harry and Leona supervise the army of mansion contractors and subcontractors. The source had voiced suspicion that Struck might have played a hand in creating the dummy Helmsley-Spear invoices. If memory served the reporter right, Struck had answered directly to Mrs. Helmsley. On November 13, the reporter gathered a pile of phone books. No "John Struck" was listed in any of them, so he began to call every "Struck" in the metropolitan area. Manhattan was a washout, but a woman in one of the other directories recognized the name.

"He's right here," she said. "Hold the phone."

"Hello?"

"Mr. Struck?"

"Yes."

"I'm from the New York *Post* and we're working on a very interesting story about the Helmsley mansion in Connecticut. We've got a lot of fake invoices—expenses for the mansion that were charged off to the Graybar Building and the Helmsley Building. And one of my sources says that *you're responsible!*"

Struck immediately became defensive.

"The cookup was not my cookup," he volunteered, saying that while he personally dreamed up descriptions of office building repairs that apparently wound up on the bogus invoices, "I was not the one who made the decision." During his eighteen months as construction manager for the Dunnellen Hall job, Struck said he routinely took detailed orders from Frank Turco and Joe Licari.

"I was told, 'Do this, John. Mr. and Mrs. Helmsley want it done this way.' Licari was the one who told everyone what property we would bill. I had a job to do and if I didn't do it I would be fired. At least that's the feeling I would get. She [Mrs. Helmsley] is a tough lady to deal with."

Asked if the Helmsleys ever spoke to him directly about the scam, Struck said, "I submitted them [the fake work descriptions] to Turco and Licari," adding that he believed "Mr. and Mrs. Helmsley would pass them down through the system."

"I know for a fact," Struck continued, "that Turco and Licari never did a thing unless they got the instruction or permission from the Helmsleys. I had to write a report and tell them [the Helmsleys] every nickel of what was spent on the house, and that's what they had to approve." Altogether, Struck estimated the fraudulent payments "probably" exceeded $1 million. Struck said accountants at Helmsley-Spear and various Helmsley office buildings refused to cut checks to mansion contractors until a fake work description was in hand. "I made it sound like a construction bill. You know, it didn't sound like an English major was writing the damned bill. I was to say which building, for how much, and for what purpose." When Struck once expressed curiosity about the strange system, he said Turco and Licari assured him it was merely an accounting procedure and that the Helmsleys would reimburse the buildings "at the end of the year" for funds paid through fictitious billings. Despite his willingness to play along, Struck said Leona fired him in December 1985 when his underlings failed to refinish several mansion doors to her satisfaction.

When the *Post* reporter confronted Licari with Struck's allegations, Helmsley's former top financial aide denied that he ever supervised Struck or had any knowledge of the billing scam.

"He [Struck] is confusing me with someone else," said

Licari, who had joined another real estate firm after being axed by Leona six months earlier. "I'm not going to be the scapegoat for John Struck. I never received any instructions from the Helmsleys to re-create a bill or falsify a bill." The *Post* was unable to reach Turco for comment on Struck's account. But Licari tried to shift suspicion his way. "Turco may have given [Struck] instructions. He was the personal representative of Mrs. Helmsley. I know he was in charge of Dunnellen Hall."

Thanks to Struck's account, the *Post* now knew for certain who concocted the elaborate descriptions of office building repairs. It had also learned the names of the likely chieftains behind the scam and had a fair understanding of how it worked. But the *Post* still needed to authenticate its mound of invoices.

"Mr. Licari," the reporter said. "How about taking a look at these invoices?"

"I don't want to get involved," he answered.

The same day the *Post* made contact with Struck, the curse of the Rosenthal family hit again. Sandra, Leona's older sister, was hospitalized in Atlanta after suffering a massive heart attack. Leona and Harry had rented a house in the Caribbean for the winter, a relative recalls, and couldn't be reached. Luckily, Alvin Rosenthal was located in Massachusetts.

"She's not going to survive," the relative told Sandra's baby brother. "It could be just a couple of days. The doctor says her heart is not reparable—all the muscles were destroyed."

"Yeah, I see," Alvin replied, seemingly unaffected by the news. The relative asked him to contact Leona right away. Surprisingly, neither Alvin nor Leona made any effort to call their stricken sister as she lay on her deathbed. For a full two weeks, Sandra clung on, conscious of her surroundings. And still no phone calls. It was unbelievably callous, the relative recalls. "This is your sister and she's dying, and they made absolutely zero contact." Rather than acknowledge the pain of being ignored, Sandra "just didn't mention them. Leona's name didn't come up once, and neither did Alvin's. It's almost like she didn't want to know they didn't care." Even after she returned to New York on November 29, Leona neglected to inquire. The next day, November 30, Sandra died.

The Queen did take notice, however, that the *Post* was continuing to interview contractors and Helmsley executives. The lawyer who had represented her in the Van Cleef & Arpels sales tax affair, Steven Hayes, sprang into action. The young attorney was a partner at Parcher, Arisohn & Hayes, a Manhattan firm known for handling the business affairs of celebrity clients such as Bruce Springsteen, Billy Joel and the Rolling Stones. The firm also took on criminal matters. On the morning of December 1, Hayes invited the reporter to drop by his Fifth Avenue office. And he specifically asked him to bring along copies of the Helmsley-Spear invoices, which he knew the *Post* had obtained.

"Forget about it!" snapped Neal M. Goldman, the *Post's* lawyer, when the reporter informed him of Hayes's invitation. "There's no way I'm going to let you go to Hayes's office. He'll sit you down at a big table and every lawyer in his firm will gang up on you." Instead, Goldman advised the reporter, "Tell them to come see you at *my* office." Hayes agreed to send two members of his law firm to Goldman's office later that afternoon.

Post metropolitan editor Al Ellenberg realized the meeting would be an important one. For weeks, ever since John Struck recounted his mansion tale, Ellenberg had been itching to drop a front-page bomb on Harry and Leona. The only thing that held him back was worry about the authenticity of the Helmsley invoices. "This is our big chance," he told the reporter, and proceeded to outline a game plan.

"Don't meet with these lawyers till after four o'clock. When they show up, tell them everything's set: 'The story's already written and we're going to press in one hour. Here's the documents; take a look. What's your explanation?' " By putting deadline pressure on the lawyers, Ellenberg hoped he could force them into providing a quick answer. Otherwise, they might take copies of the invoices with them and spend weeks or months preparing a response.

The meeting in Goldman's office began as scheduled. Two Helmsley lawyers, who asked that they not be identified by the *Post*, took their seats opposite Goldman and the reporter at a giant conference table.

"May we examine the documents?" the more talkative lawyer asked straightaway. He and his partner then divided the workload and literally speed-read the papers. Within five minutes, their task was completed.

"We're familiar with these documents," the Helmsley lawyer announced. "We've seen them before."

Goldman and the reporter glanced quickly at one another, stunned by the admission. Bingo, *Bingo*, BINGO! By admitting familiarity with the invoices the Helmsley lawyer had authenticated them.

"After talking with knowledgeable sources," the lawyer continued, "it's our belief that someone is stealing from the [Helmsley] company."

"Who's stealing from the company?" asked the reporter, while the subject was still fresh.

After conferring with his partner, the lawyer replied that it would be premature to speculate. In fact, he advised that the *Post* hold off on its story until a fuller explanation could be obtained

"Sorry," the reporter said, "but we've already interviewed everybody. We're running it tomorrow. I've only got an hour to update the story, and we'd really like to include your explanation."

"Are you serious, or are you buffaloing us?" the lawyer demanded.

"It's not up to me. My editor's ready to go."

Rather than proceed too precipitately, the lawyers asked if they could use a phone in the next room. They wanted to confer privately with Howard Rubenstein, the Helmsleys' public relations adviser. (Ironically, Rubenstein also handled p.r. for the *Post.*) When they walked off, the reporter phoned Ellenberg at the city desk.

"Al, you're not gonna believe it! They gave it to us on a platter! They say they've seen the documents before and it's a ripoff. Somebody's stealing from the company."

"Great! Fucking terrific! Where's your story?" Ellenberg asked, aware that the reporter had actually written an exposé for the next day's paper just in case the lawyers were helpful enough to authenticate the documents.

"My [computer] directory is PR-7. The slug is 'Helmsley.' "

"Okay," said Ellenberg. "We're going tomorrow no matter what! Get the rest of the story and phone in your notes as soon as you're through with the lawyers....Un-fucking believable!"

A few minutes later, after conferring with Rubenstein, the two attorneys returned. Immediately, they changed their story. It wasn't a matter of theft after all. They acknowledged that the invoices were fabricated and that the Helmsleys' initials were real. "Let's assume they're not forged," the talkative lawyer said. But the Helmsleys didn't know what they were signing, he explained. "There is no way Leona or Harry Helmsley knew that false invoices were created or paid, and insofar as their initials appear, it is clear that these invoices were presented to them as routine invoices and they were initialed as routine invoices along with many thousands of papers put before them every day."

"Then who fabricated the invoices in the first place?" the reporter asked. "And what was the motive?"

The lawyers contended that the Helmsleys had asked key employees to find a way to hide their expenditures on the twenty-eight-room mansion. The purpose was perfectly pure and legal: to protect the billionaire couple's privacy. "The Helmsleys are extremely private people, especially so with what she spent at her home," the talkative lawyer said. He explained that employees sometimes circulated memos concerning Leona's private affairs, including her art work and other home purchases, "and it offended her." To thwart prying eyes, he said, "There were discussions with her staff and Mr. Helmsley's staff and a plan was effectuated by employees of the company whereby expenses for Dunnellen Hall were charged to or paid by the Helmsley wholly owned entities." He said that senior aides independently devised the complicated scheme of false invoices, without telling the Helmsleys. Now that the scheme was on the verge of being publicized, one thing was certain. The lawyers said Helmsley had promised he "personally will pay back" his subsidiaries or buildings all monies they had advanced for his personal expenses under the scheme.

Beyond a doubt, the *Post* now had basis to proceed. Goldman followed the Helmsley lawyers out the door and hopped the first cab in sight. It was 5 P.M., an hour and a half from *Post* deadline for the December 2 "one-star," the next day's first edition. Even as the reporter continued to feed his notes by phone to a colleague on the *Post* rewrite bank, Goldman reached the city desk. He made a beeline for Ellenberg, whose sneakers and faded jeans blended perfectly with a frolicsome newsroom sometimes described as "the biggest sandbox in New York." After briefing Ellenberg, the lawyer sat down at a computer terminal and gave his green light to the updated exposé. By 6:30, Ellenberg had trimmed the story and passed it along to the copy desk, which would complete final editing and give it a headline. At 10:30 P.M., the first 700,000 copies were loaded into a fleet of bright yellow *Post* delivery trucks and scattered to the four winds.

Leona's smiling face filled the entire upper-right hand quadrant of the front page. Alongside in three tiers of bold tabloid type was the headline: "Helmsley Scam Bared." The lead paragraph announced: "Millions of dollars in renovation bills for Harry Helmsley's Connecticut mansion were falsified as business expenses and charged to his Manhattan office buildings, a Post investigation has found." It disclosed that the Post had obtained stacks of bogus invoices initialed by the Helmsleys. The exposé quoted one source, who said fake invoices were used to bill "almost all work on the mansion to various office buildings in the company"—particularly the Graybar Building at 420 Lexington Avenue and the Helmsley Building at 230 Park Avenue. "The source said top employees initiated the scam on direct orders of the Helmsleys, in the belief that 'the Internal Revenue Service, with their stupidity, would never pick this up.'" The article quoted John Struck at length, including his allegations that Frank Turco and Joe Licari had ordered him to cook up descriptions of work that was never actually performed in the office buildings. It quoted mansion contractors such as Audio Sound and LaStrada General Contracting Corp., who denied ever having worked on the Helmsley commercial properties that paid their bills. And it aired explanations by the Helmsley lawyers that Harry and Leona had unwittingly signed bogus invoices prepared for privacy's sake by their senior aides.

By midmorning of December 2, an avalanche of phone calls swamped the city desk switchboard. Emboldened by the smell of blood, former and current Helmsley employees, contractors and vendors poured out of the woodwork, giving the reporter new tales of greed and maltreatment.

Prosecutors from every jurisdiction phoned the reporter to announce they had launched preliminary criminal probes of the mansion scam as a result of the three-page Post exposé.

That same afternoon, a handful of close relatives paid their final respects as Sandra was lowered into her resting place in a New Jersey cemetery. Neither Leona nor Alvin attended the service.

Sixteen

Four giant words, standing practically on stilts, swallowed the top half of the Post front page on December 3. "Triple Trouble Hits Helmsleys." The article announced that the IRS, state attorney general Robert Abrams, and U.S. attorney Rudolph

Giuliani of New York's Southern District had assigned staff to weigh the newspaper's allegations. Giuliani's instant involvement was of particular interest to the *Post* editors because he, like Helmsley, was a living legend in his profession. Only a month earlier, the 42-year-old federal prosecutor had dispatched three of the city's five Mafia bosses to prison. The *Post* article also reported Harry Helmsley's terse denial: "Mrs. Helmsley and I have done nothing wrong, and there will be no further comment."

A companion *Post* article, headlined "Billion dollar couple 'stiffs' workers," disclosed that fake invoices were just one tool the Helmsleys used to slash their mansion renovation costs. Basing its information largely on the torrent of phone calls from the previous day, the article cited new allegations that the couple forced many contractors to work free of charge or simply refused to pay their bills. John Fahey, a Stamford, Connecticut, landscaper, complained that he had to hire a lawyer to collect his fee for mansion improvements performed two years earlier. "They owed me $6,700, and I got only about half. I'd work for the bag ladies before I'd work for someone like that again," Fahey growled. Peter Guglielmi, president of LaStrada General Contracting Corp., said he had been waiting more than a year to collect a final $70,000 payment for his work on the mansion. "We worked night and day to finish the job and we did," said Guglielmi. "And after they didn't need us anymore, they said, 'To hell with these people. We don't need them.' " The companion article also quoted Jay Nichtberger, the painting contractor. "She wanted to get work for nothing," he said, alleging that he had kept two painters at the mansion for a year, only to be told by Mrs. Helmsley that she would not pay his $88,000 fee. When Nichtberger continued to press for payment, he said Leona told him: "You cannot get paid because I consider it a commission for being able to work for the Helmsley organization." He said he was forced to release Mrs. Helmsley from the debt so he could collect an additional $800,000 "that she owed us for work at the Helmsley properties. When someone owes you $800,000" he said, "you're willing to lose $88,000." In addition, the piece alleged that the Helmsleys had economized by paying their personal mansion staff from checks drawn on their various hotels. Thomas Dupree, a former mansion security guard, said he had been paid $320 a week for eighteen months "on checks from the Harley hotel chain and the Park Lane Hotel...I was even in the Hotel Association pension plan,"

Dupree added. "They put me on it. That came with the job." Dupree said seven other security guards, as well as maids, cooks and other mansion staffers, were also confused to find themselves on hotel payrolls.

The *Post*'s splashy second-day coverage threw gasoline onto the fire, eliciting a new wave of callers. A particularly interesting one came about 11 A.M. "They're cleaning house at the Lincoln Building," whispered the tipster, who described himself as a temporary Helmsley-Spear employee hired to shred company documents. "The records are on the tenth and fifteenth floors. What they're doing is taking everything out and shredding it, getting rid of it as fast as possible so you won't have a chance to know what's going on. And they're pulling stuff out like crazy. For all kinds of buildings: the Graybar Building and Park Avenue."

The caller explained that all hell had broken loose the day before, when the *Post* exposé appeared. "All of a sudden everything's rearranged totally. Everybody went haywire. They had people pulling out stuff that wasn't supposed to be pulled out. They had things to be shredded that weren't supposed to be shredded; they never thought about it before. All of a sudden, they're covering up something. And I don't know what it is. But once I read the *Post* article, I said, 'God! I work here!' "

"Where on the tenth and fifteenth floors?" the reporter asked. "Go to Room 1551 and you'll see a shredder on the left side. You'll see a lot of file boxes. And the records are in 1032. It's a dirty and nasty office." The informant then hung up.

Another newsman sped to the office building to check out the anonymous report. He visited room 1551, whose front door was marked with a Helmsley-Spear nameplate, and saw stacks of empty trays, stuffed garbage bags and other evidence of recent shredding. The documents included financial statements dated as recently as the previous week.

When the *Post* phoned the office of attorney general Abrams for comment, his investigators were astounded by the shredding allegations. John Ryan, an assistant attorney general, and four other agents hotfooted to the skyscraper and sealed the two rooms with "evidence tape" to prevent further destruction of records. Ryan told the *Post* he had also limited access to the two floors and had asked Helmsley's lawyers for permission "to examine the premises to see if documents were shredded, if so which, and to see which remain." Permission was denied, he said, but the lawyers allowed his agents to seal the doors.

Meanwhile, callers continued to swamp the *Post* switchboard. "Leona is absolutely crazed by this scandal," an anonymous Palace executive told the reporter. "She's been caught and she doesn't want to face the fire. She's leaving tonight for Barbados."

"Why Barbados?" the reporter asked.

"I don't know," the executive replied, and hung up.

In a front page article the next morning, Thursday, December 4, the *Post* disclosed that the state attorney general's office had "sealed off document-shredding rooms at Harry Helmsley's corporate headquarters in midtown Manhattan." It quoted Steven Hayes, the Helmsley lawyer, who "adamantly" denied that the Helmsleys "ordered any shredding of any documents. They did not even know there was a shredder in the building."

Another caller was the anonymous shredder, who was persuaded to visit the *Post* newsroom. At 1 A.M., a young man wearing jeans, sneakers and a fedora came in and identified himself as Larry Early, 30, a Chicago native who had moved to New York in October. He said he had gone to work just three weeks earlier at Harry Helmsley's central accounting department on the fifty-second floor of the Lincoln Building. His job was to shred financial documents in room 1551 and he got his orders from two accounting managers. His first two weeks were slow, he said. But on Tuesday, he was bombarded with orders to destroy canceled checks, invoices and computer printouts. Within twenty-four hours, he estimated he had shredded enough material to fill a hundred thirty-gallon plastic bags—and forty larger bags. "These larger bags must have been a hundred gallons. They were huge. The amount of work went up at least four times." In frustration with the impossible workload, as well as suspicion that he "was covering shit up," he said he had quit his job around noon the day before, right after tipping off the *Post*.

Early's tale and photograph appeared the next morning in an article headlined: "I was the Helmsley shredder." For four days in a row, the Helmsley mansion scam had made the front page of the *Post*. What had begun as a tedious investigative piece had blossomed into a fast-breaking news story. Galvanized by Early's allegations, attorney general Robert Abrams ordered his agents to replace the evidence tape with padlocks to ensure that no more documents were destroyed. The following week, Abrams empaneled a state grand jury to weigh the *Post* allegations and issued the first of many subpoenas for Helmsley business records. Simultaneously, U.S. attorney Rudolph Giuliani whipped his federal probe into high gear by issuing subpoenas to numerous current and past Helmsley employees. "Giuliani has notified lots of people and they are all looking for lawyers," a former Helmsley aide told the *Post* on December 8.

As storm clouds continued to gather, where were Harry and Leona? In a December 11 article headlined "Party-Poopers!" the *Post* noted they had skipped two important soirées. Two nights earlier, four hundred Helmsley-Spear employees showed up for the annual Christmas party on the twenty-seventh floor of the Lincoln Building. But the Helmsleys, who personally hosted the event each year, were nowhere to be found. "It's the first time I can remember," one senior manager told the paper, "when they weren't there. It's a company tradition." The following evening, sixteen hundred guests flooded the observation deck of the Empire State Building to celebrate the twenty-fifth anniversary of Helmsley's and Lawrence Wien's syndicated purchase of the landmark skyscraper. Again, as champagne flowed, guests searched in vain for their would-be hosts.

A *Post* news team solved the mystery of the missing Helmsleys after scouring the island of Barbados for over a week. Harry and Leona had rented Half Moon House, a fifteen-room villa on the eighth fairway of the Sandy Lane Golf and Beach Club. They had signed a four-month lease in November, before the scandal broke, and were paying $8,000 per week to enjoy a climate agreeably warmer than their usual wintering nest in Palm Beach. Using a 300-millimeter telephoto lens, *Post* lensman Marc Vodofsky discreetly photographed them as they strolled in swimsuits along the exclusive Sandy Lane beach. Three of the photos, with Leona looking less than her Scitex best, were plastered on page one and two inside pages of the December 15 editions, in an article headlined "Life's A Beach!" It reported that the Helmsleys were "immersing themselves here in paradise" while their lawyers and accountants grappled with prosecutors up north. A separate article disclosed that Abrams, after being approached by informants, had widened his investigation to include allegations that the Helmsleys had routinely falsified expenses for many other "hotels and other businesses" not mentioned in the first *Post* revelations.

The spate of *Post* articles greatly angered the Queen, according to a former manager of the Park Lane. When the first article broke on December 2, he recalls, she ordered a security man to make sure every copy of the paper was removed from the hotel's lobby newsstand. "She told him to tell the newsstand to get it out of there and never have it again!" (Curiously, she allowed sales of the paper to continue at the Helmsley Palace.) In mid-December, the Park Lane manager says she phoned him to correct an oversight. "We used to deliver the *Post* with our breakfast room service," the ex-manager explains, "but in the third week of December she ordered us to substitute *Newsday*. She wasn't going to help Rupert Murdoch at all," referring to the Australian-born owner of the *Post*. As real retaliation against Murdoch, however, Leona yanked her hotel ads from *New York* magazine, the media mogul's glitzy handbook for the city's brie-and-quiche set. Beber and Silverstein might be gone, but the Queen owned their ads and continued to run them every week in the *Times*, airline magazines and other upscale publications. By late December, *New York* editor Edward Kosner realized that Leona had blackballed his publication. "Suddenly," he recalls, "the ads were canceled. It was a big piece of business—several hundred thousand dollars a year. It became clear that the ads were being pulled to punish the Murdoch company. Their decision showed how deeply they were wounded by the *Post*—that trouble was coming." By the end of the year, Leona hired a small new Manhattan ad agency, Taylor-Gordon, Aarons & Co., which stuck to many of Beber's previous design concepts while drawing up plans for an entirely new campaign.

Soon afterward, on January 6, 1987, the *Post* reported that the Helmsleys had returned from sunny Barbados but remained in virtual seclusion at their Park Lane penthouse. It also disclosed that at least three dozen of Harry's present and former employees had been subpoenaed to testify before a grand jury empaneled by U.S. attorney Giuliani. On January 8, the *Post* revealed that a dozen federal and state investigators had joined hands in an "unprecedented" team probe of the Helmsley mansion scam, converting the padlocked shredding and document-storage rooms at Helmsley headquarters into their command post. By working together literally in the belly of the beast, the feds and state agents could pass documents back and forth with utmost ease. "We don't want to miss one piece of evidence," a high-level state investigator told the paper. "One agency could stumble across a piece of information useless to it but of critical importance to another law enforcement agency." For example, he explained, "the federal government has a statute of mail fraud and wire fraud, whereas the state has crimes of falsifying business records that don't have exact analogies in the federal code."

As the Helmsleys shuttled back and forth between Barbados and Manhattan, the *Post* kept the Helmsley story on its front burner. On January 27, it reported that Abrams and Giuliani were probing multimillion-dollar fraud allegations against Deco. The article noted that Leona's son, Jay Panzirer, had run the Florida-based purchasing firm. "Prosecutors are probing allegations that Mrs. Helmsley and Panzirer forced the hotels and office buildings to buy from Deco at highly inflated prices."

The same day, Harry checked out of New York Hospital after a series of operations to trim back his droopy eyelids. With stitches out and vision improved, he and Leona then quietly returned to their rented Barbadian villa. Aside from warmer weather, Harry's health was surely one reason the Helmsleys had planned well ahead for a long winter stay on the island. Several former aides had noticed slight problems with his memory and his gait late the previous year, which they speculated might have been caused by a minor stoke. Joe Catania, Leona's longtime interior designer, recalls that Harry "would sometimes walk funny, dragging a foot." When Catania mentioned this observation once to Leona, he said she brushed it aside, saying, "I think it's because of his eye." And several times that year, he recalls, "I talked to Mrs. Helmsley about his memory. It seemed to be slipping." Joyce Beber recalls that Leona once mentioned "that Harry was shuffling his feet," and lamented the recent development. "She said, 'Oh, the party will be over. He's getting old.' " Beber added that Jeff Lerigo, Harry's closest hotel adviser, had noted slight memory lapses in the fall of 1986. "He said Harry would see him for the third or fourth time in one day and start a conversation over again—he had forgotten their earlier conversation." Beber never noticed any problem, however, "maybe because I usually dealt with him on one specific subject at a time and he could stay alert with it."

Back home, the scandal grew inexorably. The *Post* disclosed on February 19 that Giuliani had subpoenaed financial records of Garden Bay Manor, Harry's 759-unit apartment complex in Queens. The article quoted an anonymous *Post* source who alleged that Harry and Leona paid contractors for their mansion renovation by routing "over a million dollars" worth of phony invoices through Garden Bay Manor and Helmsley's Parkchester housing complex in the Bronx. The source said many of the fake bills were from LaStrada General Contracting Corp., the general contractor for the Dunnellen Hall pool enclosure. Peter Guglielmi, president of LaStrada, responded by pointing the finger at Harry and Leona. He repeated his earlier contention that they altered his invoices for the mansion work after he made them out. "With these people [the Helmsleys], anything's possible."

Finally, after almost three months in seclusion, Leona and Harry returned to work on February 24. Despite his legal troubles, Helmsley flashed a smile as he entered his office on the fifty-third floor of the Lincoln Building. "People were waiting with signs and balloons and applauded him as he walked in," his spokesman, Howard Rubenstein, told the *Post*. Rubenstein said the 77-year-old tycoon told his staff: "I'm here to stay for a long while," and immediately sat down to negotiate over $100 million in real estate deals. Leona, meanwhile, reclaimed command of her nationwide string of twenty-three hotels and her pink office on the fifth floor of the Palace. "There was a big bouquet of roses and a lot of letters waiting for her," Rubenstein said. He denied that the Helmsleys' long absence was due to the tax investigations. Instead, Rubenstein insisted that Harry was kept away from work by five operations on his swollen eyelids and that Leona insisted "on being at his side."

As the *Post* pressed on with its investigative series, the Helmsleys struck back on March 16 with a press release denouncing the coverage. It was the couple's first public statement since the scandal broke three and a half months earlier. "We are totally innocent of any improper actions," they insisted, and alleged that "the recurring media stories amount to unfair gross character assassination....to be viciously smeared and demeaned personally in the press and tried by innuendo violates the basic American principle of the presumption of innocence. We have done nothing wrong. We have violated no laws, and have trust in the public and confidence in its ability to keep an open mind, despite what's said in the press. We have been charitable, giving well over $33 million to one hospital alone last year. We are productive, employ at least 50,000 people, and contribute to our city, state and nation's economic well-being," the statement concluded.

Surprisingly, New York's other major daily newspapers virtually ignored the mansion scandal, even as Abrams and Giuliani paraded scores of Helmsley employees and contractors before state and federal grand juries. Perhaps they felt uncomfortable following the lead of a Rupert Murdoch tabloid whose taste level was often called into question. Millions of New Yorkers were familiar with the *Post*'s racy headlines, including the most infamous of all: "Headless Body Found in Topless Bar." Yet as frivolous and fun-loving as the tabloid might be, the *Post* routinely outpaced its more serious competitors in the arena of local news coverage. As often as not, a member of its lean news staff was the first to arrive at a fire or shooting, or to notice governmental hanky-panky. For whatever reason, the *Daily News* and *New York Newsday* contented themselves with summarizing the latest *Post* revelations in the Helmsley scandal but failed to launch independent inquiries of their own. The *New York Times* ran only one news brief about the scandal during the entire calendar year of 1987. And the *Wall Street Journal*, which had so avidly covered Harry Helmsley's rise to the pinnacle of New York real estate, reported absolutely nothing in 1987 about the two criminal investigations or their potential impact on Harry's $5 billion empire.

Although back at the Palace and working, the Queen was keeping a somewhat lower profile. Her grand entrances tapered off a bit, recalls a Madison Room waiter. "She used to get out of her limo in the garage, go to the sidewalk, and walk in under the marquee. She liked to be seen. She'd walk slowly to get attention. 'Here comes the Queen!' Then she stopped." Instead, she would enter quietly through the garage door. Her dining habits, it was noticed, also changed. Upon entering the Le Trianon dining room, many a guest over the years had looked straight ahead into the adjoining Hunt Room and seen Leona dining at table No. 7 along the back wall. But after the tax scandal hit, according to former waiter Bob Verchick, "she started hiding off to the side at table No. 44," also in the Hunt Room, "where she was out of sight. It's in a low-traffic area, so people wouldn't come up to her and say, 'You're Leona Helmsley.'"

Many things, alas, remained the same. Despite the Queen's much-publicized problems, she seemed as haughty and coldly indifferent to staff as ever. After seven years, she still refused to set aside space in the hotel for an employee cafeteria. Almost nine hundred employees had to share a dozen tables in a basement lunch room. Their bill of fare was either what they brown-bagged themselves or what happened to be stocked in a row of vending machines. Only the hundred or so employees who worked in the hotel's bars and restaurants were entitled to hot meals, which were served buffet style in an equally dismal space on the third floor. The Queen also continued to find fault with dirty fingernails and slouched shoulders. Not surprisingly, Verchick says workers expressed sheer delight that the pampered Queen was experiencing discomforts of her own. In fact, a popular fantasy among staff "was the thought of her in jail being set upon by fat black lesbians because of the way she treats [black] maids."

And Leona's bill-paying habits apparently remained unchanged, despite the *Post* articles which had described how she "stiffed" mansion contractors. That April, after the Helmsleys' Barbados sojourn, small businesses all over the Caribbean island found themselves strapped with unpaid bills. Indeed, they were the very merchants who had catered to the embattled couple and protected their privacy from reporters in the wake of the tax scandal. Ann Stoute, owner of Stoute's Car Rental, says she leased the Helmsleys a sporty red Subaru with no earthly idea they would skip off without paying the final balance of $1,329. "I submitted bill after bill," she recalls, "but got zilch response. They obviously didn't plan to pay us." The turn of events was distressing indeed, she says, "because we were told the Helmsleys were wealthy landowners from New York. We considered them reputable people." Honored to have the couple's business (presumably uninformed as yet about the Helmsley scandal), Stoute says she delivered the car right to their door and even gave them a $20-a-week discount. "Perhaps we were stupid. Maybe this is why they're billionaires."

Keith Laurie, owner of Barbados Security Kennels, is still awaiting payment of his $4,500 bill. He said he stationed three guards, a Doberman and two German shepherds near the Helmsleys' bedroom every night "to make sure they weren't disturbed." Aiming to please, Laurie said he replaced one of the guards when Leona complained that the man had "a little cough. Like a lot of wealthy people, little things irritated them." Rental agent Sam Mahon took care of the Helmsleys' every need during their stay at the Barbadian villa, yet he says they stuck him for $3,500 in unpaid food bills, overseas phone calls and other expenses. "I put out my own money for Mrs. Helmsley's comfort," he told the *Post*, "and my calls have been ignored. They're bloody unethical."

The Queen had more important matters to consider. By May,

he had returned to table No. 7, where many a business lunch concerned her hotel advertisements. Elaine Taylor-Gordon, her new ad counselor, says she suggested that Leona "soft-pedal her presence" because of the brewing tax scandal. "Absolutely not!" Leona made clear. "I don't want anybody to forget me. I am these hotels." Any embarrassment the Queen might have shown earlier had disappeared, replaced by a fighting resolve. Her attitude was that she had done nothing wrong, and that whatever she had done was done by most business people. She felt she was being persecuted by people who were jealous of her celebrity and her husband. And she was not going to let the turkeys get her down. She was determined to get up every day, put on her makeup, dress properly, do her work. She felt the Leona Helmsley connotation stood for something positive—for someone inspecting and kicking ass and making sure the guest had a wonderful stay." With Leona's input, the ad agency developed a new $5 million-a-year campaign which would compare the Helmsley Palace to ten of the world's most renowned landmarks. The most audacious ad was a three-quarter-page color photo of the Taj Mahal, with the caption: "In India, It's the Taj Mahal. In New York, It's the Helmsley Palace." A different landmark—perhaps Matsumoto Castle, Linderhof Castle, Versailles, or the Alcázar—would be featured each Sunday in the *Times* magazine section. Leona would continue to appear as the smiling Queen, but only in a two-inch snapshot at the bottom of each ad. "We convinced Mrs. Helmsley to become the logo instead of the focal point," Elaine Taylor-Gordon recalls. Yet in no way was the Queen being demoted. She was merely stepping tastefully to stage right in order to freshen up the ads and focus more attention on the Palace itself. Ads for the Palace and Leona's other five Manhattan hotels were also placed in *Connoisseur, Travel and Leisure* and airline magazines.

All the while, Taylor-Gordon says, "Mrs. Helmsley remained in the eye of the storm. But she never seemed worried about the scandal." If anything, she seemed a wee bit excited by the front-page coverage. "I don't think she enjoyed being vilified, but she enjoys that kind of exposure. You can't buy that kind of exposure. She's shrewd. My assumption is that she felt the Helmsley name was becoming more famous. I don't think it was disgraceful to her." Although her Park Lane guests might search in vain for a copy of the *Post*, Taylor-Gordon says the Queen "would want to get several copies immediately" whenever a new article appeared. "I guess she put them in her scrap book or sent them to people."

If drawn to the flame, the Queen was wise enough to recognize imminent danger. To keep state and federal investigators at bay, she and Harry had hired Stephen E. Kaufman, 56, a former chief of the criminal division for the U.S. Attorney's office in New York. Kaufman's biggest obstacle was an energetic 38-year-old antagonist by the name of James R. DeVita, an assistant to U.S. attorney Giuliani. Although he seems soft spoken and lackluster at first glance, criminal lawyers who have battled DeVita describe him as aggressive to the point of stubbornness. "DeVita is not as laid back as he appears," says Barry Slotnick, one of New York's most famous defenders of alleged mob bosses and white-collar criminals. "Don't be fooled by his appearance. He's tough, he's thorough, he's tenacious, tenacious, tenacious." DeVita had developed an expertise in tax matters in 1982, when he was part of the prosecution team that sent Korean evangelist Sun Myung Moon to prison for federal tax evasion. As soon as the Helmsley scandal broke in December 1986, Giuliani placed DeVita in charge of the federal probe.

Thanks to numerous grand jury witnesses, DeVita had already sketched the shape of a potential prosecution in the early months of 1987. Then, on May 29, he went whole hog by convincing the grand jury to slap a subpoena on Leona's secretary, Martin Goldstein, requiring him to turn over "any and all books, records or documents of any kind" related to the renovation and upkeep of Dunnellen Hall. In addition, the subpoena ordered Goldstein to deliver all statements and canceled checks relating to Leona's two alleged piggy-bank checking accounts. DeVita apparently had already learned that the New York Decco account and her more recent "Five Twenty-One Corp." account had been heavily used to pay for furnishings and luxury goods installed in Leona's various homes. According to court records obtained by the *Post*, Kaufman stalled DeVita by challenging the subpoena in Manhattan Federal Court. When the court upheld the subpoena, Kaufman tied DeVita's hands again by appealing to the U.S. Court of Appeals, Second Circuit, arguing that the subpoena "violates the Fourth Amendment because it requires [Goldstein] to conduct a warrantless search" of Mrs. Helmsley's office at the Palace.

Despite DeVita's clear presence on the trail that summer, Milton Meckler says Leona and Goldstein continued to place questionable financial demands on Deco. "It was business as usual." On several occasions, Meckler said, Goldstein ordered him "to make out Deco checks to Mrs. Helmsley" for furniture she supposedly had donated to or purchased for the hotels. "Goldstein would say, 'We just delivered a chest or a sofa' or some other kind of furniture to the Park Lane or the Palace." Meckler said he would follow orders by sending Leona a check "for $4,000 or more" although he suspected the furniture was imaginary, just another scam to provide the Queen with extra spending money. "It seemed doubtful that Mrs. Helmsley would go shopping and buy [furniture] for a hotel out of her own money. The realistic way would be for her to tell Deco to go get it." Another curious thing, he added, "was that Goldstein would never send us an invoice for the merchandise, which Deco would have to have under ordinary procedures." After paying the Queen, Meckler said Deco would be reimbursed by billing the designated hotels for furnishings he was certain they never received.

Another scam, the Five Twenty-One "circle jerk," also continued unabated, Meckler says. Between late 1986 and the summer of 1987, he said $554,000 was siphoned from the Deco treasury to pay for Dunnellen Hall expenses. He said Donald Hesselbirg, treasurer of Helmsley Enterprises, would order Deco to reimburse the parent company when money was deposited into the Five Twenty-One checking account used by Leona for her mansion expenses. In step two of the circle, Meckler said, Goldstein would give Deco a list of items recently purchased for the mansion by Five Twenty-One Corp. Deco would bill Five Twenty-One accordingly. Goldstein would then send Deco a Five Twenty-One check for that amount, creating the appearance that the Helmsleys had indeed reimbursed the purchasing subsidiary for delivered goods. Appearances were deceptive, however, because Deco would deposit Goldstein's check and immediately return the funds to Hesselbirg by separate Deco check. "And that apparently goes back into Leona's Five Twenty-One account in New York," thereby replenishing her piggy bank and completing the circle at Deco's expense. Meckler said Harry reimbursed Deco for approximately $230,000 of its losses to the "circle jerk" by summer's end, leaving Deco still approximately $320,000 in the hole.

Meckler said he complained to Harry in late July about the continuing charge-offs to Deco.

"By the way," Meckler told the tycoon, "Five Twenty-One still owes Deco $320,000 for Dunnellen expenses."

"Well, I don't know about that," Helmsley replied, sidestepping the issue. Still intent on protecting Deco's profit picture, Meckler said he then sent a letter by Federal Express to Goldstein urging him to satisfy Five Twenty-One's debt to Deco. "It was a very strong letter about a delinquent account receivable," Meckler recalls, but the bill went unheeded.

In conversations with Leona that summer, Meckler said she seemed unchanged by the scandal. "Did I see her become a humble woman after that? No way! There was no change in arrogance. We were still busy shopping for Dunnellen Hall. Cleaning supplies had to be delivered by tomorrow morning." He said Deco even had to send a free case of toilet paper every month to the mother of Leona's penthouse maid, who lived in the Caribbean. "She couldn't get a good grade of paper over there." Apparently Leona was capable of charity as long as it was not at her own personal expense. And Leona's phone etiquette remained the same: "Nasty as ever. She still threatened to pull me through the telephone."

Jim DeVita, meanwhile, continued to investigate more-distant Helmsley history. The *Post* reported on August 26 that he was studying new allegations that Harry and Leona "used fake business invoices to pay for lavish renovations" to the North Hills, Long Island, condo they had purchased for Ruth Panzirer and young Wally back in 1982. The article quoted an anonymous *Post* source, a former Helmsley supervisor, who said the condo fixup was indeed fraudulently charged to the Graybar Building, the Helmsley Building, and other business properties. "Greenwich was just like North Hills," he said, "but on a much bigger scale." DeVita turned the heat up the same week by having the Helmsleys served with subpoenas to give handwriting samples and their fingerprints as part of a mail fraud probe. With the prosecutor closing in, Leona made preparations. The *Post* reported on September 7 that her Deco aides in Florida "are frantically packing tons of subpoenaed documents in order to shift them to another location."

A Deco employee told the paper the records contained "at least $3 million worth of invoices for chandeliers, carpets, linens" and other goods installed in Dunnellen Hall and in Leona's Park Lane penthouse. "The records are being labeled and inventoried," the source said, adding that it was a "panic situation." The anonymous aide added that Leona intended to close the Florida office and move Deco's operations to the fifth floor of the Helmsley Palace in Manhattan. It was no mere rumor. On September 30, Milton Meckler received a long-distance call from James Sheehan, a former controller of the Brown, Harris, Stevens subsidiary. Sheehan disclosed that Leona indeed was moving the entire Deco operation to New York and that he, Sheehan, was the new man in charge. Vince Sclafani, the ex-cop who once served as a member of Frank Turco's investigation squad, would also become a senior Deco officer. But as of October 1, Sheehan advised, Meckler and his staff of forty would be officially terminated.

It was a terrible, but not unexpected, blow. When Meckler asked for details about severance pay, Sheehan explained the formula: "The most Mr. and Mrs. Helmsley will pay anyone leaving Deco is one week's pay per year of service, but no more than thirty-five hundred dollars." If that was the case, Meckler quickly calculated he was getting royally shafted. Compared with his salary of $135,000, the $3,500 maximum meant he would walk away with barely seven days' worth of severance pay for his nine long years of service. He phoned Harry Helmsley to protest.

"Have I done you any harm over the years?" Meckler asked.

"No, you've been a good worker, but I've decided to close Deco down," said Helmsley. "I've decided to move it."

"Mr. Sheehan just called me about the severance pay," Meckler continued, "and he's talking thirty-five hundred. That equates to about a week and a few days' pay. Do you think that's fair?"

"I'll check into it and get right back to you," Helmsley promised.

But like so many other longtime aides, Meckler never heard another word from the tycoon. When the bundle of severance checks arrived on October 1, Meckler looked in vain for his $3,500. He said Sheehan then informed him that Leona wanted to withhold even that paltry sum until a complete inventory was taken of the Deco office. He had been stiffed by the Queen. He searched his mind for an explanation, and could think of only one. "It's her usual paranoia that the whole world is cheating her" and she could compensate by returning the same treatment.

By November, with his severance check nowhere in sight, Meckler said he sued the Helmsleys as a matter of personal pride. Only after a long-drawn-out fight did he recover the

$3,500, plus $1,500 reimbursement of his legal fees. He speculated that Leona paid her own lawyers over $5,000 to pursue the lost cause. Another thing Meckler couldn't understand: Why would Leona intentionally alienate him at the very time she needed his loyalty? Prosecutors were already huffing and puffing at Deco's door, and nobody in the realm was better acquainted with the Queen's spending habits than Meckler.

Dr. Charles H. Turner, who leased two floors above his dental office to Deco for a decade, says he suffered perhaps worst of all at the hands of the Helmsleys. "They paid me ninety-six hundred dollars for their last month's rent," the 54-year-old landlord said, "but then stopped payment on the check. I practically had a nervous breakdown over the way it was done. I was so upset I was taken to the hospital. I had temporarily slurred speech and all the symptoms of a stroke." Turner's health insurance company paid the $8,000 hospital bill, but immediately tripled his monthly premium to $600. He's been uninsured ever since.

A major break in Jim DeVita's case came on December 1, when the federal Appeals Court finally upheld his blanket subpoena for Leona's checkbooks and Dunnellen Hall records. Kaufman had kept him tied in knots for half a year. Within a matter of months, however, Giuliani's designate had amassed over 500,000 pages of subpoenaed reading material. As always during the year-long probe, he shared the workload with two state prosecutors from the office of state attorney general Abrams. The two assistant state attorneys general—Diane Peress and Alfredo Mendez—had been deputized as special federal prosecutors in order to lend DeVita a helping hand. Likewise, DeVita had been deputized as a state prosecutor in order to have jurisdiction to assist Abrams in his separate state probe of the Helmsley scandal. The special "cross-designation" system truly enabled the state and federal government to double-team the Helmsleys.

Any other couple with their particular problems might have avoided sprawling estates like the plague. But Harry and Leona went shopping for yet another mansion. On March 4, 1988—Harry's 79th birthday—they closed title on a mountaintop estate in the exclusive town of Paradise Valley, outside Phoenix, Arizona. Why the need for a fourth residence? "They decided Palm Beach was much too cold in the winter time," a former Helmsley aide recalls, and plunked down $6 million for the fifteen-acre spread, which includes a Mexican-style house, a pool with rock islands, and a man-made waterfall. A week later, Leona hired a Texas interior designer, Rita Silbert Davis, to beautify her new getaway. Before color schemes or furniture styles could be agreed upon, the *Post* intruded on March 28 with disconcerting news.

"Leona Faces Indictment" was the headline of the page-one article. It disclosed that "Billionaire hotel queen Leona Helmsley is expected to be indicted by federal and state grand juries within a month on multiple tax evasion and business fraud charges." A confidential law enforcement source told the paper, "We're [only] talking about weeks and there will be many, many charges." The source said the charges would be "more or less the same" as those uncovered by the *Post* in its series of approximately three dozen articles that began in December 1986. Harry Helmsley had also been under intense investigation for over a year by state and federal grand juries, the article noted. But it said his lawyer, Stephen E. Kaufman, "reportedly plans to argue against an indictment" on the basis of the developer's advanced age and health. The grand juries had progressed rapidly in the past six weeks, the paper said, when twenty or thirty Helmsley employees testified under immunity. Kaufman refused to discuss the case, but said in a prepared statement that "any allegations that Harry and Leona Helmsley have tried to avoid taxes are groundless and grossly unfair to them. Indeed, they are among those Americans who have paid the most money in personal income taxes over the past several years… From 1981 to 1987, while many multi-millionaires and major corporations paid no taxes whatsoever, the Helmsleys paid more than $130 million in personal income taxes and that does not include over $140 million paid in taxes by their corporations, which are 100 percent owned by them." In the same period, Kaufman stressed, "the Helmsleys gave over $35 million to charities," including $33 million to New York Hospital. The following day, Joe Licari, Helmsley's former chief financial adviser, told the paper he feared he would also be indicted because— unlike many other Helmsley aides—he had not been offered immunity to testify before the grand juries. Sources close to the case predicted that Frank Turco would also be charged.

On the morning of April 14, the *Post* leaked word that indeed the Helmsleys and their two aides, Turco and Licari, had been charged with "hundreds of felony counts of tax evasion and falsifying business records by federal and state grand juries." The defendants would be arraigned in state Supreme Court that morning. In the afternoon, the mountain of state and federal charges—each carrying a possible prison term of at least four years—would be detailed at a joint press conference by Abrams and Giuliani.

Preparations commenced bright and early on April 14. At 7:45 A.M., the Queen and Harry pulled up in a silver stretch limo at the Equitable Building in lower Manhattan, where they would surrender at the office of state attorney general Abrams. Helmsley knew the building well, having brokered its purchase thirty years earlier for a syndicate headed by Lawrence Wien. Waiting for the Helmsleys in a gray Cadillac at the corner of Pine Street and Broadway was an advance team of four bodyguards. They rushed to the Helmsley vehicle and opened the doors for the indicted couple. A crowd of fifteen reporters and photographers went wild when Leona stepped out, dressed to kill in a blazing scarlet coat-dress with brass buttons and blue lapels. She flashed a smile and chirped "Good morning" to the scrambling media mass. Harry, by contrast, seemed painfully aware that serious proceedings were in store. He was frowning as he got out of the back seat and followed his wife into the lobby. There, waiting by the elevators, the embattled couple joined arms. A reporter remarked that many a kind word had been said over the years about Harry Helmsley. Harry looked grimly ahead, but Leona acknowledged, "They're all true."

"Mr. Helmsley, you've spent a lot of years in real estate," said one newsman. "What do you consider your greatest accomplishment?"

"I married her," he answered without hesitation. Leona's smile grew brighter still and she squeezed his arm and leaned closer. After being fingerprinted, the Helmsleys, each escorted by state agents, were taken a mile away to police headquarters for booking. They were in and out of Central Booking in ten minutes, jumping ahead of other defendants. Their journey continued at an eleventh-floor courtroom of state Supreme Court, where they found themselves at 10:30 A.M. amidst a swarm of accused drug peddlers and thieves. They sat patiently for thirty minutes as a half-dozen accused, including a woman who admitted forging over $10,000 worth of checks, entered their pleas before acting Supreme Court justice Carol Berkman. Finally, among the riffraff, Leona forfeited her glued-on smile and wiped away tears with a tissue. But she seemed to regain her composure after a chat and laugh with Harry. When he briefly disappeared to the bathroom she held his camel-hair coat to her breast. A new member of the Helmsley defense team, Washington tax expert Gerald Feffer, was on hand when the clerk read identical state charges handed down against the couple and their two former aides three days earlier. The 188-count state indictment alleged that the foursome billed Helmsley hotels and commercial properties for more than $3 million in fraudulent charges between June 1983 and April 1986 to finance personal expenditures and the Dunnellen Hall renovation. (If the prosecutors knew of any crimes committed after 1986, including the alleged continuance of the Five Twenty-one "circle jerk," they apparently left them by the wayside.) The charges included 139 counts of falsifying business records, 44 counts of filing false instruments for tax returns, 3 counts of scheming to defraud, 1 count of conspiracy, and 1 misdemeanor count of scheming to defraud.

"Harry Helmsley," asked the clerk, "how do you plead?"

"Not guilty," he said firmly.

"Not guilty," said Leona, louder still. Turco and Licari, each represented by his own lawyer, pleaded the same. The judge released everyone without bail, satisfied that Harry and Leona were unlikely to skip town. "If the Empire State Building or the Helmsley Palace goes on the block, I'm sure we'll all hear about it in time," she said. With the ordeal finally over, the Helmsleys walked out of court and climbed back into their limo.

That afternoon, Giuliani and Abrams held a joint news conference in the lobby of the United States Attorney's office at 1 St. Andrew's Plaza, near City Hall. Giuliani announced that a federal grand jury had handed up a 47-count indictment against the four defendants that morning on similar charges. He said he and Abrams had waited until the eve of the annual tax-filing deadline "to underscore the deterrent principle: to remind people of their obligations." Giuliani said the indictments were a result of a fifteen-month investigation resulting from articles in the *Post*. "To a very large extent," Giuliani said, "the origination of these charges was through investigative reporting on the part of Ransdell Pierson and the New York *Post*. Throughout the course of the investigation, the New York *Post* reports did at times uncover things that alerted us that we should go investigate." Abrams said, "On behalf of the state, I want to indicate as well that the New York *Post* brought it to the attention not only of the federal authorities but to the state authorities."

The list of fraudulent charges outlined in the state and federal indictments painted the picture of one chintzy Queen. Apparently even the smallest chargeoffs were worthy of her attention. She was accused, for instance, of charging the Park Lane $2,000 for "uniforms" which were actually a white lace and pink satin dress, a jacket and a white chiffon skirt. Among the grander expenditures allegedly charged to business properties was the more than $1 million spent for construction of the elaborate pool enclosure. The defendants were also accused of fraudulently charging the Park Lane, St. Moritz , Windsor and Carlton House hotels for $500,000 worth of jade figurines installed in the Queen's Manhattan penthouse. "The phony invoices paid by those hotels falsely described the merchandise covered as items of antique furniture" for the hotels, according to the federal indictment. The Queen was accused of billing the Park Lane $45,000 for a birthday present to Harry: a silver clock in the shape of the Helmsley Building (an echo of her late son, Jay, who paid for Harry's gift Monopoly table with Deco funds). Part of the cost of the $130,000 mansion stereo system mentioned earlier by the *Post* was allegedly charged as a security expense to the Helmsley Building. The four defendants were also accused of charging $290,000 worth of mansion renovations in 1984 and 1985 to Helmsley's Garden Bay Manor housing complex in Queens. Over $370,000 in mansion gardening and landscaping costs was alleged to have been fraudulently charged to the Harley Hotel in Enfield, Connecticut. More than $1 million worth of furniture, antiques, artwork and other items was alleged to have been purchased for the estate by Deco. Neither the state nor the federal indictment accused the defendants of any wrongdoing in connection with Ruth Panzirer's Long Island condo. In all, prosecutors alleged that no fewer than nineteen different business entities in the Helmsley organization had been charged for costs of renovating, furnishing, decorating and operating Dunnellen Hall from 1983 to 1986.

The most serious of the 235 state and federal counts was a federal extortion charge lodged against Leona and Turco, for allegedly demanding kickbacks and "free goods and services" from contractors and vendors. The pair faced a possible penalty of twenty years in jail for that charge alone. Each of the other federal counts carried a possible sentence of up to five years in prison. But in all likelihood, Giuliani said, the most time any of the defendants would likely serve would be "one, two, or three years because these are basically white-collar crimes."

In a separate article, the *Post* predicted that Harry Helmsley's health would be a pivotal factor as prosecutors prepared their case against the billionaire developer. "Helmsley's attorneys are expected to argue that the tycoon is in failing health and is incapable of standing trial."

Kaufman and Feffer said nothing about the health issue, but denounced the two indictments in a scalding two-page press release. "[It] represents the first time that the state and federal governments have ganged up on any American citizens to jointly prosecute them on their income tax return.... This unprecedented tactic is nothing less than an attempt to intimidate and cower the Helmsleys with a vicious 'double punch' ... based on the same set of false charges."

A week later, in a replay of their state court appearance, Harry and Leona pleaded "not guilty" in federal court, as did Turco and Licari. The foursome were informed that the federal indictment took precedence over the state charges. Uncle Sam would have first crack at prosecuting them. Their case was assigned to U.S. District Judge John M. Walker Jr., 48, a cousin of Vice President George Bush with a reputation for toughness. Before joining the court three years earlier, he had served as chief of enforcement for the U.S. Treasury Department. Rough terrain stretched ahead, but who could doubt the Helmsleys' pledge to fight the charges "tooth and nail"? Once upon a time, in a 1986 interview with *New York Woman* magazine, Leona boasted about her powers of recuperation. "I'm a Cancer," she explained, born on July 4th. "And you know what they say about the crab. When you break a claw, it grows back."

Would it, again?

Afterword

August 30, 1989

"Has the jury agreed upon a verdict?" the court clerk asked.

Hundreds of spectators, including reporters from around the globe, craned forward in the cramped benches of room 318 of Federal District Court to hear the answer.

"Yes, we have reached a verdict," replied Alvin Taylor, a black mail carrier who had served as jury foreman for thirty-five hours of jury deliberations following a sensational two-month trial.

"On count one," asked the court clerk, "how do you find defendant Leona Helmsley?"

"Guilty," said Taylor, standing alone in the still courtroom on Manhattan's Foley Square.

"On count two...?"

"Guilty."

"On count three...?"

"Guilty."

"On count four...?"

"Guilty."

A dozen sketch artists, some wearing binocular goggles, watched Leona for the slightest trace of emotion as the guilty verdicts rained unmercifully down on her. But the Queen of the Palace disappointed them, sitting ramrod straight in her green leather chair at a conference table only six feet from the jury box.

Not until count ten, when Taylor announced yet another "Guilty," did she betray a reaction. Leona slumped noticeably in her chair and bowed her head slightly. The back of her neck began turning red. For a brief moment, she glanced at the jury and shook her head in seeming disagreement as Taylor continued to read from his verdict sheet. When he finished, the billionaire hotel queen stood convicted of thirty-three felonies, including conspiracy to defraud the I.R.S., evading $1.2 million in federal taxes, filing false tax returns, and mail fraud. The racially mixed jury of six men and six women also convicted her two co-defendants, Frank Turco and Joe Licari, of thirty-three counts of aiding and abetting her tax fraud, and of mail fraud. Leona and Turco were acquitted, however, of the most serious charge: conspiring to extort kickbacks from contractors and suppliers. The three defendants were also found not guilty on seven of the seventeen counts of mail fraud.

Harry Helmsley, although indicted, was nowhere in sight as the verdict was pronounced. He had been found incompetent to stand trial three months earlier, when a Boston doctor testified during a medical hearing that the tycoon had moderate memory problems caused by a series of small strokes over the years. The tycoon awaited news of his wife's verdict at the Park Lane penthouse.

The courtroom emptied, but Leona remained seated for forty-five minutes longer as her lawyers conferred with Judge John Walker in his robing room. She was comforted by her 21-year-old grandson, Craig Panzirer, who rested his head on her left shoulder. The only other relative on hand was Leona's niece, Frances Becker, Sylvia's daughter, who had offered her support throughout the summer ordeal. (According to a top former aide to Leona, she had fired her brother, Alvin Rosenthal, earlier that spring. In addition, she reportedly removed Alvin's wife, Susan, from her longtime post as hotel "inspectress" and ordered the couple to vacate their apartment in the Carlton House.)

For nine long weeks, a harsh spotlight had shone on Leona in the dock. A parade of forty-four government witnesses, some of whom betrayed their hatred for the Queen, laid bare her peculiar lifestyle. Newspaper readers and television viewers all over the country lapped up each juicy detail and startling revelation.

And Leona, so accustomed to bending others to her own comfortable schedule, had to adjust to Uncle Sam's timetable. Morning after morning, she told one reporter, she had to awake at 3:30 A.M. in order to swim and dress in time for the 9:30 A.M. criminal proceedings. Upon returning to Harry and the Park Lane at 6 P.M., she barely had time to eat dinner before heading to bed.

The trial had started on June 26. Judge Walker's first item of business was to begin selecting a dozen jurors and six alternates from a pool of sixty candidates summoned to the federal courthouse. Leona, clutching a white alligator bag, observed the preliminaries in a yellow suit and she got a very unroyal reception from a drunk who leaned into her face and shouted: "You rich people. You all ought to go to jail. You're guilty." Courthouse security guards evicted the heckler.

When the jury was finally picked on July 5 (the day after Leona's sixty-ninth birthday), a reporter quipped: "I hope she was good to the help, because that's who's on the jury." Among those chosen to decide the Queen's fate were a baggage handler, a postal worker, a telephone company tester and an electrician. During jury selection, many noted that they knew little or nothing about the Helmsleys.

In his opening arguments to the jurors, prosecutor James De-Vita alleged that Harry and Leona had cheated the government out of "over a million dollars of taxes" from 1983 to 1985 and used Turco and Licari as their henchmen "to carry out this fraudulent deceptive scheme. When necessary, they fabricated and falsified documents." DeVita disclosed that Harry had tried to make amends on Dec. 2, 1986, the day of the *Post* exposé. "On that same day, Harry Helmsley issued eighteen checks totaling over $5 million to repay the companies" which had made the payments for Dunnellen Hall improvements. "Those frank admissions of guilt proved too little, too late, because once the scheme was exposed the criminal investigation was started and this case is the result."

Leona's silver-haired Washington lawyer, Gerald Feffer, then electrified the packed room by describing his client as a "tough bitch" in open court. Yes, he told the jurors, "She can be abrasive and she can be demanding.... And it is well known that if an employee makes a mistake, the employee pays.... If she should stumble on a speck of dirt in a hotel room, or God forbid, a roach in a hotel room, all hell breaks loose." But Feffer stressed, his hands trembling for emphasis, "I don't believe Mrs. Helmsley is charged in the indictment with being a tough bitch. In this country, we do not put people in jail because they're unpopular." His novel strategy was instantly nicknamed the "tough-bitch defense."

Amazingly, Leona kept her poise as Feffer painted her odious portrait. But in reality, according to one defense insider, "It took Feffer months to convince Mrs. Helmsley to let him call her a bitch. She wasn't at all comfortable about it," either before or after Feffer uttered the word. Right off the bat, continuing his unconventional defense, Feffer admitted to the jury that millions of dollars' worth of personal expenses had been charged to the Helmsleys' businesses, including $1 million for the Dunnellen Hall pool enclosure. And he agreed that "altered or changed invoices were frequently used," and that more than $1 million worth of Dunnellen Hall furnishings were purchased by Deco. "The facts relating to the case are really not largely in dispute," he stated, but insisted that there was no intention to cheat on taxes.

Helmsley employees independently resorted to fake invoices, he argued, so that they would not have to deal personally with the feared Queen. He said the invoices were "just a shortcut to permit the companies to pay their proportion of the expenses or Dunnellen Hall." (Apparently his rationale for expecting the companies to pay part of the mansion expenses was that Harry and Leona used it as a workplace.) He also cautioned the jury that Harry and Leona, with their "staggering" wealth, saw things a little differently than the average couple. "Let's face it —a million dollars to the Helmsleys is not a million dollars to anyone of you or to me."

Things got off to a rollicking start the next day when the first witness, a former Helmsley accountant, described how he was banished from Dunnellen Hall because of a telephone chime under Leona's bed which went "ding dik" instead of "ding dong." After Leona complained about the unmelodious chime during lunch one day, the accountant said he took it upon himself to crawl under the bed and fix it. But Leona became furious anyway, he said, because he entered her bedroom without permission.

On July 12, the trial grabbed national headlines when a former head housekeeper of Dunnellen Hall, Elizabeth Baum, testified that Leona once told her in 1983: "We don't pay taxes. Only the little people pay taxes." Leona silently challenged the damaging testimony by shaking her head back and forth. Baum, middle-aged and plump, also testified in a heavy European accent that she and other mansion employees were paid by check from the Park Lane or from the Harley hotel chain's Cleveland headquarters. The next day, fired senior engineer Jeremiah McCarthy recalled for the court how Leona forbade him in 1983 to pay contractor Eugene Brennan for masonry work at the Greenwich mansion, and how Leona forced him to repay Helmsley-Spear out of his own pocket after he went ahead anyway and had a company check cut to Brennan. In a devastating parting blow, he described how Leona reamed him out in 1986 for daring to refuse her orders to charge mansion improvements to the Garden Bay Manor apartment complex. "She said, 'You fuck, you're not my partner. You don't tell me how to spend my money. You sign what you're told to sign.' "

The soap opera frothed onward when a former Helmsley-Spear engineer described Leona's 1984 dream to build an outdoor stereo system like the one she had seen at Disney World, with underground speakers planted in the front yard, tennis, gazebo and barbecue areas of Dunnellen Hall. The engineer testified that Leona and her advisers disguised the amenity as an electronic security system for the Helmsley Building, as the *Post* had disclosed in 1986. Spectators tittered as he described

Leona's utter inability to control the sophisticated sound system, which came alive of its own accord one morning at 4:30 A.M.

Even Leona's courthouse wardrobe became titillating news when *New York Newsday* published a front-page sizzler on July 19, headlined "The Queen's New Clothes." The article, accompanied by five color photos of Leona's colorful fashions, disclosed that Feffer had scolded his client two days earlier for wearing "a glamorous, attention-getting Chanel suit" with shiny buttons. "What are you, crazy?" Feffer asked in a low voice, apparently fearful that Leona's elegant attire might alienate the blue-collar jury. "Think this is a fashion show?" he added sarcastically. "We'll get a runway and bring in models.' A more sedately dressed Leona arrived at the courthouse the following day, the paper noticed, clad in an "oatmeal-colored V-collared dress with a wide belt of the same color."

Milton Meckler took the witness stand on July 24 and buried Leona under a mountain of incriminating testimony. For two full days, he described how Deco had to "eat" the cost of "every conceivable or inconceivable item that would go into a mansion-type place...Antiques, carpeting, furniture, fabrics, televisions, appliances, golf carts." And all orders, he testified, "had to be initialed by Mrs. Helmsley." He told the court that Harry Helmsley had been well aware, since buying Dunnellen Hall in 1983, that Deco was supplying free goods to the mansion. When Meckler complained that the policy was destroying Deco's profit picture, he said Harry replied: "Don't worry about it. I know about it, and you're doing enough business. I'm not holding you personally responsible for this." The former Deco boss also explained how Leona had abused him on the job, including her occasional threats to "pull me through the telephone." At one point, Meckler halted his marathon testimony and complained to the judge that Leona was making nasty faces at him. "I apologize for that," Feffer told Judge Walker. "I will talk to her and make sure that does not happen again." And it didn't.

Mayor Edward Koch, not one to stand on the sidelines of any public controversy, enlivened the summer circus on July 31 by branding Leona "The Wicked Witch of the West" during an impromptu press conference. "A billionairess to be so chintzy distresses people," he said. "The things that she did are so vile...." Donald Trump followed suit on August 2 by denouncing the Queen as a "sick woman. I can feel sorry for my orst enemy, but I cannot feel sorry for Leona Helmsley. She deserves whatever she gets."

One of the true highlights of the trial came on August 10, when court records revealed Leona's most intimate shopping habits. The *Post* reported that "the hotel queen wears cheap girdles, curls her hair with rollers, waxes her legs and smears ople mousses on herself...[And] of course, the billionairess didn't pay for any of it." An IRS agent testified that her rollers, pins and a $12.99 girdle from Bloomingdale's were all billed the Park Lane between 1983 and 1986, along with another $20,000 worth of personal goods and services. A $21 subscription to a crossword puzzle club and a $58 Itty Bitty Book Light also went on the hotel books. By now, the trial had become an international affair. "The basic elements—greed, avarice and sheer nastiness—are just too wonderful, aren't they?" a reporter om England's *Daily Telegraph* exulted.

After putting on only four defense witnesses, Feffer rested is case on August 21. Three days later, in his closing arguments, Feffer implored the jury to let God judge the Queen. "If a fact she has abused or has mistreated people, I beg you to ave that decision to a higher authority." The jury rendered its own jarring judgment on the fifth day of deliberations.

Juror Stephen Maier, a Westchester County electrician, recalls that the panel decided on its first day of deliberations "that l three defendants were guilty of tax conspiracy." One of the rst invoices they examined, for housekeeper Elizabeth Baum's oving expenses charged to a Helmsley business and approved y Leona as well as Turco and Licari, "pointed us in that direction." He said the jurors immediately discounted Feffer's entire "tough bitch" theory—that executives concocted invoices dependently to minimize their contact with Leona—because e Baum invoice proved that Leona participated directly in the lling scam. Maier said the jury battled for two days over the xtortion count, but voted to acquit Leona and Turco on the arge because liquor and television salesmen "came out ead" even if they had to kick back goods and cash to the two efendants. Everyone on the jury liked Joe Licari "like a favorite uncle," Maier says. "Nobody who testified had a bad word say about him." By contrast, Maier said, "Turco looked like weasel, and nobody had anything nice to say about him." Nor, said, did anyone have a kind word for Leona. "Here's a oman that has everything, but has nothing. She has no friends. he has nobody. She's a very decadent person. She's obsessed

393

with making money and keeping everything she's got. I'm no a psychiatrist," Maier adds, "but I think she's a sick woman."

As the reporter who broke the Helmsley scandal, I have grappled with the riddle of Leona Helmsley for almost four years. What motivated a woman of her immense wealth to cheat and lie to save such relatively paltry amounts of money? Why did she so totally distrust and suspect other people? How could she take so much pleasure in humiliating others? She seemed to lack any feeling for other people. Yet, on occasion, wasn't she capable of showing great kindness, even affection, to such key employees as Joyce Beber and Jane Maas? (Then at the drop of a hat, they too could be disposed of like toilet tissue.) And if everyone else was treated so miserably, what could explain the single, salient exception: her unflagging devotion to Harry? Was there ever a more paradoxical, more enigmatic human being?

A psychological condition known as narcissistic personality disorder might just explain the riddle of Leona Helmsley. The late Heinz Kohut, a Vienna-born psychoanalyst, coined the phrase in the 1960s. He theorized that the disorder resulted from a disruption of early child development, caused by the mother's failure to show empathy for the child's emerging personality. As a result of the blow to its self-esteem, Kohut believed such a child would become permanently stripped of a sense of self. To fill the void, from infancy onward the child would unconsciously overcompensate by taking on a grandiose, unrealistically powerful self-image. Only by placing itself above everyone else could the child cope with an overwhelming fear of having no real connection with the world. A hallmark of the syndrome is a related trait: intense rage when others fail to recognize your exalted position or abilities.

Narcissistic personality disorder is described at length in the *Diagnostic and Statistical Manual of Mental Disorders* of the American Psychiatric Association:

> The essential feature is a personality disorder in which there are a grandiose sense of self-importance or uniqueness; preoccupation with fantasies of unlimited success...and lack of empathy....[When the goals of unlimited power and success are actually pursued], it is often with a "driven," pleasureless quality, and an ambition that cannot be satisfied.

Individuals with this disorder are constantly seeking admiration and attention, and are more concerned with appearances than substance. For example, there might be more concern about being seen with the "right" people than having close friends....

Entitlement, the expectation of special favors without assuming reciprocal responsibilities, is usually present. For example, surprise and anger are felt because others will not do what is wanted; more is expected from people than is reasonable.

Frequently there is painful self-consciousness, preoccupation with grooming and remaining youthful, and chronic, intense envy of others....

One of the classic diagnostic criteria cited in the AMA manual is "lack of empathy: inability to recognize how others feel, e.g., unable to appreciate the distress of someone who is seriously ill."

Dr. Otto F. Kernberg, perhaps the most respected living authority on the narcissistic personality, writes in *Severe Personality Disorders* (Yale, 1984):

[T]hey obtain very little enjoyment from life other than from the tributes they receive from others or from their own grandiose fantasies, and they feel restless and bored when external glitter wears off and no new sources feed their self-regard. In general, their relationships with other people are clearly exploitative and sometimes parasitic. It is as if they feel they have the right to control and possess others and to exploit them without guilt feelings—and, behind a surface which very often is charming and engaging, one senses coldness and ruthlessness....[T]hey are completely unable really to depend on anybody because of their deep distrust and depreciation of others.... They are especially deficient in genuine feelings of sadness and mournful longing....

At the worst extreme, which Kernberg calls "malignant narcissism," such individuals show a "lack of anxiety tolerance...and a disposition to explosive or chronic rage reactions of severely paranoid distortions." Indeed, says Kernberg, their feeling of superiority is reinforced "through inflicting fear and pain on others." Predictably, says Kernberg, these individuals display an "absence of an ordinary sense of morality," and many have "the feeling that the gratification of aggression is the only significant mode of relating to others."

Kernberg also notes that their basic isolation from other people leads to paranoid features, including the fear of being overcharged.

Dr. Kernberg has said that although narcissists are unlikely to form lasting relationships with other people, they often admire a hero and form a seemingly dependent relationship with the person. "They really experience themselves as part of that outstanding person...The admired individual is merely an extension of themselves...There is no real involvement with the admired person and a simple narcissistic use [getting some status or benefit] is made of him." If Leona is indeed a narcissistic personality, Kernberg's theory might explain her ability to remain true to at least one person: Harry.

They will need each other more than ever for years to come. Leona was due to be sentenced on November 14 on her thirty-three federal felony counts. The offenses carry a total penalty of 127 years in prison, but as a practical matter, white-collar criminals rarely are sentenced to more than a few years. She also faces fines of up to $7.75 million. Mayor Koch and others have publicly stated that Leona deserves to go to jail. But others, such as gossip columnist Liz Smith and juror Stephen Maier, have argued that prison would serve no purpose other than to satisfy a public itch to further humiliate the Queen.

For the near future, Leona's punishment may be that she will be required to endure many, many more hours in the courtroom. Feffer has already stated Leona's intention to appeal her federal conviction. Furthermore, the 188-count New York State indictment returned in 1988 against the Helmsleys, Turco and Licari is very much alive, and pending.

Regardless of how things go in court, the Queen of the Palace will be no more, for it is likely Leona will have to relinquish her throne and title as president of the Helmsley hotel empire. Warren B. Pesetsky, former general counsel for the New York State Liquor Authority, explains that a convicted felon "can't be an officer, shareholder, or partner in any entity that holds a liquor license." The Palace, Park Lane and New York Helmsley could hardly survive if they were unable to serve liquor.

Perhaps the most inventive penalty would be the one proposed by Arthur Wang on the editorial pages of the *New York Times* the day after the verdict:

I propose that the Queen be sentenced to work in her own palace—in each of the dominions over which she reigns.

So many weeks in the laundry, folding towels she helped make so fluffy, soft and clean.

Then another long stint, this time in the guests' rooms, working as a chambermaid, cleaning bathrooms, changing beds, dealing with hard-to-please guests.

Then several more weeks serving as a busboy (busgirl) doling out rolls and water and clearing tables.

Finally, in the kitchen, she should work under a demanding chef, peeling potatoes, scrubbing pots and pans.

Menial work.

She should rub elbows and take orders from the minions over whom she has so long stood guard.

Yes, an eye for an eye—a punishment that fits the crime. But there's one missing ingredient.

While serving this part of her sentence, the autocratic Queen would not be standing guard. Alas, she'll never know how it is to work for herself.

Author's Note

The writing of this book would have been impossible without the patience and trust of hundreds of sources, many of whom made themselves available despite personal fear during my years of research. To them, including those who must remain anonymous, I'll always be grateful.

It would be impossible to adequately thank Genevieve Young, my editor at Bantam Books, for her insights and skill with a sharpened pencil; I count her rare as a Palace craftsman. Special appreciation also to Stephen Rubin, Stuart Applebaum, Lauren Field, Tom Dyja and Dolores Simon for their help at 666 Fifth Avenue.

I am indebted to my agent, Sterling Lord, for many brainstorming sessions in his clocktower office and for keeping my spirits high during the tough early stages of the manuscript. Prodigious thanks also to his assistants, Elizabeth Kaplan, Jody Hotchkiss and Michael Goff.

For valuable early advice, I would like to thank Harriet Fier, Paul Manning and Mike Pearl. For special assistance, my gratitude to Steve Ryan, Frank Sommerfield, Karen FitzGerald, Joan Tedeschi and Victor Cabrera.

For information on the birth of Manhattan skyscrapers, an

invaluable reference was *New York 1930—Architecture and Urbanism Between the Two World Wars*, by Robert A. M. Stern, Gregory Gilmartin and Thomas Mellins.

For tolerating my excessive curiosity, keen thanks to my friends in the New York *Post* library: Merrill Sherr, Jack Begg, David Hacker, Donald Curci, Mary Beth McGeary, Billy Heller and Beatrice Green.

And how could I fail to mention my sounding boards: Alan Harris, Eve Stoddard, Marty Mandell, Patricia J. Howard, Leslie Gevirtz, Peg Byron and Esther Pessin?

DON'T MISS
THESE CURRENT
Bantam Bestsellers